INDIGENOUS WOMEN AND FEMINISM

Women and Indigenous Studies Series

The series publishes works establishing a new understanding of Indigenous women's perspectives and experiences, by researchers in a range of fields. By bringing women's issues to the forefront, this series invites and encourages innovative scholarship that offers new insights on Indigenous questions past, present, and future. Books in this series will appeal to readers seeking stimulating explorations and in-depth analysis of the roles, relationships, and representations of Indigenous women in history, politics, culture, ways of knowing, health, and community well-being.

Other books in the series:

Being Again of One Mind: Oneida Women and the Struggle for Decolonization, by Lina Sunseri
Taking Medicine: Women's Healing Work and Colonial Contact in Southern Alberta, 1880-1930, by Kristin Burnett

INDIGENOUS WOMEN AND FEMINISM
Politics, Activism, Culture

Edited by Cheryl Suzack, Shari M. Huhndorf,
Jeanne Perreault, and Jean Barman

UBCPress · Vancouver · Toronto

20 19 10

Printed in Canada on FSC-certified ancient-forest-free paper (100% post-consumer recycled) that is processed chlorine- and acid-free.

Library and Archives Canada Cataloguing in Publication

Indigenous women and feminism : politics, activism, culture / edited by Cheryl Suzack ... [et al.].

Includes bibliographical references and index.
ISBN 978-0-7748-1807-0 (bound)
ISBN 978-0-7748-1808-7 (pbk.)

1. Indigenous women – Political activity. 2. Indigenous women – Social conditions. 3. Feminism. 4. Feminism and the arts. I. Suzack, Cheryl

HQ1155.I64 2010 305.48'8 C2010-902167-3

e-book ISBNs: 978-0-7748-1809-4 (pdf); 978-0-7748-5967-7 (epub)

Canadä

UBC Press gratefully acknowledges the financial support for our publishing program of the Government of Canada (through the Canada Book Fund), the Canada Council for the Arts, and the British Columbia Arts Council.

This book has been published with the help of a grant from the Canadian Federation for the Humanities and Social Sciences, through the Aid to Scholarly Publications Programme, using funds provided by the Social Sciences and Humanities Research Council of Canada.

Printed and bound in Canada by Friesens
Set in Futura Condensed and Warnock Pro by Artegraphica Design Co. Ltd.
Copy editor: Lesley Erickson
Proofreader: Deborah Kerr
Indexer: Heather Ebbs

UBC Press
The University of British Columbia
2029 West Mall
Vancouver, BC V6T 1Z2
www.ubcpress.ca

Contents

Acknowledgments

We are grateful to the many individuals and institutions that in various ways supported this project. We thank several individuals for productive conversations that enhanced our thinking about the challenges and possibilities of Indigenous feminism: Ellen Arnold, Virginia Carney, Janice Gould, Patricia Penn Hilden, Janet McAdams, Danika Medak-Saltzman, and Dory Nason. We are also greatly indebted to a number of people who supported this project at key moments in its development: Kris Calhoun, Patricia Demers, Len Findlay, Gary Kelly, Andrea Ruskin, and Norman Shaw. The idea for this book emerged from the "Indigenous Women and Feminism Conference," which received generous institutional support from the Social Sciences and Humanities Research Council of Canada, the Alberta ACADRE Network, and from numerous units at the University of Alberta: the Office of the Vice-President (Research); the Faculty of Arts; the Office of Human Rights' Employment Equity Discretionary Fund; the Women Writing Reading Program; the Canada Research Chair, Department of English and Film Studies; the School of Native Studies; and the Departments of English and Film Studies, Political Science, Sociology, and Women's Studies.

At UBC Press, we are grateful to Jean Wilson for comments on an early version of the book and for soliciting it for publication. We thank Darcy Cullen and Ann Macklem for valuable support at key stages and for guiding the project through the acquisitions process. We are also indebted to the Aid to Scholarly Publications Programme for its support of this publication project.

Three essays in this volume have appeared in different forms elsewhere: Shari M. Huhndorf's "Indigenous Feminism, Performance, and the Politics of Memory in the Plays of Monique Mojica" is drawn from *Mapping the Americas: The Transnational Politics of Contemporary Native Culture* (Cornell University Press, 2009); Jeanne Perreault's "'Memory Alive': An Inquiry into the Uses of Memory by Marilyn Dumont, Jeannette Armstrong, Louise Halfe, and Joy Harjo" appeared in Renee Hulan, ed., *Native North America: Critical and Cultural Perspectives* (ECW, 1999); and an earlier version of Julia Emberley's "To Spirit Walk the Letter and the Law" was published in *Defamiliarizing the Aboriginal: Cultural Practices and Decolonization in Canada* (University of Toronto Press, 2007). We thank the publishers for permission to reprint them here.

Indigenous Feminism
Theorizing the Issues

SHARI M. HUHNDORF AND CHERYL SUZACK

Since the 1970s, Indigenous politics have increasingly encompassed issues that cut across boundaries of nation, language, and culture. As these shifts have facilitated critical engagement with women's shared experience of the collusions between colonialism and patriarchy, they have laid the foundation for the conceptualization of Indigenous feminist cultural and political practices, practices in which this volume participates. For Indigenous women, colonization has involved their removal from positions of power, the replacement of traditional gender roles with Western patriarchal practices, the exertion of colonial control over Indigenous communities through the management of women's bodies, and sexual violence. As gender has begun to reshape Indigenous politics, the growing legal recognition in settler-colony countries of the rights of Indigenous peoples to cultural and political autonomy has brought to the fore questions about Indigenous women's access to civil rights and sovereignty claims. Since the late 1980s and 1990s, developments in feminist theory and practice have enabled scholars to recognize how nationality, race, class, sexuality, and ethnicity inform axes of gender differentiation. Despite these interventions and the urgency of gender analysis specific to Indigenous communities, Indigenous women and feminist issues remain underexamined in contemporary feminist theory. Although presumed to fall within normative definitions of women of colour and postcolonial feminism, Indigenous feminism remains an important site of gender struggle that engages the crucial issues of cultural identity, nationalism, and decolonization particular to Indigenous contexts. An emerging generation of scholars and writers has only begun to analyze the unique political and social positions of Indigenous women, at times from a feminist perspective. Yet Indigenous feminism to date has generated little published scholarship.[1] This volume adds to the small but growing body of work on this critical topic. Together, the essays that follow address a range of issues central to emerging Indigenous feminist inquiry.

Despite the critical importance of gender in Indigenous contexts, the process of conceptualizing theories and practices of Indigenous feminism remains controversial for a number of reasons. As other women of colour, both scholars and activists, have long contended, feminism as a political movement and academic practice originated as a means to address the social problems of the white middle classes. To a certain extent, feminism, especially in academia, remains white-centred, despite the active involvement of women of colour in the second- and third-wave feminist movements. For Indigenous women, the marginalization of their issues is compounded by the fact that a critical component of colonialism throughout the Americas involved the imposition of Western gender roles and patriarchal social structures. Those who struggle for gender equality are often seen, sometimes erroneously, as opposing traditional Indigenous practices and forms of social organization. Thus, Indigenous feminism frequently elicits accusations that it fractures communities and undermines more pressing struggles for Indigenous autonomy. Consequently, feminist research and politics often appear to be irrelevant to the concerns of Indigenous communities and may even seem to be implicated in ongoing colonial practices.

The need to address the urgent social, economic, and political problems confronting Indigenous women remains critical, however. These problems stem from ongoing colonial practices of the dominant culture and, at times, from the internal dynamics of Indigenous communities. We propose Indigenous feminism as a rubric under which political and social organizing can and should take place. Yet a single, normative definition of Indigenous feminism remains impossible because Indigenous women's circumstances vary enormously throughout colonizing societies, where patriarchy dominates, and in Indigenous communities with distinct histories and cultural traditions. Differences among Indigenous communities have always impeded collective political action, but this is perhaps especially true in the post-1960s era, during which the political autonomy and cultural distinctiveness of individual communities have been emphasized.[2] This emphasis on nationalism has devalued issues of gender, and one of the most pressing challenges for Indigenous feminism today is to find a basis for collective political action and engagement in broader anti-colonial struggles that also addresses the particularities of Indigenous women's social positions. Although Indigenous women do not share a single culture, they do have a common colonial history, and our conception of Indigenous feminism centres on the fact that the imposition of patriarchy has transformed Indigenous societies by diminishing Indigenous women's power, status, and material circumstances.

Indigenous feminist analysis and activism must aim to understand the changing situations, the commonalities, and the specificities of Indigenous women across time and place; it must seek ultimately to attain social justice not only along gender lines but also along those of race, class, and sexuality.[3] Social justice, in our view, can be attained only through specific attention to gender and must be considered as an integral part of, rather than a subsidiary to, struggles for national liberation. The individual essays that follow address the specificities of Indigenous women's situations; taken together, however, they uncover commonalities that unite Indigenous women across cultural and national boundaries and create the possibility of collective feminist political action. At the same time, Indigenous traditions and social organizations, as Emma LaRocque warns, must not be exempt from critical scrutiny and the struggle for social justice. Although traditions "help us retain our identities as Aboriginal people," she writes, "as women we must be circumspect in our recall of tradition. We must ask ourselves whether and to what extent tradition is liberating to us as women."[4] Indeed, Fay Blaney observes, "patriarchy is so ingrained in our communities that it is now seen as a 'traditional trait,'" and a key goal of Indigenous feminism must therefore be "to make visible the 'internal oppression' against women within our communities" as well as in the dominant society.[5] While most of the essays in this collection address the material or ideological dimensions of Indigenous women's lives in the post-contact era, they also attend to the gendered dimensions of cultural traditions that remain central in contemporary communities.

This volume takes up the challenge of conceptualizing Indigenous feminist theories and practices. Rather than representing a unified vision of Indigenous feminism, the essays engage with questions that limn emerging Indigenous feminist inquiry. Our title, *Indigenous Women and Feminism,* acknowledges the fraught historical relationship between Indigenous women and mainstream feminism as it opens discussion about the ways Indigenous women can construct a theory and practice specific to their interests. The essays thus cohere around a series of interrelated questions: What are the stakes and controversies in conceptualizing Indigenous feminism? How do feminist endeavours relate to Indigenous politics centred on land and sovereignty? Is it possible to recover the obscured historical presence and agency of Indigenous women, and if so, how might we go about the task? What lessons does the past carry for contemporary situations? How do Indigenous women confront ongoing violence and social and political marginalization?

Our hope is that this volume will at once contribute to these discussions and debates and underscore the critical importance of emerging Indigenous feminist endeavours. The idea for this volume arose from the conference "Indigenous Women and Feminism: Politics, Activism, Culture" held at the University of Alberta in 2005. The conference was the first large-scale event to bring together scholars, activists, and community members to conceptualize an Indigenous feminist theory and political practice. The immense interest the conference garnered expressed the timeliness of questions surrounding Indigenous feminism in academic, activist, and community circles. Drawing several hundred participants from the United States, Canada, Latin America, Australia, Aotearoa New Zealand, and other locations throughout the world, the conference demonstrated the urgency of conceptualizing an Indigenous feminist project that crosses national and disciplinary boundaries as well as those between academia and the broader community.

Both the conference and this volume arose from collaborations among Indigenous and non-Indigenous women (two of us are Indigenous, two are not) who speak from different intellectual trajectories and personal histories but are drawn together by our commitment to Indigenous feminist issues. Our choice to proceed collaboratively reflects our shared conviction that although Indigenous women must shape Indigenous feminism, Indigenous feminism – as a political strategy and project – also requires the alliances that are built through the engagement, contributions, and support of Indigenous men and non-Indigenous men and women.

Histories of Indigenous Feminism

Although Indigenous feminism is a nascent field of scholarly inquiry, it has arisen from histories of women's activism and culture that have aimed to combat gender discrimination, secure social justice for Indigenous women, and counter their social erasure and marginalization – endeavours that fall arguably under the rubric of feminism, despite Indigenous women's fraught relationship with the term and with mainstream feminist movements. Indigenous women's activism has taken shape around a series of issues related to social transformations that have resulted from colonial policies. While women's traditional roles in Indigenous communities vary widely, colonization has reordered gender relations to subordinate women, regardless of their pre-contact status. In the early colonial period, political and economic relationships between settlers and Indigenous communities favoured Indigenous men, betraying the colonizers' unwillingness or inability to recognize women's authority and disturbing established social patterns within these communities (see, for example, Rebecca Tsosie's contribution to this volume). Beginning in the nineteenth century, residential school policies eroded women's status further by imposing patriarchal gender roles as part of the assimilation process.

In Canada, the 1876 Indian Act redefined Indigenous identity in ways that disenfranchised and dispossessed large numbers of women, and the 1887 General Allotment Act in the United States broke up reservation lands into privately held property that was held disproportionately by men. The sexualization of Indigenous women, which Jean Barman in this volume identifies as an integral part of colonization, worsened the effects of governmental policies and left women particularly vulnerable to violence. This problem endures in the present: recent Amnesty International reports have exposed that Status Indian women in Canada are up to five times more likely than other women to die of violence, and their counterparts in the United States are 2.5 times more likely than non-Indigenous women to be raped.[6] While the reports show that problems in the legal system and the ability of perpetrators to evade justice have contributed to this violence, they also point to women's economic, political, and social marginalization, which has been shaped by government policies, as a key source of vulnerability. The systematic disempowerment of Indigenous women, in all of its dimensions, has provided grounds for women's activism in recent decades.

Although women have always played key but often overlooked roles in Indigenous political campaigns, their activism gained momentum in the 1960s and 1970s and began to focus more heavily on issues of gender. Legal claims and social movements have provided necessary tools for protest and empowerment. In Canada, in particular, the legislative dominance of the Indian Act, with its explicitly gendered provisions, mobilized Indigenous women to seek legal remedies for inequalities to achieve the "most basic incidents of citizenship: equal status and membership within Aboriginal communities, equal entitlement to share in matrimonial property, and equal participation in Aboriginal governance."[7] The gains for Aboriginal women through the courts, however, have been double-edged.[8] As Sharon McIvor explains, "the use of the courts to advance women's collective and individual rights has pitted these women not only against Canadian and Aboriginal patriarchy, but also against other women in the Aboriginal community who do not share their view of women's equality."[9] An additional tension has emerged from the limited goals that Aboriginal women are permitted to claim for themselves. Verna Kirkness describes this limitation as discrimination-within-discrimination, whereby "the adoption of sex equality guarantees in any form at all helps make even more invisible the sex equality of women in traditional Native culture."[10] These challenges have generated the formulation of new terminological, activist, and political strategies premised on the broadly defined goal of gender justice for women. The strategies include using the courts and the media as tools of protest, articulating a collective identity that takes account of gender, and connecting struggles for gender justice to broader Indigenous quests for self-determination.[11] Indian Act and band membership provisions and matrimonial property rights remain vital issues around which Aboriginal women in Canada continue to organize.[12] A crucial underlying concern, as Bonita Lawrence and Kim Anderson explain, is that these struggles should not be "reduced to 'women's issues' by the formal male leadership, and then presented as a wholesale threat to sovereignty."[13] Marie Anna Jaimes Guerrero also notes the oppositional logic between Indigenous feminism and struggles for sovereignty and asserts that "any feminism that does not address land rights, sovereignty, and the state's systematic erasure of the cultural practices of native peoples, or that defines native women's participation in these struggles as non-feminist, is limited in vision and exclusionary in practice."[14] These issues of political representation and limited choice mark an important tension around which Indigenous women organize transnationally (see also Shari Huhndorf's contribution to this volume). Human rights activist Elsie B. Redbird argues, for example, that "stereotyping, misconceptions and abuse of Indian women come from the fact that they were not allowed to speak for themselves, express their own identities or participate in the development of policies which affected them." For these reasons, as Redbird states, "If the erosion of sovereignty comes from disempowering women, its renewed strength will come from re-empowering them."[15]

Despite the breadth of their issues, movements for gender justice have, however, developed differently around the world.[16] In Canada, major national organizations have furthered women's struggles to achieve political and social justice.[17] The Native Women's Association of Canada (NWAC) was founded in 1974 in response to gender inequalities in the Indian Act, particularly women's status. It has since expanded its mission to exert an influence on all legislation that affects Indian women, provide leadership and educational opportunities, expose and combat sexual violence, ensure representation in the justice system, and address a host of other issues, including those with an international dimension. Whereas the NWAC serves primarily First Nations and Métis women, Pauktuutit formed in 1984 to represent Inuit women in Canada. It identifies sexual violence among its most important priorities.[18] Although national organizations are better known, most social organizing around Indigenous women's issues has appeared in local contexts. The Aboriginal Women's Action Network of Vancouver (AWAN), British Columbia, for example, engages the myriad social, political, and legislative challenges confronting Indigenous women. By doing so, it has increased awareness and understanding of Indigenous feminism.[19] The Institute for the Advancement of Aboriginal Women, founded by current president Muriel Stanley Venne, one of Canada's most respected activists, has also been instrumental in bringing women together to discuss their concerns through local organizing. Like the NWAC and the AWAN, the institute has a broad political mandate to change stereotypical attitudes in Canadian society toward Aboriginal women, address issues at all levels of government that impact women, and serve as an advocate for the human rights and dignity of Aboriginal women.[20]

Gender has been less central in social movements in the United States, where nationalist endeavours remain dominant and have a complicated relationship with feminism. Women of All Red Nations (WARN) organized in 1974 as an extension of the American Indian Movement (AIM) to address issues that have special relevance to women – health, education, and violence – within the context of broader campaigns for political sovereignty, land rights, and environmental justice. In its early years, the group exposed the forced sterilization of Indigenous women in the 1970s by the Indian Health Service, and it published a study about the dangers to women of radiation contamination on the Pine Ridge Reservation. Some of the women affiliated with WARN went on in 1985 to found the Indigenous Women's Network (IWN), which defines itself as "a global movement that achieves sustainable change for our communities" by supporting women's leadership and perpetuating traditional knowledge.[21] Winona LaDuke, perhaps the best-known Indigenous woman activist in the United States, has participated in both organizations, and much of her current work addresses land recovery and environmental justice issues, often with a particular focus on women.

Although these examples point to continuities of interest between women's and Indigenous organizations, the two political projects have come into conflict as women's organizations have identified examples of patriarchy in Indigenous communities, their political organizations, and the dominant society. In both contexts, women confront sobering rates of domestic and sexual violence along with political under-representation and social marginalization, and their efforts to address these inequalities frequently elicit accusations of divisiveness. These tensions came to the fore in the court case *Native Women's Association of Canada v. Canada* (1994), in which the NWAC argued that the groups that had participated in the Charlottetown Accord had primarily represented men and that the government was required to provide equal representation for women.[22] The Supreme Court of Canada ultimately decided against the NWAC. These conflicts, complicated by the fraught relationship between Indigenous and mainstream feminism, have created a predicament for Indigenous women, who are frequently pressed to oppose feminist and Indigenous political commitments. This dual marginalization underlies recent scholarly arguments for making space for Indigenous feminism: the particular forms of racist and sexist oppression brought to bear on Indigenous women, as Joyce Green insists, necessitate that Indigenous feminism be considered a valid and necessary political stance.[23]

Among the most promising reconciliations of feminist concerns with those of broader Indigenous struggles for autonomy is the political project of the Zapatista National Liberation Army (EZLN), which emerged in 1994 in the Chiapas region of Mexico. Its Women's Revolutionary Law enumerates the rights of Indigenous women, including political leadership and participation, freedom from violence, reproductive choice, health care and education, and fair wages. Extending beyond mere rhetoric, this declaration paralleled the material restructuring of women's places within and outside the home, including the sharing of domestic labour and significant political participation within the Zapatista movement. In this context, writes one observer, "indigenous women have maintained a double militancy, linking their gender-specific struggles to struggles for the autonomy of indigenous communities." This double militancy allows "us to speak of the emergence of a new indigenous feminism."[24] Also significant in this regard is the transnational Indigenous movement, which began in the 1980s and brought to the fore issues that extend beyond the tribal.[25] Women's organizing in particular has gained significant momentum in this new constellation of relationships,[26] and this development suggests the possibilities that transnationalism is creating for Indigenous feminism.

Indigenous women's cultural production has also played a key but neglected role in the development of feminism. While activism aims to accomplish material social change, culture fosters critical consciousness by attending to the meanings of history and social relationships and imagining political possibilities. Unsurprisingly, then, Indigenous women's literature, art, film, and performance often addresses the same issues that preoccupy activists. Colonial transformations of Indigenous communities, the meanings of traditions, and contemporary social issues such as sexual violence are frequent themes of women writers and artists. In addition, culture has gained particular importance as it has confronted the silencing, marginalization, and invisibility of Indigenous women in patriarchal narratives and social practices.[27] As they scrutinize the effects of colonialism and patriarchy, writers and artists render Indigenous women visible by shifting their voices and cultural authority to the foreground and by reimagining their roles within and outside Indigenous communities. One purpose of this book is to consider how culture complements and extends Indigenous women's activism and political work; it seeks to draw out connections that have received little attention in the scholarship on Indigenous feminism.

Although Indigenous women struggle for parity in activist groups and politics, in the realm of culture they have managed to forge a significant presence in recent decades. Yet, even in the cultural realm, they receive less critical consideration than their male counterparts. Although several Indigenous women artists and intellectuals attained early prominence,[28] women writers in particular did not gain widespread attention until the 1970s and 1980s, decades when women's activism around issues of gender emerged. Paula Gunn Allen, Jeannette Armstrong, Louise Erdrich, Joy Harjo, Linda Hogan, Wendy Rose, and Leslie Marmon Silko are among the many American and Canadian Indigenous women who began to publish in this era, often to widespread acclaim, and Erdrich is today usually cited as the bestselling and Silko as the most widely read of all Indigenous authors in Canada and the United States. In many ways, the work of these writers complemented Indigenous activism of the period. For example, Armstrong's novel *Slash* (1985) – the first novel by an Indian woman in Canada

– scrutinizes the effects of the residential school system and racism in the dominant society on its protagonist, Tommy Kelasket. As the novel progresses, Tommy, renamed Slash, develops a critical consciousness that leads him to participate in a protest movement reminiscent of AIM and to become an Indigenous rights activist. In a parallel project, Silko's *Ceremony* (1977) tells the story of the reintegration of its protagonist, Tayo, into Laguna Pueblo after the church, mission schools, and his service as a soldier during the Second World War had severed his social and cultural connections to his community. This narrative of individual and communal identity reconstruction in the wake of colonialism, along with the novel's valorization of cultural traditions, linked directly with the goals of Indigenous activism during the Red Power era.

These path-breaking novels centred, however, on the stories of male protagonists, and along with the majority of Indigenous texts of this period, they mirrored in troubling ways the social marginalization and invisibility of Indigenous women. This circumstance began to change in the 1980s as Indigenous women writers and intellectuals increasingly asked and sought answers to questions about gender. Paula Gunn Allen's *The Sacred Hoop: Recovering the Feminine in American Indian Traditions* (1986) represents an early attempt to expose the patriarchal dimensions of colonization and to retrieve what she called "gynocratic" Indigenous traditions as a basis for contemporary feminist practice. Women writers also began to revise the gendered paradigms of Indigenous literature. Most famously, Erdrich's stories almost invariably focus on women and place them at the centre of Indigenous communities; in the process, the stories often engage with issues of gender exploitation. The same can be said of Hogan's work, Silko's recent novels, and the writing of a newer generation of authors such as Janet Campbell Hale, LeAnne Howe, Heid Erdrich, Lee Maracle, and Winona LaDuke. Indigenous women, some of whom identify as feminists, have also made significant forays into cultural realms that remain more resiliently male. These include filmmakers Alanis Obomsawin, Sandra Osawa, and Christine Welsh; dramatists and performers such as Monique Mojica, Marie Clements, and the members of the Spiderwoman Theater; and artists Shelley Niro and Rebecca Belmore.

Despite the significant accomplishments of these writers and artists and the attention they have drawn to Indigenous women, they nevertheless have had to contend with scholarly narratives that privilege men's work and deflect attention away from issues of gender. Some critics, however, have begun to pay particular attention to the work of Indigenous women, at times from a feminist perspective. Others have made crucial contributions to this endeavour by publishing anthologies of Indigenous women's writing that present alternative genealogies of cultural and intellectual history to male-centred narratives and raise questions pertinent to Indigenous feminism.[29]

Indigenous Feminist Practices

This volume takes up these issues – politics, activism, and culture – as they bear on Indigenous women. Not only do we see these topics as essential interrelated components of Indigenous feminism as it now exists, we also seek to initiate conversations across disciplinary, national, academic, and activist lines. The breadth of this project also reflects the nature of Indigenous feminist endeavours over time. Although the focus is on Canada and the United States, some of the chapters explore other Indigenous contexts, and the volume as a whole, we believe, has implications for Indigenous feminist efforts around the globe. The contributors do not seek to create a singular or unified definition of Indigenous feminism but rather to explore the myriad, sometimes conflicting questions that result from Indigenous feminist inquiry.

"Politics," the first section of the volume, begins with Minnie Grey's examination of the relevance of feminism to cultural traditions and to her own involvement in Inuit politics. Her chapter was initially delivered as a keynote address at the "Indigenous Women and Feminism" conference. Rebecca Tsosie, in another keynote speech, broadens the questions raised by Grey about the interconnections of feminism and politics by analyzing women's leadership in contemporary society. Laura Donaldson brings a historical perspective to these issues by considering gender and tribal politics in early Cherokee writing, particularly the work of Nancy Ward. Drawing inspiration from the writings of Laura Cornelius Kellogg, an influential but largely forgotten activist and intellectual, Patricia Penn Hilden and Leece Lee define the project of Indigenous feminism as they scrutinize the place of academe in the creation and maintenance of racial and gender inequalities.

In the essay that opens the section "Activism," Kim Anderson argues for the centrality of feminism in Indigenous communities and women's organizations. Jean Barman's chapter extends this argument by contending that Indigenous women's behaviours at the time of contact are consistent with feminist principles and practices. Interrogating the work of the African American feminist writer Anna Julia Cooper, Teresa Zackodnik considers feminism as a basis for coalitions between Indigenous and African American women. In her chapter, Cheryl Suzack argues that Yvelaine Moses' bids to have her band membership reinstated reveal how the law has reinscribed Indigenous women's subjectivities and feelings in colonial terms. In turn, ann-elise lewallen examines how Ainu women's activism in regard to traditional culture and natural resources constitutes a feminist practice distinct from feminism in the dominant Japanese community.

"Culture," the final section of this volume, begins with Shari Huhndorf's examination of scholarly debates about Indigenous feminism and the ways that women dramatists, including Monique Mojica, define an Indigenous feminist project. Jeanne Perreault analyzes the significance of memory in the poetry of Indigenous women writers Marilyn Dumont, Joy Harjo, Louise Halfe, and Jeannette Armstrong. Julia Emberley's essay considers how Rudy Wiebe and Yvonne Johnson's *Stolen Life: The Journey of a Cree Woman* addresses issues of colonial violence and the problems that Indigenous peoples confront in the justice system. Pamela McCallum argues that the work of visual artist Jane Ash Poitras reclaims cultural memory as it scrutinizes colonial and patriarchal representations of gender and community in Indigenous contexts. Katherine Evans traces the work of the Spiderwoman Theater, the first Indigenous feminist drama group, and suggests that the theatre has used performance to revitalize contemporary Indigenous communities. Elizabeth Kalbfleisch examines the significance of space, place, and borders in Rebecca Belmore's *Vigil,* a performance in protest of the murder of Indigenous women in Vancouver. The volume concludes with Patricia Demers' analysis of what indigeneity and feminism means in the work of Indigenous women filmmakers.

The diversity of the topics and issues explored in this book demonstrates the range of questions through which Indigenous feminist inquiry can be taken up. Any attempt to reduce this book to a work of cultural feminism will miss the mark.[30] Nevertheless, any attempt to construct a theoretical framework to study Indigenous feminism must also address the following questions: What term – *Indigenous* or *feminism* – should take precedence? Can feminism inhabit discourses that marginalize the question of gender?[31] How can the debates and conflicts surrounding Indigenous feminism allow the movement to advance as other women of colour feminisms have done? How can Indigenous feminism resist assimilation to either male or mainstream feminist norms? By what power structures do Indigenous women's feminist positions become visible, and by what alliances can these power structures be changed?[32] Ultimately, we hope that, as Indigenous feminist practices are built through the work of this anthology, these questions will be taken up together rather than separately to develop Indigenous women and feminism as a field of study.[33]

NOTES

1 Thus far, only two books focus explicitly on Indigenous feminism in Canadian contexts: Joyce Green, ed., *Making Space for Indigenous Feminism* (Black Point, NS: Fernwood, 2007), and Grace Ouellette, *The Fourth World: An Indigenous Perspective on Feminism and Aboriginal Women's Activism* (Halifax: Fernwood, 2002). On the US context, see the "Native Feminisms without Apology" forum in *American Quarterly* 60, 2 (June 2008). A number of relevant articles are also cited in this Introduction.

2 In the American Indian Movement in the late 1960s and 1970s, for example, pantribal alliances proved fragile, as Vine Deloria Jr. and Clifford Lytle explain, because of conflicts between traditional people, who "preached the doctrine of tribal integrity," and urban Indians, who created community identities and common political cause by foregoing tribal differences. See *The Nations Within: The Past and Future of American Indian Sovereignty* (Austin: University of Texas Press, 1984), 236.

3 We are influenced by Ipshita Chanda's contention that third world feminism must aim primarily to achieve collective rather than individual rights and that this endeavour necessarily involves preserving historical and cultural specificity while also finding bases for collective political action. See "Feminist Theory in Perspective," in Henry Schwarz and Sangeeta Ray, eds., *A Companion to Postcolonial Studies* (Oxford: Blackwell, 2000), 486-507.

4 Emma LaRocque, "The Colonization of a Native Woman Scholar," in Christine Miller and Patricia Marie Chuchryk, eds., *Women of the First Nations: Power, Wisdom, and Strength* (Winnipeg: University of Manitoba Press, 1996), 14.

5 Fay Blaney, "Aboriginal Women's Action Network," in Kim Anderson and Bonita Lawrence, eds., *Strong Women Stories: Native Vision and Community Survival* (Toronto: Sumach Press, 2003), 158.

6 See Amnesty International, *Maze of Injustice: The Failure to Protect Indigenous Women from Violence* (New York: Amnesty International, 2007), and *Stolen Sisters: A Human Rights Response to Discrimination and Violence against Indigenous Women in Canada* (New York: Amnesty International, 2004).

7 Sharon McIvor, "Aboriginal Women Unmasked: Using Equality Litigation to Advance Women's Rights," *Canadian Journal of Women and the Law* 16, 1 (2004): 108. The political status of Indigenous women is both fraught and complex due in part to legislative policies that contributed to their historical erasure through imposed status categories. Scholar Jo-Anne Fiske explains some of the terminology that has followed from these changes to the Indian Act, terminology that conflates the political with gender identity in key ways, thus challenging the straightforward assertion of any rubric through which to organize socially and politically. See "Political Status of Native Indian Women: Contradictory Implications of Canadian State Policy,"

American Indian Culture and Research Journal 19, 2 (1995): 1-30. As Fiske explains, the Indian Act is "administered by the Department of Indian and Northern Affairs Canada [DINAC] and exercises exclusive power (allocated to the Canadian Parliament by the Constitution Act, 1867) to determine who shall be recognized as Indian, the criteria by which this status shall be accorded or lost, and the conditions under which said Indians must live in order to benefit from special treatment in federal law." Fiske notes that "from 1876 onwards, the terms *legal, registered,* and *status* have been used interchangeably to denote Indians recognized by the federal government and regulated by the Indian Act" (5).

Distinctions between First Nations, Métis, and Inuit are equally complex. For a record of this evolving terminology, see Indian and Northern Affairs Canada's website at http://www.ainc-inac.gc.ca/ap/tln-eng.asp.

8 One of the most contentious pieces of legislation affecting Aboriginal women, section 12(1)(b) of the Indian Act, removed Indian status from Indian women who married Non-Status Indians or non-Indians. See Green, "Sexual," and Weaver, "First Nations Women and Government Policy, 1970-92: Discrimination and Conflict," in Sandra Burt, Lorraine Code, and Lindsay Dorney, eds., *Changing Patterns: Women in Canada* (Toronto: McClelland and Stewart, 1993), 92-150. Although 1985 amendments to the Act repealed this and other sections, discrimination against Aboriginal women has not been remedied. As Val Napoleon has argued, discrimination has simply been delayed a generation and borne instead by the children and grandchildren of these women. See "Extinction by Number: Colonialism Made Easy," *Canadian Journal of Law and Society* 16, 1 (2001): 113-45.

9 McIvor, "Aboriginal Women Unmasked," 109.

10 Verna Kirkness, "Emerging Native Woman," *Canadian Journal of Women and the Law* 2, 2 (1987-88): 413.

11 McIvor, "Aboriginal Women Unmasked," 133; Myrna Cunningham, "Indigenous Women's Visions of an Inclusive Feminism," *Development* 49, 1 (2006): 56; Val Napoleon, "Aboriginal Self-Determination: Individual Self and Collective Selves," *Atlantis* 29, 2 (2005): 14.

12 These issues have attracted a great deal of attention. For an analysis of the intersection between law, social policy, and gender identity, see Joyce Green, "Sexual Equality and Indian Government: An Analysis of Bill C-31 Amendments to the Indian Act," *Native Studies Review* 1, 2 (1985): 81-95; Delia Opekokew, "Self-Identification and Cultural Preservation: A Commentary on Recent Indian Act Amendments," *Canadian Native Law Reporter* 2 (1986): 1-25; Sally Weaver, "First Nations Women and Government Policy, 1970-92: Discrimination and Conflict"; Val Napoleon, "Extinction by Number"; Joanne Barker, "Gender, Sovereignty, and the Discourse of Rights in Native Women's Activism," *Meridians: Feminism, Race, Transnationalism* 7, 1 (2006): 127-61; and Mary Ellen Turpel, "Home/Land," *Canadian Journal of Family Law* 10, 1 (1991): 17-40. For a comparative analysis of the regulation of Aboriginal identity in Canada and the United States, see Bonita Lawrence, "Gender, Race, and the Regulation of Native Identity in Canada and the United States: An Overview," *Hypatia* 18, 2 (2003): 3-31. Lawrence raises the crucial point that "we need to dare to

look in different ways at Native identity" (23). Val Napoleon also supports this argument in "Aboriginal Self-Determination," 10. In this article, she proposes an activity-based citizenry model as an alternative to basing membership on the Indian Act.

13 Bonita Lawrence and Kim Anderson, "Indigenous Women: The State of Our Nations," *Atlantis* 29, 2 (2005): 3.

14 Marie Anna Jaimes Guerrero, "Civil Rights versus Sovereignty: Native American Women in Life and Land Struggles," in M. Jacqui Alexander and Chandra Talpade Mohanty, eds., *Feminist Genealogies, Colonial Legacies, Democratic Futures* (New York: Routledge, 1997), 101.

15 Elsie B. Redbird, "Honoring Native Women: The Backbone of Native Sovereignty," in Kayleen M. Hazlehurst, ed., *Popular Justice and Community Regeneration: Pathways of Indigenous Reform* (Westport, CT: Praeger, 1995), 135-36. Andrea Smith makes a similar point when she states that "gender justice is often articulated as being a separate issue from issues of survival for indigenous peoples." See "Native American Feminism, Sovereignty, and Social Change," *Feminist Studies* 31, 1 (2005): 121.

16 The term *gender justice* is used widely to mark a key differential positioning between Indigenous women and men. Deborah Bird Rose describes the differential double bind as the "encounter between Indigenous knowledge systems which include boundaries of exclusion and silence and the colonising demand for information ... that entraps women and men differently." See "Land Rights and Deep Colonising: The Erasure of Women," *Aboriginal Law Bulletin* 3, 85 (1996): 6. See Rose and Hannah McGlade, "Aboriginal Women and the Commonwealth Government's Response to *Mabo* – An International Human Rights Perspective," in Peggy Brock, ed., *Words and Silences: Aboriginal Women, Politics and Land* (Crows Nest, NSW: Allen and Unwin Academic, 2001), 139-56, especially 141, for more extensive discussions of this problematic in the Australian context. See also Anveshi Law Committee, "Is Gender Justice Only a Legal Issue? Political Stakes in UCC Debate," *Economic and Political Weekly* (March 1997): 453-58.

17 For a history of Indigenous women's organizing in Canada, see also Joyce Green, "Balancing Strategies: Aboriginal Women and Constitutional Rights in Canada," Joyce Green, ed., *Making Space for Indigenous Feminism* (Black Point, NS: Fernwood, 2007), 140-59.

18 A brief account of the NWAC's history and descriptions of its ongoing activities may be found on its website. See also Pauktuutit's website.

19 Blaney, "Aboriginal Women's Action Network," 157.

20 See the Institute for the Advancement of Aboriginal Women's website for a complete list of its objectives.

21 See the IWN's website. For a fuller history of Indigenous women's organizations and their objectives in the United States, see M. Annette Jaimes and Theresa Halsey, "American Indian Women: At the Center of Indigenous Resistance in North America," in M. Annette Jaimes, ed., *The State of Native America: Genocide, Colonization, and Resistance* (Boston: South End Press, 1992), 311-44, and Donna Hightower, "American Indian Women's Activism in the 1960s and 1970s," Indybay, 21 March 2006, http://www.indybay.org/newsitems/2006/03/21/18095451.php.

22 Sharon McIvor explains that the Charlottetown Accord was a constitutional reform agreement that included negotiations among the federal, provincial, and territorial governments and representatives from the AFN (Assembly of First Nations), the NCC (Native Council of Canada), the Inuit Tapirisat of Canada, and the MNC (Métis National Council). See McIvor, "Aboriginal Women Unmasked," 126.

23 Joyce Green, "Indigenous Feminism: From Symposium to Book," in Joyce Green, ed., *Making Space for Indigenous Feminism* (Black Point, NS: Fernwood, 2007), 14.

24 R. Aída Hernández Castillo, "Zapatismo and the Emergence of Indigenous Feminism," *NACLA Report on the Americas* 35, 6 (2002): 42.

25 Ronald Niezen, *The Origins of Indigenism: Human Rights and the Politics of Identity* (Berkeley: University of California Press, 2003).

26 Guillermo Delgado-P., "The Makings of a Transnational Movement," *NACLA Report on the Americas* 35, 6 (2002): 38.

27 Rayna Green shows the pervasively gendered representation of Indian women in colonial texts that fashioned the virgin-whore paradox to transform Old World images into New World terms that symbolically justify conquest. See "The Pocahontas Perplex: The Image of Indian Women in American Culture," *Massachusetts Review* 16, 4 (1975): 698-714. Green's work contests what Jo Carrillo describes as myths America, myths that rely on fictional and symbolic perceptions of Indigenous women rather than the material realities. See "Tribal Governance/Gender," in Jo Carrillo, ed., *Readings in American Indian Law: Recalling the Rhythm of Survival* (Philadelphia: Temple University Press, 1998), 208.

28 The best-known examples of early writers and performers are E. Pauline Johnson in Canada and Zitkala-Ša (Gertrude Bonnin) and Ella Deloria in the United States. Indigenous women also gained prominence in traditional cultural practices. See, for example, Karen Kilcup's edited collection, *Native American Women's Writing, c. 1800-1924: An Anthology* (Cambridge, MA/Oxford, UK: Blackwell, 2000).

29 See Paula Gunn Allen, *Spiderwoman's Granddaughters: Traditional Tales and Contemporary Writing by Native American Women* (Boston: Beacon Press, 1989); Anderson and Lawrence, *Strong Women Stories;* Joy Harjo and Gloria Bird, eds., *Reinventing the Enemy's Language: Contemporary Native American Women's Writings of North America* (New York: W.W. Norton, 1998); Kilcup, *Native American Women's Writing 1800-1924;* and Jeanne Perreault and Sylvia Vance, eds., *Writing the Circle: Native Women of Western Canada* (Edmonton: NeWest, 1990).

30 See Nancy Fraser's use of the term *cultural feminism* and her critique of feminist cultural politics as being too focused on struggles for identity and recognition, struggles that Fraser argues have subordinated the social to the cultural and the politics of redistribution to recognition. It is the representation of these struggles as "cultural" that we object to. We note that decolonization as an objective does not appear in Fraser's assessments of feminist cultural politics. And concepts such as participatory parity and public reason (see p. 32), which are applied to progressive forms of recognition for collectivities such as Indigenous women, do not adequately conceptualize what Indigenous feminist inquiry proposes to achieve. These problems draw attention to forms of culturalism *within* the dominant feminist movement that remain to be addressed and that impede strategic alliances and political affiliations among

feminists. See Nancy Fraser, "Feminist Politics in the Age of Recognition: A Two-Dimensional Approach to Gender Justice," *Studies in Social Justice* 1, 1 (2007): 23-35.

31 See Sara Ahmed's analysis of this question in "Beyond Humanism and Postmodernism: Theorizing a Feminist Practice," *Hypatia* 11, 2 (2006): 71-93. Whereas Ahmed answers this question with an emphatic no, we prompt further discussion by asking whether it might be construed differently by and for Indigenous feminist politics.

32 Other topics have been suggested by the anonymous readers of this volume, and we thank them for sharing their astute insights. These subjects include Indigenous women and environmental activism, Indigenous women's writing and the formation of ethics, and storywork as a form of gender empowerment.

33 Some of this work is already under way. For an excellent analysis of how Indigenous women's activism is reshaping traditional definitions of state-based diplomacy to enact intersectionality as a diplomatic strategy through which Indigenous women can "represent themselves on their own terms," see Laura Parisi and Jeff Corntassel, "In Pursuit of Self-Determination: Indigenous Women's Challenges to Traditional Diplomatic Spaces," *Canadian Foreign Policy* 13, 3 (2007): 83.

PART 1

POLITICS

1

From the Tundra to the Boardroom and Everywhere in Between

Politics and the Changing Roles of Inuit Women in the Arctic

MINNIE GREY

I have long grappled with the word *feminism.* What is feminism? Does it mean different things to different women from different backgrounds? In my private deliberations and in discussions with close female friends, I think what it really boils down to is this: women deciding who women are and who or what they want to be.

Having said this, I also asked myself how this fits into being an Aboriginal woman today and being a feminist in Aboriginal and Canadian society. I cannot pretend to speak for all my fellow Aboriginal women, but I will attempt to express my views as an Inuk woman who was raised in a traditional culture, in a way of life not practised by as many people today. And, most importantly, I will offer my views as an Inuk woman raised by an incredibly strong mother.

My mother was widowed at a young age and raised five children on her own. She was a very traditional woman who provided food and clothing for her children and her fellow Inuit. She worked her dog teams as a young woman and was a provider, hunting and fishing to help her extended family during times when her brothers were absent from the family, acting as guides to the newly arrived mineral explorers in our region. She was a midwife, a traditional caretaker, and later, during my childhood, she embraced the modern world of her day by becoming an income earner. She was a housemother to young girls who were taken from their traditional camps to start school in the federal day-school system. She worked as a cook and cleaning woman for the Hudson's Bay Company and for construction companies, and later in her life she cooked for the tourists who came to the fishing camps in Kangirsuk. My mother passed away on New Year's Day 2005 at the age of eighty-three. Give it to my mother to go out with a bang. She maintained her independence and refused to be helpless to the very end. After celebrating the coming of the new year with her community, she went peacefully alone the next morning in her living room. Even in her death, my mother left a message to me and others: that she was present and, above all else, cared about her family and her community to the very end.

I wanted to disclose this little story of my mother because she is one of many women who have lived through so many changes. The title of this chapter is "From the Tundra to the Boardroom and Everywhere in Between: Politics and the Changing Roles of Inuit Women in the Arctic," but my mother probably would have said of her life, "From the igloo and the dog teams to the kitchen of the white man – changes that Inuit have seen." She would not even have thought of herself as *the woman* who has gone through all of these changes, but would rather have seen the changes as what her people, Inuit, have gone through together.

It is true that the roles of women in Inuit society have changed drastically in the last few decades. We have moved our families from the land into established communities, and many of us have taken on positions that my mother and grandmother never entered into, positions that were never even thought of among their generation. Historically, the Inuk woman was central to the family. She was never the spokesperson, but was the silent advisor. She raised her family, making sure the food brought by the men was prepared and preserved for the days ahead. She made clothing that protected her family from the severe cold. She was a teacher who gave advice and guidance. And, most of all, she was an entertainer through her stories and songs. She was central to the day-to-day life of the family, from the parkas they wore on their backs and the kamiks they wore on their feet, to what they had in their belly, to the reason they smiled when they came home.

It is not difficult to argue that the changes that happened during my grandmother's and mother's lifetimes were drastic, sometimes so much so that they are difficult to comprehend. But what is surprising, perhaps, is that these changes continue today. My own life and the lives of the women of my generation continue to adjust to the ever-evolving role of being an Inuk woman in contemporary Inuit society.

My journey from the tundra began in 1971, when I was sent away to Ottawa. At that time, the schools in our communities did not go beyond

Grade 8, so my teacher took it upon himself to call the Department of Education in Ottawa and decided that I would be a good candidate to continue my high school in the south. Some official came to meet my mother, and I left in April of that year to attend a Grade 8 class for the last two months of the school year. The reasoning behind this move was to see if I was going to be able to adjust to a new life so different from the one I knew in Nunavik. I guess I not only adjusted but adapted – and successfully it seems! – to living my life in both worlds: that of the Inuit community that I came from and this new and somewhat strange southern community where I ended up. After leaving Ottawa, I went back to Nunavik to join a very exciting time for the Inuit in my region.

In 1975, the Quebec government decided to construct a major hydroelectric project in James Bay. At this time, the Inuit and the Cree of our region went to court to fight this development for a number of reasons. Eventually, we entered into negotiations with the Canadian and Quebec governments and the development corporations, and as a result of a long and difficult process, the first modern-day comprehensive land claims agreement with an Aboriginal group in Canada was created. This was the James Bay and Northern Quebec Agreement (JBNQA).

I was recently interviewed by a student from France who wanted to know how I got involved in politics. I answered her by saying that I don't know how I got involved, it just happened. My first job out of school was as a receptionist-secretary to the Northern Quebec Inuit Association, and things just started happening from there. With the signing of the JBNQA, public organizations were created for the first time in our region for the region. Inuit were now responsible for administering their education, health services, and municipal organizations. It was a significant change from the past.

In order to ensure that our rights and our interests in our land and its resources were protected and addressed, land-holding corporations were created in each of our fourteen communities. The corporations, which still exist today, are ethnic in nature, specifically to represent the beneficiaries of the JBNQA. It was through one of these corporations that I arrived in the boardroom for the first time. I became a manager and secretary on the board of the Nayumivik Landholding Corporation.

I cannot leave out the fact that during this time I was already a mother of two young boys. This is the part where the "everywhere in between" in my title comes in.

I soon aspired to learn the traditions of my mother. With my new family, I took every opportunity to live on the land and pass this experience on to them. I learned the art of food preparation and preservation as well as cleaning skins for the clothing I eventually learned to make. I can honestly say that learning these skills, the traditional and essential skills of an Inuk woman, has been one of the most gratifying accomplishments of my life. It has helped me to become more of who I am. Although today it is not my common practice to be doing these tasks, what I learned through my traditional education helps me cope with my modern-day challenges that I face every day. The challenges of motherhood, working outside the home, and trying to get the best out of both of these worlds have not been easy but have become a way of life for me.

After my involvement at the local level in my community, I ventured into regional politics by becoming vice-president of the Makivik Corporation. As vice-president, I took part in economic development, education, and self-government, all the while still raising my family.

In case you don't know, the Makivik Corporation was also created under the JBNQA and is an ethnic organization solely representing the rights of the Inuit as opposed to the public bodies established at that time. Makivik's mandate and objectives are as follows:

- to receive, administer, use, and invest the compensation money intended for the Inuit as provided for in the James Bay and Northern Quebec Agreement
- to relieve poverty and to promote the welfare, advancement, and education of the Inuit
- to foster, promote, protect, and assist in preserving the Inuit way of life, values, and traditions
- to initiate, expand, and develop opportunities for the Inuit to participate in the economic development of their society
- to exercise the functions vested in it by other Acts or the JBNQA
- to develop and improve the Inuit communities and to improve their means of actions
- to assist in creating, financing, or developing the business, resources, properties, and industries of the Inuit.

These were pretty tall orders for Inuit in those days. But we now run our own airlines, have modern schools in our communities, and teach our children in our language, Inuktitut, as well as in English and French, with our youth becoming trilingual people. We also now manage all of our municipal affairs and health services.

Well, by the time I had come to this point in my life, I had worked at the local and regional levels. So what next? The next part of my journey opened my eyes to the role and place of Inuit in the world. I joined the Inuit Circumpolar Conference (ICC) as a Canadian Council member and became engaged in action at the international level. In this capacity, I was privileged to become involved in issues that are of major concern to the Inuit today. I have been involved in issues related to the protection of our rights as Indigenous peoples and the protection of our wildlife and environment, among other topics. My work with the ICC has taken me to the far reaches of the world, and I can honestly say that it has kept me nomadic, which the Inuit are well known for. So, I guess some things don't change – it's just that today I am earning frequent flyer miles for being nomadic. That's all.

The tug of war I feel of wanting to maintain my connection to traditional and cultural activities within my modern-day life is so different from the same struggle of my mother and previous generations of Inuit. My tug of war eventually led me back to my region, so that I could once again be in my community and have the freedom to be out on the land. It was at this time that I went back into working within my region in the health sector. I took a job as the first Inuk executive director of a regional hospital, where I ended up staying for ten years before going on to become the executive director of the Regional Health Board. In that role, I had the privilege of being engaged in developing policies, programs, and services relevant to the realities faced by our people. I have to mention here that the Inuit of Nunavik, as elsewhere in the circumpolar Arctic, have had to endure a very fast and drastic change over the past four or so decades, which has not always been healthy in many respects. Our communities and my people have suffered the effects of these changes, and in some cases still do. Alcohol, drugs, violence, crime, abuse, and suicide are results of these changes, but they are also challenges that we can face and address as a people, together. In facing these very real challenges in their communities, many Inuit women are at the forefront of leading the fight for the well-being of our people, and I commend them for their work throughout the North.

In my work in the health sector, I became involved in research related to contaminants in our environment and our traditional food resources. This initial research, which identified that Inuit were exposed to higher-than-normal levels of harmful chemicals coming up from industrial, southern regions of the world, led to investigation of how these contaminants affect the health of the people living in my and other northern regions. As it turns out, it is the mothers who are most at risk from the impacts of these substances as they find their way into our bodies from the traditional food we eat. And we then pass some of these contaminants to our babies while they develop during pregnancy. You can imagine that this has been a very sensitive issue in Nunavik, but one that we must know about, and I am proud to say that Nunavik has become the leader on these issues in the circumpolar world. The communities in my region are intensively engaged in this research, more and more as partners and directors of the work than simply as participants in the studies. And this work continues today. Our work in this area led to our involvement in the International Union for Circumpolar Health, an international organization for research on northern health issues. This was an extremely busy time of my life, and I am glad I was able to work with and for my region – all the while still trying to get some time out on the land and raising two more children.

What has been my motivation? This is another question that has been asked of me. Well, honestly, I just happened to be there when so many new things were coming into place. Inuit were taking over all of the things that the government once controlled for them. There were just so many things happening at that time that – for someone like me who wanted to be involved and wanted to be active in the Inuit life, development processes, and progress – it was a very good opportunity and a very exciting time. That opportunity and desire to be involved became my motivation. But perhaps the greatest motivation I have had was my mother, who raised me to be a doer. My motivation also came from my children, for whom I wanted to make the region and the world a better place, my family that I wanted to care for in the best way I knew, and from my vision or belief that no matter what the challenge was, things would always come out for the better. I am a very optimistic person, and I believe that is what drives me: the hope and belief that things can be better and that one person can make a difference if she tries.

I am proud to be with all those women out there who are the doers. Many Inuit women are involved at their local and regional level, but we also have to recognize those women who continue to represent their people by tackling the big issues at the international level on our behalf. We have Inuit women speaking out against pollutants, working for the causes of our environment, our wildlife, and our health. They are helping to create international laws and speaking up against issues like global warming because our fragile world needs to be cared for, and our way of life, the way of life that sustained so many Inuit that came before me and the way of life that my mother taught me to respect, is being threatened and needs to be protected. We have Inuit women who have dedicated their lives to fighting for the rights of Indigenous peoples. I have recently been involved in sessions discussing the UN Draft Declaration on the Rights of Indigenous Peoples, and I pray that the last twenty years will have been worth it and that some state governments that continue to resist will come around and realize that we are only doing our part to make it a better and safer world for everyone.

I cannot say that my work in politics has always been easy. There will always be barriers for women in politics, but I see them more as stumbling blocks that we can overcome. I cannot speak for all Inuit women, but I have been very lucky to have been able to work well with both men and women. My own experience has shown me that it is not a competition between men and women but rather that it is a very complementary working relationship. What I cannot do on my own, my male counterpart can; and what he cannot do, I can. It is not about gender but rather ability, people's ability. I have been privileged to work among very dynamic people who respect my opinions, and I think this respect is absolutely important.

Today, I am heading the Inuit negotiating team for the creation of the Nunavik government, which will become the first of its kind in Canada and Quebec. We are working with the federal and provincial governments in mapping out a public government that will have decision-making powers over the region above the fifty-fifth parallel but that will remain within the jurisdiction of Quebec. This is just another step for my people to achieve their aspirations and to be able to make decisions relevant to our traditions, culture, and our everyday lives. My life and my work continue to be a challenge, and this is one of the more interesting tasks I have become involved in so far.

We, as Inuit women, have been striving for such things as equal pay for equal work, equal sharing of roles for the good of the family, equal rights to participate in the decision-making processes of our governments, equal rights for the hiring of women at all levels of commerce and science, equal rights in education, and most importantly, equal rights to raise our children in safe, healthy, and positive conditions. This means, among other things, above the poverty line. I look at these aspirations not as women's liberation, but as people's liberation. In fact, we need and love our men, and similarly, we need to liberate them from the concepts that bind them to unbreakable traditional roles that, in turn, keep the status quo intact in many regions of the world.

During my lifetime and that of my mother, we, as Inuit women, have moved from the land into established communities. Many of us have taken on positions in local organizations or in community, regional, national, and international politics as Inuit have gained more control over the issues that affect us today. As mothers and wives, we continue our role in nurturing our families, but we do so for our communities, as we are also midwives, nurses, counsellors, teachers, social workers, church vestries, police officers, administrators, and politicians. We are playing a very important role in the establishment of land claims and in shaping the future face of our communities. And in so doing, we are ensuring the place of Inuit in Canada and the circumpolar world. But we are doing these things in a very different way from our ancestors. Many Inuit women across the Arctic hold these important positions in very new and rapidly changing Arctic regions, but they do these jobs while still taking on their traditional roles of caretaker and provider at home.

If I have any advice to the young women and youth in general, I would like to tell them that it is now a very different world for Indigenous youth today. They are now provided wonderful opportunities that as a youth I did not have. Things have changed and will continue to evolve. Youth in my communities now have a place and a role to play in making the future even better for our people. It is so good to see our leadership embracing the youth and having them join their deliberations. Our youth are our future, and we need their involvement. I know that life can be a struggle, especially in trying to find a place and an identity, but be optimistic and know that things have a way of turning out for the better. Our youth need to take advantage of the best of both worlds, as my mother taught me and as I continue to strive to do today.

NOTE

This is a slightly revised version of a keynote address presented at "Indigenous Women and Feminism: Culture, Activism, Politics," August 2005, Edmonton, Alberta.

2 Native Women and Leadership
An Ethics of Culture and Relationship

REBECCA TSOSIE

The impact of colonialism upon Native women and families is a very important subject and is deserving of full exploration. In this chapter, I want to address the policies of colonialism and their impact upon Native women in the United States and Canada. However, I will use the lens of leadership to evaluate this. In focusing on the ethics of leadership, I examine the profound capacity of the human spirit that is exemplified by the leadership of Native women. This is an ethics of survival, of connection to the past generations, of responsiveness to the needs of this and future generations. It is present in all Native cultures, and it is present in the leadership that I have studied. That spirit is what sustains Native peoples, what inspires us and gives us hope for the future.

This chapter is based upon research on Native leadership that my colleague at Arizona State University, Carol Lujan, and I have been involved in for the past four years. Our study examines the construction of leadership among contemporary Native men and women from various tribal backgrounds and regions. In doing this research, I became particularly interested in the expression of leadership among Native women and how this ties into notions of land and community and cultural views of relationship and responsibility. I offer an account of what I consider to be Native feminist ethics, which I believe frames these women's responses to leadership and also ties into traditional epistemologies. This account provides a template for understanding the cultural perspectives of leadership that inform contemporary

Native women's experiences and how they differ from the construction of a feminist ethics that has emerged from scholars in women's studies. This account will engage a community-based vision of female leadership within the legal and ethical framework that governs Native peoples' rights in the United States. It represents my responses as a Native woman, as a legal scholar, and as a tribal court judge.

Joy Harjo, a Creek (Muskogee) poet, writes, "I have lost my way many times in this world, only to return to these rounded, shimmering hills and see myself recreated more beautiful than I could believe." For me, this poem evokes a great deal about how we, as individual Native women, live our lives. But it also evokes the collective existence of Native women as tied to land, culture, and community. There is a sense in which many of us feel lost at times, disconnected from those critical aspects of our identity as Native people. That feeling of loss can become almost overwhelming and is certainly exacerbated by being raised in an urban environment, schooled in an Anglo educational system, and having to work and live in predominantly non-Indian communities and situations. On a broader scale, we recognize that there is a pervasive history of colonialism and dispossession that affects our lives on a daily basis. We see that in our court cases, our social institutions, and the ways in which we interact with each other and with outsiders.

However, as Joy Harjo's poem affirms, we can return to the lands, cultures, and communities that we came from. We may not do this in exactly the same ways as our grandparents and great-grandparents. But we have the capacity to re-create ourselves, as contemporary Native women, by acknowledging the beauty of those things that give content to our existence and learning to heal the things that have caused us to feel pain and loss. Land, culture, and community are enduring components of who we are; they are vital to our self-determination, as individuals and as peoples.

Native Women and Leadership: Traditional Cultural Roles and Ethics

It is important to understand where we began. In the Southwest, many tribes look at the corn plant as a symbol of our lives. It is fundamental to the survival of our people, and there are many ceremonies that accompany the growing of corn and its preparation for eating. Corn pollen and cornmeal are used in prayers. For many tribes – such as Navajo, Hopi, and the many Pueblo nations – women have the responsibility to grind corn. There are certain songs that accompany corn grinding. Those songs, according to Paul Enciso (Taos Pueblo/Apache), a cultural leader and artist, remind women that what they are grinding is sacred. When a woman puts herself in tune with the spirit of the activity, it becomes part of her, and not just a chore. She is creating something, and as she works in the rhythm of the song, of the grinding, the feeling flows through her and results in something of great value to her family. The grinding songs often tell stories that

> remind you of life itself, how you must go through life, how you must walk, just like the corn has come up from the stalk, and also be thankful, not only to Mother Earth and Father Sky, and also to the sun for what it provides, but also to the Creator ... for creating these things ... Eventually what comes from the ground goes back to the ground, and we just keep exchanging, and so the grinding song tells the whole story, and so it shows our gratefulness for all of this, the cycle. The cycle is never broken. It is an eternal thing, and the grinding song makes us part of it.[1]

If you think about this story, you see that in many traditions we are taught an ethic of responsibility in connection with our life's work. We are taught that the cycle of rebirth and regeneration that we all are part of places a great responsibility on us, to be appreciative, to remember what is important, and to serve our families and communities. We are taught that one aspect of our world – in this case, corn – enables our survival and that survival depends upon our ability to honour the core values that serve individuals in our relationship to ourselves, our families, our communities, and the Creator.

One can see that set of ethics at work in the descriptions of the traditional gender roles and responsibilities of Native women. A woman's identity among traditional Native cultures was "firmly rooted in her spirituality, extended family, and tribe."[2] Native women understood their existence as holistic – involving biological, social, and spiritual dimensions – and related through time and tradition to their lands, cultures, families, and communities. There is notable variation among tribes in how these aspects of Native women's existence are realized in social and cultural institutions. However, there are also some very consistent features. As I read the work of Paula Gunn Allen, Shirley Witt, Teresa LaFramboise, and others, I saw certain common themes among Native women from the many respective nations of this land. I do not want to essentialize but merely to draw out three common patterns that are associated with many, if not most, Native cultures and peoples.

In most tribes, gender roles were perceived as complementary and not as dichotomous. While Europeans tended to rank gender duties hierarchically, placing domestic duties in an inferior status and privileging public duties (politics, economics), Native societies largely viewed these tasks as complementary. For example, in the Southwest, men and women have complementary roles in planting, growing, harvesting, and preparing corn. The ceremonial duties of women are complementary to those of men. The distribution of the corn can occur through family or clan lines, which often are associated with the woman's side of the family. So, it would be inappropriate to say that one gender has primary responsibility for growing corn. It is an obligation of both genders, but it manifests in distinct duties and responsibilities.

Even where more traditional gender-differentiated roles were established for the society, Native cultures were often quite tolerant of individual women transcending gender roles. Again, tribal variations make it very difficult to generalize. But there are historically documented instances of certain Native women assuming military leadership roles, political leadership roles, and economic leadership roles that may not have been the norm for all women in the tribe but were sanctioned for these individuals at particular points of time. In addition, unlike the women of many European societies that legally determined men to be the owners of resources such as property, Native women often owned property, including land, agricultural products, and the means of economic production. Even if they were not the political leaders in a particular tribe, they were entitled to rights of ownership and control of resources that are more typically associated with political and economic power in European societies.

The central role of Native women within their societies is often reflected by the religious or spiritual content of their cultures. The social and political power of Native women was often sanctioned by tribal religious traditions that emphasized the powerful essence of the feminine aspects of creation. Unlike the Judeo-Christian religions, which are guided by an omnipotent male God, most Native religions are guided by a pervasive sense of spirituality. The Creator is an essence rather than an individual, and that essence is embodied within all of creation: the earth, sky, thunder, animals, rocks, plants, stars, and so on. To live in the right way requires individuals to have a sense of respect for and relationship with the natural world. The creative powers of the natural world are brought to assist human beings through song, ceremony, and ritual. Some of these spirit powers are perceived as having a male essence and some as having a female essence. It is quite clearly the case, however, that life depends upon a balance of both male and female energies.

Jennie Joe, a Dine (Navajo) anthropologist, has written of how traditional spiritual norms inform the actions of contemporary Navajo women. She tells of how, in the traditional Navajo creation stories, a male spirit entity associated with thought unites with a female spirit entity associated with speech to create Changing Woman, who personifies the life force of the universe and gives birth to the ritual structure that is still used by the Dine people. In contemporary Dine culture, Changing Woman is still perceived as being responsible for the growth of crops and the continuation of life. She is also a protector of what she has created. Dr. Joe says that this ethic underlies the strong protective feelings that Navajo women have for their land, which is passed down matrilineally through clan ties. This ethic is what is responsible for the refusal of a core group of Navajo people (including several women who are Elders) to vacate their lands at Big Mountain after a legal resolution of the land dispute with the Hopi Tribe found that they were no longer the owners of this land, which the United States now deems to be under the ownership of the Hopi Tribe.

According to Dr. Joe, "The defensive actions that these women continue to take fit their perceptions of the appropriate role for themselves. This concept includes the role of a warrior. For example, most traditional Navajo women have names that contain the word *baa,* which signifies 'female warrior.' As a female warrior, she is expected to fight off whatever poses a threat to the well-being of her family and home."[3]

The Impact of Colonialism on Native Women's Leadership

I believe that colonialism had substantial impacts upon Native women's leadership. I think most scholars agree that the overwhelming result of colonialism has been to try to acculturate Native peoples to the Anglo society's norms. This means that acculturation policies – which in the United States included military-style boarding schools, the suppression of Native languages, the suppression of Native religions and enforced Christianity, the suppression of Native economies and inculcation of forced dependency (a welfare economy), and supplanting traditional governments and judicial systems with structures modelled upon Anglo governance – took on similar values and norms to those of the Anglo-American society, including gender hierarchies and systems of oppression.

Consider this quote from US Indian Commissioner Medill, who in his annual report of 1848 spoke of the positive effects of the campaign to "civilize and Christianize the Indians," which was intended to convince Indian men to give up their "desire for war and ... love of the chase" (hunting) and to replace them with a desire for the "advantages possessed by the white man," including schools for their children and the "cultivation of the soil." With respect to Native women, Commissioner Medill noted that "the most marked change ... when this transition takes place, is in the condition of the females. She who had been the drudge and the slave then begins to assume her true position as an equal; and her labor is transferred from the field to her household – to the care of her family and children."[4]

This quote illustrates the government's tendency to perceive women's role in ownership of land and production of crops as slavery and to place the ownership of resources in the hands of a male head of household, which supplanted the importance of families, clans, and women in a major portion of the economy. Women might be eligible to take some forms of property ownership, through allotment, but the favoured individuals were definitely the male heads of household, a practice that was quite consistent with prevailing gender roles.

Without belabouring the history of colonialism and its consequences for Native women and families, let me highlight some of the policies that have had a lasting impact on Native women and that continue to pose challenges for contemporary leaders.

The historical policy of the European nations, and then of the United States, was to recognize male political leaders only. In some treaty negotiations, male leaders were asked to sign away tribal rights to land that, under traditional custom, was within the ownership and control of Native women. An example of this occurred within the Cherokee Nation, as has been documented by Wilma Dunaway.[5] Traditional Cherokee society was organized according to matrilineal clans, and control over the land resided with the women. Because the matrilineal clan was the fundamental social unit, women had a significant role in the agrarian economy and controlled the means of production. Dunaway finds that the introduction of the market system changed the economics of Cherokee society to include a dominant role for Cherokee men. First, the fur trade opened up the trade economy, which Cherokee men then transformed into livestock raising (horses and cattle). Dunaway claims that capitalism fostered a market-based economy in which men were labourers who produced surplus commodities for export, and women's labour was concentrated into arenas that were *not* incorporated within the male-dominated export economy. Because of this, Cherokee men assumed the dominant role in all trade, including agricultural trade.

Not surprisingly, Dunaway finds that the traditional government was reorganized to incorporate the emerging role of Cherokee men in intercultural dealings with the white society, which had a marked effect on traditional clan systems and Cherokee women. Between 1808 and 1825, male leaders instituted a series of laws that transformed marriage, property rights, family lineage, and the political rights of women. This enabled these leaders to transfer Cherokee lands and resources to the United States government. Dunaway describes the resistance of one of the traditional Cherokee women leaders, Beloved Woman Nancy Ward, who urged male leaders not to cede these lands. The Cherokee women organized a strong opposition to the National Council's negotiations with the US government and presented a petition to the council, which read in part, "We have raised all of you on the land which we now have ... Your mothers and your sisters beg of you not to part with any more of our lands, we say ours [for] you are our descendants ... Therefore, children, don't part with any more of our lands but continue on it ... Hold out to the last in support of our common rights."[6] Eventually, the National Council responded to this plea by enacting laws that precluded white husbands from selling the lands of their Cherokee wives and made it treasonous for any individual to negotiate a sale of Cherokee lands without the approval of the National Council.

The impact of colonialism upon domestic relations, family relationships, traditional norms, and values that guide those relationships. Dunaway describes the leadership of Cherokee women as founded on an ethics of responsibility and respect for the cultural values of the traditional Cherokee people. She describes how Cherokee women organized a strong resistance to Christianization and cultural change and fought to keep control over the education of their children. Cherokee women traditionally controlled marriage, divorce, child-bearing, and child rearing. However, the missionaries were attempting to inculcate a norm of patrilineal family leadership whereby men would make decisions about child rearing and divorce. As Dunaway describes this leadership, Cherokee women instituted a religious revitalization movement and stressed the importance of the ceremonies that accompanied the growing and harvesting of corn and healing. This became quite difficult as the traditional villages were reorganized into political districts, and the movement also suffered upon the tribe's removal to the Oklahoma Indian Territory in the 1830s.

Dunaway's findings with respect to the Cherokee are also applicable to other Indian nations. The US government, as part of its reservation policy, placed Indian agents in charge of reservations and established the Courts of Indian Offenses (which became known as CFR courts) and a Code of Indian Offenses for the agents to utilize to force compliance with Anglo-American norms. The Code of Indian Offenses criminalized many tribal customs, including traditional marriage practices and religious ceremonies. There are cases out of the nineteenth-century CFR courts in which Indian women were criminally punished for adultery when they left their spouses according to customary tribal practice and entered a new marital relationship.

The boarding school system had several serious consequences for Native women and Native families. Native women traditionally maintained much of the responsibility to educate children on their appropriate role as adult members of the tribe. The removal of Indian children from their families prevented this transmission of cultural education and often impaired the normal development of interpersonal relationships among extended family members. In addition, the physical, psychological, and emotional trauma suffered by many Native children in residential boarding schools gave rise to dysfunctional family relationships and patterns such as substance abuse, domestic violence, and sexual abuse, which are still present in many Native families and communities. Finally, Native parenting, which typically included substantial roles for members of the extended family, was often viewed as inappropriate and provided justification for the removal of Native children from their parents and their placement with non-Native adoptive families. Until the enactment of the Indian Child Welfare Act in 1978, many Native children were removed from their families and placed with non-Native families, leading to problems of social and cultural alienation and isolation.

The enforced dependency that resulted from nineteenth- and early twentieth-century federal Indian policy has manifested in a host of contemporary problems related to poverty and a welfare consciousness. Many tribes continue to struggle to combat rampant unemployment and high rates of substance abuse (today, methamphetamine abuse is even more prevalent than alcohol abuse), alcohol- and drug-related fatalities, domestic violence, and suicide. Because of the Supreme Court's decisions on tribal sovereignty, tribes no longer possess jurisdiction over non-Indian criminal offenders on the reservation, who are overwhelmingly involved in domestic violence incidents with Native women and children. Most of those cases will never be prosecuted because of the lack of federal resources to prosecute "misdemeanours" on the reservation.

Native Women's Leadership in Contemporary Society

Native people have endured largely as a result of the dedication of Native women to nurturing our cultures, our people, and the lands we belong to. Native women leaders today face a significant challenge, because they must successfully negotiate between the dominant Anglo-American culture and their own Native culture. Each of these cultures emphasizes different values and priorities. The majority culture espouses a leadership ethic centred on individual achievement, competitiveness, and the accumulation of property and prestige. Cultural traditions and family ties are considered of secondary importance compared with personal social and professional mobility. They may even be disadvantageous for political candidates who are assumed to be biased because they actively identify with a particular religion (e.g., Catholicism) or ethnic group and are, therefore, perceived as not being truly capable of representing a diverse constituency. In comparison, Native communities place a great deal of value upon the observance of tradition, the responsibility for extended family and friends, and cooperation and group identification. Leaders are expected to reflect these values, and if they are viewed as not adhering to them, they may lose a considerable amount of credibility with their constituents.

With respect to Native women, these values are often interpreted as having a political and cultural dimension. Cultural survival is perceived as fundamental to physical survival. LaFramboise refers to this dynamic among contemporary Native women as a process of retraditionalization, in which the women extend their traditional roles in caring for their relatives and transmit their culture to include activities vital to the continuation of Native communities within the larger non-Indian society. In my own work on leadership, I have examined sovereignty as both a political and cultural phenomenon. Tribal political sovereignty is typically understood as encompassing some concept of inherent sovereignty, for example, political autonomy as a distinctive government. However, that concept has been greatly modified by doctrines within federal Indian law that speak of the plenary power of the federal government to modify, limit, or even eliminate the political sovereignty of the tribes, as well as by the concept of diminished tribal sovereignty, which holds that Indian tribes have been implicitly divested of certain aspects of their inherent sovereignty as a result of their dependent status and incorporation into the United States. Thus, as domestic dependent nations, tribes are viewed as having lost the ability to criminally prosecute non-Indians, and they possess only limited civil jurisdiction over non-Indians on the reservation or over lands that are no longer within tribal ownership.

The concept of cultural sovereignty, on the other hand, is represented by the "effort of Indian nations and Indian people to exercise their own norms and values in structuring their collective futures."[7] Indian nations are fighting to preserve not only their remaining lands and resources but also their cultures and lifeways. In order to achieve self-determination, we must rebuild Native nations by probing the philosophical core of our belief systems as Native peoples to understand what sovereignty means and what rights, duties, and responsibilities are entailed in our relationships to ourselves, to each other, to our ancestors, and to our future generations.[8] There is important work taking place on language revitalization and cultural maintenance in the tribal colleges that exist on many reservations. As many participants in tribal language restoration projects have noted, Native languages are repositories of important knowledge about tribal concepts of spirituality and about the norms and values that structure tribal philosophies and metaphysics. There are important linkages between language, culture, law, spirituality, and education that are featured in tribal college curriculums.

Many Native people today are calling for a cultural healing in order to overcome the negative legacy of colonialism. This process involves many different institutions, including education, politics, law, and the arts. Native women are in key leadership positions in all of these institutions, within tribal institutions as well as within state and national institutions.

Summary of Research

Carol Lujan and I have interviewed several Native women who are in leadership positions within the various institutions constitutive of tribal cultural sovereignty.[9] The women are from different regions and different Native nations. They have different educational and cultural backgrounds. They are from different age groups. However, they share some striking similarities in their description of what inspired them to seek leadership positions, the challenges they have faced, and what qualities enabled them to overcome the challenges and enjoy the rewards of these positions. In short, the responses give rise to a Native feminist ethics of leadership, one that emphasizes the role of culture and community and a shared sense of responsibility.

What Motivates Native Women to Seek Leadership Positions?

Throughout each of the narratives runs a tribal story as well as an individual story. It is clear that each of the women took strength from the history and traditions of her tribe, and each woman expressed a sense of responsibility to ensure a secure future for the tribe. This appeared to be the most significant motivation for women to seek leadership positions. There was a marked lack of focus on personal accomplishment or seeking a particular status or privileged position.

In fact, the women who served their tribes as political leaders overtly rejected the idea of power politics and expressed discomfort with feeling that they had to fit into an old boy's network or that they ought to trade off their personal values for professional advancement. They agreed that it was not appropriate to set oneself above the people. They did not come from families that groomed them for leadership. They cited their love for their people and their desire to create a better future for the tribe as the inspiration for leadership. They also said that they had been repeatedly asked by other members of the tribe to run for leadership positions prior to their decision to assert their candidacy.

In some cases, leadership has had a personal toll that the women acknowledged as a sacrifice. They said that Native women are held to a higher standard in leadership than Native men. Some women fear this and will not seek leadership positions. Those that do, acknowledge this as one of the sacrifices they must make.

What Role Does Culture Have in Establishing the Standard for Leadership?

The traditional conception of leadership is still alive in many communities, but there are unique challenges for contemporary leaders. Contemporary leaders must be knowledgeable about the external society, and they must be able to function within the state, federal, and local structures. They must understand a complex universe of legal principles, economic principles, and technology and global interconnections that did not exist in the past. This complex environment is compounded by social pathologies that did not exist in the past and by external pressures that often jeopardize cultural survival.

The Native women whom we interviewed identified several qualities of effective leadership, including,

- being a visionary and having the ability to see things beyond tomorrow
- the ability to articulate goals and work toward them
- integrity and honesty, as well as the ability to honour personal values in one's professional life

- courage, which comes from conviction, from intuition, and from careful thought
- a strong sense of self, including an obligation to "be yourself" and "don't take a job to be somebody; take it to do something"
- the ability to turn things over to faith when the challenges seem too great to bear.

Each of the women placed a high value on tribal culture, as well as a strong sense of spirituality and the right way to live. They described their culture as an inspiration for how they ought to live and what ought to be in place for the future. What was particularly remarkable about the women, however, was their creativity and flexibility. They looked to their own traditions as well as to external sources for guidance. This is an active use of culture rather than a passive understanding of it.

What Is the Relationship of the Individual Leader to the People Whom She Serves?

Each of these women displayed a strong sense of personal sovereignty. They all spoke of the necessity to make independent decisions. They had a strong sense of their own purpose in leadership that enabled them to withstand criticism from other tribal members. In particular, the women who served as political leaders were not deterred by the comments of detractors who claimed that pursuing political leadership was inconsistent with the traditional ideal of a Native woman within these respective cultures. The women all had simultaneous traditional roles (as wives, mothers, or both) but understood these roles as being compatible with their leadership responsibilities. They also expressed a deep understanding of and commitment to tribal sovereignty. In Native cultures, the group is often seen as taking precedence over the individual. Our interviews demonstrated that these women had an equal commitment to their purpose to care for their families and for the members of the tribe. They did not place one role in an exalted position but described the necessity to do both.

What Enables These Women to Overcome Challenges and Succeed as Leaders?

The women agreed that an inner sense of self (i.e., who they are as people) has an important bearing on the external part of one's life (i.e., who they are as community leaders). They also agreed that leadership is earned through action, such as sharing knowledge or experience with the community and working hard to serve it. They stressed the importance of having a purpose and direction in life based on values that are meaningful.

Uniformly, the women said that their biggest challenge was harmonizing their internal role within the community with their external roles in society, and they described the many diffuse and pervasive pressures that tend to accompany modern leadership.

How Do These Women View Success?

The women spoke of the need to be a whole person, that is, balanced physically, emotionally, intellectually, and spiritually. They did not tend to measure success by external standards but by how well they thought they had achieved these goals. They stressed the necessity to not give up and to insist on interfacing with the people who have the power to make decisions. Over and over, we heard that it is important to have a vision and not to back down if it is something that you really believe in.

Conclusion

The Native women we studied were part of a larger tradition in which Native leadership is much more a reflection of the development of one's inner self than of how many degrees one has accumulated or what level of material resources one has. Leadership is earned through acts that develop a reputation for wisdom and generosity. Leaders are respected as humble people. They do not hold themselves out as leaders or brag about their accomplishments; they are always willing to help out when asked, and they make valuable contributions to their communities through this assistance. Leaders belong to the people in a way that imposes great responsibility upon them. They are expected to act for the interest of the group and not merely out of self-interest. It is a difficult life but also one that has many rewards. These rewards are not necessarily economic but personal – the sense of living a life with purpose and direction according to values that are meaningful.

Dr. Henrietta Mann, a noted scholar and woman of prayer for her people, the Northern Cheyenne, has spoken of the teachings of her grandparents, which emphasized that each of us has an identity, a purpose, and a responsibility, and that as we travel along life's road, we are each responsible for tomorrow and all that the future holds. It is this ethic of responsibility that defines the contemporary leadership of Native women. The women we interviewed had been profoundly influenced by their parents, grandparents, and their children. They developed their own values about leadership in the context of these relationships and the norms and values that they learned through them. The result is an "ethics of culture and relationship" that embodies the core of traditional thought about cultural survival and the obligations we owe to future generations.

NOTES

This is a slightly revised version of a keynote address that was presented at "Indigenous Women and Feminism: Culture, Activism, Politics," August 2005, Edmonton, Alberta.

1 Interview with Paul Enciso, in Marcia Keegan, *Southwest Indian Cookbook* (Santa Fe: Clear Light, 1987).

2 Teresa D. LaFramboise, Anneliese M. Heyle, and Emily J. Ozer, "Changing and Diverse Roles of Women in American Indian Cultures," *Sex Roles* 22, 7-8 (1990): 455-76, 457.

3 Quoted in Rebecca Tsosie, "Changing Women: The Cross-Currents of American Indian Feminine Identity," in Vicki L. Ruiz and Ellen Carol DuBois, eds., *Unequal Sisters: A Multicultural Reader in U.S. Women's History,* 3rd ed. (New York: Routledge, 2000), 568.

4 *Annual Report of the Commissioner of Indian Affairs,* 30 November 1848. Reprinted in Francis P. Prucha, ed., *Documents of U.S. Indian Policy,* 2nd ed. (Lincoln: University of Nebraska Press, 1990), 77-80.

5 Wilma Dunaway, "Rethinking Cherokee Acculturation: Agrarian Capitalism and Women's Resistance to the Cult of Domesticity, 1800-1838," *American Indian Culture and Research Journal* 21, 1 (1997): 155-92.

6 Ibid., 171, quoting Records of the Office of the Secretary of War, 25 July 1818.

7 Wallace Coffey and Rebecca Tsosie, "Rethinking the Tribal Sovereignty Doctrine: Cultural Sovereignty and the Collective Future of Indian Nations," *Stanford Law and Policy Review* 12, 2 (Spring 2001): 196.

8 Ibid.

9 The text in this section of the chapter provides a summary of our interview questions and the responses we received, with individual identities redacted, pending publication of the collective work.

3

"But we are your mothers, you are our sons" Gender, Sovereignty, and the Nation in Early Cherokee Women's Writing

LAURA E. DONALDSON

> *You know that women are always looked upon as nothing; but we are your mothers; you are our sons. Our cry is all for peace; let it continue. This peace must last forever. Let your women's sons be ours; our sons be yours. Let your women hear our words.*
>
> *– Nancy Ward to the US treaty commissioners, 1781*

These poignant words are from an oral petition presented by the woman known as Nan-ye-hi to the Cherokee and as Nancy Ward to the Euro-American men who had gathered to sign the Treaty of Holston in July 1781. At the time of the treaty's composition, Ward was the *Ghigau,* or most beloved woman, of the Cherokee – a title bestowed only in recognition of a woman's extraordinary merit and service. Wilma Mankiller, former principal chief of the Western Cherokee Nation, believes that the term is most probably a corruption of the Cherokee words *giga* (blood) and *agehya* (woman).[1] Scholars of Cherokee language and history concur that the title, when conferred before menopause, actually meant "war woman" and became "the most beloved woman" only after a woman's child-bearing years were over. Whether she was a war woman or a most beloved woman, however, the Ghigau sat in council meetings with both the peace and war chiefs, decided the fate of war captives, prepared the purgative Black Drink at the centre of many Cherokee ceremonies, and led the women's council.[2] In his *History of the American Indians*, which was published originally in 1755, James Adair derided this unique political institution as a petticoat government – a direct jab, according to Paula Gunn Allen (Laguna Pueblo), at the power of the Ghigau.[3] Indeed, Allen argues that the honour accorded her by the Cherokee people offended the Euro-American belief in universal male dominance.[4] Although there is some disagreement about whether the female council consisted only of clan mothers, or clan mothers plus other war and beloved women, all agree that it gave women a substantial voice in Cherokee politics and society.[5]

Nancy Ward received her designation as a Ghigau when she was only seventeen years old. After Ward's husband, Kingfisher, died during the battle of Taliwa, reportedly one of the bloodiest conflicts that the Cherokee ever fought with their ancient enemies, the Muskogee (Creek), she seized his rifle and rallied the warriors to a decisive victory. Because of her courage and the crucial role she played in winning the conflict, the Cherokee honoured Ward with the title of war woman. Like many American Indian groups both past and present, the Cherokee considered blood to be an extremely powerful and potentially dangerous substance. At least some of Ward's power and recognition derived from the way that this young Wolf Clan mother with children had experienced different kinds of blood – the female life-giving blood of menstruation and the male life-taking blood of battle – and thus became a particularly powerful blood woman. As Theda Perdue observes, such commingling permitted war and beloved women to move between the worlds of men and women and generated a phenomenal source of spiritual authority.[6] If the cultural work of mythologizing concentrates the entire history of a people or person into one epitomizing event, as Richard Slotkin argues, then settler mythologies of Nancy Ward collapse her power as Ghigau into a single act: saving a white woman from being burned by Cherokee warriors.[7]

In 1776, Mrs. William Bean was taken captive and held for some weeks at Tocqua, a town near Chota where Nancy Ward lived. When the war chiefs decided to burn their female prisoner, an interpreter informed Ward, who reportedly strode to the mound where Mrs. Bean was tied, kicked out the fires at her feet, and cut the ropes that bound her. In a popular variant of this story that probably contains at least some historical truth, Ward takes the freed woman back to Chota and learns from her how to make butter and cheese from cows' milk. In a contemporary novel based on Ward's life, Mrs. Bean offers to teach Ward dairying so that the Cherokee can become independent from the English.[8] Unlike this fictitious explanation, however, most non-Indigenous accounts of Lydia Bean's rescue have transformed Ward into "the Pocahontas of Tennessee, and the constant friend of the American Pioneer" – to quote the plaque that the Daughters of the American Revolution placed at her burial site in 1923. Just as Pocahontas chose the English over her own people by saving (and allegedly loving) John Smith, Ward cast her lot with white society by saving (and learning dairying from) Mrs. Bean.[9] This parallel between Pocahontas and Nancy Ward not only constructs Indigenous women as the facilitators of colonization, it also greatly distorts the historical roles of both Matoaka (Pocahontas' Indian name) and Nan-ye-hi as beloved women. Ward's rescue of Mrs. Bean nevertheless raises troubling questions even among her most informed and sympathetic admirers – questions that become clearer as the gendered history embedded in this event is uncovered.

William Bean, Lydia's husband, was a hunting partner of Daniel Boone and most certainly also a participant in the land speculations of the Transylvania Company, which had employed Boone to explore the potential of Cherokee territory in Kentucky and Tennessee. In 1768, Bean and his family returned through the Cumberland Gap to the recently explored Watauga River area (near what is now eastern Tennessee) to set up a homestead. The brothers of Mrs. Bean and other settlers followed, and the white population on the Watauga soon grew considerably. The newcomers engaged in hostile skirmishes with the inhabitants of nearby Cherokee towns and ultimately left several thousand Cherokee homeless and fleeing for safety to the southwest. The Watauga settlement (and others like it) was illegal under existing treaties, for it was built well within the territorial boundaries guaranteed to the Cherokee by the British. The infamous Treaty of Sycamore Shoals, signed in 1775 by the Transylvania Company and several Cherokee headmen – who, without tribal consent, transferred millions of acres in Kentucky and Tennessee to Euro-American control – further inflamed tense relationships at Watauga. Led by Dragging Canoe, Nancy Ward's cousin, the Cherokee war chiefs decided to evict the homesteaders by force, and it was at this point that Ward sent a warning about the coming attack to both the settlers and British forces. Lydia Bean was captured because she failed to heed Ward's alarm and was too slow in leaving the settlement. Rather than being innocent bystanders captured by hostile Indians, then, the homesteaders participated in – or at least acquiesced to – an illegal land grab: they threatened to expropriate the very centre of *Elohi,* Cherokee land and culture.

Although one of Ward's biographers has remarked that "Nancy Ward's reason for seeming to turn against her people can be known only by conjecture," a greater understanding of cultural mediation and the traditional duties of the Ghigau would certainly help to clarify her rationale.[10] Choctaw scholar Clara Sue Kidwell notes that historians – and, I would add, those who mythologize Ward – have often misunderstood the role of Indigenous women as intercultural mediators. For example, Cherokee towns were structured according to cosmic principles of balance: some were designated as red, or war, towns and others as white towns of peace. The mother town, Chota, was white, a fact that leads Kidwell to contend that, instead of choosing Euro-American over Cherokee culture, Nancy Ward "played her role [as Ghigau] as it was defined in her own culture – advocate for peace. To that end, she protected American settlers and informed British military agents of the hostile intentions of Cherokee men."[11] The unlikely testimony of Colonel Arthur Campbell to then governor Thomas Jefferson corroborates this view. According to Campbell, "the famous Indian woman Nancy Ward came to Camp, she gave us various intelligence, and made an overture in behalf of some of the Cheifs [sic] for Peace."[12] However, although Kidwell's point about the beloved woman of Chota as a peacemaker partially explains Ward's actions, it does not tell the whole story. Ward's role as a beloved woman meant that she was not only an advocate for peace but also for women: as the head of the female council, Ward assumed the responsibility of speaking on behalf of women during town deliberations and in the public sphere more generally.

One should also be mindful of the fact that in pre-contact Cherokee society, the penalty for killing a woman was double that of killing a man. These contexts imbue with new meaning the words reportedly spoken by Nan-ye-hi when she liberated Lydia Bean: "It revolts my soul that Cherokee warriors would stoop so low as to torture a squaw. No woman shall be tortured or burned at the stake while I am *Honored Woman*." I frankly doubt whether Ward would have described any woman with the term *squaw,* and the corroboration of this incident by a military officer's written records should prompt readers to regard with suspicion the rhetoric of savagism that it imports into Ward's speech. Despite these obvious distortions, Ward's statement nevertheless yields a kernel of social truth about the position of Cherokee women and the Ghigau in an era that witnessed the transition of the Cherokee from a decentralized confederation of independent towns to the much more centralized political entity known as a nation.

Several interpreters of Native women's history have persuasively challenged the field's domination by the declension model, or the belief that cultural contact with Euro-Americans inevitably resulted in the erosion of women's status. There can be no doubt, however, that the decades from the American Revolution to the beginnings of the nineteenth century negatively affected the standing of Cherokee women. Indeed, Ward's oral petition to the Treaty of Holston conference foregrounds some of the most important aspects of this adverse nexus of social processes. In his official response to Ward, Colonel William Christain confidently affirmed that since "we are all descendants of the same woman," the Euro-Americans would heed her words.[13] Christain was obviously not listening closely enough, however, because he failed to hear both the critique and the bold assertions in Ward's statement that "you know that women are always looked upon as nothing." For Christain, the "same woman" from whom all humans descend is Eve, an ancestress whose alleged transgression in Eden resulted in millennia of diminished standing for Jewish and Christian women. Ward was not a daughter of Eve but of Selu, the Cherokee corn mother, who gifted the Ani-yun-wiya (the people) with sustenance and thereby ensured that women would always be regarded with respect. Indeed, Ward's famous uncle, Ada-gal'kala (transliterated as Attacullaculla), once chastised members of the South Carolina Governor's Council because they had excluded women from an important diplomatic meeting between the Cherokee and the British. Ward herself possessed an intimate knowledge of the troubling attitudes about woman espoused by the newcomers. Although she never converted to Christianity, Ward did marry a Christian Anglo-Irish trader and thus had ample opportunity to observe this religion's ideology of female subservience – or at least the notion of true Christian womanhood prominent in the late eighteenth and early nineteenth centuries.

Contrary to these views, I hear the following in Ward's opening challenge to the Holston treaty commissioners: "you" (Euro-Americans) "know" (insist) "that women are nothing." She then interjects the contradiction followed by the Cherokee perspective: "but, we are your mothers." In her book on Eastern Band Cherokee women, Virginia Moore Carney notes that Ward often used a device known in Greek rhetoric as *epideictic,* the establishment of a common ground as the basis for persuading the listener to do what the speaker deems necessary.[14] This was undoubtedly the intent of Ward's claim that they (members of the Cherokee Women's Council) were the mothers of the treaty commissioners and that those men were their sons. Even more importantly, the petition asserts a political authority through kinship – most particularly, through the kinship of Cherokee mothers to their Euro American sons. This directs us to the only written petition composed by Ward – an 1817 document opposing the sale of Cherokee land by her own tribal government:

> The Cherokee ladys now being present at the meeting of the chiefs and warriors in council have thought it their duty as mothers to address their beloved chiefs and warriors now assembled.
>
> Our beloved children and head men of the Cherokee nation, we address you warriors in council. We have raised all of you on the land which we now have, which God gave us to inhabit and raise provisions. We know that our country has once been extensive, but by repeated sales has become circumscribed to a small track, and [we] never have thought it our duty to interfere in the disposition of it till now. If a father or mother was to sell all their lands which they had to depend on, which their children had to raise their living on, which would be indeed bad & to be removed to another country. We do not wish to go to an unknown country [to] which we have understood some of our children wish to go over the Mississippi, but this act of our children would be like destroying your mothers.[15]

In her landmark book *Women of the Republic: Intellect and Ideology in Revolutionary America,* feminist historian Linda Kerber notes that although the United States refused women "the technical machinery of political expression," there still remained available a "most archaic" mode of political behaviour – the petition. The right of petition – a request (usually written) made to an official, legislature, or court for the granting of a favour or the redress of a grievance – has been recognized in British jurisprudence since the days of the Magna Carta and in the United States since the 1776 rebellion against the British Empire. The revolutionary architects of the first Bill of Rights thought the right to petition so important that it became part of the First Amendment. According to Kerber, "the formulation of a petition begins in the acknowledgement of subordination; by definition the petitioner poses no threat. The rhetoric of humility is a necessary part of the petition as a genre, whether or not humility is felt in fact. Occasionally, the restiveness of the petitioner peeps out from the smothering rhetoric, and the petition approaches the broadside."[16] Euro-American women petitioned revolutionary governments and local committees of safety for permission to join their husbands across enemy lines, to claim property, and to travel to ports from which they might embark for Europe. Whatever their form or goal, Kerber argues that women's petitions were usually authored by a single woman and were only rarely the product of a female constituency. It is unfortunate that Kerber's historical vision limited itself to white female communities during the Revolutionary War era. If she had looked further – to the petitions of the Cherokee Women's Council, for example – she would have discovered that Indigenous women's use of the petition challenged many of her deeply held conclusions.

Even though they were not US citizens, Indigenous women readily grasped the power of the petition and appropriated this textual form "not only to resist dispossession, but to recount parts of their own history, describe the nature of their present lives, and assert their Native identities."[17] Legislative petitions consequently provide contemporary scholars with a provocative source of information about the impact of colonization on daily life and the complex ways that American Indian women and men struggled with one another for control within their own communities. This is particularly true of the 2 May 1817 petition that Nancy Ward submitted on behalf of the Women's Council – not to the US government but to her own Cherokee National Council. Ward was nearly eighty at the time and too infirm to attend, so she sent her personal walking cane along with the written document. This constituted her last officially recorded act as the Ghigau of Chota. The conclusion of the War of 1812 and the Creek War had been followed by both a revival of nationalist sentiment and a cotton boom in the South – and each of these developments combined to spawn a catastrophic political environment for the Cherokee. In the spring and summer of 1817, Andrew Jackson negotiated a treaty with several Lower Town headmen from northeastern Alabama and southwestern Tennessee by which they agreed to exchange 650,000 acres of their land for an equivalent parcel in the territory of Arkansas. For the first time, a treaty officially dictated the removal of the Cherokee from their ancestral homelands as a sanctioned, albeit voluntary, remedy. Further provisions of this agreement stipulated that those Lower Town residents who did not relocate to Arkansas would accept individual land allotments and the laws of the US government as well as those of the states of Georgia and Alabama. It was this threat that prompted Ward's petition, which was also signed by a dozen members of the Women's Council, including Ward's daughter Caty Harlan and granddaughter Jenny McIntosh.

In the petition, Ward laments the cumulative effect of white contact upon the Cherokee and their daily lives – "We know that our country has once been extensive, but by repeated sales has become circumscribed to a small track" – and reminds her listeners of the parallel between the sustaining role of this "land which we now have, which God gave us to inhabit and raise provisions" and the duty of parents to sustain their children by maintaining the land. Indeed, she argues, it is the duty of mothers to remind fathers, husbands, and brothers on the National Council about the stakes of their decision: "We have understood some of our children wish to go over the Mississippi, but this act of our children would be like destroying your mothers." For Ward and the other women who signed the document, the Lower Town decision to sell Cherokee lands and emigrate to Arkansas was nothing less than an act of matricide. Although some scholars have acknowledged the 1817 petition by Ward, they have consistently underestimated not only the trauma but also the gendered context that spawned the actual writing of the text. The Euro-American failure to understand the equivalence between land dispossession and matricide is vividly demonstrated in President Jackson's second State of the Union Address (delivered on 6 December 1830), in which he declares that it would doubtless "be painful [for the Cherokee] to leave the grave of their fathers; but what do they more than our ancestors did or than our children are now doing. To better their condition in an unknown land our forefathers left all that was dear in earthly objects. Our children by thousands yearly leave the land of their birth to seek new homes in distant regions."[18] For Jackson, land functioned as an exchangeable commodity – a notion that was utterly foreign to Ward and the Women's Council.

Duane Champagne (Turtle Mountain Chippewa) notes that Ward – and presumably the Women's Council – endorsed the Cherokee towns' decision to create a centralized government and a binding national constitution in order to prevent further sale of their collectively owned land by local or regional leaders. Champagne – who describes Ward as a wealthy innkeeper, farmer, and slaveholder – concludes that the women's petition "favored a constitutional government modeled after the male-dominated American system if it would enhance the nation's capacity to resist removal and preserve the Cherokee homeland."[19] This characterization is no doubt accurate, but Champagne's dispassionate rhetoric significantly underestimates the depth of the trauma in Ward's equation of land sale or removal and matricide. It also blunts the trauma embedded in the petition by misconstruing its genesis. For Champagne, Ward's intervention originates in a practical acculturationist desire to stem the effects of colonization. I would argue, however, that Ward and the Women's Council conceived their petition when the struggle between Lower Town Cherokees who desired removal to Arkansas and those who adamantly opposed them produced an appalling act of gender violence.

In 1817, the American Board of Commissioners for Foreign Missions (ABCFM) sent the Reverend Cyrus Kingsbury to oversee the opening of the Brainerd Mission School, an institution it had established at the invitation of Cherokee leaders. As the initial leader of this enterprise, Kingsbury kept a school journal, which recorded the following entry on 13 February 1817:

> Go out to day on business – Meet with Charles Hicks, one of the principal Chiefs. He informs me an Indian on Highwasse [Hiwasse] murdered his wife and children about a week since; supposed to be occasioned by a disagreement respecting removing over the Mississippi, he wishing to go, she not. The women in these parts are about to draw up a memorial to the National Council against an exchange of country. This is done in cognizance of the hardships & suffering to which it is apprehended the women & the children will be exposed by a removal.[20]

According to additional primary sources, a Cherokee man murdered his wife and three children, locked their bodies in the potato cellar, shut all the doors of the house, and then went to a relative's house at several miles distance.[21] Neighbours became suspicious when the house's doors remained closed. After they found the bodies of the mother and her children, the neighbours found the husband, who was sitting by the fire at his relative's dwelling. One can imagine the horror felt by Ward and members of the Women's Council when they were confronted with a kind of violence exceedingly rare in Cherokee society. A domestic quarrel over removal to Arkansas had engendered nothing less than an act of matricide. I suggest that a close relationship exists between this episode and the decision of Ward and the Women's Council to write their petition as well as their rhetorical equation of land dispossession and matricide. At the very least, it lends their statement "this act of our children would be like destroying your mothers" a newly poignant meaning.

The petition's rhetoric of motherhood also yields other, and thankfully less disturbing, insights. Theda Perdue has argued that the maternal concern manifested in Ward's speech to the treaty commissioners at Holston emerged from an expansive notion of kinship rather than a strictly biological connection. According to Perdue, Ward believed that peace could be sustained only if the Cherokee and their adversaries became bound by the ties of kinship – and, in Cherokee society, only women could accomplish this. Clan identities passed from mothers to their children, and households centred on the mother and her extended family. This leads Perdue to conclude that "the political power of Ward and other Cherokee women rested on their position as mothers in a matrilineal society that equated kinship and citizenship. In such a society, mothers – and by extension, women – enjoyed a great deal of honor and prestige, and references to motherhood evoked power rather than sentimentality."[22] The women's petition manifests much more than simply maternal concerns, however, and in this sense Perdue emulates Champagne in underrating Ward. An investigation of the Indigenous treaty protocols prevalent in eighteenth- and early nineteenth-century political discourse foregrounds the boldness of Ward's kinship gestures. Daniel Richter identifies nine basic stages through which virtually all Native North American participation in treaty conferences east of the Mississippi passed. The sixth stage involved a recitation of the parties' relationship with one another, the basis of their peaceful interaction, and the way in which their ancestors had taught them to behave. Richter observes further that American Indians described the connection among treaty aspirants in terms of the kinship relationships of uncle and nephew, father and son, or brother and brother. Unlike Ward's uncle Ada-gal'kala, however, Richter does not question the exclusively masculine nature of these relationships. This use of kinship terms functioned in an educative rather than literal sense; that is, they asserted to all participants what their attitudes toward each other ought to be.[23]

One striking example of this type of diplomatic education is the subversive way that the Haudenosaunee (Iroquois) often deployed the kinship category of brother when dealing with their Euro-American adversaries. As Richter comments, "brethren might be older and younger, temporarily stronger or weaker, than each other. They might often be rivals and sometimes come to blows. But, in a way no imperious English governor liked to acknowledge, they were fundamentally equals; none of the obedience fathers and uncles could expect of children and nephews applied. Just as important, as Brethren, the two parties were supposed to be inescapably bound to one another despite short-term quarrels."[24] Viewed in this context, the rhetoric of the Women's Council petition takes on new meaning. If the kinship relationships that American Indians used in treaty negotiations articulated ideals rather than realities, then the women's insistence on establishing a mother-son relationship with the treaty commissioners of Holston as well as with the exclusively male Cherokee government suggests a radical turning, or more accurately a re-turning, to those core Cherokee values that affirmed women's cultural and social authority. These values were demonstrated most fully in the establishment of the Women's Council. In contrast to the Haudenosaunee appeal to brotherly equality, however, Ward's assertion "we are your mothers; you are our sons" demands a respectful deference. In the kinship relationship of Cherokee mothers to their British (and Cherokee) sons, the Euro-American children acknowledge the greater wisdom of their Indigenous mothers – the women who birthed them as symbolic and social members of the larger Cherokee household. "We have raised all of you on the land which we now have, which God gave us to inhabit and raise provisions." Ward's petition reminded those who wanted to sell the ancestral homelands and remove to Arkansas that the traditional basis for Cherokee sovereignty lay in recognizing the Cherokee's responsibilities to, rather than exercising power over, one another. And the originary basis for this recognition was their relationship with their mothers – both *E:-tsi,* their human mother, and Elohi, "the repeatedly along place" of Earth.

It is difficult to assess the precise impact of Ward's petition. Although the Cherokee did surrender land to the US government in 1817 and 1819, they refused to accept the system of individual allotments, which the Women's Council had opposed, and ceded no more land until 1835.[25] Whatever its historical influence, the women's voices it embodies speak eloquently to contemporary debates about self-determination. If, as Taiaiake Alfred contends, the promotion of traditional perspectives on power, justice, and relationships is essential to the survival of Indigenous peoples, then the petition of the Cherokee Women's Council offers a case study of these viewpoints.[26] In his self-described Indigenous manifesto, *Peace, Power, Righteousness,* Alfred presents a sustained challenge to what he describes as the largely uncritical acceptance of Euro-American sovereignty in American Indian/First Nations communities. While acknowledging that this acceptance has effectively enabled an Indigenous critique of state control, Alfred also challenges Indigenous leaders to "de-think" sovereignty and replace it with a notion of power based on more appropriate standards: "We have a responsibility to recover, understand, and preserve these values, not only because they represent a unique contribution to the history of ideas, but because renewal of respect for traditional values is the only lasting solution to the political, economic, and social problems that beset our people."[27] This chapter reveals one historical attempt by Indigenous women to de-think the

Euro-American conception of sovereignty – most especially its articulation of nationhood or personhood in terms that degrade women.

The legacy of Nan-ye-hi consequently endures – not as the so-called Pocahontas of the West but rather as an example of why women's participation is so important to any discussion of sovereignty and the meaning of the Indigenous nation. More importantly, her written intervention in the early nineteenth-century struggle over Cherokee removal gestures simultaneously toward the past and the future: a past in which acts of matricide – the murders of both E:-tsi and Elohi – were inconceivable, and a future in which we will once again love our mothers.

NOTES

1 Wilma Mankiller and Michael Wallis, *Mankiller: A Chief and Her People* (New York: St. Martin's Press, 1993), 19.

2 Virginia Moore Carney breaks this down even further: beloved women sanctified food, drink, and places in the landscape by singing, dancing, and praying, while war women were chosen to control the activities of their warriors. See *Eastern Band Cherokee Women: Cultural Persistence in Their Letters and Speeches* (Knoxville: University of Tennessee Press, 2005).

3 James Adair, *The History of the American Indians* (Johnson City, TN: Watauga Press, 1930 [1755]), 133.

4 Paula Gunn Allen, *The Sacred Hoop* (Boston: Beacon Press, 1986), 32, cited in Carney, *Eastern Band Cherokee Women,* 24.

5 For the former position, see Grant Foreman, *Indian Removal: The Emigration of the Five Civilized Tribes of Indians* (Norman: University of Oklahoma Press, 1972); for the latter position, see Pat Alderman, *Nancy Ward, Cherokee Chieftainess, Dragging Canoe, Cherokee-Chickamauga War Chief* (Johnson City, TN: Overmountain Press, 1978).

6 Theda Perdue, *Cherokee Women: Gender and Culture Change, 1700-1835* (Lincoln: University of Nebraska Press, 1998), 39.

7 See Richard Slotkin, *Regeneration through Violence: The Mythology of the American Frontier, 1600-1860* (Norman: University of Oklahoma Press, 1973).

8 Marlene Sosebee, *Warrior Woman: Based on the Story of Nancy Ward* (Bloomington, IN: Xlibris, 2001), 74-75.

9 It seems clear that the ceremony described by John Smith in his diary was one in which "Pocahontas" adopted him as her kinsman and thus secured his loyalty for Powhatan.

10 Ben Harris McClary, "Nancy Ward: The Last Beloved Woman of the Cherokees," *Tennessee Historical Quarterly* 21, 4 (1962): 357.

11 Clara Sue Kidwell, "Indian Women as Cultural Mediators," *Ethnohistory* 39, 2 (1992): 103.

12 See Julian P. Boyd, ed., *The Papers of Thomas Jefferson* (Princeton, NJ: Princeton University Press, 1951), 4:361.

13 General Nathanael Greene Papers, Library of Congress, quoted in Alderman, *Nancy Ward,* 65.

14 Carney, *Eastern Band Cherokee Women,* 26.

15 This document is located in the *Jackson Papers,* Book 29, no. 17, vol. 14, 6452-3.

16 Linda K. Kerber, *Women of the Republic: Intellect and Ideology in Revolutionary America* (New York: W.W. Norton, 1986), 85.

17 Amy Den Ouden, "Gender, Culture and Colonialism: A Critical Feminist Perspective on Native-Angloamerican Struggles over Land in Eighteenth-Century Connecticut" (paper presented at "Contemplating Sex: Inferences, Strategies, Meanings," Rutgers University, Camden, New Jersey, 23 March 1996).

18 Theda Perdue and Michael D. Green, eds., *The Cherokee Removal: A Brief History with Documents* (Boston: Bedford Books of St. Martin's Press, 1995), 119.

19 Duane Champagne, *Social Order and Political Change: Political Governments among the Cherokee, the Choctaw, the Chickasaw, and the Creek* (Stanford, CA: Stanford University Press, 1992), 131.

20 Joyce B. Phillips and Paul Gary Phillips, eds., *The Brainerd Journal: A Mission to the Cherokees, 1817-1823* (Lincoln: University of Nebraska Press, 1998), 29. Charles Hicks was assistant principal chief of the Cherokee Nation from 1817 to 1827. When Pathkiller, the principal chief, died on 6 January 1827, Hicks briefly became principal chief until his own death on 20 January.

21 This is described in the Moravian Mission Diary on 10 February 1817, quoted in ibid., 436.

22 Perdue, *Cherokee Women,* 101.

23 Daniel K. Richter, *Facing East from Indian Country: A Native History of Early America* (Cambridge, MA: Harvard University Press, 2001), 135.

24 Ibid., 138.

25 Perdue and Green, *The Cherokee Removal,* 122.

26 Taiaiake Alfred, *Peace, Power, Righteousness: An Indigenous Manifesto* (New York: Oxford University Press, 1999), 141.

27 Ibid., 5.

Indigenous Feminism
The Project

PATRICIA PENN HILDEN AND LEECE M. LEE

History is the fruit of power, but power itself is never so transparent that its analysis becomes superfluous. The ultimate mark of power may be its invisibility; the ultimate challenge, the exposition of its roots.

– *Michel-Rolph Trouillot,* Silencing the Past: Power and the Production of History

Our theme stems from Michel-Rolph Trouillot's words and from the work of Nĝuĝi wa Thiong'o. To Trouillot's call to expose power, Nĝuĝi adds a model for decolonizing the worlds created by Europeans – in our case, worlds created by Europeans who became Americans.[1] Inspired by their call to action, we look at Indigenous feminism within the academy, its promise, and its problems. We then offer two examples of Indigenous feminist work. First, we examine the ideas of Laura Cornelius Kellogg, a political leader and activist of the early twentieth century. Our goal is to recapture this forgotten woman's significant critique of US bourgeois society. We then analyze some recent work on women in the Blackfoot world, a subject much studied and much mischaracterized by anthropologists, ethnographers, and historians. In both examples, we read against the grain to decolonize scholarship and history. In both cases, we suggest the importance of insider work, work written by Indigenous women themselves. Insider work, we argue, validates the real history of Native people rather than reiterating Euro-American stereotypes. We conclude with some brief comments on Indigenous feminist historians whose work could rescue from historical invisibility or marginality millions of Indigenous women, women who have disappeared from the historical landscape because of the work of generations of non-Native historians. As Indigenous feminist academics, we situate ourselves in a new space – a space that is separate from what has become the hegemonic white feminist world of women's or gender studies and, to some extent, separate from the practices of some women of colour feminists who are lost in the fogs of a trendy, but hopelessly obfuscatory, postmodernism.

Two Genealogies

Patricia Penn Hilden: When I was small, my sister and I lived in the same housing project as my grandparents. While my grandmother cleaned other people's houses, my unemployed grandfather, a Nez Perce Indian man who was six feet five inches tall, looked after us. We thought he was a god. Years later, while a student at Berkeley in the 1960s, I wrote my grandparents every week. Usually, my grandmother wrote back. One week, though, I got an envelope with handwriting I didn't recognize. Inside was a crooked piece of orange-coloured paper with a short note explaining that my grandmother had been called home for a sister's funeral. My grandfather signed his letter "Love Gramps" but at the bottom added a postscript that I shall never forget: "Forgive the paper, the handwriting, and your stupid old Gramps." I cried then: I cry now. Who taught my grandfather he was stupid? Who taught this man – then in his eighties – that he should apologize to the little granddaughter who thought he hung the stars? I had always believed that he had escaped the shame that came with being called "Hey, Chief" wherever he went. I had not realized that they had gotten him, too. This was, after all, the man who, as a young boy, had been put in one of the first locked-up boarding schools that Indian children were forced to attend. It was here, as Ngũgĩ wa Thiong'o writes of colonial Kenya, that "the night of the sword and the bullet was followed by the morning of the chalk and the blackboard." In colonizers' schools, children were hit with a culture bomb that annihilated their belief in their names, languages, heritage of struggle, unity, abilities and, ultimately, themselves.[2] Indian children were forbidden their religion and languages. They were forced to take white names. (Many – the stories creep out of the shadows – were sexually abused.) My grandfather hated Haskell Indian School, and he rarely spoke of it. I didn't know then about the techniques used to colonize these children, to "kill the Indian and save the man."[3] We didn't find out until after he died that he had become, at the age of thirteen, one of the rare successful runaways. (His school record is stamped with the word *deserter;* his character is described as incorrigible.) Watching my father's efforts to be accepted by white society as I grew up, I gradually began to realize the physical and mental entirety of colonization. | PPH

Leece M. Lee: Once, after I had presented at a conference, a Blackfeet man said to me, "So, you said you're Blackfeet. What do you know about being Blackfeet?" I laughed a little and said, "Well, that's quite a question." I wanted to say, "You first," but instead I told him our family name. He turned to me and quietly said, "That's one of the oldest Blackfeet names ... We didn't know any of you survived. We thought you were all ghosts. Gone." This has stuck with me ever since. I have great love and respect for my grandfather, my mother, and all of my family who survived great odds and gave me more than a name.

My grandfather was Blackfeet. He was tall, lanky, beautiful, and funny, and he had the driest sense of humour. He taught us certain ethics, and this is one of them: never say anything about someone you can't say to him or her directly, in every aspect of life. Although he was not college-educated, he taught my mom that "life is your college" and taught us all that we are intellectuals. He lived a quiet life and for the most part kept his heritage locked up like a secret. Luckily, other members of our family were not silent, though they all shared in a kind of tender solitude. My grandfather was a war veteran who was staunchly anti-war. He was gentle. But he became brittle at the mention of race. What racism, disenfranchisement, and war brought into his life, he mitigated with fishing, cooking, humour, and alcohol. He died of cancer when I was twelve. What are the causes of cancer? I don't know, but I would guess that colonial subjugation of the human spirit is one. | LML

Honouring the Past

These brief genealogies help to situate us and honour our families and those Native people who struggled so that we could be here, those people who survived, kept the stories, kept the languages, remembered the songs and the dances, the patterns of the face paint, the ways of making baskets, of beading, of weaving, those who held on to what it is to be who we are. So we begin by pausing to remember them, to hear their words, and sometimes to find their lost voices and make them heard again. Second, we who are inside the academy are trying to use our privileges to decolonize both minds and bodies. The tools? More stories. We who have attended US schools know the mind-colonizing road. At the University of California, Berkeley, we walk straight from our homes into a hyper-European world. Look at the catalogue of courses taught at this great university – or any university, for that matter. There is an entire department dedicated to Dutch studies, in which students can learn Dutch and the arts, culture, and history of the Netherlands (though perhaps not the history of Dutch colonization in North America, the Pacific, Africa, the Caribbean, Latin America, and Asia). There is a French Department, an Italian Department, a Spanish and Portuguese Department, a Department of Asian Languages – and so on. You can learn almost any European or Asian language on this campus. But you can't learn an Indigenous language – no Native American languages, no Pacific Island languages and, indeed, no African languages. The History Department teaches dozens of courses on European subjects that range from "our" origins in ancient Greece and Rome, to the European Middle Ages, to the early modern period (when the European-created United States heaves into view) and, finally, to the modern era. There are lots of US history courses as well, which are broken up into tidy periods that privilege the experiences of men and non-Natives. Nodding at people of colour and white women, the History Department adds a few token courses about those not usually considered, but they are taught almost exclusively from a European perspective. And the English Department is no different.

Patricia Penn Hilden: Majoring in English when I was young, this child of a barrio in the San Fernando Valley learned that so-called real literature, which was written by men, came from England or – and this was considered a bit dicey – from white (still all-male) US writers, most of whom were New Englanders and, so, almost the real thing. | PPH

Since the emergence of women's literature and women's history courses, the work of white women has also been privileged over that of women of colour – and this development is part of the continuing oppression. (This practice is evident in the fields of women's and gender studies, disciplines in which we find allies but at the same time find white feminist scholars whose histories of suffrage and feminism fail to acknowledge the influence of women of colour on their collective consciousness and political apparatuses.) White feminists' archives preserve a history that almost entirely omits the historical influence of Indigenous women on white suffragists and the feminist rights agenda. The profound influence of the Haudenosaunee clan mothers on the development of a women's rights forum is an important part of this overlooked history.[4] In the 1920s, Laura Cornelius Kellogg wrote, "I see no hope in the party politics of the United States until the women of the land get the suffrage and form a no-party organization."[5] As with other Indigenous women leaders, however, Kellogg's name never appears in the US feminists' pantheon.

During the same period, many white suffragists and feminists did not recognize the particular problems of women of colour. Indeed, the so-called Pocahontas loophole – which allowed the presence of a little Indian blood in white families to be represented as a heroic coming together of two great peoples, Native Americans (usually female) and Europeans (usually male) – skilfully transplanted the indigeneity of Native American women into the genealogies of white families. These erasures have yet to be discussed and explained adequately within feminist discourse. Instead, the silencing of Indigenous women enables the integrity of white genealogy, rooted in patriarchy, to go unchallenged.[6]

Anyone examining a map of the university's intellectual world will see immediately who belongs and who does not. Of course, there are still subtler indications of these exclusions. Inside Western, usually male-focused classes, we learn that only Western-produced knowledge is real, that our stories, dances, arts, and languages are not real repositories of scholarly knowledge but rather myths and legends. (These stories and practices are quaint and interesting, of course, especially when Westerners borrow them for their own entertainment, as is the case when tikis, hulas, and tataus are used to represent a conquered Pacific.) Mythologized young Native females appear as icons on coins and stars in cartoons of the Conquest. Old ones disappear from sight. Young Indian male figures live as larger-than-life movie heroes or as cherished sports mascots. Old men become wise Elders, raising pipes to the Creator and selling sweats or secret ceremonies to white consumers. For us, our stories and our languages and our songs, our dances and our traditions of face painting or other markings, and our ways of maintaining our relationships with the greater creation and the seemingly intangible realities hold histories that go deep into our unique and diverse pasts.

We recognize and we rename. We reclaim and learn our languages, reversing the process Leslie Marmon Silko describes in *Ceremony.* In this novel, Auntie realizes that "reconciling the family with the people," which once would have meant "gather[ing] the feelings and opinions that were scattered through the village ... gather[ing] them like willow twigs and [tying] them into a single prayer bundle that would bring peace to all of them," is now impossible because "the feelings ... [are] twisted, tangled roots, and all the names for the source of this growth ... [lie] buried under English words, out of reach." Auntie – and Silko – know that "there would be no peace and the people would have no rest until the entanglements had been unwound to the source."[7] All the myriad self-mutilations – which all of us educated in English in these Western knowledge-purveying places have experienced – *can* be unwound, and through the linguistic eyes of our ancestors, we can begin to remake ourselves. But as we try to grasp anew, tell our stories, and reclaim our words, problems remain, especially within the academy and even in the recent feminist scholarship on the history of women of colour.

Patricia Penn Hilden: In recent years, postmodernism has entered the groundwater of academic thought. In the case of women of colour feminists, postmodernist methods were first used in the laudable work of dismantling the essentialism of the early movements of racialized peoples. Unfortunately, subsequent work has effectively dismissed all epistemological claims, or indeed historical truths, based in experience, whether past or present. I find this endlessly deconstructive approach dangerously apolitical, focused, as it inevitably is, on texts without contexts or the individual and her putatively infinite possibilities for identity formation. Not only are the assumptions underlying this work mistaken, most of it is couched in impenetrable jargon understood only by select people. In much of this work, both "ethnic identity" and "woman" are mere categories, readily invented, readily dismissed. The most distressing effect of the spread of these academic practices is that they stifle historical consciousness, which is always fragile in these United States of Amnesia.[8]

A second consequence has been even more dire. Enraptured by exotic and secretive languages and techniques, captivated by the claims of the evanescent and fragmentary nature of experience, and terrorized by postmodernists who dominate contemporary scholarship, hundreds of feminist scholars have drowned their politics in increasingly wild deconstructions of epiphenomena. Words such as *subjecthood, signification, performance, fragmentation, hybridity,* and *representation* fly around like Tinkerbell on Ecstasy, rarely landing long enough even to be questioned by skeptical, old-fashioned hardliners like me.

At the same time, of course, some of this work has led to stimulating and important insights. Many Indigenous scholars, including me, have explored issues of representation. We have examined, for example, representations of Indian women in the ethnographic dioramas that are so ubiquitous in US museums and mark bodies with both sex and race.[9] In the most extreme of such practices, a single female body can occupy many spaces: as a real life victim of the European conquest, as an involuntary provider of so-called authentic artifacts (beads, moccasins, and dresses), as a transformed real body (bones or remains for scientific study) and, finally, as a series of unreal representations. In the latter case, there are myriad possibilities: for example, the Sacajawea dollar coin, which depicts a female figure modelled on a "real" Shoshone woman, now represents the success of the European conquest as new multicultural money. It is an apotheosis worthy of this money-driven nation wherein Sacajawea has become the sole "real historical female" on US currency. Unlike her less successful white predecessor, Susan B. Anthony, Sacajawea is even gold.

Sacajawea has recently undergone yet another transformation into a figure created by Sherman Alexie. The 8 July 2002 issue of *Time* celebrates "Lewis and Clark: How an Amazing Adventure 200 Years Ago Continues to Shape How America Sees Itself." In this story, who speaks for Sacajawea? No Shoshone woman. No Native American woman. In fact, no woman at all. Instead, we have "What Sacagawea Means to Me (and Perhaps to You)," by Sherman Alexie. Alexie smarms a bit about the difficulties of Sacajawea's life – she was kidnapped by other Indians while still a child, then quickly sold to a French Canadian man who had her in his possession, as one of his wives and the mother of his child, when Lewis and Clark appeared. In a fit of faux-feminism, Alexie notes that this young woman not only guided the explorers, she also breast fed her baby along the way, as though this was her most heroic activity, her greatest triumph. Rather than evoking admiration for Sacajawea, Alexie's conclusion effectively renders her historyless; it transforms Sacajawea into just another female commodity. "As a Native American," Alexie writes,

> I want to hate this country and its contradictions. I want to believe that Sacagawea hated this country and its contradictions. But this

> country exists, in whole and in part, because Sacagawea helped Lewis and Clark. In the land that came to be called Idaho, she acted as diplomat between her long-lost brother and the Lewis and Clark party. Why wouldn't she ask her brother and her tribe to take revenge against the men who had enslaved her? Sacagawea is a contradiction. Here in Seattle, I exist, in whole and in part, because a half-white man named James Cox fell in love with a Spokane Indian woman named Etta Adams and gave birth to my mother. I am a contradiction. I am Sacagawea.[10]

We of the first generation of feminist historians were, perhaps, likewise overly addicted to employing a kind of politically conscious ventriloquism, to interpreting what we believed to be the genuine voices of the dead. Yet our subjects were not merely mirrors. We acknowledged their real existence and their real struggles even as we recognized the problematic nature of our sources. Members of succeeding generations, however, seem to have accommodated themselves to the new postmodernist temperament by confessing to the limitations of their sources upfront. They claim that no truth can possibly be discovered and then proceed to substitute their own voices for those of their historical subjects. In this case, to employ the words of Gayatri Spivak, Native women have been "made to unspeak (themselves) posthumously."[11] Self-reflexivity, made trendy by guilt-stricken anthropologists, has therefore caused real people to disappear from history. Structures, categories, and processes, cloaked in the universe of increasingly postmodernist language, have appeared in their place. | PPH

For us, however, there are voices that cry out from the margins of this people-dismissing work. There are terrible looming facts in our contemporary lives that cannot be overlooked. To narrate these stories, to find and rearticulate the words of our peoples and reclaim their histories from the silencing blanket of white forgetfulness, we need a language that they, and others, can read and employ in their struggles for recognition and change.

Many feminists of colour offer alternatives to the dominant postmodernist system of feminist analysis. We rely on the work of two of them – Patricia Hill Collins and Paula Moya. Collins proposes a dialogic relationship between the articulated experiences of the everyday lives of all black women and the scholarly work of black women intellectuals. All black women's experiences, in Collins' analysis, are an intellectual work and politics. Because this work depends on the rearticulation of the ordinary experiences of black women, it must be discussed in fully accessible language. Collins notes, "I was committed to making this book intellectually rigorous, well researched, and accessible to more than the select few fortunate enough to receive elite educations. I could not write a book about Black women's ideas that the vast majority of African-American women could not read and understand. Theory of all types is often presented as being so abstract that it can be appreciated only by a select few. Though often highly satisfying to academics, this definition excludes those who do not speak the language of elites and thus reinforces social relations of domination."[12]

Collins makes an argument for accepting black women's experiences as knowledge. Paula Moya agrees and insists that women of colour in the academy should both validate and express – in accessible language – the learning that comes from our experiences. Echoing Collins, Moya sees intellectual work *as* activism. She argues, as we do, that we must reclaim our pasts and articulate our lives and our work. Her words about her own community could equally apply to ours: "The texts and lived experiences of Chicana/os and other marginalized people are rich sources of frequently overlooked information about our shared world ... [Thus] Chicana identity should be seen not as a principle of abstract oppositionality, but as a historically and materially grounded perspective from which we can work to disclose the complicated workings of ideology and oppression."[13]

Methods and Project

To articulate the broader project of our scholarship, we begin by rejecting two additional manifestations of our colonization that are potentially crippling, beginning with the widespread belief that intellectual work is self-indulgent, useless in the real world. We respond with the words of the prophet Smoholla, leader of one of the many Indian religions at the end of the nineteenth century. Smoholla had one essential rule that Patricia Penn Hilden heard first from her grandfather: "My young people," he said, "will never work, for those who work cannot dream." We, then, are destined to be the dreamers (the university calls these people theorists), obligated to offer our dreams, our analyses, our histories, our surveys, and our stories. Second, to overcome the silence wrought by the double deformations of racism and patriarchy, we embrace our place as feminists struggling both politically and intellectually *as women* to find our voices – and those of so many others.

Rereading Laura Cornelius Kellogg

Patricia Penn Hilden: A little confession as context. I am a historian, and even a historian of previously silenced women. Still, it was only as I sat in Cambridge, writing my second book about Europe's forgotten socialist feminist workers, that I finally had my "going home" moment. What had I been doing? I had been sitting in archives in Mons, Charleroi, Tourcoing, Roubaix, Lille, Verviers, and Liège – cold, alone, and poor but determined to gather all the little pieces to write the histories of these Belgian and French women workers. I asked myself why was I not instead at home, at tribal headquarters, in tribal museums and archives and boarding school libraries? Why had I learned French and Flemish and not Nez Perce? No answer. Except, perhaps (to refer again to the European knowledge validation process) I *had* thrown off the patriarchal, which had me firmly in its grip. So I went home, where I found a great vacuum. "They" said that the Indians had vanished, and then they wrote us out of history, leaving only traces of this or that warrior, wise chief, or unspeakable savage. And these traces were all masculine. The women? Gone. | PPH

So at last we seek our own pasts. In this chapter, we offer only a glimpse of the necessary future of Indigenous feminist scholarship, work that *must* reclaim and rearticulate the voices of all our forebears, whose intellectual work offers a solid foundation for our own and for that of our daughters. We reclaim Laura Cornelius Kellogg, a major critic of American capitalism who, by focusing on the Indian Bureau's terrible depredations and on the dire need to retain the practices that had kept her nation and its partners in the great Iroquois Confederacy strong throughout centuries of conquest, produced as thoroughgoing an analysis of the ills of the spread of global capital as was available in those decades. At the centre of an important group of Native leaders (a group that included her better-known colleagues, Charles Eastman, Carlos Montezuma, and two other women reformers, Zitkala-Ša and Sarah Winnemucca), Kellogg produced work that was important for several reasons, although both she and her words have been almost entirely forgotten. Indeed, a recent work that purports to have collected the writings of significant Native American women who worked in the period from 1800 to 1924 completely ignores Kellogg's brilliant critiques of American society and politics.[14] Moreover, the rhetorical methods used by non-Indian editors and publishers to frame Kellogg's work contributed to the dismissal of her ideas. Yet Kellogg's work in fact offered a startlingly prescient critique of US society, the outlines of which can be seen in two samples of her work, a speech given before the Society of American Indians in 1913 and a book published in 1920, *Our Democracy and the American Indian.*

Kellogg's speech is excerpted in Frederick E. Hoxie's collection *Talking Back to Civilization: Indian Voices from the Progressive Era.* Excerpts here are a problem as they are in all such collections. They exclude all nuance and many details. Native American writers and speakers seem to be particularly afflicted by this practice as countless non-Native editors cut Native texts into little pieces and arrange them according to an editor's thematic plan. Hundreds of randomly sorted collections of myths and legends, the wise words of Indian chiefs, authentic traditional stories, and descriptions of the spiritual practices of American Indians (heavily illustrated with authentic Indian art) grace America's coffee tables. Hoxie's *Talking Back to Civilization* collects Native voices and groups them according to chronological periods so that they do not stream wildly across time – just across space. At least, however, Hoxie has included women's voices. Of the twenty-three authors represented, two are women. Laura Cornelius Kellogg is heard once; Zitkala-Ša appears twice. Hoxie's editorial frames for Kellogg's words shape readers' responses to this so-called controversial woman. He does allow that negative opinions about the Indian Office's educational efforts "*probably* reflected the view of most members [of the Society of American Indians]."[15] He concludes that Kellogg's radicalism (he does not term it that) led to her marginalization. "During the 1920s and 1930s," Hoxie argues, "Kellogg's fierce opposition to the Indian Office alienated her from other Indian leaders." As a result, "She eventually retreated to her Wisconsin home, stirring little notice when she died in 1949."[16]

One wonders, who were the other Indians? Whose notice was absent at Kellogg's death? The Oneidas certainly took note of her many activities after her so-called retreat. Laura Kellogg's engagement in Oneida and Six Nations political life continued for many years and was regularly reported in the Midwest's major newspapers. On 21 January 1933, for example, the *Chicago Daily Tribune* reported the installation of new tribal chiefs and named Kellogg as the executive secretary of the Six Nations. The article notes that she was also the executive secretary on the Oneida Council. According to the article, Kellogg had been instrumental in forcing the Oneidas to follow Six Nations practices to choose and install a new chief. The newspaper quoted

Kellogg: "If any group of people want to elect officers according to the white man's rules, no one can stop them ... But they cannot be called Oneida chiefs." As this and subsequent stories attest, far from disappearing into some wilderness, ostracized by other Indian leaders, Kellogg had merely returned to the smaller stage of her own tribe and the Six Nations Confederacy.[17] There, after the death of her clan mother in 1922, she resumed her family's traditional responsibilities, working for the tribe, pushing land rights claims, and promoting a painstaking adherence to Six Nations laws.[18] It is clear, then, that not only did the Oneidas notice her work but so too did newspapers across the Midwest. Citizens of the Six Nations Confederacy and many of Kellogg's fellow Wisconsinites mourned the passing in 1949 of this key figure in tribal and national politics.

At least Hoxie included some of Kellogg's words. In the excerpted speech, Kellogg offers a clear claim to a separate Native American epistemology, a system of knowledge production held and expressed, she argued, in Native languages. (She spoke two languages, Mohawk and Oneida.) She insisted passionately on the validity and necessity of Native languages in Native education. Furthermore, Kellogg recognized an essential difference in Native people: "There is something behind the superb dignity and composure of the old bringing up; there is something in the discipline of the Red Man which has given him a place in the literature and art of this country, there to remain separate and distinct in his proud active bearing against all time, all change."[19]

Kellogg therefore rejected the sameness – called universality – so beloved of Euro-American multiculturalists of a later day. Kellogg also underscored the fact that Indian leaders had long recognized these differences and, from them, enacted their powerful resistance. They all knew that white men were stupid and ignorant when they viewed Indians as lesser beings. Their attempts to patronize or to infantilize Indians had always failed: "When Tecumseh was called to Vincennes, and intrigue and defeat were staring him in the face, in the open council, an aide to General Harrison called him to the General's side by saying, 'Your *white father* wishes you to sit beside him.' Tecumseh answered, 'My father? The sun is my father, the earth is my mother, upon her bosom I will recline,' and seated himself with the ease of one who dares to be himself."[20] Like Tecumseh, Kellogg recognized that that essential self was not a white man with red skin. Rather, that Native self was embedded in a world very different from the human-centred, bourgeois individualist world of the whites. The Indian world was alive – and from its life, Tecumseh's resistance to white power arose.

Kellogg's argument also included an extraordinary theory of Indian aesthetics. "It has not been appreciated that the leisure in which the American Indian lived was conducive to much thought and that the agitations and the dangers of the wilderness gave him a life rich in emotions. These combined with his clear first principles and the stringent discipline to a high standard of character, really gave him an aesthetic education. His choice, when it is native, and not borrowed, is fine, always the artistic thing in preference to the unattractive practical. He loved the beautiful because he had an educated sense of things."[21]

Not surprisingly, Kellogg roundly rejected Western teaching (later decried by Ngũgĩ wa Thiong'o). Despite her years of European-style education (she attended several prestigious Ivy League universities and travelled widely in Europe), Kellogg recognized the mind colonization that inevitably accompanied such teaching. She insisted instead on a pedagogy grounded in the Native world: "I ... say that there are noble qualities and traits and a set of literary traditions he had which are just as fine and finer, and when he has these, for the sake of keeping a fine spirit of self-respect and pride in himself, let us preserve them."[22]

In these smart and sophisticated claims, Kellogg also validated the essential place of intellectuals in traditional Indian life. As she put it, "The leisure in which the American Indian lived was conducive to much thought." In her words lie a key argument against those who might argue that our Indian world has too many practical needs to allow time for intellectual work. Moreover, Kellogg added, with their greater thinking, more intense dreaming, and broad and rich feelings, Indians lived better, more intellectual, and altogether richer lives than they would if they followed the narrowly focused, hyper-individualistic, materialistic, and competitive lives prescribed by white Indian Bureau schoolteachers.

Kellogg similarly condemned the worship of material wealth, the defining characteristic of the pre-eminently capitalist value system in the United States. Those who worship at this temple should not, Kellogg told her audience, make prescriptions for Indians: "Where wealth is the ruling power and intellectual attainments secondary, we must watch out ... that we do not act altogether upon the dictates of a people who have not given sufficient time and thought to our own peculiar problems, and we must cease to be dependent on their estimates of our position."[23] As for the boarding schools, Kellogg was pitiless, her metaphors calling to mind both prisons and that favourite pastime of white school children, butterfly collecting:

"The inmates lead restricted lives ... pinned too closely to the monotony of daily routine."[24]

Our Democracy and the American Indian: A Comprehensive Presentation of the Indian Situation as It Is Today, which was published after the First World War in 1920, explored the appalling conditions of Native Americans (conditions that led to a congressional investigation, which was published as *The Meriam Report* in 1928). Typically, Kellogg proposed a highly original solution, a plan called Lolomi, which in Hopi means "perfect goodness be upon you."[25] This book was also framed by an anonymous author. The anonymous Introduction effectively diminishes and marginalizes Laura Kellogg's work by locating Kellogg squarely within a genealogy of anomalous Indian women. Kellogg's critique of American policy comes "like the historic heroism of Pocahontas, from a woman." A stereotypical physical description of Kellogg follows: "Laura Cornelius Kellogg is a real daughter of the race, as we [!] like to think of the Indian, the tall lithe figure of the forest type, whose quickness of body and mind never deserted him [!] in the hour of need." The author of the Introduction concludes that Kellogg was driven by a quirky hostility to social injustice: "She loves to champion a helpless people, to her it is a sacred right and she is flamingly sincere."[26] The final words of this "frame" will resonate with every Native American reader: "We are made to feel through this [book] the undaunted spirit of an indestructible race."[27] Such a patronizing and sexist Introduction does everything to undercut this remarkable woman's intellectual authority.

Kellogg's Lolomi plan anticipated, in several important ways, the most successful contemporary Native Alaskan organizations. Convinced that the world of US capitalism was impervious to moral or ethical attack but equally hostile to Bolshevism (then roiling in Russia), Kellogg chose a third way to live as Natives in the twentieth century. Her approach was corporate. If all the assets of all the members of a given Indian nation were collected into one pool and then used to meet democratically identified goals based on the economic needs of the whole nation, the people would survive *as Indians.* Kellogg did acknowledge barriers to the plan that had been erected by a US government intent on keeping Indians colonizing themselves: "The Bureau as a school for sycophants has a method of destroying natural leadership in the race which has no equal."[28] To characterize people trained by Indian Bureau schools, Kellogg quotes one so-called blanket Indian: "The mind of this generation is like a broken reed, it cannot say no – a smile, and a pat, and our cause is undone!"[29] When the government welcomed colonized Indians to its service, it granted them the status of "competent" (i.e., able to own their land outright) in a humiliating ceremony that marked the leaving of the Indian life and the assumption of whiteness. Each new Indian Bureau recruit shot the last arrow. Then, under the auspices of the secretary of the interior, he kissed the plough.[30] What was the result of creating a group of competency commissioned private landowners? "I have been told," Kellogg wrote, that they "have all lost their property and are shifting around."[31]

Given her own intensive schooling, how had Kellogg escaped the deleterious effects of the Indian Bureau's colonizing practices? She wrote, "I had been preserved from the spirit-breaking Indian schools through my father's wonderful foresight. My psychology, therefore, had not been shot to pieces by that cheap attitude of the Indian Service, whose one aim was to 'civilize' the race's youth by denouncing his parents, his customs, his people wholesale, and filling the vacuum they had created with their vulgar notions of what constituted civilization."[32] In Kellogg's view, the Indian Bureau was an unmitigated disaster, staffed by Indian agents who "have become a type of historic criminal."[33] So egregious were their crimes against the Indian people that even a generally lackadaisical Congress ("all its energies are consumed acting upon piecemeal legislation that is either remedial of former acts, or the legalizing of loot") had ordered two investigations of the bureau, one undertaken to expose corrupt business methods, and the other (by the US Public Health Service) to report on contagious and infectious diseases among the Indians.[34] Both investigations exposed numerous crimes, and the latter resulted in a few changes in health services. In the end, however, they joined countless so-called investigations over the years that have "whitewashed the glaring facts, except such as do not concern the interests or good repute of the political personnel of Congressional Committees. As such, they merely license corruption." "Of what concern," Kellogg added, "is this pauper's cause before the supreme greed of the American nation?"[35] It remained to Indians themselves to take control, by joining the Lolomi project, pooling their resources, and forming tribal corporations with sufficient resources (particularly capital) to shape a viable economic future. Land could not then be alienated – as it could be under the Dawes Act – and corrupt whites would no longer be able to cheat or harm credulous or helpless people. (Linda Hogan documents the theft of Osage land by whites. And Kellogg participated in an investigation into the Osage murders.)[36]

Wise woman. All but forgotten. The intricate processes of colonization were laid open for her analysis; the problems faced by a world epistemologically unsuited to capitalism were laid open for her proposed solution.

That Kellogg is forgotten in much of today's scholarly world is a tragedy. With us, then, sits the responsibility to discover, reclaim, and publish her wisdom and radicalism. Given subsequent events, wasn't Kellogg right? Wasn't she one in a long and growing line of Indian women who have warned, planned, and acted against the deleterious policies of white Indian Bureau bureaucrats? For Native feminist intellectuals, Kellogg was surely one of us.

Recolonizing the Colonized: Women in the Blackfoot World

We turn now to a much-studied world that has fascinated countless scholars since the late nineteenth century, when anthropologists and ethnographers set out to re-create the histories of Native peoples. Taken as a whole, the scholarship on Blackfoot peoples suggests that the lure of this subject was the much-vaunted war-making capacities of Blackfoot warriors, unbowed before other Indians or the cavalry.[37] Not surprisingly, then, non-Native scholars' ideas about the role of Blackfoot women were preordained. Women could play only subordinate roles lest the supermale image of Blackfoot men be compromised. We look at some of this scholarship to analyze scholarly methods that – in the guise of objective research into the past – have effectively recolonized history. We also seek to identify and fracture several distorting lenses through which Blackfoot society, particularly women's society, has been observed and to offer successful counterpoints. Only then will a project that can uncover a more complete and deeper understanding of this world – one in which Blackfoot women's lives play a central role – be possible.

Most narratives of the Blackfoot world have produced interpretations that are, in the words of M. Annette Jaimes and Theresa Halsey, little more than a "vast and complex set of myths imposed and stubbornly defended by the dominant culture as a means of 'understanding' native America, both historically and topically."[38] The majority of these historical accounts (most written by ethnographers) appeared in the nineteenth century. The social scientists (predominantly men) who produced these accounts were typically fascinated by Blackfoot men – as the quintessential Plains Indian warriors. Their attentions were also captured, however, by women's activities that challenged Western patriarchal norms. Naive iterations of these women's so-called anomalous behaviours helped to create the mythical world of the Indian. Attempting to situate Blackfoot epistemology while not knowing the language, or because they unadmittedly looked through blinkered Western eyes, Western academics saw nothing of Blackfoot concepts of gender. Indeed, the cultural-intellectual frameworks of the Blackfeet proved Western lenses insufficient for framing Indigenous cultural-intellectual systems. As a counter-narrative, notable anthropologist Alice Kehoe's work on this subject demonstrates the limitations of wrongly associating and globalizing Western notions of gender as the measure of power, via personal agency and social influence. Kehoe writes, "Algonkian languages do not distinguish male and female through lexical gender. Instead, they distinguish animate from inanimate ... Everything that exhibits volition through movement ... is marked by the animate gender. Within that gender, the various species have differing degrees of power ... The fact that gender, in Blackfoot, distinguishes animate from inanimate subordinates 'gender roles' to the basic prerogative of living beings, the exercise of autonomy."[39]

Without recognizing these key epistemological distinctions, Euro-American observers became intrigued by members of the misnamed *Man*ly Hearted Women's Society. Evidently troubled, ethnographers, anthropologists, and other outsiders questioned whether these curious unwomanly women were accepted within what they believed to be the male-dominated society of their European fantasies. Most argued that these women who lived like men existed only on the fragile edges of the Blackfoot world.

Blackfoot Musical Thought, published in 1989 by ethnomusicologist Bruno Nettl, is a recent example of the tenacity of this view. Nettl describes Blackfoot women's activities in several, often contradictory, ways – as though he is mystified by what he cannot understand. He begins with the taxonomy of music, in which he finds that "there is ... the significant difference in cultural roles between men and women; and while the explicit taxonomy of musical persons does not include gender, my own Blackfoot consultants, male and female, made it clear that men's and women's participation in music is different." Does this difference signal a secondary or marginal role for women? Nettl writes,

> The existence of a women's society, the Buffalo Society, is acknowledged in the literature, but the description of its activities and rituals ... indicates that the singing was done by men while women danced, blew whistles and played rattles. On the other hand, there are indications that women had their own songs and singing functions. For example, McClintock ... describes the Crow Water Ceremony, in which women did 'most of the singing while men beat drums and helped in songs.' McClintock ... describes 'night singing,' in which young men *and their wives or sweethearts* ride around the encampment, singing in unison, and Ewers ... mentions women's

> mourning chants. Hatton ... makes a point of showing that the development of women's singing groups in the pow-wow culture is to be seen as a continuation of, not a departure from, cultural tradition.[40]

Despite all this complicated and often contradictory evidence – all of it drawn from dated sources (1912, 1913, 1930, and 1958) produced by white males – Nettl is unable to consider women's independent agency.

By contrast, Alice Kehoe's "Blackfoot Persons" describes the role of women in the ceremonial system of Blackfoot peoples. At the metaphysical level, Blackfoot cosmology includes a sacred woman who "move[s] between the Holy People of the Above World and the people below."[41] Many sacred practices were born to Blackfoot society "through the agency of human women." These central figures transmitted the "power [that] has been granted to humans" and were charged with caring for ceremonial material tools.[42] In this world, and in stark contrast to Western renderings, both male and female are cornerstones of sacred beliefs.

Although this is but an abbreviated rejoinder to these male scholars' misinterpretations, Kehoe's work points the way to a larger research project that would utterly transform scholarship on Blackfoot women's purportedly subordinate status in both the so-called traditional world and the world of contemporary Blackfoot society. Moreover, a paradigmatic shift in analysis would contribute to the evolution of research in the social sciences and humanities. As with other aspects of Blackfoot society, Blackfoot social, economic, and sacred practices defied Western conceptions of gender roles and women's subordination. According to Blackfoot history, "the economic role of women was clearly recognized by the Blackfoot in that women owned the products of their labor." Strong Hearted Women, Kehoe writes, "owned property, and were active in religious rituals. [They] specialized in certain crafts, such as tipi making, and exchanged or sold their work in the specialty to other women ... Wealth – ownership of horses, clothes, and other objects of fine craftsmanship, medicine bundles, and in the reservation era, cattle and cash (used to support ceremonies and gift giving) – distinguish leading families from commoners among the Blackfoot. Both men and women are admired for wealth and the power it brings."[43]

Despite Kehoe's work, negative ethnographic references to Blackfoot women's roles abound. In a 2002 interview, one professor's research on Blackfoot society is drawn upon to demonstrate that Manly Hearted Women stood out because "in a time when the ideal Blackfoot woman was quiet, submissive and stayed out of public affairs, these women held office, told bawdy jokes and owned horses. They were politically active, and many were medicine women." Although the scholar interviewed declares that evidence exists to suggest that Western notions of a gendered hierarchy in Blackfoot society were probably unfounded, she introduces a Blackfeet student who is "better qualified as a cultural insider to research the Blackfeet perspective on the manly-hearted women."[44] The term *Manly Hearted* and the dialectic between Native informants and non-Native scholars continue to validate Western myth as fact. The myopic tendencies of Western scholars that situate gender rather than disrupt the predominant positionality of Western ideology in research investigations is evidenced herein. Apparently, Alice Kehoe's work has not altered tenacious stereotypes. Worse, few scholars in the US context even bother to seek Blackfoot archives that hold traditional stories and songs and ceremonial practices. Few trouble themselves to learn what the Blackfoot language, and its history, might reveal. Instead, twisted beliefs about Blackfoot women continue to be promulgated and disseminated – evidence, again, of what Patricia Hill Collins (with an addition by Julia Sudbury) has called the "Eurocentric [patriarchal], knowledge validation process."[45]

Conclusion

This chapter offers three brief examples of our feminist project to reclaim, reread, and rearticulate. We must continue this work, first, to rediscover the ideas and practices of Native women leaders such as Laura Kellogg, women whose critiques of US society, capitalist materialism, and the effects of Western pedagogies all foreshadow more recent work and, in many cases, drive beyond what has been published. We need, too, to continue to delineate and deconstruct the myriad flows of power that limit and control our vision. Decades of stereotyped patriarchy-driven (and validated) images of Native women must be revealed as such so that a fresh, new, insider perspective will emerge. Finally, we need historians who will delve into the archives to give us portraits of politically astute, active, culturally essential Native women. Without histories of these women, the past remains the story of victors, and our true past will remain forever beyond our reach. As we come to an end, out of space for further musings about our collective project, we each have a last word:

Leece M. Lee: I quote the words of Albert Memmi: "Oppression is the greatest calamity of humanity. It diverts and pollutes the best energies of man – of oppressed and oppressor alike. For if colonization destroys the colonized, it also rots the colonizer."[46] After centuries of oppression, the task at hand remains the practice of decolonization, which first requires recognition of who we are today and recognition of the heart and intellectual core of our peoples before colonization was deployed to subsume us. | LML

Patricia Penn Hilden: I end by quoting my Nez Perce language teacher's friend Harry Wheeler: "wa.qo? w?qis kye wisí.x. kaló? Yox." Now we are alive. That's all.[47] | PPH

ACKNOWLEDGMENTS

We thank many people for their ideas, their conversation, their support, and their work. The Red Feminist Collective, which is represented in this collection by two of the editors, Shari Huhndorf and Cheryl Suzack, tops our list. Shari Huhndorf deserves our special thanks. We thank her for her work, her years of support and conversation, and her mentoring of so many Native students. In addition to this group and those we have named in the course of the chapter, we would like to thank our Indigenous colleagues at the University of California (some of whom are members of the Red Feminist Collective), including Majel Boxer, Danika Medak-Saltzman, Tim Molino, Dory Nason, Fuifuilupe Niumeitolu, Vika Ga'oupu Palaita, Kim Richards, Dewey St. Germaine, Marilyn St. Germaine, Harriett Skye, and Michael Tuncap. Special thanks as well to Wilma Crow and Twila and Dwight Souers. And, as always, we'd like to thank Timothy J. Reiss for his help.

NOTES

1 Ngũgi wa Thiong'o, *Decolonising the Mind: The Politics of Language in African Literature* (London: James Curry, 1986), and *Moving the Center: The Struggle for Cultural Freedoms* (London: James Curry, 1993).

2 Ngũgi, *Decolonising the Mind,* 9, 3.

3 Richard Henry Pratt, quoted in Gregory Nobles, *American Frontiers: Cultural Encounters and Continental Conquest* (New York: Hill and Wang, 1997), 236.

4 Laura Cornelius Kellogg (Wynnogene), *Our Democracy and the American Indian: A Comprehensive Presentation of the Indian Situation as It Is Today* (Kansas City, MO: Burton, 1920); Sally Roesch Wagner, "Is Equality Indigenous? The Untold Iroquois Influence on Early Radical Feminists," *On the Issue* 5, 1 (Winter 1996): 122-26; M. Annette Jaimes and Theresa Halsey, "American Indian Women: At the Center of Indigenous Resistance in North America," in M. Annette Jaimes, ed., *The State of Native America: Genocide, Colonization, and Resistance* (Boston: South End Press, 1992), 311-44.

5 Kellogg, *Our Democracy and the American Indian,* 56.

6 State of Virginia, Racial Integrity Act, 1924. This Act authorized the State of Virginia to register each of its inhabitants according to regulated racial designations, with an explicit directive to control who would be deemed as "white." American Indian ancestry of one-sixteenth or less was subsumed into the white category.

Because these relationships were typically between white males with particular political interests and American Indian females, the Act has become noted as "the Pocahontas loophole."

7 Leslie Marmon Silko, *Ceremony* (New York: Penguin, 1986 [ca. 1977]), 69.

8 Fuentes, in George Szanto, *Inside the Statues of Saints: Mexican Writers on Culture, Corruption, and Daily Life* (Montreal: Vehicule Press, 1997), 153.

9 Shari M. Huhndorf, *Going Native: Indians in the American Cultural Imagination* (Ithaca, NY: Cornell University Press, 2001); Patricia Penn Hilden, *From a Red Zone: Critical Perspectives on Race, Politics, and Culture* (Trenton, NJ: Red Sea Press, 2006); and Patricia Hilden, with Shari M. Huhndorf, "Performing 'Indian' in the National Museum of the American Indian," in *From a Red Zone,* 75-102. See also Danika Medak-Saltzman, "Trading Colonial Knowledge, Reclaiming Indigenous Experience: Native Peoples, Visual Culture, and Colonial Projects in Japan and the U.S. (1860-1904)" (PhD diss., University of California at Berkeley, 2009).

10 Sherman Alexie, "What Sacagawea Means to Me (and Perhaps to You)," *Time Magazine,* 8 July 2002, 56-57.

11 Gayatri Spivak, "History," *A Critique of Postcolonial Reason* (Cambridge, MA: Harvard University Press, 1999), 273.

12 Patricia Hill Collins, *Black Feminist Thought: Knowledge, Consciousness, and the Politics of Empowerment* (New York: Routledge, 2000), vi-vii.

13 Paula Moya, *Learning from Experience: Minority Identities, Multicultural Struggles* (Berkeley: University of California Press, 2002), 3, 18.

14 Karen L. Kilcup, ed., *Native American Women's Writing, 1800-1924: An Anthology* (Oxford: Blackwell, 2000).

15 Frederick E. Hoxie, ed., *Talking Back to Civilization: Indian Voices from the Progressive Era* (Boston: Bedford/St. Martin's, 2001), 52, emphasis added.

16 Ibid., 53.

17 See also "Oneidas Plan to Name New Chiefs by Ancient Practice Soon," *Green Bay Press Gazette,* 18 January 1933. Kristina Ackley has published a thorough discussion of many of our points in "Renewing Haudenosaunee Ties: Laura Cornelius Kellogg and the Idea of Unity in the Oneida Land Claim," *American Indian Culture and Research Journal* 32, 1 (2008): 57-81. This latter article was published after we wrote this piece.

18 Darren Bonaparte, "The St. Regis Mohawk School and the Cultural Revival of 1937," *People's Voice,* 1 July 2005.

19 Laura Kellogg, "Laura Kellogg Attacks the Government's System of Indian Education, 1913," in Hoxie, *Talking Back to Civilization,* 53.

20 Ibid.

21 Ibid.

22 Ibid., 54.

23 Ibid.

24 Ibid., 56.

25 Kellogg, *Our Democracy and the American Indian,* 34.

26 Anonymous, Introduction to ibid. 8-9.

27 Ibid., 10.

28 Kellogg, *Our Democracy and the American Indian,* 52-53.
29 Ibid., 30.
30 It should be noted that there was an equivalent women's ceremony of citizenship readiness, performed across the west around the turn of the nineteenth century. These are discussed in Patricia Penn Hilden, "Timi:pn'it – Remembrance: Space, Surveillance, Stories," in Timothy J. Reiss, ed., *Ngugi in the Americas* (Trenton/Asmara: Africa World Press, forthcoming).
31 Ibid., 67.
32 Ibid., 38-39.
33 Ibid., 41.
34 Ibid., 56.
35 Ibid.
36 Linda Hogan, *Mean Spirit: A Novel* (New York: Atheneum, 1990). These matters are also discussed in Lawrence J. Hogan, *The Osage Indian Murders* (Frederick, MD: Amlex, 1998); Dennis McAuliffe, *Bloodland: A Family Story of Oil, Greed, and Murder on the Osage Reservation* (San Francisco: Council Oak Books, 1994); and Terry Wilson, *The Underground Reservation: Osage Oil* (Lincoln: University of Nebraska Press, 1985).
37 We use the terms *Blackfoot* and *Blackfeet* as they are used by the authors cited. At the same time, we are aware of the controversies surrounding the differentiation of those who lived inside the borders of the United States, generally known as Blackfeet, and those who live in Canada, generally known as Blackfoot.
38 Jaimes and Halsey, "American Indian Women," 314.
39 Alice Kehoe, "Blackfoot Persons," in Laura F. Klein and Lillian A. Ackerman, eds., *Women and Power in Native North America* (Norman: University of Oklahoma Press, 1995), 120, 124.
40 Bruno Nettl, *Blackfoot Musical Thought: Comparative Perspectives* (Kent, OH: Kent State University Press, 1989), 83-84, emphasis added.
41 Kehoe, "Blackfoot Persons," 117.
42 Ibid., 116-17.
43 Ibid., 116.
44 Evelyn Boswell, "MSU Scholar Intrigued by Legend of Manly-Hearted Women," *MSU News,* 6 February 2002.
45 Collins, *Black Feminist Thought,* 253; Julia Sudbury, "Women of Color Feminist Theory" (lecture, Ethnic Studies Program, University of Oregon, 11 April 2000).
46 Albert Memmi, *Decolonization and the Decolonized,* trans. Robert Bononno (Minneapolis: University of Minnesota Press, 2006 [1965]), vii.
47 Haruo Aoki, *Nez Perce Texts* (Berkeley: University of California Press, 1979), 76.

PART 2

ACTIVISM

5 Affirmations of an Indigenous Feminist

KIM ANDERSON

"I'm not a feminist" is a remark I often hear from Indigenous women – even though many of the people I associate with are advocates of women in one form or another. When I told friends and colleagues that I was working on an essay on Indigenous feminism, their responses were in keeping with this dismissal. Some seemed bored, others indicated it was a waste of time, and still others saw it as an exercise in negativity. As one friend put it, "Feminists are always arguing *against* something." In this view, Western feminism is unpalatable because it is about rights rather than responsibilities and because it emphasizes individual autonomy. Some see Western feminism as erroneously striving for an equality that implies sameness with men, and some feel that feminism represents an attack on our responsibilities as women, particularly as mothers. There is also the argument that we cannot employ feminism, because it will exclude men from our struggle for health and well-being as peoples.[1] These sentiments make it difficult for an Indigenous woman such as myself to identify with feminism – and certainly to write an essay about it! Yet there are many kinds of feminism, and as I will argue, Indigenous feminism in my own thought and practice is anything but negative or exclusive. My intention is to open a dialogue about how Indigenous feminist thought can help us re-create a world that validates life in all its forms.

I begin with the notion that Indigenous feminism is linked to a foundational principle in Indigenous societies – that is, the profound reverence for life. Although life-affirming practices and beliefs are still operational to varying degrees in contemporary Native societies, our land-based societies were much more engaged with ways of honouring and nurturing life all life. Our relatives had ways of giving thanks when life was taken, as is evident in traditional hunting practices. Indigenous nations throughout the Americas had protocols to ensure that they maintained respectful relationships with the animals they hunted. I have been particularly struck by the respect inherent in the practice of *notokwew mâcîwin* (old lady hunting) as described by Cree Métis Elder Maria Campbell. Campbell remembers that it was the grandmothers who were the first teachers of hunting and trapping. Children as young as three or four would go out with their grandmothers to set snares because it was the grannies' job to teach children to be thankful, respectful, and gentle with the animals at this time and in this context. Old ladies were deemed to be the most appropriate first teachers of hunting because of their experience and wisdom as life givers. Notokwew mâcîwin was the name given to the careful practice of taking life, as learned by young children and taught by the senior life givers.

In cases where life was given, there were also ways of paying respect. In particular, women were recognized for their unique contributions in the life-giving process. Indigenous creation stories taught that all life was born of the female, and Indigenous ceremonies replicated the cycles of renewal and rebirth that femininity represented. Indigenous philosophies and practices ensured that healthy life was maintained through balance between the various life forms, including men and women. These principles were built into all of our political, social, and economic systems and underpinned the health and well-being of the people and the environments they lived in.

Living as we currently do in a violent and militarized world, a world that operates on hierarchical systems and in which women and children suffer disproportionate levels of poverty and abuse, I am struck by the thought that we have much to learn from the systems our ancestors created to protect themselves and Kā wee ooma aski, their original mother, the earth. Perhaps they understood that systems of dominance and control are not sustainable and therefore created the checks and balances that they deemed necessary for survival. In any case, I believe that what we now call feminism – which the Merriam Webster's online dictionary defines as "the theory of political, economic and social equality of the sexes" – was simply a way of life to our ancestors.[2] Feminism was simply one plank in the platform of life-affirming values that kept us alive.

My own venture into Indigenous feminist thought began with my first pregnancy, which brought home in a visceral way teachings about the sacredness of life. In carrying, giving, and then nurturing new life, I also began to understand the significance of women in the life-cycle process. I was overwhelmed by the responsibility and by the magnitude of physical, emotional, mental, and spiritual work involved in mothering. Being responsible for someone else's life was undoubtedly the most significant and the toughest thing I had done, and yet there was so little acknowledgment of this in the public domain. Although I was lucky to have support in my own home, I began to think about how small children and their caregivers (who are mostly women) are not validated or recognized by society. I was haunted by thoughts of the abuse and neglect that mothers and young children suffer on a daily basis. I wondered how we could possibly hope for a better future without due attention to the ways upcoming generations are living out their early years.

It was the emotional intelligence of mothering that really transformed me into an Indigenous feminist. I had for years been involved in social justice and policy work for Indigenous peoples, but I had not been particularly interested in so-called women's issues. In spite of knowing the statistics about how Indigenous women are doubly oppressed, I had not considered whether the oppression of women was connected to the overall state of disease in our societies. For me, pregnancy was a wake-up call about how far we have strayed from life-affirming principles in mainstream and Indigenous societies alike.

These feelings and thoughts led me to explore how Indigenous cultures validated women and their mothering work in the past. I was able to link the deplorable conditions of many contemporary Native women and children to colonization and its handmaiden, patriarchy. I learned that one of the biggest targets of colonialism was the Indigenous family and that our traditional societies had been sustained by strong kin relations in which women had significant authority. There was no such thing as a single mother, because Native women and their children lived and worked in extended kin networks. In the case of matrilineal societies, the father or partner would move in with the woman and her kin. This system protected the women from abuse and isolation, allowing her to raise children with the support of her own family. Women were not dependent economically on a single male, and because of this, separation (divorce) was much more feasible than it is for women today. Women were considered the head of the household because they were primarily responsible for the work involved in child rearing and in managing the home and home community. Empowered motherhood was not only a practice but also an ideology that allowed women to assert their authority at various political levels. In a number of Indigenous societies, it was older women who made decisions that set the direction for all of the people, which they did as clan mothers, through women's councils, and as head women of their own extended families.

My early musings about motherhood coincided with one of my other areas of interest: the participation of Indigenous women (or lack thereof) in governance. Before my first pregnancy I had spent three years working for a chiefs' organization. This job inspired my thinking about the role of Indigenous women in our contemporary governance systems, for it was there that I gained first-hand experience with the machinations of a male-dominated political organization. The hierarchical nature of the system places chiefs, who are primarily men, at the top of the pecking order, followed by technical people (policy analysts and the like) and their assistants, who are often women. I was hired initially to write a policy paper, but because of my gender and tenuous position in the organization, I found myself more than once being asked (if not expected) by visiting chiefs to get coffee and change airline tickets. Having moved from a female-run Indigenous organization in which rank was not immediately apparent by the space one occupied in the office, I found it odd to be in an environment that was organized by status and, ultimately, gender.

I eventually moved into a full-time position – developing social policy for children. We worked hard in our unit, and there were many admirable male chiefs who worked with us to raise the profile of children's social and health concerns. Yet time and again I was disappointed when we took our work to the regional assembly, only to have the social issues placed on the last day, where they would inevitably fall off the table because of lack of quorum. There seemed to be a fault line between the women who were doing much of the work at the community level (and with whom I consulted) and the men who did not raise the social issues we had been working on as political priorities. In turn, I don't recall any discussion about the need to address sexual inequality as part of our liberation as peoples. The gender equity plank was missing, but no one seemed to be paying much attention.

I hope that I am not dating myself with these experiences, and I certainly give credit to some of the current initiatives coming out of the male-dominated national political organizations in Canada. At the very least, there are women's councils at the Métis National Council and the Assembly of First Nations, and the Inuit Tapiriit Kanatami now has a female president who has been vocal about children's needs. Matrimonial real property on reserves has become an issue in national politics, and awareness of this issue may help to alleviate the losses incurred by First Nations women and children who flee their homes because of family violence. The Assembly of First Nations has engaged in a campaign to make poverty history and is working on a gender-based analysis framework. One can even find some decidedly feminist statements in its charter, including "the equality of men and women has always been a guiding principle ... Both men and women must be involved in the advancement of an equitable society." Yet actions, as the saying goes, speak louder than words.

I raise these anecdotes and issues in the context of arguments that Indigenous peoples should sidestep feminism because we have bigger issues at hand. Decolonization, healing, sovereignty, and nation building are areas of priority. If we work in these areas, so the logic goes, then the dire conditions in which many Native women find themselves will improve.[3] Yet, in spite of our efforts to achieve self-determination since the middle of the twentieth century, the lives of Indigenous women continue to be plagued by violence and poverty. Going back to my mother's heart, I am disturbed to think that a staggering number of Native children are being raised in situations of violence and poverty by women who are not supported by the body politic. Contrary to the trickle-down logic that says Indigenous women's lives will improve when we address the bigger issues, I would argue that until we seriously address the political, social, and economic inequities faced by Indigenous women, we will never achieve full healing, decolonization, and healthy nation building.

This was the premise of my book *A Recognition of Being: Reconstructing Native Womanhood* (Sumach Press, 2000), the writing of which was another key factor in the development of my Indigenous feminist consciousness. In *A Recognition of Being,* I wrote about a four-part process of Indigenous female identity development that included resisting oppression, reclaiming Indigenous tradition and culture, incorporating traditional Indigenous ways into our modern lives, and acting on responsibilities inherent in our newfound identities. This process is now useful to me as I think about how Indigenous feminist thought can help build healthier nations.

As I have noted, my journey began with feelings of resistance to some of the inequities and injustices that began to preoccupy me as a young mother. I began by resisting the violence and poverty in the lives of Aboriginal women and children. I resisted the failure to address gender equity as a key component in decolonization, and I resisted the lack of Indigenous women's voices in governance. Reclaiming involved taking a look at our history and understanding how Indigenous women traditionally had authority in all areas of society – political, social, economic, and spiritual – areas that I explored in *A Recognition of Being*. Incorporating traditional elements into our modern lives is more complicated, and it is at this stage that I find feminist thought to be critical. Feminism of all stripes can help us to tease out patriarchy from what is purportedly traditional and to avoid essentialist identities and systems that are not to our advantage as women. Studying feminist theory and history has been helpful to me, for I can draw parallels between some of what we call traditional and that which has been undoubtedly patriarchal in other contexts worldwide.

Lately, I have been able to call on feminist work to help me think through my ongoing interest in motherhood and nation building and how these two institutions work together.[4] Motherhood, both in practice and as an ideology, was the source of Indigenous female authority in the family and in the governance of our pre-colonial nations. Contemporary Indigenous peoples now call on these teachings as part of the political discourse related to healing and rebuilding.[5] As mothers of the nations, Indigenous women are supposed to be revered for birthing the upcoming generations and for being their first teachers. Women are also said to be carriers of the culture – a responsibility that we have by virtue of our connection to the very young. We are championed as the strength of the nation, a principle that is supported in often-quoted sayings such as "a nation is not lost until the hearts of its women are on the ground."[6] These ideologies of Indigenous womanhood are called upon by advocates for women's presence in contemporary political processes. The Native Women's Association of Canada, for example, has identified motherhood as a way of seeking authority in national Aboriginal politics.[7]

Calling on traditional ideologies of motherhood is challenging because the relationship between respect for Indigenous motherhood and women's roles in the present day is not straightforward. By virtue of their position as mothers of the nations, Indigenous women in many pre-contact cultures had the authority to call up or halt a war, allocate the wealth of the community, and determine membership through decisions such as those related to inter-nation adoption. With this in mind, we have to ask what kind of decision-making power our contemporary mothers of the nation truly carry. We have to ask whether Indigenous male leaders are not only open to listening to but also to taking direction from their mothers, grandmothers, aunts, and their affiliate organizations. In cases where there are no systems for women to exercise their authority, how is the motherhood discourse being used? If women are seen as mothers of the nations but are devoid of political authority, what *are* our roles and responsibilities?

One area worthy of examination is our literal role in birthing the nations. Because we are survivors of smallpox, massacres, eugenics, enforced sterilization, residential schools, and child welfare intervention, it is not surprising that there has been some pro-natalist (i.e., encouraging women to bear children) sentiment in our communities.[8] The American Indian Movement, an early manifestation of the drive for Indigenous self-determination, certainly had members who espoused this concept.[9] With higher than average birth rates, Native women of today are, indeed, taking up their responsibilities in child-bearing. Yet child-bearing can easily slide into an overwhelming responsibility for women, for there are plenty of women who end up without support from either the fathers of their children or the nations that supposedly value them. What, we may ask, are the fathers of the nation doing for children who no longer have the type of support from extended family that we knew in traditional societies?

Feminist literature exposes how pro-natalist movements and ideologies related to the mothers of the nation have been common in countries worldwide during war or postwar periods and within liberation movements.[10] Feminist history has shown just how disempowering these movements have been for the women involved, because they typically confine women to motherhood roles within the patriarchal family. Sadly, dominance and control of women have been the classic response to nations struggling with liberation movements, war, or postwar recovery. Immersed as we are as Indigenous peoples in our own battle and recovery movements, we have to ask ourselves how our states of national crises have influenced the image of our women and the expectations we place upon them. It is also worthwhile to consider how well we can be served by maternal feminism, for maternal feminism practised in a patriarchal environment can be limited in its success.[11]

These notions related to motherhood spill over onto Indigenous female identities in general. The less frequently stated, but often implied, corollary to the traditional motherhood discourse is that women are responsible for upholding tradition and cultural continuity through their identities, practices, and actions. The roles and responsibilities of Native women are purportedly grounded in Indigenous traditions. Women in other countries have been similarly employed as the keepers of tradition, a role that casts them as inherently static and relegates them to the backburners of political development. Men, by contrast, are charged with the forward movement of the nation.[12] As we fervently recover our spiritual traditions, we must also bear in mind that regulating the role of women is one of the hallmarks of fundamentalism. This regulation is accomplished through prescriptive teachings related to how women should behave, how they should dress and, of course, how well they symbolize and uphold the moral order.

When I think about how our women are cast as the strength and foundation of the nation, I have to ask how well this is serving us. My Indigenous feminist red flag goes up because we hear so comparatively little about the roles and responsibilities of Native men, particularly in relation to their families. My worry is that what we celebrate as our responsibility is really a question of overwork for Native women. Without a doubt, Native women have demonstrated tremendous strength in sustaining themselves and their children throughout centuries of oppression. This should not, however, be used as an excuse to put off taking care of them or their needs.[13]

This circumstance brings us back to the criticism of feminism in general and the question of how we can carve out an Indigenous feminism that is more suited to us. If Western feminism is unpalatable because it is about rights rather than responsibilities, then we should take responsibility seriously and ask if we are being responsible to *all* members of our societies. If we are to reject equality in favour of difference, then we need to make sure those differences are embedded in systems that empower all members. If we see feminism as being too invested in Western liberalism and individual autonomy, then we need to ensure that our collectivist approaches serve everyone in the collective. And if we want to embrace essential elements of womanhood that have been problematic for Western feminists (such as motherhood and the maternal body), then we have to ensure that these concepts don't get stuck in literal or patriarchal interpretations. We need to give the essentials of Indigenous womanhood the full metaphorical power they once had and figure out ways to act on them now.

As is evident, I have more questions than answers about how we can incorporate our traditional feminist ways into the modern world. But we don't have to have all the answers before we begin to act, for the wheel is constantly turning, and we continue to resist, reclaim, and construct as we move through our life journey. *Acting* in my case has meant working with other women and men in community organizations and in publishing to advance Native women's health and well-being, which I always link to the advancement of our people as a whole. This being said, I most often work with women's groups because I am interested in how women organize and work when left to themselves. I don't see this as being exclusive or as part of the negative man-hating rhetoric that still seems to hang around popular and ill-founded notions of Western feminism. To our own people, I would say that women's organizing is an Indigenous thing: our pre-colonial societies were sustained by women's work, women's councils, women's ceremonies, and women's languages. In practice today, it means creating the space for women to get together and to do work that will ultimately benefit all our relations.

In publishing, I have enjoyed collaborating with other women and men to work through questions of resistance, reclamation, construction, and action. In 2003, Bonita Lawrence and I published a collection of essays, *Strong Women Stories: Native Vision and Community Survival* (Sumach Press, 2003), with the intention of raising some of the prickly questions that are rarely publicly discussed in Indigenous communities. We gathered together some of our favourite thinking women to contribute to that anthology, women who were strong enough to point out the patriarchal underpinnings in what is often said to be traditional, women who could examine topics such as homophobia or the unrecognized contributions of women's leadership in our communities, women who were bold enough to withstand the negative repercussions of asking for change. Other contributions related to incorporating an Indigenous feminist vision into society. The last chapter was an essay we solicited from a young Anishinaabe man, Carl Fernandez. We deliberately sought out the voice of a young man to conclude this Indigenous feminist volume because we wanted to envision a future world in which men and women, young and old, would come together to work in balance and harmony among themselves and with all of creation. As Fernandez so eloquently stated in the final sentence of *Strong Women Stories,* "Our path must come to create a spiral, one that turns back to the past while at the same time progressing forward in order to survive in a different world."[14]

For me, Indigenous feminism is about creating a new world out of the best of the old. Indigenous feminism is about honouring creation in all its forms, while also fostering the kind of critical thinking that will allow us to stay true to our traditional reverence for life. If we want to avoid some of the ideological pitfalls encountered by other women and children worldwide, we would do well to become acquainted with feminist theory. Feminist theory can help us to be vigilant in protecting our own teachings, lest they reappear as patriarchy with an Indigenous face. We especially need to learn about the feminist elements of our various Indigenous traditions and begin to celebrate and practise them. As we spiral forward, we can only gain from considering some of these teachings of Indigenous feminist thought.

ACKNOWLEDGMENTS

I wish to thank Maria Campbell, Nahanni Fontaine, and Sylvia Maracle for reviewing this essay for me. Thanks also to the editors of this anthology who provided valuable feedback.

NOTES

1 Indigenous feminists worldwide have run into the same arguments. See contributions to Joyce Green, ed., *Making Space for Indigenous Feminism* (Black Point, NS: Fernwood, 2007). These arguments have also been used to denounce black feminism. See bell hooks, *Ain't I a Woman: Black Women and Feminism* (Boston: South End Press, 1981); and Patricia Hill Collins, *Black Feminist Thought: Knowledge, Consciousness and the Politics of Empowerment* (London: Routledge, 1991).

2 The term *equality* is problematic to many Indigenous women who assume that it means women should be the same as men. The argument is that we should not be seeking equality, because we have our own unique identities, roles, and responsibilities. I don't take *equality* to mean "like in nature" but rather "like in status." More often, I use the term *equity*, which Merriam Webster's online dictionary defines as "justice according to natural law or right; freedom from bias or favouritism."

3 In her article on feminism and Indigenous Hawaiian nationalism, Haunani-Kay Trask has articulated sentiments that I have heard in Canada. Trask states, "Sovereignty for our people is a larger goal than legal or educational or political equality with our men. As we struggle for sovereignty, our women come to the fore anyway." See Trask, "Feminism and Indigenous Hawaiian Nationalism," *Signs* 21, 4 (1996): 14. These arguments have been made in Indigenous communities worldwide, as is evident from the essays in Green, *Making Space for Indigenous Feminism*.

4 See Patricia Albanese, "Territorializing Motherhood: Motherhood and Reproductive Rights in Nationalist Sentiment and Practice," in Andrea O'Reilly, ed., *Maternal Theory: Essential Readings* (Toronto: Demeter Press, 2007); Patricia Albanese, *Mothers of the Nation: Women, Families, and Nationalism in Twentieth-Century Europe* (Toronto: University of Toronto Press, 2006); Ann Taylor Allen, *Feminism and Motherhood in Western Europe, 1890-1970* (New York: Palgrave Macmillan, 2005); Ann Taylor Allen, *Feminism and Motherhood in Germany, 1800-1914* (New Brunswick, NJ: Rutgers University Press, 1991); Anne McClintock, *Imperial Leather: Race, Gender and Sexuality in the Colonial Contest* (New York: Routledge, 1995); Miranda Pollard, *Reign of Virtue: Mobilizing Gender in Vichy France* (Chicago: University of Chicago Press, 1998); Raffael Sheck, *Mothers of the Nation: Right-Wing Women in Weimar Germany* (Oxford: Berg, 2004); and Nira Yuval-Davis, *Gender and Nation* (London: Sage, 1997).

5 I have written more about this in Kim Anderson, "Giving Life to the People: An Indigenous Ideology of Motherhood," in O'Reilly, *Maternal Theory*.

6 These popular sentiments are voiced in a recent collection of scholarly essays edited by D. Memee Lavell-Harvard and Jeannette Corbiere Lavell, *Until Our Hearts Are on the Ground: Aboriginal Mothering, Oppression, Resistance and Rebirth* (Toronto: Demeter Press, 2006).

7 Jo-Anne Fiske has written about the use of a motherhood discourse in Indigenous politics and argues that it has been more effective at the local level. See Fiske, "Carrier Women and the Politics of Mothering," in Gillian Creese and Veronica Strong-Boag, eds., *British Columbia Reconsidered: Essays on Women* (Vancouver: Press Gang, 1992), 198-216; "Child of the State, Mother of the Nation: Aboriginal Women and the Ideology of Motherhood," *Culture* 13, 1 (1993): 17-35; and "The Womb Is to the Nation as the Heart Is to the Body: Ethnopolitical Discourses of the Canadian Indigenous Women's Movement," *Studies in Political Economy* 51 (Autumn 1996): 65-95.

8 Lisa Udel reports that, in light of our history, having Indigenous children can be interpreted as an act of resistance. She states, "Given the history of the IHS campaign to curtail Native women's reproductive capacity and thus Native populations, Native women emphasize women's ability, sometimes 'privilege,' to bear children. Within this paradigm, they argue, Native women's procreative capability becomes a powerful tool to combat Western genocide. Motherhood recovered, along with the tribal responsibility to nurture their children in a traditional manner without non-Indigenous interference, assumes a powerful political meaning when viewed in this way." See Udel, "Revision and Resistance: The Politics of Native Women's Motherwork," *Frontiers* 22, 2 (2001): 50-51.

9 See Mary Crow Dog (Brave Bird) and Richard Erdoes, *Lakota Woman* (New York: HarperPerennial, 1990), 78.

10 See references in note 4. See also Wenona Giles Malathi de Alwis, Edith Klein, and Neluka Silva, eds., *Feminists under Fire: Exchanges across War Zones* (Toronto: Between the Lines, 2003); Lois Ann Lorentzen, *The Women and War Reader* (New York: New York University Press, 1998); and Rita Manchanda, *Women, War, and Peace in South Asia: Beyond Victimhood to Agency* (New Delhi: Sage, 2001).

11 Lisa D. Brush has reviewed international historical studies on motherhood to explore the potential for maternalist politics in the present day. See Brush, "Love, Toil and Trouble: Motherhood and Feminist Politics," *Signs: Journal of Women in Culture and Society* 21, 2 (1996): 429-54.

12 See McClintock, *Imperial Leather*, 359, and Yuval-Davis, *Gender and Nation*, 6.

13 Nahanni Fontaine has written an interesting essay that demonstrates how contemporary Indigenous youth gang culture rolls patriarchy and popular notions of Indigenous women's strength into a justification for violence. Women in gangs are cast as either matrons or whores (i.e., as old ladies or as bitches and "hos"). Old ladies are expected to stay home and refrain from doing drugs and to endure beatings from their partners. In the words of one old lady, "We couldn't stop it because we had to take it like a woman." See Fontaine, "Surviving Colonization: Anishinaabe Ikwe Gang Participation," in Gillian Balfour and Elizabeth Comack, eds., *Criminalizing Women: Gender and (In)Justice in Neo-Liberal Times* (Halifax: Fernwood, 2006).

14 Carl Fernandez, "Coming Full Circle: A Young Man's Perspective on Building Gender Equity in Aboriginal Communities," in Kim Anderson and Bonita Lawrence, eds., *Strong Women Stories: Native Vision and Community Survival* (Toronto: Sumach Press, 2003).

Indigenous Women and Feminism on the Cusp of Contact

JEAN BARMAN

Indigenous women's outlooks prior to contact with Europeans are impossible to know. Archaeologists probe the material remains and anthropologists the non-material dimensions of past cultures through interviews with informants and other means. Their findings tell us quite a lot about ways of living but very little about attitudes and perspectives before contact or, for that matter, on the cusp of contact.[1]

Another source exists for exploring Indigenous women's lives on the cusp of contact. Outsiders wrote about their encounters for their own purposes, and in doing so they left traces that open up possibilities. Almost all of these accounts are by men. Not only did men comprise the virtual entirety of arrivals, the assumptions they brought with them meant that they considered themselves the keepers of the written word. As a very broad generalization, male newcomers depicted Indigenous men in terms of their physicality and Indigenous women in terms of their sexuality.

In a groundbreaking and seminal article titled "The Double Standard," published in 1959, the distinguished English historian Keith Thomas reflected on outsiders' attitudes toward Indigenous women. In Britain and throughout much of the colonizing world, "both before and after marriage men were permitted liberties of which no woman could ever avail herself, and keep her reputation." Generally held assumptions about gender in what Thomas termed *patriarchal society,* being a society in which politics and the economy were male purviews, gave men sexual freedom denied to women. Acknowledging the fundamental link that exists between gender and sexuality, Thomas considered this double standard to be but one component of "a whole code of social conduct for women which was in turn based entirely upon their place in society in relation to men."[2]

The process by which Europeans took control of virtually all the world between the sixteenth and nineteenth centuries gave men access to a huge new pool of women who were seemingly there for the taking. Historian Stephen Garton crisply sums up this perspective in his observation that "sex was both a signifier and a practice for asserting dominance over other peoples." As he explains, "prostitution was tolerated and even accommodated by British colonial authorities as a legitimate means of regulating the sexual needs of the colonists – to protect their health, act as an outlet for natural desires and ensure social order."[3]

The unintended consequence of this attitude was considerable attention to Indigenous women in accounts from the cusp of contact. They reveal writers' perspectives on Indigenous women's behaviour, both within their own societies and in their interactions with newcomers. In the course of doing so, the various accounts hint at women's perceptions of themselves in relationship to these outsiders in their midst. The accounts tell us that, in some circumstances, Indigenous women acted independently of both Indigenous and newcomer men. Indigenous women gave the appearance of exercising agency. They took the initiative when it was in their interest to do so. We glimpse Indigenous women on the cusp of contact behaving in ways not wholly incompatible with notions of feminism.

The concept of feminism is most often employed relationally as the means by which women emancipate themselves from the subordination to men that is the hallmark of patriarchal and colonial societies. Some scholars go so far as to argue that "feminist analysis only arises in conditions of patriarchy, as a response to oppression and as a prescription for change."[4]

This limitation of the concept of feminism appears to have two principal causes. The first is the particular historical circumstances of patriarchy and colonialism in which the term came to prominence. The generation that coined the term has been reluctant to let go of the definition attached to it based on those experiences. The second cause is an assumption that men have always, so far as they are able, subordinated women. In this thinking, because patriarchy is assumed to be inherent to the human condition, feminism must by its very nature be adversarial.

Both of these reasons close off, rather than open up, possibilities in thinking about feminism. They discourage us from paying attention to times and places where women may have acted in ways consistent with the goals of feminism without necessarily doing so within conditions of patriarchy and colonialism. As well as being adversarial, feminism as it is usually defined is a state of mind. It emerges out of an attitude in which women take themselves seriously, value themselves as comparable or equal to men, and act accordingly.

It may be that on the cusp of contact some Indigenous women were not subordinated to men. At the least, they did not consider themselves to be. This circumstance does not make their actions any less feminist in the sense of their viewing themselves first and foremost as women, respecting themselves as women, and behaving accordingly in their relationships with others.

The three glimpses presented here are of Indigenous women on the cusp of contact in one of the last parts of North America to attract the attention of outsiders – British Columbia on the Northwest Coast. The earliest came by sea in the late eighteenth century as part of ongoing maritime expansion around the world. Others soon arrived overland in search of furs. Only in the mid-nineteenth century did a third wave of outsiders looking for gold move British Columbia from the cusp of contact to a colonial place.[5] The three vignettes come from these three time periods.

Record keeping was taken for granted by the time the first outsiders reached British Columbia. Ships' officers and the men in charge of the land-based fur trade were tasked with recording on a daily basis all and anything that came to their attention. During the gold rush, private and newspaper accounts served much the same purpose. The tedium of writing, whether by mandate or choice, about events as they occurred meant that happenings out of the ordinary sometimes received more attention than might otherwise have been the case. Encounters with Indigenous women fit into this category.

These three vignettes gleaned from the written record are in no way conclusive or definitive; nor are they necessarily representative of some larger phenomenon. They are presented much as they appear in the original documents. Our interpretations of their larger meaning will perforce differ depending on the personal backgrounds and scholarly apparatus we bring to their interpretation. However we approach these three vignettes, their telling brings us a bit closer to some Indigenous women's lives on the cusp of contact than we would otherwise come. They are, therefore, worth pondering.

The No-Nonsense Nootkan Women

It was the arrival of Royal Navy captain James Cook in 1778 in search of a fabled Northwest Passage across North America to facilitate British trade with Asia that first brought today's British Columbia to the attention of the outside world. The visit had two consequences. One was the almost immediate publication of accounts of Cook's travels; the other was the chance discovery that sea otter pelts acquired from Indigenous peoples were much valued in China to trim garments.

Cook's month-long visit and the resulting maritime scramble for furs by entrepreneurs from Britain and, later, the United States were both centred at Nootka Sound on the west coast of Vancouver Island. The journals men kept reveal they were searching not only for the non-existent route, and then for furs, but also for local women to bed. The situation was exacerbated by many of the officers and men on board being relatively young in age, at a time in their lives when their sexuality was an especially potent force.

The generally held assumptions that Indigenous women's sexuality should satisfy male wants and that the world of work was a man's prerogative both hit a snag at Nootka Sound. As the twenty-six-year-old surgeon with Captain Cook mused, Nootkan women did not conform to stereotypes formed by "the beautiful Nymphs of the South Sea Islands."[6] After a week in the area, David Samwell lamented that "we had seen none of their young Women tho' we had often given the men to understand how agreeable their Company would be to us & how profitable to themselves."[7] It was taken for granted that, like men in the society from whence the newcomers had come, Nootkan men controlled the sexuality of Nootkan women.

Samwell eventually recorded that a couple of women were "prevailed upon to sleep on board the Ship, or rather forced to it by their Fathers or other Relations who brought them on board" and thereby "received the price of the Prostitution of their Daughters."[8] It soon became obvious that something was amiss. The surgeon's assistant grew suspicious as other women followed in their wake. William Ellis came to realize that at least some of the women "were not of their own tribe, but belonging to some other, which they had overcome in battle."[9]

Other observations from Cook and his officers similarly attest that Nootkan women themselves saw no reason to cavort with the visitors. Their refusal was so unexpected as to invite positive comparisons with women at home. Cook remarked in his journal that "the women were always decently cloathed, and behaved with great propriety; justly meriting all commendation for a modest bashfulness, so becoming in their sex."[10]

Men on board the next British ship to visit Nootka Sound, a trading vessel captained by thirty-three-year-old James Strange, had a similar experience. A twenty-year-old officer on board wrote that "on our arrival, when the Men were absent, which frequently happened, the Women shut us out of their houses, and Barricaded the doors with Chests and Planks." Young Alexander Walker attributed this action to the women's common sense, as he put it, to "the fears of the Women, who took this method of freeing themselves from our coarse importunities." He described how "the frequent attempts, that were made to debauch the Women, and the tempting bribes that were offered for this purpose, were with a very few exceptions constantly rejected." In his view, "the behaviour of the Women was uniformly exemplary."[11]

Strange was very impressed that the Nootkan women were not going to be bought: "As a tribute due to the Virtue & Fidelity of the female part of this Society (and indeed to the honor of the Sex in general) I cannot help Observing, that it stood the test of, & resisted bribes, which by a Comparison of local Value, I am sure could not be estimated at less then fifty thousand Pounds."[12] As had occurred during Cook's visit, Walker noted that "three or four poor wretches were produced for prostitution." He likewise concluded the women "were Captives, taken in War, and reduced to a state of Slavery."[13]

British adventurer John Meares, who arrived at Nootka Sound a couple of years later, similarly concluded about Nootkan women that "in their characters they are reserved and modest; and examples of loose and immodest conduct are very rare among them." The thirty-year-old seemed a bit astonished that "there were women in Saint George's Sound [his name for Nootka Sound], whom no offers could tempt to meretricious submissions." A bit further north along the Vancouver Island coast, he was similarly impressed by how "no entreaty of temptation in our power could prevail on them to venture on board the ship."[14]

Nootkan women attracted attention not only for their control over their sexuality but also for an appearance of equality with men quite different from expectations for women back home in Britain. Captain Cook wrote about the everyday behaviour of Nootkan women: "They are as dexterous as the men in the management of their canoes; and when there are men in the canoes with them, they are paid very little attention to on account of their sex, none of the men offering to relieve them from the labour of the paddle. Nor do they shew them any particular respect or tenderness on other occasions."[15]

The next British seafarer to visit Nootka Sound, James Strange, who arrived in 1785 in search of sea otter pelts, made a similar observation but went further. In his view, the Nootka "seemed to live with each other on terms the most amicable & friendly possible." He observed that "in the married state, they appeared exemplary in love & attachment to each other."[16] To Alexander Walker, the officer on board Strange's vessel at Nootka Sound, "it would appear that the Women at Nootka are highly esteemed and treated with as much tenderness, as in the most civilized Countries of Europe." He described how "the Men were always very careful to protect the Women from our insults, whether they proceeded from violence or ignorance."[17]

Not only were Nootkan women respected by their menfolk and by themselves, they also acted accordingly. Nootkan women saw no reason why they should not participate alongside Nootkan men in the new market economy in pelts. Not only that, they were much more effective as traders than were their menfolk. Strange complained: "The Deserved Ascendancy which the Females have over the minds and actions of their husbands, appeared accordingly in several instances to be very considerable, for my part, in my Mercantile capacity. I dreaded the sight of a Woman, for whenever any were present, they were sure to Preside over & direct all commercial transactions, and as often as that was the case, I was obliged to pay three times the Price for What in their Absence, I could have procured for One third the value."[18] Meares' observation, made a few years later, was virtually identical in relationship to the trade for sea otter pelts, which had brought these men to Nootka: "The women, in particular, would play us a thousand tricks, and treat the discovery of their finesse with an arch kind of pleasantry that baffled reproach."[19]

These accounts challenge the easy stereotype held at the time, and into the present day, of Indigenous sexuality as a commodity. Except for women taken in war or otherwise exploited, Nootkan women on the cusp of contact controlled access to their bodies. Nootkan women also exercised power in other ways. They gave the appearance of leading somewhat independent lives in the everyday. They confidently entered the market economy of newcomers and had no qualms about exacting as much benefit as they could from the sea otter trade.[20]

The Uppity Women of Fort Langley

During the land-based fur trade that succeeded its maritime counterpart, Indigenous women came to be viewed by outsiders as useful sexually for more than a single night. From 1821, the fur trade in British Columbia and across the Pacific Northwest was controlled by the Hudson's Bay Company, based in London. Although many of the surviving records are limited to brief factual entries, the daily post journal kept during the first several years of Fort Langley, founded in 1827 in southwestern British Columbia, is pithy.

As with ships stopping along the coast, Fort Langley was male space, managed and regulated by men in their own interests. Indigenous people were banned from the post except to trade and in the case of men as short-term employees. Local women were invited in, but the manner in which they responded to the invitation did not always accord with the traders' intentions for them. Like the no-nonsense women of Nootka Sound, the uppity women of Fort Langley knew their own minds.

Fort Langley's head during the late 1820s, Archibald McDonald, who was then in his late twenties, quickly realized local women's utility in acquiring pelts. One of the best means to establish "intercourse with the natives here" was using women with whom traders had sexual relationships as intermediaries.[21] He set a proposition before the post's second in command, thirty-year-old James Murray Yale: The "Quaintkine [Kwantlen] ... being the principal Indians of the neighbourhood & [the only ones] who at all exert themselves to Collect Beaver, we have thought it good Policy in Mr. Yale to form a Connection in that family – and accordingly he has now the Chiefs daughter after making them all liberal presents."[22]

This unnamed young woman, whom Yale bought and bedded, turned out to have ideas of her own. Initially, it was her father who acted on her behalf. He repeatedly used his new status to make demands on McDonald and Yale, and it may have been in part for this reason she decided she had had enough of being a pawn.

In the story handed down in his family, Yale returned home after spending two days away supervising construction of a new home for his wife and young daughter to discover that his wife had left: "Reaching his cabin he found the small Eliza wailing away to herself. Her mother was not to be seen. James knew without further thought that the thing he had feared from the first had finally come to pass."[23] The phrasing of the last sentence suggests that the departure was not of the moment or unexpected. It was, rather, the culmination of a long-term situation that this young Indigenous woman chose to end by leaving her daughter behind to ensure her own freedom.

Archibald McDonald's utilization of Indigenous women to advance the fur trade went well beyond his luckless clerk. Post employees were almost all young men in their sexual prime who were already employing various enticements to persuade local women to spend the night with them. Realizing that "those of the men that had not been lucky enough to Come in for a

Chance of this kind have no inducement at all to remain at the place," McDonald devised a new policy.[24] He permitted men who were two years into their three-year contracts "to take a woman" on a more or less permanent basis.[25] By early 1830, he reported to his fur trade superiors that "all our Men have taken Women," which "has had the effect of reconciling them to the place and removing the inconvenience and indeed the great uncertainty of being able to get them year after year replaced."[26] Men now renewed their contracts for another three years as a matter of course.

Although they were enclosed in male space, these women also inhabited a much larger Indigenous space. McDonald wrote somewhat idealistically in the post's journal that "it behooves us to ... keep these dames always within due bounds," by which he meant the post and its near vicinity.[27] The restraint McDonald assumed was women's place was, in practice, impossible. These Indigenous women were accustomed to freedom of movement, and they continued to be their own persons. When a perceived danger of attack caused them to be locked in at night, "allowed out only morning and evening for water & firewood," they "contrive[d] to Create a little disturbance among the Indians about the beach with their batter of words."[28] A few days later, still locked up at night, the women "created a most unconscionable row among themselves, & two Couples actually proceeded to blows."[29]

Another time, some of the women stole some gunpowder from a storeroom, but apart from getting it returned, the post head acknowledged "tis all we can make of it."[30] The fur traders expected deference from their womenfolk as a matter of course and were repeatedly at a loss as to how to manage uppity women. Dissatisfied women simply left; by doing so, they put men at an immediate disadvantage, for the men either had to enter Indigenous space to retrieve the women or lose face.

In July 1829, a woman who had been "remonstrated with" by her so-called husband for talking with her mother near the gates to the post "watched her time and walked off to the [nearby Indian] camp." The husband wanted her back, and "after his work was over he followed her, & requested her return, which with the Concurrence of her relations and others around was positively refused under frivolous pretexts that She was not Kindly treated or entirely Secured as yet with the necessary property."[31] Reflecting colonial assumptions of male superiority, the post's head fretted over the best course of action. If this woman was not returned, there were consequences for the other men in their relationships. It would mean "the husbands are bound down never to Correct them."[32]

So Archibald McDonald acted. He described in his daily journal how he "called 5 men under arms immediately & with them proceeded to the Village when with very little gallantry in my address I ordered the lady to the Fort & acquainted the Natives that it would be best for them never to put us to Such trouble again."[33] The woman was forcibly returned, and although we do not know for certain what happened next, we get a hint of what might have occurred from a journal entry ten days later. It noted curtly, without elaboration as to whether it was the same woman, that "one of our men's wives decamped this morning."[34]

This glimpse of Indigenous women on the cusp of contact at Fort Langley is partial and one-sided. Even so, it suggests that women did not lose their sense of selves on agreeing on their own accord or after being persuaded by their families to cohabit with newcomers. Some of these relationships were long-lived or lifelong and resulted in large families that descend to the present day.[35] Other women became uppity, and when they did so, they were not afraid to act in what they perceived to be their own best interests as women and as human beings.

The Women Who Danced

The critical event that moved British Columbia from the cusp of contact toward settlement was a gold rush that erupted in 1858.[36] A fur trade population numbering in the hundreds grew many times over as upward to thirty thousand men rushed in from around the world in the hopes of getting rich quick. Many were experienced miners of the California gold rush, which had begun a decade earlier; others were young men in their early twenties newly arrived from homes in North America, Britain, or China. Vancouver Island had been a British colony under fur trade oversight since 1849, and the mainland now became the separate British colony of British Columbia. The two colonies would be amalgamated in 1866, and five years later British Columbia would join the new Canadian Confederation.

The most scrutinized phenomenon speaking to Indigenous women's attitudes during this rapidly changing time was the dance hall. Dance halls were an everyday feature of gold rushes, be it in California in 1849, Australia in the early 1850s, or the Klondike in the late 1890s. Dance halls encouraged miners to put aside, for the moment, the hardships of the gold fields, even as they were parted from their newly got gains. The phenomenon was much the same everywhere: men paid to dance with women who were there especially for that purpose, and they were expected to treat the women to drinks during the intervals.

The difference in British Columbia was that newcomer women were in such short supply that the women who danced were almost all Indigenous. The two to three dozen dance halls that sprang up during the half dozen years of the gold rush were, as elsewhere, economic ventures intended to serve newcomer business interests. The women were the necessary sidebars to the dance halls' successful operation.

All the same, dance halls gave Indigenous women real opportunities to exercise control in a world that, for many of them and their families, was being turned upside down by rapidly changing times. Dance halls gave women the means not only to make a bit of money but also to dress like their newcomer counterparts. By doing so, some of them may have hoped to secure a measure of acceptance or even respectability. Indigenous women had to adopt patterns of behaviour already familiar to many of their dancing partners by virtue of their earlier participation in the Californian or Australian gold rushes. These expectations were not easy to meet, yet women appear to have done so.

The dance halls that operated in the colonial capital of Victoria on Vancouver Island, where many of the miners passed the winter months when the weather made it impossible to mine, and elsewhere did so in a fairly similar fashion. Women were expected to learn cotillions, waltzes, and the lancers, and Julien's quadrilles, dances led by "the dulcet strains of a fiddle," by "a violin, bass viola, and a brass instrument," or perhaps only by a "fifer."[37] A participant recalled that "25 cents (about a shilling) was the entrance fee, and there was a kind of master of ceremonies who called out the figures – 'first gent to the left with the left hand round, back again and turn' – 'balance in a line' – it was really wonderful what a good time they all kept and how serious they all were about it."[38]

Even more important than the dances themselves was the expected behaviour between the dances, which was the most profitable aspect of the evening from the perspective of dance hall owners. A local writer described how "each man paid fifty cents for a dance, and had to 'stand drinks' at the bar for himself and his dusky partner after each."[39] The gold fields account explained how "When the Quadrille was finished 'Waltz up to the bar' was shouted out in a very loud voice – when every one did so at once, and we all had a drink and our partners generally took lemonade, or ginger ale. 50 cents was charged for each drink whatever it might be so one can easily understand what a good profit was made. Sometimes champagne was ordered. I should be sorry to say what it was made of but it always cost $10 a bottle."[40] At another dance hall, according to a newspaper account, "a buff of conversation and a rush to the bar" was quickly followed by "the poppings of soda-water corks and the munchings of apples."[41]

The common means of communication was Chinook. This jargon of a few hundred words had emerged during the fur trade out of French, English, and Nootkan, Chinookan, and other Indigenous languages.[42] Virtually everyone during the gold rush picked it up as a matter of course. A dance hall attendee recalled how the women "had learned a little English and all the men could speak Chinook more or less, which was the lingua franca."[43]

Indigenous women not only had to act suitably, they also had to dress appropriately. One account describes participants as being "well and in some instances tastefully dressed," wearing "the silk dress and the dainty garter, with the air of a Parisian dame."[44] Many women sewed their own outfits. The newly arrived Anglican bishop observed at an Indigenous encampment "a woman making up a dress" for the dance house that night.[45]

Contemporary accounts indicate that women not only responded well to their new circumstances, they took the initiative to ensure dance halls operated as they were supposed to. One attendee wrote, "I recollect asking one of the Kitty's in Chinook to dance with me and she drew herself up in a very dignified manner and said 'Halo introduce' which signified I had not been introduced to her! And I couldn't help laughing which made her very angry."[46] Another account includes a similar observation: "A strange miner going in one night, went to one of these 'maids of the forest' and intimated his desire for the pleasure of a dance with her. She eyed him with scorn and remarked, 'Halo introduce.' He accordingly had to hunt up some one who would do him the favor."[47] Indigenous women ensured that the rules were followed, not only by themselves but also by the miners and others who sought to dance with them. By doing so, they exercised a measure of control over the new circumstances in which they found themselves.

It is critically important to distinguish Indigenous women's resourcefulness from contemporary responses to them grounded in patriarchy and colonialism. Not unexpectedly, Indigenous women's mimicry of their newcomer counterparts became of itself cause for scorn. Postcolonial theorist Homi Bhabha, in an explanation of the fundamental nature of colonialism, comments that the women could become "the same, but not quite," almost white, but not quite.[48] The Anglican bishop had no qualms about ridiculing "the young women decked out in every sort of vulgar finery – even to the wearing of crinoline & hoops."[49]

Gender had become intertwined with race in the bishop's and others' responses. It was during these years that race became a cornerstone of colonialism. "By the middle of the nineteenth century," the respected historian of science Nancy Stepan explains, "everyone was agreed, it seemed, that in essential ways the white race was superior to non-white races."[50] Newcomers' paler skin tones came to be equated with a right to rule that was seemingly confirmed, in a conveniently circular fashion, by the very fact of colonialism and the unequal power relationship that had grown up between rulers and ruled.

All the same, even the most condemnatory responses, and there were many of them, sometimes incorporated an element of respect for the initiative these Indigenous women who danced took as women.[51] An anonymous poem penned in 1862 about the women who danced in the Vancouver Island colonial capital of Victoria was intended to be satirical. It was satirical, but at the same time it was quite flattering in that it evoked both the fundamental shift the gold rush had facilitated for Indigenous women and the competent way in which they had met the challenge of changing times:

> Only three years since, in blankets,
>   Slovenly they rolled along,
> Like old-fashioned Dutch-built vessels
>   Lurching surging, in a storm.

Now Indigenous women had a very different appearance:

> Sound the voice of exultation,
>   Let it everywhere be known,
> That the Indians round Victoria
>   Almost civilized have grown.
> That the squaws in radiant colors,
>   Dress'd in ample crinoline,
> And with graceful tread of turkeys,
>   And with proud and stately mien.
> Down the streets like gay gondolas
>   Gliding o'er Venetian stream
> Every day and in all seasons,
>   May thus constantly be seen.

The poem's author attributed the reason for this change directly to the dance halls:

Now they trip the gay cotillion,
With an elephantine prance,
In the Market Company building,
Glide they through the mazy dance.

The rhyme attested to women's independence of character. The poem also emphasized that it was the women who ensured that the dance halls operated in a respectful manner:

Without form of introduction,
They will not allow their forms
To be clasped in waltzing graces
Or in polkas flighty charms.
Not without a Caribooite [miner]
On himself the task doth take,
To present a brother miner
Will a foot the klootchman [Chinook jargon for an Indigenous
woman] shake.[52]

The expectations dance halls put on Indigenous women were considerable, yet, as contemporary accounts indicate, Indigenous women largely met them. They were amazingly resourceful in ways that speak to a self-confidence in themselves as women that is consistent with feminism.

In the event, the women who danced were undone not by the critiques levelled against them grounded in patriarchy, colonialism, and racism but by changing times. The gold rush was in decline by the mid-1860s. Most miners departed. The handful who remained were not sufficient for dance halls to continue in operation.

Conclusion

At Nootka Sound, at Fort Langley, and in the dance halls, Indigenous women on the cusp of contact in British Columbia demonstrated a sense of autonomy apart from men that is consistent with feminism as the concept is sometimes conceived. Nootkan women and those living at Fort Langley exercised a degree of control over their sexuality and their everyday lives that was at odds with the gender assumptions Britons and others brought with them to British Columbia. It was not only in relationship to their sexuality that Indigenous women acted. They were comfortable entering the market economy that outsiders had introduced at Nootka Sound and in the dance halls.

In retrospect, we know these women's efforts were in vain and served only to complete the equation favoured by newcomers that, as one contemporary put it in reference to the dance halls, "they wear hoops and are prostitutes!"[53] As to the choice of that term, the historian Anne McClintock usefully reminds us, in line with Keith Thomas' double standard, that "prostitutes flagrantly demanded money for services middle-class men expected for free."[54] The equation of Indigenous women's initiative with prostitution freed men to act toward them as they would rather than as Indigenous women's behaviour suggested they should. To a considerable extent, men have continued to treat Indigenous women as they please into the present day.[55]

Indigenous women's easy dismissal by others should not be equated with our dismissal of the agency they appear to have employed in these three discrete circumstances on the cusp of contact. What happened elsewhere may or may not have been similar. As historical geographer Richard Phillips reminds us, "imperial sexual politics ... were fundamentally *situated*, shaped by the material and imaginative geographies in and between which they unfolded: geographies of domination (concentrations of imperial power) and resistance (with scope for agency)."[56]

Because we are dealing with the past, we know the end of the story, so to speak. When these women acted, they did not. The attitudes displayed toward Indigenous women at that time and since then must not prevent us from considering Indigenous women, as far as possible, on their own terms within the historical contexts in which events occurred. We also know we can never retrieve the past in its entirety; rather, we can only catch glimmers of it. The limited nature of the sources means we can make inferences only to a limited extent, and we are inevitably left with more questions than answers.

Indigenous women's lives on the cusp of contact, as we glimpse them in these three British Columbian vignettes, are nonetheless instructive as we reflect on the changing nature of, and possibilities for, Indigenous feminism. The distant past merits attention alongside yesterday and today.

NOTES

1 Among the exceptions from a British Columbian perspective are Wendy Wickwire, "To See Ourselves as the Other's Other: Nlaka'pamux Contact Narratives," *Canadian Historical Review* 75, 1 (1994): 1-20; Louis Miranda and Philip Joe,

"How the Squamish Remember George Vancouver," in Robin Fisher and Hugh Johnston, eds., *From Maps to Metaphor: The Pacific World of George Vancouver* (Vancouver: UBC Press, 1993), 3-5; and some of the essays in John Sutton Lutz, ed., *Myth and Memory: Stories of Indigenous-European Contact* (Vancouver: UBC Press, 2007), especially Lutz, "First Contact as a Spiritual Performance: Encounters on the North American West Coast," 30-45.

2 Keith Thomas, "The Double Standard," *Journal of the History of Ideas* 20, 2 (1959): 195, 210, 213.

3 Stephen Garton, *Histories of Sexuality: Antiquity to Sexual Revolution* (New York: Routledge, 2004), 130, 137.

4 Joyce Green, "Taking Account of Aboriginal Feminism," in Joyce Green, ed., *Making Space for Indigenous Feminism* (Black Point, NS: Fernwood, 2007), 21. Several of the authors in this collection (Verna St. Denis, "Feminism Is for Everybody: Aboriginal Women, Feminism and Diversity," 37, 45; Andrea Smith, "Native American Feminism: Sovereignty and Social Change," 102; and Denise K. Henning, "Yes, My Daughters, We Are Cherokee Women," 189-90) discuss women's role prior to and on the cusp of contact without specifically categorizing their perspectives as feminist or non-feminist. The closest an author comes to doing so is Henning's reference to "early forerunners of modern feminism" (189).

5 For the history of British Columbia, see Jean Barman, *The West beyond the West: A History of British Columbia,* 3rd ed. (Toronto: University of Toronto Press, 2007).

6 David Samwell, in John Beaglehole, ed., *The Journals of Captain James Cook* (Cambridge: Cambridge University Press, 1967), 3:1095, also 1089. The people living at Nootka Sound refer to themselves as the Mowachaht.

7 Ibid., 3:1094-95.

8 Ibid., 3:1095.

9 William Ellis, *An Authentic Narrative of a Voyage Performed by Captain Cook and Captain Clerke* (London: G. Robinson, 1782), 1:216.

10 James Cook and James King, *A Voyage to the Pacific Ocean* (London: John Stockdale, Scatcherd and Whitaker, John Fielding, and John Hardy, 1804 [1784]), 2:258.

11 Robin Fisher and J.M. Bumstead, eds., *An Account of a Voyage to the North West Coast of America in 1785 and 1786, by Alexander Walker* (Vancouver/Seattle: Douglas and McIntyre/University of Washington Press, 1982), 85-87.

12 James Strange, *James Strange's Journal and Narrative* (Fairfield, WA: Ye Galleon Press, 1982), 84.

13 Fisher and Bumstead, *Account of a Voyage,* 87. In *A Narrative of the Adventures and Sufferings of John R. Jewitt* (Middleton: Loomis and Richards, 1816), 89, Jewitt, who lived with the Nootka from 1803 to 1805, makes much the same point.

14 John Meares, *Voyages Made in the Years 1788 and 1789, from China to the North West Coast of America* (London: Logographic Press, 1790), 251, 149.

15 Cook and King, *Voyage to the Pacific Ocean,* 2:258.

16 Strange, *Journal and Narrative,* 84.

17 Fisher and Bumstead, *Account of a Voyage,* 85, 86.

18 Strange, *Journal and Narrative,* 84.

19 Meares, *Voyages,* 149.
20 For examples of descriptive and ethnographic accounts of the Nootka based later in time, see Gilbert Malcolm Sproat, *The Nootka: Scenes and Studies from Savage Life,* ed. Charles Lillard (Victoria: Sono Nis, 1987 [1868]); Philip Drucker, *The Northern and Central Nootkan Tribes* (Washington, DC: Smithsonian Institution, Bureau of American Ethnology, Bulletin 144, 1951); and Eugene Arima and John Dewhirst, "Nootkans of Vancouver Island," in Wayne Suttles, ed., *Northwest Coast,* vol. 7 of William C. Sturtevant, ed., *Handbook of North American Indians* (Washington, DC: Smithsonian Institution, 1990).
21 Morag Maclachlan, ed., *The Fort Langley Journals, 1827-30* (Vancouver: UBC Press, 1998), 3 March 1829, 99.
22 Maclachlan, *Fort Langley Journals,* 13 November 1828, 85.
23 James Andrew Grant, "An Unsung Pioneer: Life and Letters of James Murray Yale and His 30 Years at Fort Langley," 55, typescript, British Columbia Archives, Add. MS. 182, pt. 3.
24 Maclachlan, *Fort Langley Journals,* 3 March 1829, 99.
25 Ibid., 14 January 1830, 137.
26 Ibid., Archibald McDonald, Report, 25 February 1830, 222.
27 Ibid., 3 July 1829, 118.
28 Ibid., 16 March 1829, 101.
29 Ibid., 20 March 1829, 102.
30 Ibid., 28 May 1830, 149.
31 Ibid., 3 July 1829, 118.
32 Ibid.
33 Ibid., 118-19.
34 Ibid., 13 July 1829, 120.
35 See Jean Barman, "Family Life at Fort Langley," *British Columbia Historical News* 32, 4 (1999): 16-23. Descendants under the leadership of Lisa Pepin maintain an active website titled "The Children of Fort Langley" at http://www.fortlangley.ca/.
36 This time period is probed incisively in Adele Perry, *On the Edge of Empire: Gender, Race, and the Making of British Columbia, 1849-1871* (Toronto: University of Toronto Press, 2001).
37 "Dance-Houses," *British Colonist,* 29 December 1861; "The Squaw Dance House," *Evening Express,* 20 January 1864; "Police Court," *Daily Press,* 22 July 1862; "A Relapse into Barbarism," *Evening Express,* 15 October 1863; "Fire Department," *Daily Press,* 15 January 1862.
38 Philip J. Hankin, "Reminiscences," British Columbia Archives, microfilm.
39 Francis E. Herring, *In the Pathless West with Soldiers, Pioneers, Miners, and Savages* (London: T. Fisher Unwin, 1904), 173.
40 Hankin, "Reminiscences."
41 "Squaw Dance House."
42 For a succinct introduction, see Charles Lillard and Terry Glavin, *A Voice Great Within Us* (Vancouver: New Star, 1998).
43 Hankin, "Reminiscences."

44 "Squaw Dance House."
45 Bishop George Hills, Diary, 1 February 1862, in Anglican Church, Ecclesiastical Province of British Columbia, Archives.
46 Hankin, "Reminiscences."
47 Herring, *In the Pathless West,* 173.
48 Homi Bhabha, "Of Mimicry and Man," in Homi Bhabha, *The Location of Culture* (London: Routledge, 1994), 86.
49 Hills, Diary, 12 August 1860.
50 Nancy Stepan, *The Idea of Race in Science: Great Britain, 1800-1960* (London: Macmillan, 1982), 4.
51 This topic is examined more fully in Jean Barman, "Aboriginal Women on the Streets of Victoria: Engendering Transgressive Sexuality during the Gold Rush," in Myra Rutherdale and Katie Pickles, eds., *Contact Zones: Aboriginal and Settler Women in Canada's Colonial Past* (Vancouver: UBC Press, 2005), 205-27.
52 Prince Albertiana, "A Civilized Song of the Solomons," *Daily Press,* 10 March 1862.
53 "Prostitution Recognized by Government," *British Colonist,* 2 June 1862.
54 Anne McClintock, *Imperial Leather: Race, Gender and Sexuality in the Colonial Contest* (New York: Routledge, 1995), 56.
55 This point is elaborated on in Jean Barman, "Taming Aboriginal Sexuality: Gender, Power, and Race in British Columbia, 1850-1900," *BC Studies: The British Columbian Quarterly* 115-16 (1997-98): 237-66, reprinted in Mary Ann Irwin and James F. Brooks, eds., *Women and Gender in the American West* (Albuquerque: University of New Mexico Press, 2004), 210-35, and in Mary-Ellen Kelm and Lorna Townsend, eds., *In the Days of Our Grandmothers: A Reader in Aboriginal Women's History in Canada* (Toronto: University of Toronto Press, 2006), 270-300.
56 Richard Phillips, *Sex, Politics and Empire: A Postcolonial Geography* (Manchester: Manchester University Press, 2006), 220.

Reaching Toward a Red-Black Coalitional Feminism
Anna Julia Cooper's "Woman versus the Indian"

TERESA ZACKODNIK

Too often we despise the past, forgetting that the things which are to be must develop from what is now, as the things which now are the enlargement and development of that which was.

– *Anna Howard Shaw, "The Heavenly Vision," speech given at the International Council of Women, Washington, DC, 25 March 1888*

In 1891, Anna Julia Cooper, born a slave only to become one of the most radical African American feminists of her day, wrote an essay titled "Woman versus the Indian." This essay was subsequently published in the first book-length black feminist treatise, Cooper's *A Voice from the South,* in 1892. Much of *Voice* consists of reprintings of Cooper's speeches, for she was a popular public speaker whose engagements took her around the United States and, indeed, the world. As an educator, journalist, activist for the poor, and leader in the social settlement movement and the black women's club movement, Cooper has occupied an ambivalent position in scholarship on early black feminism. Hailed by some scholars as the prototypical black feminist for her sustained consideration in *Voice* of the intersection between race and gender, Cooper is considered an elitist by others because of what appears to be her wholesale endorsements of the standards and values of bourgeois or true womanhood. Others consider her to be an astute critic of imperialism because she was the first black feminist to "identif[y] the link between internal and external colonization, between domestic racial oppression and imperialism."[1] These opposed readings of Cooper are made possible, in part, by her subtlety, for she preferred to catch her readers and audiences off guard with what some have called rhetorical traps.[2] I argue that although it appears to be wholly occupied with the indignities African American women suffered in the late nineteenth century, particularly in the American South, Cooper's "Woman versus the Indian" in fact makes an argument for the importance of a black and red feminist coalition, a coalition not only in opposition to racism within the woman suffrage movement but also in and for itself. Indeed, Cooper's essay is itself an enactment of a coalitional feminism, for it urges readers to recognize the linked oppressions of Native Americans and African Americans as it contemplates the railway, American manners, and competition for citizenship, which was so central to the woman suffrage movement, at the close of the nineteenth century.

Searching for coalitions among women of colour during the first wave of American feminism is hampered not only by incomplete resources but also by the possibilities those resources have allowed us to consider. Archives of white reform organizations and individual reformers are more complete than are comparable institutions for African Americans and Native Americans. But perhaps more significant is the way that resources such as the *History of Woman Suffrage,* the multivolume history of first-wave American feminism edited by Elizabeth Cady Stanton and Susan B. Anthony, have been treated as both an artifact and *the* record of the woman's rights struggle, even as they excise important details from that history by, for example, selectively choosing which African American feminist addresses to reprint. Similarly, those Native American women whose writing, speaking, and activism have been included or lauded by white feminists of the first wave are those whose positions can be easily accommodated to that movement's political purposes.

We therefore know Sarah Winnemucca (Paiute) primarily through her autobiographical work *Life among the Piutes: Their Wrongs and Claims* (1883) [sic], edited by white feminist Mary Peabody Mann. Mann and her sister Elizabeth Peabody secured speaking engagements for Winnemucca around Boston and in the Northeast,[3] raised funds for the manuscript's publication, and ensured that prominent politicians received a copy. They did so, in part, because the book narrated the position of women among the Paiutes, and their position, much like that of women in the Haudenosaunee (Iroquois) Confederacy, was promoted by white feminists as an alternative to women's exclusion from public politics in America: "The women know as much as the men do, and their advice is often asked. We have a republic as well as you. The council-tent is our Congress, and anybody can speak who has anything to say, women and all ... If women could go into your Congress I think justice would soon be done the Indians."[4] Winnemucca would also have been an acceptable figure to white feminists because she is said to have supported allotment and the Dawes Act of 1887 and was opposed to the reservation system.[5] Yet her criticism of boarding school education and the larger project of assimilating the Indian would position Winnemucca directly against the so-called civilizing efforts most white feminists supported. However, characterizing Sarah Winnemucca as a woman and activist who "positioned herself on the border," as Cheryl Walker argues, by "advocating accommodation rather than assimilation, preservation of Indian traditions and language but transformation of the hunter-gatherer culture into an agricultural one" is a relatively recent critical turn in scholarship on a figure who was praised by her white contemporaries for helping white settlers and Indigenous people to live together in peace.[6] Indeed, Winnemucca's contemporaries declared that her name "should have a place beside the name of Pocahontas in the history of our country."[7] Sarah Winnemucca's complexity was thus reduced to willing support of Native American assimilation, and the complexity of Paiute tribal structure and practices was reduced to an ideal promoted by white suffragists.

Unless the politics of women of colour were accommodated to those of first-wave feminists, they were rarely acknowledged. Our ability to imagine that an African American feminist such as Cooper not only critiqued the white feminist movement but also did so with a view to marking important links between African American and Native American women has therefore been affected by the narratives of the first wave that we have inherited. When we do hear voices of dissension within the first wave, they are often black feminist critiques of white racism that are presented in a way that avoids discussion of whether the critiques are an end in themselves or a call for affiliations outside white feminist networks and their power dynamics.

Perhaps, then, it comes as little surprise that although "Woman versus the Indian" is often cited as the essay Cooper viewed as the centrepiece of

A Voice from the South, it has been poorly contextualized in ways that limit our understanding of the work Cooper may have been pursuing through it. Cooper opens the essay by indirectly accusing Anna Howard Shaw, Susan B. Anthony, and the woman suffrage movement in general of being racist. She notes a discrepancy between Shaw's address "Women vs. Indians" to the National Council of Women in 1891, in which Shaw called for the white woman's vote in baldly racist terms, and Shaw's earlier repudiation of an effort to exclude an African American woman from Wimodaughsis, a woman's club of which Shaw had been president. As Cooper writes with biting sarcasm, the Kentucky secretary of Wimodaughsis had failed to "calculate that there were any wives, mothers, daughters, and sisters, except white ones," and upon seeing a "solitary cream-colored applicant" before her, refused the woman membership.[8] Charles Lemert and Esme Bhan – editors of the only collection of Cooper's essays, papers, and letters, including *Voice* – speculate that Wimodaughsis was Cooper's creation and that the African American woman rejected by the club was simply an example of the racism black women experienced in the feminist movement at the time.[9] Wimodaughsis was indeed a suffrage-oriented national woman's club that had been founded in 1890 by Emma Gillett and was headquartered in Washington, DC.[10] Its name was an amalgam of wife, mother, daughter, and sister, and it purported to disregard members' race, religion, or class. Wimodaughsis was incorporated as an educational society to help working women further their education, and its DC headquarters provided courses for women in subjects such as French and journalism. Stockholding members had contributed five dollars per share to build the Washington clubhouse, and its members included Elizabeth Cady Stanton and Susan B. Anthony.

Cooper continues by noting that although "Susan B. Anthony and Anna Shaw are evidently too noble to be held in thrall by the provincialisms of women who seem never to have breathed the atmosphere beyond the confines of their grandfathers' plantations," they nonetheless have stooped "from the broad plateau of light and love" to become "as fearful of losing caste as a Brahmin in India."[11] To Cooper, Shaw's "Women vs. Indians" was nothing "less than a blunder," for in delivering it, Shaw had failed her responsibility as a feminist and leader of the suffrage movement: "Miss Shaw is one of the most powerful of our leaders, and we feel her voice should give no uncertain note. Woman should not, even by inference, or for the sake of argument, seem to disparage what is weak."[12] By implication, Susan B. Anthony had likewise failed, for she too, out of expediency, had argued that the suffrage for white women should take precedence over suffrage for all other groups, including the Indians in Shaw's title.

Yet Lemert and Bhan fail to document that Shaw's speech was, in fact, given at the first meeting of the National Council of Women of the United States in Washington, DC, on 22-25 February 1891 and instead suggest that it, too, may have been Cooper's creation, an amalgam of Shaw's speeches while she was the national lecturer for the National American Woman Suffrage Association: "It is possible that Cooper's reference to the 'National Woman's Council' could have been a mistaken allusion to the NWSA before which Shaw was a prominent lecturer in 1891."[13] Although Shaw's speech is not included in the National Council of Women's transactions for this meeting, it can be found in the account of the gathering in *The History of Woman Suffrage,* though neither Lemert nor Bhan note this. Far from being a convenient straw man for Cooper's purposes, Shaw's speech is part of the established mainstream account of the American suffrage movement compiled by its leaders.

Shaw circulates phantom-like in the editorial apparatus of Cooper's collected work, leaving the reader to wonder what Shaw did say and to which audience. This lack of clarity in turn raises the possibility that Cooper's critique of white feminists and racism within the suffrage movement may have been a convenient creation for her own purposes. The failure to contextualize Cooper and her work extends from Shaw's address to the larger discourse of Native American rights that circulated in the early 1890s. To understand how Cooper moved from an indictment of white women reformers to a call for coalitional feminism, we must take into account how her extended treatment of discrimination against African American women on the railway connected to discourses on Native American civility and to the effects of the transcontinental railway on Native Americans. In addition, Cooper's work cannot be completely understood unless it is placed in the context of images of Native American women that were circulating in suffragist speeches and writings at the time and rooted in imagery put forward by advocates for women's rights earlier in the century. Our readings of historical figures and the feminist coalitions they may have called for or participated in are therefore limited not only by the documents that have been preserved and can be accessed but also by the way they are presented. If a feminist as established as Cooper can be presented in scholarship as the author of the political climate she contested, how many other women of colour and their politics have been misrepresented or lost to us altogether?

Before turning to my reading of Cooper's "Woman versus the Indian," I set out what I see as being the necessary context for understanding the essay: an examination of Shaw and her remarks at the National Council and an examination of Indian reform as white women's organizations and individual reformers were practising it at the time.

Touted as the most renowned American woman speaker of all time and queen of the suffrage platform, Anna Shaw was one of the strongest voices for reform and suffrage heard at the close of the nineteenth century. Like those of many of her contemporaries, Shaw's reform roots were in abolition. Shaw became a licensed Methodist preacher in the early 1870s, and by 1885 she was a full-time lecturer for suffrage, temperance, and social purity. She was appointed national lecturer of the National American Woman Suffrage Association (NAWSA) in 1890, vice-president in 1892, and president from 1904 to 1915.

On 23 February 1891 Shaw addressed suffragists in Washington, DC, on "Women vs. Indians." Focusing on the enfranchisement of Indians in South Dakota in 1890, Shaw noted that "45 per cent of the votes cast the preceding year were for male Indian suffrage and only 37 per cent for woman suffrage." Going on to complain that "Indians in blankets and moccasins were received in the State convention with the greatest courtesy" whereas "Susan B. Anthony and other eminent women were barely tolerated," Shaw depicted Native Americans in South Dakota as undeserving of the ballot: "While these Indians were engaged in their ghost dances, the white women were going up and down in the State pleading for the rights of citizens." Then, wilfully ignoring that in South Dakota (at least) the so-called Indian was now the political better of the white woman, Shaw declared that the Indian question should be left to a commission of white women, headed by Indian reformer and suffragist Alice Fletcher, whose aim would be to "mete out to the Indian, to the Negro, to the foreigner ... the justice which we demand for ourselves."[14] Shaw's denigration of Native Americans and their spiritual and cultural practices was a bald and obvious attempt to position white women not only as more deserving of the ballot but also as engaged in their civic responsibilities. The image of the responsible white woman, as opposed to the irresponsible Indian, carries through to Shaw's deliberate selection of Alice Fletcher as the head of her proposed commission to solve the Indian question. Fletcher, a respected anthropologist, had some ten years earlier drafted what became the blueprint for a national severalty program that would exchange Native American lands for Native American citizenship.

Through plans such as Fletcher's, the Indian could prove his fitness for citizenship only by being a responsible individual landowner; the Indian could not achieve this status without the guidance of the more civilized nation-state (in this case represented by the white woman who acted on behalf of and in the interests of that state).

Commissions formed in the interests of Indian reform were, as Shaw well knew, already in place and "met[ing] out to the Indian" a rather different type of justice from the one Shaw was demanding for white women. One such commission was the Woman's National Indian Association (WNIA), founded in 1879 by white women ostensibly to protest the encroachment of railroads and settlers into Indian territory in violation of federal treaties.[15] By 1883, the WNIA had called for recognition of Native American rights under the law, the universal education of Native American children, the dismantlement of the reservation system, and the reallotment of tribal lands to individual Native Americans. Under the Dawes Severalty Act of 1887, in exchange for renouncing their tribal holdings, Native Americans received individual land grants of 160 acres for family heads, 80 acres for single adults, and 40 acres for dependent children. After twenty-five years, individual landholders would be given title to the land and citizenship.[16] After the allocations were made, the extensive lands remaining were declared surplus and opened for sale to non-Native Americans. As Mrs. William E. Burke's address to the 1893 World's Congress of Representative Women on the work of the WNIA makes clear, the Dawes Severalty Act was the result of a combined effort by the WNIA and the Indian Rights Association.[17] The land allotment the WNIA agitated for cost Native Americans millions of acres of land and tribes and nations their legal standing, and it divided tribal communities. By 1934, allotment had exacted from Native American tribes and nations over 90 million acres of former reservation lands and left a hundred thousand Native Americans without land.[18] And although the WNIA had also been an advocate for the legal protection of "suffering, undefended, ever-endangered Indian women and children" in the early 1880s, the so-called protection, which was the goal of the WNIA's domestic missionary work, encroached on Native American homes and tribal communities by introducing Christianization schemes ostensibly to hasten Native American civilization and enfranchisement.[19] Indeed, as Burke's address to the World's Congress of Representative Women argued, "Good women everywhere are waking to a moral consciousness that we have yet within our borders aboriginal tribes still in their native savagery, and that this results ... from lack of opportunity for civilization."[20] In the 1890s, the Board of Indian Affairs introduced field matrons, many of whom were sponsored by the WNIA.[21]

The WNIA pursued a politics of colonization that depended upon and actively perpetuated an image of Native American women as "primary civilizing influences" upon Native American culture and tribal communities.[22] Although the WNIA was unwilling to pursue woman suffrage and in 1888 withdrew its membership from the Woman's National Council of the United States because its president, Frances Willard, and vice-president, Susan B. Anthony, were perceived by WNIA members as too radical,[23] the image of the civilizing Native American woman was central to the suffrage politics they rejected. As Gail Landsman has documented, the civilizing Native woman was widely promoted by white woman's rightists such as Lucretia Mott, Lydia Maria Child, and Matilda Jocelyn Gage who saw assimilation as a route to saving Native Americans even as they extolled Native American culture – particularly the social structure of Haudenosaunee (Iroquois) society – as a "matriarchal alternative to American white patriarchy."[24] Images of Native American culture as a matriarchal ideal and of the Native American woman as empowered to civilize and further the assimilation of her people into American society persisted from the mid-1830s, in Child's writing, to the early 1890s, in the writing and speeches of white suffragists.[25] In fact, in her address to the National Council of Women in 1891, titled "The Matriarchate, or Mother-Age," Elizabeth Cady Stanton referred to woman's position "among different numbers of the American aborigines" as an ironic example of "our barbarian ancestors['] ... higher sense of justice to woman."[26] For Cady Stanton, Native American men were more civilized than white American men because they recognized women's natural rights. White women such as Cady Stanton and Gage saw no contradiction in extolling cultural practices and social structures that they also believed should be eradicated through civilization schemes. Indeed, by extolling Native American women as the primary and ideal civilizing influences within Native American communities, suffragists such as Cady Stanton and Gage were arguing, by extension, for white women's larger influence in American society.[27] The white woman was a moral and civilizing agent for the nation who must be accorded her rights and privileges as citizen.

The question of citizenship and enfranchisement for Native Americans in the late 1880s and 1890s was fraught, linked as it was to forced assimilation and the promotion of citizenship as individualism at the expense of Native American sovereignty and lands. Fraught, too, was the framing of arguments for women's citizenship and enfranchisement in the 1890s. The argument presented in "Women vs. Indians" was not simply made out of expediency following the reunification of the white suffrage movement, when certain reformers contended that a scarcity of resources in the struggle for political rights made it expedient to enfranchise (white) women before "dependent races."[28] Rather, Shaw's speech, given her status and reputation, functioned as the NAWSA's justification for the racist and nativist politics it was only beginning to embark on as it made its move to draw white Southerners into the movement, thereby expanding and securing its base and support for the struggle ahead. Shaw's speech also reveals the wilful ignorance upon which white feminists' anxiety over limited resources rested. Shaw and the NAWSA had little to fear from Indian reform, which harnessed potential citizenship to land reallotment.

The National Council of Women's transactions at its annual meeting in 1891, however, reveal just how successful an anxiety-causing appeal to competing rights among the oppressed classes could be. At the meeting, one of the greats of African American feminism, Frances Harper, addressed the gathering on the subject of the duty to dependent races.[29] Her address followed Alice Fletcher's remarks on the American race problem, which focused on the "Red Man" and his ability to "breed evil among" whites "by turning loose the lightly-leased savage elements of our nature," as evidenced by "the conduct of white men ... in the West among the Indians."[30] While Fletcher urged white women's duty to the Indian, Frances Harper reminded white women of their duty to "the Negro," who was then being lynched because of white fears of "Negro supremacy" following black male enfranchisement. Harper opened her speech by refusing to include the Negro in the category of dependent races. She instead argued that African Americans should be regarded as "member[s] of the body politic who ha[ve] a claim upon the nation for justice, simple justice, which is the right of every race, upon the government for protection, which is the rightful claim of every citizen, and upon our common Christianity for the best influences which can be exerted for peace on earth and good-will to man."[31] Not once did Harper mention the Indian; she instead made an argument for the Negro's greater claim on the white woman and the nation. Harper's reference to lynching reinforced her argument, for it suggested that attending to the greater claim of the Negro could put an end to the butchering and burning alive of hundreds of black men, women, and children.[32] Indeed, Harper's stress in the speech is on the nation's claim to civilization, an ironic choice given Fletcher's sketch of Indian savagery as a contagion that was spreading among whites in the West. "Our first claim upon the nation and government is the claim for protection to human life," urged Harper: "That claim should lie at the basis of our civilization, not simply in theory but in fact. Outside of America, I know of no other civilized country ... where men are still lynched, murdered, and even burned for real or supposed crimes."[33] It is hardly surprising that Harper focused on lynching; however, I argue that it is significant that she did so at the expense of an opportunity to align African American claims on the nation's civility with those of Native Americans.

Given Frances Harper's focus on the greater claim of the Negro at the National Council of Women in 1891, it is all the more significant that Cooper's essay, published a year later, not only indicted the racist treatment of African American feminists within the woman's rights movement but also critiqued how white suffragists had leveraged an ostensible climate of scarcity into a battle over rights that pitted themselves against the so-called dependent races and black against red. Cooper's intended audience for "Woman versus the Indian," and for *A Voice from the South* more generally, undoubtedly included white women reformers and suffragists and fellow black feminists and fellow black intellectuals, both male and female, for *Voice* was published by Aldine Publishing House.[34] Cooper's essay marks her astute reading of not only Shaw's but also Fletcher's speech and white women's reform of the Indian more generally.

Appearing to focus on the indignities that African American women suffered on the South's railway system, Cooper's essay plays on the railway as a historical source of oppression for Native Americans and African Americans and as a symbol of national progress. Cooper clearly recognized that the development of the railway in the United States came at a severe cost to Native Americans that extended well beyond the Railroad Enabling Act of 1866, which had appropriated Native American lands for corporate use. It is therefore quite to the point that Cooper casually observes that "there can be no true test of national courtesy without travel." Seemingly offhand, she continues by commenting that although white Americans see "our well-nigh perfect railroad systems" as the epitome of "the comfort and safety of American travel, even for the weak and unprotected," there is "some material [she] could furnish" on the realities of the railways, "though possibly it might not be just on the side" the American public may "wish to have illuminated."[35] Cooper then elaborates on the discrimination she endured while riding the railway of the Jim Crow South; she subtly shows her readers that this mode of comfortable and safe American travel is, in fact, a tool of oppression. The "weak and unprotected" of her essay, who at first glance appear to be the (white) women who are reassured that they can travel safely by rail, are in fact those dependent races that are such a concern to white female reformers. Far from being comfortable and safe as a result of the railway's expansion across the nation, the Indian and the Negro are kept in a state of dispossession because of it.

Cooper argues that the exploitation and dispossession of African Americans and Native Americans is a burden for white American women to shoulder. If the railway is a true test of national courtesy, and if, as Cooper argues in the vein of domestic feminism at the time, the "American woman ... is responsible for American manners," then the oppression of Native Americans and African Americans can no longer be viewed as competing with the oppression of white women in a hierarchy of victimization fuelled by arguments in support of the suffrage movement.[36] Cooper argues that the condition of the so-called dependent races is instead the direct result of the American woman's now questionable efforts to civilize the nation: "Like mistress, like nation."[37] The white woman, Cooper writes, is responsible for the way that America treats her "weak and unprotected"; she is not simply one of the nation's victims. Consequently, argues Cooper, the white woman's civilizing impulse should be turned not to the uncivilized and unChristianized Indian but rather to her own back yard. To highlight the effects of white American incivility, Cooper refers to the conductor who ejects her from the ladies' car as "an American citizen who has been badly trained ... sadly lacking in both 'sweetness' and 'light.'" She then turns her gaze out the car window to a chain gang of African American youths, "working on private estates ... not in 1850, but in 1890, '91 and '92." Cooper makes a mental note that "the women in this section should organize a Society for the Prevention of Cruelty to Human Beings, and disseminate civilizing tracts, and send throughout the region apostles of anti-barbarism." She exclaims under her breath, "What a field for the missionary woman."[38] Indeed, a richer field for the missionary women of the WNIA would be the nation itself, the "least courteous ... on the globe," according to Cooper, and one in need of a "national ... department for ... GOOD MANNERS."[39] Under Cooper's witty and able pen, then, that bugbear of disqualification for citizenship and fair treatment, incivility and barbarism, becomes the state of white Americans, and it is best witnessed on that symbol of national and imperial progress – the railway.

Anna Shaw's "Women vs. Indians" is all the more dangerous in Cooper's opinion because it tries to manipulate its audience into seeing the white woman as a potential victim, rather than an active oppressor, of the Indian. Cooper instead contends that "woman's cause" is to see the struggle for rights as an affiliated rather than competing one: "When the weak shall have received their due consideration, then woman will have her 'rights,' and the Indian will have his rights, and the Negro will have his rights, and all the strong will have learned at last ... the secret of universal courtesy which is after all nothing but ... regarding one's neighbor as one's self."[40] The effect of a scarcity of rights on African American feminists themselves is also Cooper's target in this essay. She contends repeatedly that "the cause of freedom is not the cause of a race or a sect, a party or a class": "it is not the intelligent woman vs. the ignorant woman; nor the white woman vs. the black, the brown, and the red" but rather "the cause of human kind."[41] In what is surely a caution against positions such as that taken by Frances Harper, who argued for the greater claim of the Negro on the nation, Cooper calls instead for connections between races and classes. Refusing to recognize opposition between white women and "the black, the brown, the red," Cooper also implicitly calls for affiliations among those women of the so-called dependent races, women whom white suffragists such as Anna Shaw were trying to pit not only against the white woman but also against one another. Just as white women should not rest their pleas on "Indian inferiority" or "Negro depravity," African American feminists should not seek to capitalize on the suffrage movement's racism by turning their backs on other women of colour to argue the Negro's "greater claim."

In a larger sense, by refusing to accept competing claims, Cooper refused individualism itself. Her stance was no small gesture for a feminist at the close of the nineteenth century, for as Joan Scott has noted, "the revolutionary promise to realize the individual human rights of liberty, equality, and political participation has been the basis for woman's claim for citizenship in Western democracies since the eighteenth century ... Feminism, even as we know it today, would not exist without abstract individualism."[42] Given that the era of assimilation and Indian reform was marked, as we have seen, by "an intense struggle over individualism and community," Cooper's rejection of individualism was itself an enactment of coalitional feminism, rather than a betrayal of feminism's promise. As Siobhan Senier has argued, Native American writers "oscillated between individualistic models ... and communal models" and paid attention to their "distinct *political* uses."[43] Cooper's rejection of individualism reflected her awareness of how it was being employed to reform Native Americans; consequently, her stance was marked by an awareness of what individualism exacts in the claim for and realization of citizenship. Effectively, the condition for Native American citizenship under the Dawes Act and Indian reform, as it was promoted by the Indian Rights Association and the WNIA, was individualism through individual landownership. Individual Native American landowners were promised inclusion in the US nation at the expense of Native American sovereignty, culture, and tribal community. The Dawes Act was the first of a series of Acts and declarations that characterized Native American citizenship as potential, a potential that could be realized only through the adoption of "the habits of civilized life," which would ensure "the absorption of the Indians into our national life, not as Indians, but as American citizens." Citizenship for Native Americans, then, rested on "one's own actions," as Walter Benn Michaels puts it, on the individual's potential and choice to *become* civilized, to become a citizen.[44]

If Cooper had focused on the railway and the experiences of African American women under its Jim Crow policies to advance an argument for a citizen's rights of access, she too would have been pursuing a politics of individual rights, one that would have, by necessity, ignored that the railway was both a tool for and the realization of imperial expansionism and exploitation. Cooper quite rightly recognized that any black feminist who sought right of access as a marker of citizenship risked colluding with a white imperialist project. She understood that the recognition of the black woman as an individual citizen who was due "comfort and safety" would come at the continued exploitation and dispossession of Native Americans. This may be why Cooper subtly, though with devastating acuity, revises Shaw's speech title, changing it from "Women vs. Indians" to "Woman versus the Indian." By doing so, she not only nods to the individualism as the underlying driver of rights arguments based on expediency in the white suffrage movement, she also warns against the adoption of a similar individualist ethic in a black feminist politics that would favour the Negro's greater claim at the expense of the rights of other oppressed classes.

Cooper ends her essay by reminding her readers that the wrongs that she has outlined will always be "indissolubly linked with *all* undefended woe."[45] The so-called civility of the nation is a direct consequence of its barbarity to the Indian and the Negro; it, rather than the reservation or the South, is in need of the white woman's missionary work. By linking the position of African Americans and Native Americans within the nation throughout history, Cooper makes the need for coalition rather than competition between black and red all the more urgent at the dawn of the woman's era.[46] Yet references to the Indian are rare in the work of nineteenth century black feminists. Were coalitions limited because it was difficult to overcome the effects of arguments for woman's suffrage that rested on, indeed created, anxieties about competing rights in a climate of scarcity? Did red-black coalitions even develop? Or were understandings of rights within black and red feminism so different that they had difficulty coming together at the close of the nineteenth century?

The more challenging question may not be how to find evidence of these coalitions – though that is, of course, important work – but how to grapple with what may have affected their formation. Ironically, the excerpt from Anna Howard Shaw's "The Heavenly Vision" that stands as this chapter's epigraph is prescient. However much we may despise the past that Cooper's essay and Shaw's speech returns us to, it is a past that tells us much about the ongoing challenge of building coalitions among women. And it is a past that in many ways may continue to echo even as we seek to move beyond it. As Cooper made clear, if unrestricted access to the protections and privileges of citizenship, including unhampered access to the railway, was to become a goal of black feminism, would a black feminist agenda not also risk capitalizing on imperialist expansion and its effects? Cooper indirectly suggested that an unexamined black feminist politics would not only risk succumbing to the competition over rights, it would also risk colluding with the larger imperialist project and its production of citizenship. This is the larger challenge that Cooper's "Woman versus the Indian" offers its readers, past and present. It not only challenges white women to eradicate racism from the women's movement, it challenges black feminists to seek coalitions between black and red rather than solely between black and white.

NOTES

1 Hazel V. Carby, *Reconstructing Womanhood: The Emergence of the Afro-American Woman Novelist* (Oxford: Oxford University Press, 1987), 101. For arguments that Cooper was elitist, see, for example, Mary Helen Washington, "Introduction," in *A Voice from the South, by a Black Woman of the South,* by Anna Julia Cooper (Oxford: Oxford University Press, 1988), xlix.

2 See, for example, Cathryn Baily, "Anna Julia Cooper: 'Dedicated in the Name of My Slave Mother to the Education of Colored Working People,'" *Hypatia* 19, 2 (2004): 56-73.

3 Siobhan Senier, *Voices of American Indian Assimilation and Resistance: Helen Hunt Jackson, Sarah Winnemucca, and Victoria Howard* (Norman: University of Oklahoma Press, 2001), 79.

4 Sarah Winnemucca, quoted in Cheryl Walker, *Indian Nation: Native American Literature and Nineteenth-Century Nationalisms* (Durham, NC: Duke University Press, 1997), 154.

5 Senier notes that although scholars have characterized Winnemucca as being in staunch support of the General Allotment Act, her *Life among the Piutes* contains "no explicit endorsement of that legislation." Senier, *Voices of American Indian Assimilation and Resistance,* 80.

6 Walker, *Indian Nation,* 154. Senier argues that Winnemucca should be understood as employing "dramatically oscillating rhetorical strategies." Senier, *Voices of American Indian Assimilation and Resistance,* 74. Similarly, Carol Batker argues that Native American women's journalism in what she calls the Dawes era engaged in a "complex negotiation between Native and non-Native practices" that at times "reproduce[d] ... dominant assimilationist discourse" but did "not predicate assimilation on a rejection of Native identity and culture." See Batker, "Overcoming All Obstacles: The Assimilation Debate in Native American Women's Journalism of the Dawes Era," in Helen Jaskoski, ed., *Early Native American Writings: New Critical Essays* (Cambridge: Cambridge University Press, 1996), 190. See also, Batker, *Reforming Fictions: Native, African, and Jewish American Women's Literature and Journalism in the Progressive Era* (New York: Columbia University Press, 2000). For a critical consideration of scholarship that presents Winnemucca as a mediating figure, see Senier, *Voices of American Indian Assimilation and Resistance,* 80-82.

7 General Howard, quoted in Walker, *Indian Nation,* 141.

8 Anna Julia Cooper, "Woman versus the Indian," in Charles Lemert and Esme Bhan, eds., *The Voice of Anna Julia Cooper, Including "A Voice from the South" and Other Important Essays, Papers, and Letters* (Boston: Rowman and Littlefield, 1998), 88.

9 Charles Lemert and Esme Bhan, "The Colored Woman's Office," in Lemert and Bhan, *The Voice of Anna Julia Cooper,* 28-29. Lemert and Bhan footnote Cooper's reference to Wimodaughsis by writing, "It is hard to imagine that Cooper is not joking here, either by making up the ridiculous acronym or, if it was indeed the name of a club, by using it without comment" (28n50).

10 In 1881, Gillett became the first female notary public in the United States and, in 1890, the seventh female member of the Supreme Court. She was active in drafting married women's property legislation enacted in 1896 and co-founded, with Ellen Spencer Mussey, the Women's Law Class at the Washington College of Law that same year.

11 Cooper, "Woman versus the Indian," 89, 91.

12 Ibid., 105.

13 Lemert and Bhan, "The Colored Woman's Office," 28n50.

14 Anna Howard Shaw, "Women vs. Indians," in Susan B. Anthony and Ida Husted Harper, eds., *The History of Woman Suffrage,* vol. 4, *1883-1900* (New York: Arno Press, 1969), 182-83.

15 Mary Lucinda Bonney founded the WNIA at a meeting of the Woman's Home Mission Circle of Philadelphia's First Baptist Church. Her friend Amelia Stone Quinton joined the organization, bringing with her experience as a state organizer for the Woman's Christian Temperance Union in the mid-1870s. Bonney funded the

WNIA's efforts and Quinton undertook the research that fuelled their petitions to Congress. The WNIA's first petition in February 1880 was signed by thirteen thousand citizens in fifteen states. See Valerie Sherer Mathes, "Nineteenth-Century Women and Reform: The Women's National Indian Association," *American Indian Quarterly* 14, 1 (1990): 1-2.

16 Allotment, as with Indian reform more generally, was gendered. Three-quarters of adult men on a reservation had to agree to allotment before it could be enacted. See Bonita Lawrence, "Gender, Race, and the Regulation of Native Identity in Canada and the United States: An Overview," *Hypatia* 18, 2 (2003): 17. Because title to allotted land was held by the male head of the family, a patriarchal and nuclear family model was forced on those Native Americans who "elected" allotment. See Eric N. Olund, "Public Domesticity during the Indian Reform Era; or, Mrs. Jackson Is Induced to Go to Washington," *Gender, Place and Culture* 9, 2 (2002): 154.

17 Mrs. William E. Burke, "Women's National Indian Association," in May Wright Sewall, ed., *World's Congress of Representative Women* (Chicago: Rand, McNally, 1894), 514. The Indian Rights Association (IRA) was founded by Herbert Welsh in 1882 in Philadelphia. It took over the "political activities of the WNIA thus allowing the women to pursue their new missionary endeavors." See Mathes, "Nineteenth-Century Women and Reform," 4. The IRA's objective was the education, citizenship, and "complete civilization of the Indian population" (ibid.).

18 Arlene Hirschfelder and Martha Kreipe de Montano, *The Native American Almanac: A Portrait of Native America Today* (New York: Macmillan, 1993), 22.

19 Mathes, "Nineteenth-Century Women and Reform," 5.

20 Burke, "Women's National Indian Association," 514-15.

21 Mathes, "Nineteenth-Century Women and Reform," 5.

22 Gail H. Landsman, "The 'Other' as Political Symbol: Images of Indians in the Woman Suffrage Movement," *Ethnohistory* 39, 3 (1992): 268.

23 Mathes, "Nineteenth-Century Women and Reform," 6.

24 Landsman, "The 'Other' as Political Symbol," 259.

25 See, for example, Child's *Hobomok* (1824); "History of the Condition of Women, in Various Ages and Nations" (1835); "Letters from New York" (1843); "An Appeal for the Indians" (1868); "A Legend of the Falls of St. Anthony" (1846); and "She Waits in the Spirit Land" (1846). Cited in Landsman, "The 'Other' as Political Symbol," 259.

26 Elizabeth Cady Stanton, "The Matriarchate, or Mother-Age," in Rachel Foster Avery, ed., *Transactions of the National Council of Women of the United States, Assembled in Washington, D.C., February 22 to 25, 1891* (Philadelphia: J.B. Lippincott, 1891), 220.

27 For examples of Gage's writings that invoke Native American matriarchy and Iroquois society as an alternative to patriarchy, see "The Onondaga Indians" (1875); "The Remnant of the Five Nations: Woman's Rights among the Indians" (1875); and her speech for the fiftieth anniversary convention of the Woman Suffrage Movement in 1898. Cited in Landsman, "The 'Other' as Political Symbol," 269.

28 The American Woman Suffrage Association (AWSA) merged with its rival, the National Woman Suffrage Association (NWSA), to become the National American Woman Suffrage Association (NAWSA) in 1890. The merger healed a fracture that

had been caused by passage of the Fifteenth Amendment, which enfranchised black men.

29 By the late nineteenth century, Harper, who had been a formidable abolitionist and supporter of freedmen's rights, was a nationally recognized temperance leader and was active in the struggle for women's rights and black civil rights.

30 Alice C. Fletcher, "Our Duty to Dependent Races," in Avery, *Transactions of the National Council of Women,* 83-84. Fletcher, an anthropologist and Indian reformer, was active in implementing land allotment among the Omaha and Nez Perce. She drafted the Omaha Severalty Act of 1882, which is regarded as a precursor to the Dawes Act.

31 Frances Ellen Watkins Harper, "Duty to Dependent Races," in Avery, *Transactions of the National Council of Women,* 86.

32 The Tuskegee Institute's records indicate that, in 1891, 113 African Americans were lynched. Lynching was at its height in the 1890s, when anywhere from 85 to 134 African Americans were lynched per year. See University of Missouri-Kansas School of Law: http://www.law.umkc.edu/faculty/projects/ftrials/shipp/lynchingyear.html. In the 1890s, Ida B. Wells, black feminist and anti-lynching activist, brought international attention to the use of lynching as political intimidation in the United States and to its victims, who were not only black men but also black women and children.

33 Harper, "Duty to Dependent Races," 86-87.

34 Aldine was located in Xenia, Ohio, home of Wilberforce University. It would later publish leading black intellectuals and feminists such as Hallie Quinn Brown. See Brown, *Homespun Heroines and Other Women of Distinction* (Xenia, OH: Aldine, 1926).

35 Cooper, "Woman versus the Indian," 94, 92.

36 Ibid., 90.

37 Ibid., 92.

38 Ibid., 95.

39 Ibid., 96.

40 Ibid., 105.

41 Ibid., 106 and 107.

42 Joan W. Scott, "Universalism and the History of Feminism," *Differences* 7, 1 (1995): 1.

43 Senier, *Voices of American Indian Assimilation,* 8-9, emphasis in original.

44 Walter Benn Michaels, *Our America: Nativism, Modernism, and Pluralism* (Durham, NC: Duke University Press, 1997), 31.

45 Cooper, "Woman versus the Indian," 108, emphasis added.

46 For example, slave owners perceived the proximity of Native American tribal communities and nations as dangerous potential refuges for escaped slaves (which they frequently were), and they feared armed revolt could come from the affiliation of Native and African Americans. William Katz documents the Chickasaw Nation's support for black insurrectionists in Louisiana in 1729. See Katz, *Black Indians: A Hidden Heritage* (New York: Atheneum, 1986).

Emotion before the Law

CHERYL SUZACK

In November 2003, Yvelaine Moses of the Lower Nicola Indian Band in British Columbia applied for a second time to the Federal Court of Canada for a judicial review of her reinstatement status. Moses, who had been reinstated to Indian status under section 6(2) of the 1985 amended Indian Act, "took exception to the fact that her illegitimate brother, a full brother, was registered as an Indian pursuant to section 6(1)(a) ... [whereas] she, [his illegitimate full sister], had merely been granted registration pursuant to section 6.2."[1] Moses claimed that her reinstatement under section 6(2) provided her with a "lesser class of registration than her full brother" and subjected her to unequal treatment on the basis of sex, for under the provision of section 6(2) of the amended Act, "she did not have a registration status which she could pass to her children."[2] Moses argued that the "specific provisions of the 1970 Indian Act set a different test and outcome for who may and may not be registered as an Indian," and she sought a declaration that "her registration breached sections 15 and 28 of the *Canadian Charter of Rights and Freedoms*," which prohibit discrimination based on sex.[3] In her first application, the court noted the substance of Moses' claim to differential treatment under the 1985 Act but struck out her notice for review of the registrar's decision because of want of jurisdiction. The court urged her instead to protest her reinstatement status under the terms provided for in the revised Act and informed her that it would review her application once it had been amended by the registrar's protest decision.[4]

On her next appearance before the court, Moses again asserted that the category of reinstatement she had been granted following her successful protest and reinstatement under section 6(1)(f)[5] imparted a "lesser class of registration than [the category that had been accorded to] her full brother," and she once more sought reinstatement to Indian status under section 6(1)(a).[6] Moses expressed concern that her reinstatement lacked security because the registrar had determined her enrolment status based on the assumption that "[her] mother would be entitled to registration as an Indian."[7] Counsel for Moses also questioned the basis on which the registrar had reached her decision, noting a sense of doubt "that the mother of Ms. Moses ha[d] any Indian ancestry."[8] In spite of the court's reassurances that Moses' registration was "in no way conditional on whether or not her mother ever in fact bec[a]me a registered Indian,"[9] and despite the court's insistence that Moses and her brother held "the same rights but by a different approach,"[10] Moses insisted that her registration appeared "in some way provisional or conditional" and that should her mother "not be registered as an Indian" her own registration "might be reopened and her status revoked."[11] The court again acknowledged Moses' concerns but dismissed her second application by citing the issue of mootness.[12] It noted that the relief Moses sought was not to "strike down the legislation" under section 6 of the Act but rather to obtain "some form of an individual remedy based on insecurity."[13] The court struck her claim for judicial review and dismissed her challenge to the "general constitutionality of the Indian registration scheme."[14] In its conclusion, the court stated that "Counsel for Ms. Moses has not convinced me of any reasons or utility in the Court expending resources to review the decision of the Registrar, which final decision granted to Ms. Moses the status and rights she sought."[15]

Yvelaine Moses' legal challenge to her reinstatement status on the grounds that it constitutes a lesser category of Indian registration is one of many that have been launched by Aboriginal women and their children in the post–Bill C-31 era. The 1985 amendments to the Indian Act, known informally as Bill C-31, were intended to return status to descendants of women from whom status had been removed upon marriage to a non-Indian person, but these amendments have failed to alter the Act's discriminatory provisions. The challenges brought by women, such as Yvelaine Moses, demonstrate a range of situations in which Aboriginal women have been forced to seek judicial review of Indian Act amendments to secure legal recognition of their claims, and they illustrate a number of distorting circumstances that have transformed Aboriginal women's attachments to identity, kinship, culture, and community into contestations over legal meaning. These claims include protests of disentitlement based on prior legislation that barred status to the descendants of Aboriginal women;[16] claims concerning enfranchisement undertaken without consent that, upon reinstatement, has prevented the transmission of status to children and grandchildren;[17] claims of wrongful deregistration because of marriage, despite proof of entitlement and Indian ancestry;[18] and claims of breach of women's status rights as self-constitutive Aboriginal rights that remain embedded from pre-contact times.[19]

What distinguishes Moses' narrative from these other cases is her attempt to restore a human face to these struggles. By insisting on her feelings of insecurity in light of the registrar's authority to challenge her status, and by expressing her concern that future amendments could challenge or revoke her identity as a Status Indian,[20] Moses worked to convey a sense of the vulnerability of her position as an Aboriginal woman and the gendered characteristics of the legislation that made her vulnerable as such. In so doing, she endeavoured to overlay her argument with what Susan Bandes categorizes as an emotive cast.[21] She tried to appeal, through affective language, to the court's empathy and value system to register her experiences of disentitlement and reinstatement as forms of discrimination that are not only unconstitutional but also gendered, evaluative and, ultimately, a consequence of how Aboriginal women are understood to matter in society.

In this chapter, I explore how these cases articulate stories of gender discrimination that mark out a critical terrain in legal discourse that introduces a more complex, ambiguous, and undertheorized gender identity for Aboriginal women, an identity made visible by its legal framings but not reducible to its representation in legal narratives. This figure, which I call the Aboriginal-woman-as-feeling-subject, emerges as an ephemeral presence in legal narratives, one whose voice attempts to express her experiential understanding of how Indian Act categories are lived as gender-specific forms of injury but whose voice is often overwhelmed by legal norms that reinscribe the objectivity of legal discourse at the cost of setting aside her story. My purpose is to map out this representation and unpack its implications for Indigenous feminism. Feminist legal scholars such as Kathryn Abrams argue that "establishing previously unheard perspectives as credible accounts of a social problem" can "shed new light on legal questions" and, in so doing, "reveal a neglected perspective or theme that needs to play a role in legal decisionmaking."[22] The figure of the Aboriginal-woman-as-feeling-subject, I argue, represents such a standpoint. She is a figure that, on the one hand, is constrained by law because she is subject to law's regulatory authority, and on the other hand, generative before the law because she inaugurates new forms of social understanding. I call this figure the Aboriginal-woman-as-feeling-subject because she performs paradoxically political work. In submitting to the law's authority to regulate identity, she shows how law overlooks aspects of Aboriginal women's gendered experience; in storytelling before the law, she generates new understanding about how identity as defined by the Indian Act matters to Aboriginal women. This figure of the Aboriginal-woman-as-feeling-subject marks a dialogical process of meaning making that connects Indigenous feminist politics to stories about Aboriginal women's social disempowerment. Her presence requires Indigenous feminists to develop strategies for hearing these gendered forms of expressive agency in order to define the political objectives of their struggles. I suggest that legal empathy represents a concept that may best help to undertake this work.[23]

In what follows, I explore how the Aboriginal-woman-as-feeling-subject has emerged in enfranchisement cases, such as that launched by Yvelaine Moses, and analyze its implications for understanding gender discrimination as emotional harm. I draw on the McIvor case, also based in the Lower Nicola Reserve and handed down by the Supreme Court of British Columbia in 2007, to demonstrate the value of reading for affective understanding.[24] My purpose in reading these cases is to provide a more nuanced awareness of what Indian Act identity means to Aboriginal women and thus to develop gendered understandings about gender discrimination that show how this legislation has introduced new forms of emotional harm.

Aboriginal Women in the Legal Context

Although it is widely acknowledged that the Indian Act is an instrument of bureaucratic regulation, it is also important to recognize it as a dehumanizing structure, engendering consequential emotional, social, and political effects that Aboriginal women bear. Its dehumanizing outcomes are visible in its gendered and racialized status categories and in its continuing disempowerment of Aboriginal women. This disempowerment has taken the form of ongoing political distress and obstructed political possibility. As Fay Blaney explains, "The confusion surrounding identity from section 12(1)(b) was not resolved with Bill C-31. The powers of this bill were shared between the federal government that controlled 'status' and the band that controlled 'membership' ... The personal crisis associated with identity confusion can be traced directly to systemic discrimination and internal oppression. This silences Aboriginal women and, by so doing, increases their level of vulnerability."[25] New categories of Indian Act identity have not ameliorated this uncertainty or addressed their vulnerability. The Native Women's Association of Canada clarifies why the amended Act continues to discriminate and make Aboriginal women vulnerable in socially and legally systemic ways. Its report states,

> All status Indians are now categorized as falling under section 6(1) or 6(2) of the *Indian Act.* The major distinction between 6(1) and 6(2) status is that people classified in the latter category cannot transmit their status to their children. The following scenario depicts a very simple but clear example of the impact of the new classifications. A woman who lost her status upon marriage to a non-Indian man can apply for reinstatement and regain her status under section 6(1); her children are then classified as having 6(2) status, but her grandchildren are not entitled to status. Second generation descendants must have both parents registered under section 6(1) or (2), or at least one parent with 6(1) status, in order to be registered. This also applies to the registration of future generations, thereby establishing a cut-off point for determining status, as well as creating two distinct classes of Indian status – one which allows the direct transmission of status to children, and one which does not. Through Bill C-31, the *Indian Act* was amended to ensure that no one gains or loses status through marriage, and individuals who lost status through sexual discrimination and enfranchisement can apply to regain their status ... While the overtly discriminatory provisions have been removed from the *Indian Act* through Bill C-31, the new system of distinguishing between and classifying types of Indian status means that discrimination has been maintained.[26]

Yvelaine Moses' case and those of other Aboriginal women similarly situated demonstrate how these provisions continue to discriminate against Aboriginal women in comparably gendered ways. They also tell a gender story about the devaluing of Aboriginal women's knowledge claims and their experiences of discrimination within the legal context.

These cases make apparent the uneasy relationship that Aboriginal women have with Aboriginal identity when the authority to regulate and bestow Indian Act identity is accorded to the courts. Because of this authority and regulatory power, Aboriginal women's claims to Aboriginal inheritance depend on the court's power to situate and define their claims within a legal order rooted in non-Aboriginal laws rather than one rooted in Aboriginal laws of kinship. As legal scholar John Borrows asserts, one set of laws exists to dismantle Aboriginal community, whereas the other exists to build community.[27] Despite the important recognition of these opposing aims, Aboriginal women confront a further dilemma in their appeal to legal discourse and their use of it as an agency language structured within the adversarial and mediating context of law.[28] Even as these women assert that their identity is verifiable, historical, and concrete, the legal context works to separate this identity from them by objectifying its felt characteristics and by making exterior what may be understood only as an "interior and unsharable experience."[29] Their bodily experience of attachment to identity and the law's regulation of this experience as an objectified sign are affectively structured within a context of doubt, a context that the law is then forced to interpret, for it would be impossible, given the legal setting, for the interiority of identity to conform to its outward manifestation as legal statute. This structure of doubt, rather than the attributes of identity, is what the law ultimately decides and what essentially works to displace these women's claims into "deeper obscurity."[30] The structure of representation determined by the language of legal agency thus produces a double bind: Aboriginal women must use the legal language in place to assert their claims to Indian Act identity even as this language works to displace their identities from them. This form of structural displacement has been theorized by Elaine Scarry as fundamental to the problematic nature of the language of agency, because of "its inherent instability, [which] arises precisely because it permits a break in the identification of the thing to which the attributes belong."[31] Altering this context of doubt is one of the key goals that Indigenous feminist politics must address, and the courts must also recognize it in order to reform their understanding of Aboriginal identity from a concept to be used against Aboriginal communities to a value and form of identification to which Aboriginal peoples aspire.[32]

Aboriginal women, like other racialized groups, are doubly disadvantaged through law's claims to universality, which distorts their identities, and forms of legal reasoning and analysis, which elide the issue of gender discrimination that motivates their claims. Problems of definition and representation affect Aboriginal communities more generally through law's pervasive "devaluative ideology of Indianness,"[33] yet disenfranchised Aboriginal women are even more vulnerable to these effects because they cannot point to the specificity of different First Nations practices to support their Indian status claims, since their membership is in dispute, nor to an ideology of "Indianness" for strategically locating their rights, since the dominant forms of these claims concern "land claims, treaty rights, and hunting and fishing rights cases."[34] Confronted with these analytical and ideological blind spots, Aboriginal women require different capacities and registers of understanding in order to challenge the aptness of their representation before the law and to shift law's assessment practices concerning their experiences of race and gender discrimination. An Indigenous feminist practice that uses case law stories to theorize the issues confronting disenfranchised Aboriginal women may generate new insights about how these practices may be reformed.

Aboriginal Women and Feminist Politics

One of the problems in situating case law as grounds for constituting a subject of Indigenous feminist politics is reconciling Indigenous feminism's goals with Aboriginal women's life stories and experiences. This issue has been made more urgent by debates among Aboriginal women about the status of feminism and its utility as a political movement.[35] Joyce Green provides an insightful analysis of these debates, noting, in particular, the accusation that "feminism is un-traditional, inauthentic, non-liberatory for Aboriginal women and illegitimate as an ideological position, political analysis, and organizational process."[36] The tension that Green perceives is also made more complex by the fact that the women whose stories are told through these cases do not claim feminism as an identity; nor do they contextualize their rights to reinstatement as feminist aims. They also have little in common that might form the basis for a coalitional politics, for they share no affiliations or alliances with one another across tribal identity, age, social location, or membership that might connect them together as a group. And they may be largely unaware of one another's struggle for entitlement to Indian Act status, aside from references to other cases that may arise in their own claims. What they do have in common is a commitment to the preservation and recognition of their Aboriginal inheritance and a struggle against Indian Act provisions that discriminate against them based on gender.

The agency that might be attributed to Aboriginal women as feminist subjects before the courts, therefore, is both complex and contradictory. On the one hand, Aboriginal women are asserting their right to their Aboriginal inheritance and to the authority to transmit this inheritance to their children. On the other hand, they are seeking legal intervention for formal recognition of this claim. Their agency as Aboriginal women thus raises a paradox: what connects them together as women – Aboriginal identity and identity determined by the Indian Act – is also the source of their common oppression. To situate their struggles as feminist based *solely* on their shared oppression, therefore, is to risk appropriating and essentializing their voices and experiences by conflating Indigenous feminism's political goals with their gender identities. Such an act would prioritize the space of feminist politics at the expense of theorizing and conceptualizing the meaning of gender struggle and would call into question the political stakes of an Indigenous feminism that is unreflective about its organizing aims.

For Indigenous feminism to assert a political voice and establish a political grounding for itself, however, it must, like other feminisms, represent a subject on whose behalf it speaks. As one feminist critic explains, "Feminism has assumed that it can be neither theoretical nor political without a subject. Female gender identity and experience delineate that subject. Feminist politics, it is assumed, speaks for or in the name of someone, the group of women, who are defined by this female gender identity."[37] The question that arises, then, is the following: how does one analyze these stories of oppression and theorize their implications to delineate forms of gender identity and agency specific to Aboriginal women, while at the same time establishing the grounds for an Indigenous feminist politics?

One answer to this dilemma is offered by Iris Marion Young, who, in "Gender as Seriality," proposes a twofold approach to gender analysis that conceptualizes women as a social group, without requiring them to conform to a feminist identity in advance of their social struggles, and that analyzes women's relationships to the social field, without appropriating their struggles for empowerment as feminist commitments. Young argues that this approach begins by establishing the pre-political ground of feminism and by developing "some conception of women as a group prior to the formation of self-conscious feminist politics."[38] This approach also permits feminism to develop a theory of women's oppression without foreclosing its need for a normative subject. Noting the criticisms that have been directed against feminism for appropriating women's experiences through a search for common characteristics, and troubled by "normalizations and exclusions" within feminist theory that prevent "a common commitment to a politics against oppression," Young proposes a pragmatic orientation toward women that enables feminists to think about women not only as a strategic formation, "without identifying common attributes that all women have" but also as a purposeful, coherent social positioning that does not rely on "identity or self-identity for understanding the social production and meaning of membership."[39] The serial collectivity, Young suggests, best articulates this approach.

As a serial collective, women are united through their common oppression ("members are unified passively by the objects around which their actions are oriented") and directed toward a common purpose ("individuals pursue their own individual ends with respect to the same objects conditioned by a continuous material environment").[40] In being brought together by a material object or goal, women have no essential characteristics or affinities that define them: "Their actions and goals may be different, and they have nothing necessarily in common in their histories, experiences, or identities."[41] Their membership in the collective is also contingent, historically variable, and context-specific: "They understand themselves as constituted as a collective, as serialized, by the objects and practices through which they aim to accomplish their individual purposes," but they do not necessarily know one another, even though "their actions take into account their expectations of the behavior of others in the series whom they nevertheless do not encounter."[42] Because their shared political ground is represented by the practice toward which the group is oriented, each collective "treat[s] people as individuals, [as] variable and unique," and serial membership is defined "not by something [members] are" but rather "by the fact that in their diverse existences and actions they are oriented around the same objects or practico-inert structures."[43] The strategically formed, goal-oriented collective thus achieves two important objectives for Indigenous feminist politics: it shows how disadvantages and exclusions are structural and not merely personal or natural, and it names the project around which women can organize and through which feminist theory can establish its politics.

A second concern for Indigenous feminist politics is to specify its object of analysis without reducing women's stories of struggle to already established feminist claims. What makes these struggles political, then, must also account for what makes them specific to Aboriginal women. To foreground the specificity of Aboriginal women's struggles and to fulfill the objectives of Indigenous feminist analysis that I am proposing, I rely on case law about Aboriginal women's reinstatement claims to theorize the politics of their voice and agency. Yet case law represents an especially challenging narrative form for two reasons. First, insofar as these narratives achieve a radical individuation by describing the storytelling subject before the court, they also disavow an understanding of Aboriginal women as historical subjects and obscure recognition of their collective historical oppression.[44] Second, insofar as legal narratives are highly ambiguous about their social implications, they may also contribute to "the reproduction of existing structures of meaning and power" and thus "effac[e] the connections among persons and the social organization of their experiences."[45] Legal narratives, because of their "demand for narrative particularity," do not in themselves provide a prescription for conceptualizing voice and experience, and they do not inherently show subversive strategies within individual stories. Instead, they may potentially reinforce the status quo by "hobbl[ing] collective claims and solutions to social inequities" and by obscuring the institutional source of women's oppression.[46]

Despite this tension, law remains a crucial site of political intervention for Aboriginal women,[47] and legal narratives do provide insight into the "everyday practical engagements" through which "individuals identify the cracks and vulnerabilities of institutionalized power such as the law."[48] What matters to "hearing the call of [these] stories" is the dialogic relationship established by their telling.[49] Patricia Ewick and Susan Silbey describe this relationship as "transactions between speaker and audience, text and reader" that create "collaborative productions offered within overlapping relational contexts."[50] The stories transact, they claim, "by combining first-hand knowledge that is valued because it is direct, unmediated, and emotionally salient (the story) with what is more widely shared and culturally dispersed (familiar language, tropes, and experiences)."[51] These stories can thus generate insights into human experiences and have the potential to become acts of resistance by "underwrit[ing] subsequent social action" through the knowledge about encounters with the law that they convey.[52]

Not just any storyteller or storytelling situation within legal contexts can reveal these negotiations; therefore, not all stories can be claimed as politically relevant. To distinguish among a storyteller's accounts, one must also focus on and contextualize the story's counterhegemonic potential, by describing "the social marginality of the narrator," by analyzing "the hegemonic [as it] is constituted as an ongoing concern," and by incorporating "the circumstances of [the story's] telling where particular institutions create both a common opportunity to narrate and a common content to the narrative, thus revealing the collective organization of personal life."[53] This approach potentially creates "openings for resistance" in the "regular exercise of power" that generate new understanding about the situation of the speaking subject and the formation of a political project toward which these stories might be directed.[54]

The Aboriginal-woman-as-feeling-subject, I would argue, represents such an opening in legal discourse, an opening that has been achieved by Aboriginal women who have appropriated legal contexts as storytelling sites, who have expressed their experiences of living under the regulatory workings of Indian Act law, and who have endured the consequences of the law's decision-making authority. Her presence, however fleeting, summons into being the need for an Indigenous feminist politics that must be receptive to the call of affective listening. Affective listening is necessary to conceptualize the human situations represented by Aboriginal women's stories. It has been theorized as a form of affective understanding, by legal scholars such as Lynne Henderson, that, in its reliance on emotion and description, "convey[s] human situations created by, resulting from, or ignored by legal structures" and as a mode of embodied diversity, by Jennifer Nedelsky, that "explores how both body and emotion are essential to reason and judgment."[55] Nedelsky makes the additional point that for feminist and other emancipatory movements, "the need to see human beings as fully 'embodied' in order to understand their reasoning supports the feminist claim that the diversity of embodiment must be central, not peripheral, to the concepts underlying law."[56] Affective listening is thus a mode of receptive listening and reflective insight that may generate a form of political intervention that is not enabled by legal contexts but is urgently needed by them.

Affective Understanding and Feminist Politics

The dialogic reading practice that I am developing here depends on conceptualizing how emotion and representations of vulnerability can facilitate affective understanding as a cognitive capacity that expresses knowledge and insight into women's lives.[57] Emotions, however, have not always been accepted as reliable grounds for theorizing women's experience. Despite the recent outpouring of interest in the study of emotions, which one critic describes as "a wave – even a tsunami – of interest in emotions,"[58] feminist critics have been conscious of the way that women's use of emotions as expressive agency has called into question their knowledge claims.[59] They have remained wary about the opposition between emotion and reason as an irreducible difference – "between thought and feeling, mind and body, rationality and irrationality, conscious and unconscious, nurture and nature" – that has polarized to include women and men.[60] Sue Campbell, for example, points to the problems that arise because "the association of the feminine with feeling has been a long-standing historical ground on which to dismiss women."[61] Alison Jaggar foregrounds the distinction between reason and emotion conveyed by "stereotypes of cool men and emotional women" that continues to flourish because stereotypes "are confirmed by an uncritical daily experience."[62] Catherine Lutz tracks the ideological work that these stereotypes perform in generating taken-for-granted cultural beliefs. By "identifying emotion primarily with irrationality, subjectivity, [and] the chaotic ... and in subsequently labeling women as the emotional gender, cultural belief reinforces the ideological subordination of women."[63]

Feminist theorists of emotion have countered these dismissals by emphasizing the social insights that emotional expression can convey. For example, Campbell urges feminists to consider the "conditions under which our psychological states can be successfully formed or discriminated and how much control we can exercise over these circumstances."[64] Jaggar suggests that feminists cultivate outlaw emotions to develop a critical perspective on the world. She writes, "Feminists need to be aware of how we can draw on some of our outlaw emotions in constructing feminist theory ... and also how the increasing sophistication of feminist theory can contribute to the re-education, refinement, and eventual reconstruction of our emotional constitution."[65] Catherine Lutz proposes to "reclaim the language of emotion from the unexamined terms of the dichotomies – with thought and estrangement – in which it has participated."[66] The work of these critics challenges the dismissal of emotions by emphasizing emotional knowing as a value that enables women "to perceive the world differently from its portrayal in conventional descriptions."[67] These critics also propose that the use of emotion, far from undermining the intelligibility of the subject, will lead to a less restrictive understanding of public life and to women's reflective knowledge about their social positionings.[68] As Campbell explains, "when someone does something that we call 'expressing a feeling,' she is attempting to articulate or communicate the significance of some occasion or set of occasions within the context of how she views her life."[69]

These gains in feminist theorizing have, however, also faced setbacks as their insights have been appropriated by competing political agendas that undermine the specificity of women's knowledge claims. Feminists such as Lorraine Code have noted that shifting bureaucratic demands have eroded the potential for feminist alliances between women by transforming feminism's affiliative qualities into practices of social manageability.[70] Code argues that because bureaucratic values and observational knowledge have appropriated empathetic practices and people-friendly epistemologies, "knowing just how you feel," which at one time conveyed "affirmative, comforting, and consolidating ... bond[s] [and] a sense of mutuality," has become a form of "empiricist social science."[71] "In their monologic, unidirectional character, their privileging of a spectator, observational model of evidence gathering," she explains, "these epistemologies tacitly construct a picture where empathetic knowing finds no place."[72] Although Code warns that "a society or any practice within it that devalues empathy is poorer, in human terms, for so doing," she insists, nonetheless, that empathy "is not an unqualified good" and that any would-be advocates need to develop a self-critical politics to remain cognizant of its pitfalls and its promise.[73]

However, dispelling emotion, Catherine Lane West-Newman insists, works hand-in-hand with privileging reason in instrumental thinking and sanctions the use of emotions for competing political ends. She argues that "under practical rationality these emotions allow the action that calculation and logic alone could not produce ... Having, then, either expelled emotion or absorbed and renamed it, capitalist instrumental rationality can rest on a comfortable, but ultimately unsustainable, illusion that reason prevails."[74] Jennifer Harding and E. Deirdre Pribram also point out that abandoning emotion's valence in the formation of progressive politics has a direct social cost that women and cultural others bear. Because the study of emotions can reveal "the culturally constructed discourses of appropriate and inappropriate responses and behaviours, whose purpose is to govern the individual, construct the subject, and position categories of subjects within power relations,"[75] the presence of emotions and their social deployment also reveal socially sanctioned forms of behaviour that determine "where, when, and with what degree of intensity specific emotions may be considered reasonable, appropriate, and healthy."[76] "The ideological function of discourses," they argue, has therefore worked "to keep members of dominant political, social and cultural groups in dominance – where they are almost invariably aligned with reason while subordinate groups are associated with emotions."[77]

Because the political work of emotions and their institutional expression do not represent an unqualified good, scholars have struggled to determine what status emotion-knowledge should be accorded in both feminist philosophy, as the preceding debates illustrate, and in law. Feminist legal scholars have been especially concerned to create a dialogic space for emotion-cognition in its own right in order to argue for law's capacity to be receptive to the emotions, especially to aspects of suffering.[78] As Lynne Henderson explains, "A scholar or a judge *may* react to the pain and anguish caused actual human beings by a given law or doctrine, but she will seldom point to the painful or existential consequences of that law as reason to change it. This is because the ideological structures of legal discourse and cognition block affective and phenomenological argument."[79] An additional concern raised by feminist legal scholars points to legal reasoning's reliance on objectivity and detachment to weigh issues. Kathryn Abrams notes that "scholars started to ask what argument abstracted from any emotional resonance occluded, and what emotional knowledge might bring to the fore."[80]

Law is thus pervaded by emotion in complex ways, as Henderson and Abrams point out, through its contextual framing of legal issues, and in emotion's capacity to motivate new forms of understanding about how law impinges on social discrimination and vulnerability. Susan Bandes' work has been crucial to showing these intersections.[81] In particular, Bandes argues for the importance of experiential knowing as a capacity that feminist legal scholars have developed but one that may also inform how other constituencies shift law's practices. Bandes states, "It is entirely predictable that those who experience themselves as excluded from the law's reach, or misportrayed by the law's notions of human behavior, will be those with the impetus to challenge its claims of universality."[82] Shifting law's assessment practices in order to account for their experiences of being overlooked or misportrayed represents precisely the legal struggles that Aboriginal women have been forced to take up in order to regain their Indian status. The Supreme Court of British Columbia's decision in *McIvor v. The Registrar, Indian and Northern Affairs Canada* elucidates this final aspect of my argument.

McIvor v. The Registrar, Indian and Northern Affairs Canada

The *McIvor* decision provides an extended engagement with Aboriginal women as women, a critique of Indian Act discrimination that targets them as such, and the costs they bear because of their attachments to their Aboriginal homeland, their concern to pass on their culture to their children, and their efforts to empower their cultural identity and values by taking part in community rituals and events. These struggles appear with stark and moving urgency in the case narrative, a narrative that shows an Aboriginal woman's struggle to tell how law shaped and gendered her life story. The plaintiffs – Sharon Donna McIvor and her son, Charles Jacob Grismer – argued that the "registration provisions contained in s. 6 of the 1985 Act discriminate on the basis of sex and marital status contrary to ss. 15 and 28 of the Charter and that such discrimination has not been justified by the [Canadian] government."[83] The Supreme Court of British Columbia agreed. Indeed, the court found that disenfranchised Aboriginal women and their children had suffered losses to both the tangible and intangible aspects of their cultural identity, losses (representative of culture, belonging, identity, and access to financial and other benefits associated with registration to Indian status) that it regarded as necessary to Indian cultural identity and that are protected by law.[84] Despite its finding of discrimination, by incorporating extensive statements by McIvor and Grismer, the court narrative also showed how Indian Act identity has ritualized and valued aspects that situate it as part of the social structure through which Aboriginal communities understand and define themselves. As the case shows, this knowledge extends to social relations for identifying community members and to community protocols for including members in cultural practices. As McIvor explains,

> For my siblings and me it was lonely and painful to be excluded from the Indian community on the one hand and to be the only Indian children in any of the school, social, and recreational activities that we attended. My family and I suffered various forms of hurt and stigmatization because we did not have status cards. For example, members of my family wanted to observe our traditional lifestyle[,] including the harvesting of berries, roots, and hunting and fishing ... We did our best to engage in these traditional activities. But because we lacked status cards we were required to do it covertly.[85]

Accounts by both McIvor and her son show that their loss of status invoked feelings of pain and injury as a consequence of what they refer to as legal banishment.[86] When asked by the court to describe how she felt in being made unwelcome at important events such as marriages, funerals, and healing ceremonies, McIvor responded, "It affected me profoundly. It is hard to describe just how much it hurts to be in a place where you are told that you do not belong when it is the home of your ancestors."[87] Grismer also expressed a profound sense of dislocation and exclusion that the court recognized as "demeaning to human dignity."[88] He stated, "Because I was not registered under the Indian Act, I could not participate in programs for status Indians in the schools and community ... Being excluded from these programs further undermined my sense of self-worth and self-identity ... It also caused me to doubt who I was. Finally, being excluded from the status Indian community made me feel as though I did not belong anywhere."[89] The statements by McIvor and her son express in powerful and moving terms the personal costs of exclusion and vulnerability that they experienced because of their loss of cultural identity and Indian status. The statements also attest to violations of their human dignity and self-worth caused by pre-existing disadvantages enacted by the state. Significantly, the court asserted that the responsibility for remedying these disadvantages resided with the state. As indicated by Justice Carol S. Ross, "status is now purely a matter between the individual and the state."[90]

Although the case incorporates considerable information about discrimination through its analysis of historical amendments to the Indian Act, its most compelling voice is that of McIvor, who explains why Indian Act identity is so important within Aboriginal communities and why it has a value that matters in ways that political debates do not fully capture, especially debates that focus on the language of universal rights rather than the language of human values, dignity, and identity.[91] McIvor asserts, for example, that her "identification as an Aboriginal person" has never been in doubt and that she has "never ... never denied that [she] was of Aboriginal ancestry."[92] The force of her repetitive phrasing, assertions, and determination generates the sense that Aboriginal ancestry is indelible to her identity. The effect of this repetition, McIvor's firm voice, and the painful disclosures about what banishment meant to her show how fostering empathy can facilitate understanding of a woman's experience of discrimination and how this discrimination led to social suffering for her and her family. This suffering widens the terrain of discrimination by demonstrating its lingering effects and emotional complexity for the narrating subject. When asked how banishment has continued to be consequential for her, McIvor states, "Although I am now able to live on the Lower Nicola Reserve, I have chosen not to do so because of the hurt of so many years of mistreatment."[93]

Such a poignant statement raises the question, how can the court's recognition of status as "a matter between the individual and the state" promote understanding of the long-term social suffering that McIvor and her son have endured?[94] I would suggest that it is the effect of empathy and affective understanding generated by McIvor's narrative that raises this insight. What the Aboriginal-woman-as-feeling-subject contributes to Indigenous feminist politics, then, is the recognition that affective understanding, through experiential narrative, exposes aspects of discrimination that are present before the court yet unresolved by it. McIvor's narrative, in its emotional complexity and ability to elicit empathy in the reader, opens up a space for determining the grounds of an Indigenous feminist politics that can engage with these struggles.[95]

It is important to note that Yvelaine Moses failed to elicit a response from the court that can be characterized as empathetic or as promoting an understanding of the affective aspects of the injury she suffered.[96] Instead, she was portrayed as a woman who had benefitted from her reinstatement status, who had gained access to a right that she now enjoyed, and who had been granted a resolution to the "live controversy" in "leaving aside the feeling of an insecure registration."[97] The court's language conveys the sense that, like

McIvor, Moses was being provided with a remedy that was her due through law and that she would benefit from this recognition, it does not convey the sense that Moses was confronting a distinction that continues to discriminate on the grounds of gender, that she was outraged by the discrimination and wished to challenge it, and that she was worried about future amendments that could, yet again, revoke or alter her registration. Legal scholars note that it is the work of courts to distinguish between the emotional contexts of a claim and the legal regulation under scrutiny.[98] By setting aside Moses' concerns as an "insecure registration," however, the court sidestepped the distinction at the heart of the legislation that discriminates against Aboriginal women on the basis of gender, leaving the social costs of worry and anxiety for them to bear.[99] They must worry about legislation that revokes their Indian status because, historically, this was precisely the legislation's intent.[100]

As we establish the objectives for Indigenous feminist politics, we need to recognize that it takes courage to enter into these legal processes and that the outcomes are often costly to women because of the burden of representation that they bear and because they may not achieve their goals.[101] By incorporating these stories into the narratives that Indigenous feminists claim, we must also recognize that we can learn from these struggles and act on the integrity they demonstrate about women who must make their private emotional selves public in order to retain their Aboriginal identity and inheritances. The political object toward which emotional capacity and understanding is directed – to show how affective meaning can lead to public political action – should therefore be informed by the following set of consciousness-raising concerns.[102] If the Aboriginal-woman-as-feeling-subject represents a dialogic critical stance toward stories of disempowerment narrated by Aboriginal women, how am I affected by this disempowerment? What is the injustice at work? How can I organize for change? What difference will my political stance make to the social field? Am I prepared to accept my lack of implication in these debates, knowing that my inclusion may be at the expense of these women and their children? To formulate critical work that addresses these issues, an Indigenous feminist practice could begin with research that takes up these questions to propose a project and forms of activism by and for Aboriginal women who are similarly situated. This project would represent a politically important and inclusive feminist goal.[103] To value each story's expressive force and subversive meanings, one could begin with the following questions: How does the woman express her story? What contradictions in Indian Act legislation does she draw attention to? How were these contradictions expressed and applied to her own situation? How did the court decide? Was there continuity or discontinuity with other decisions? Who erred in preventing the woman's reinstatement? Can her strategy work to facilitate a future case? By generating forms of knowing that situate an Indigenous feminist readership and by developing a critical language attentive to emotional injury and harm that "certain kinds of knowing demand,"[104] we may find a way to enter into public debates and render unnecessary the epistemic status of the Aboriginal-woman-as-feeling-subject.

ACKNOWLEDGMENTS

I am grateful to my co-editors – Jean Barman, Shari Huhndorf, and Jeanne Perreault – for their insightful comments and support during the writing of this piece. I was fortunate to receive feedback at critical moments during the drafting stages. I wish to thank Benjamin Berger, John Borrows, Luis Campos, Jeff Corntassel, Rita Dhamoon, and Jeannine DeLombard for their tremendously helpful comments and suggestions.

NOTES

1 *Moses v. Canada,* 2003 FC 1417 at para. 2 (hereafter *Moses II*).
2 Ibid., paras. 9 and 2. Under ss. 6(1) and 6(2) of the amended Act, persons entitled to be registered fall within two categories or classes of Indians: those who were "entitled to be registered immediately prior to April 17, 1985" and those who have a parent who is "or, if no longer living, was at the time of death entitled to be registered under subsection (1)." *Indian Act,* R.S.C. 1985, c. I-5 (hereafter *Indian Act*).
3 *Moses v. Canada,* 2002 FCT 1088 at para. 2 (hereafter *Moses I*).
4 Ibid., paras. 14 and 16. Sections 14.2(1) and (2) of the amended *Indian Act* allow for protests in the definition and registration of Indians within a three-year time period by the council of the band to which the person is applying, by any member of the band, and by the person or his/her representative by notice, in writing, to the registrar, with a statement of the grounds for protest.
5 This category of status "extends registration to an individual if both parents were or could have been registered as Indians." *Moses II,* para. 6.
6 Ibid., para. 9.
7 Ibid., paras. 14 and 6.
8 Ibid., para. 22.
9 Ibid., para. 7.
10 Ibid., para. 8.
11 Ibid., paras. 14 and 9.
12 Meaning, "having no practical significance."
13 *Moses II,* para. 14.
14 Ibid., para. 18.
15 Ibid., para. 27.

16 See *Sanderson v. The Queen* (Registrar, Indian and Northern Affairs), 2002 MBQB 239 (CanLII), concerning an application for review of an order made by the registrar "refusing to add [the applicant's] name to the Register" because of the alleged ineligibility of the applicant's great-grandmother to registration under s. 6(1)(c) of the Act (paras. 1 and 6).
17 See *R. v. Etches,* 2008 CanLII 8610 (ON S.C.), concerning a challenge to the enfranchisement of three generations of women based on the registrar's error in failing to take into account that the appellant was enfranchised without her knowledge (para. 9).
18 See *Marchand v. Canada* (Registrar, Indian and Northern Affairs), 2000 BCCA 642 (CanLII), concerning an appeal by the registrar to deny registration on the grounds that the applicant was not "validly registered" (para. 22).
19 See *Perron v. Canada (Attorney General of),* 2003 CanLII 44366 (ON S.C.), concerning a motion by the attorney general to strike out parts of a claim asserting breach of Aboriginal rights and a claim for remedies as a result of the plaintiff's and her children's inability to pass on "'status' under the *Indian Act* to her grandchildren and her children to their children" (paras. 3 and 4). Plaintiffs claimed a self-constitutive Aboriginal right and argued that "all Aboriginal people pre-contact enjoyed ... constitutional Aboriginal rights" (paras. 29 and 37).
20 *Moses II,* para. 14.
21 Susan Bandes, "Fear and Degradation in Alabama: The Emotional Subtext of *University of Alabama v. Garrett,*" *Journal of Constitutional Law* 5 (2002-03): 520.
22 Kathryn Abrams, "Hearing the Call of Stories," *California Law Review* 79, 4 (1991): 1030, 1031.
23 I use the terms *emotion* and *feeling* interchangeably in my argument, although I understand that there are important distinctions between them in other disciplines. See Robert C. Solomon, "The Philosophy of Emotions," in Michael Lewis and Jeannette M. Haviland-Jones, eds., *Handbook of Emotions,* 2nd ed. (New York: Guilford Press, 2000), 3-15, for an overview of these debates. I follow Sianne Ngai's practice in discussing feeling, or affect, and emotion interchangeably, for it keeps with Ngai's understanding of these terms as "modal difference[s] of intensity or degree, rather than a formal difference of quality or kind." See Ngai, *Ugly Feelings* (Cambridge, MA: Harvard University Press, 2005), 27.

Debates about terminology are key to the field of law and emotion theory, as important research by Terry Maroney has shown. Whereas some critics distinguish "emotions" as "a series of nonconscious processes mapped in the body and brain in response to emotionally competent stimuli," and "feelings" as "the conscious experiences of happiness, sadness, and so on that are triggered by emotions" (referring to Antonio Damasio's distinctions), others classify emotions and feelings according to the same "psychological phenomena." Maroney, "Law and Emotion: A Proposed Taxonomy of an Emerging Field," *Law and Human Behavior* 30 (2006): 119-42, 124. Although Maroney astutely calls for law and emotion studies to define carefully "emotion-related terminology," my analysis tends to sidestep the "taxonomy-within-the-taxonomy issue" (127) and to address itself solely to the reason/emotion distinction as it informs legal reasoning. This focus says more about the preliminary claims of the research represented here than about the tremendously insightful methodological frameworks and new directions for theoretical and empirical research proposed by Maroney's study.

24 Lynne N. Henderson, "Legality and Empathy," *Michigan Law Review* 85, 7 (1987): 1592.

25 See Fay Blaney, "Aboriginal Women's Action Network," in Kim Anderson and Bonita Lawrence, eds., *Strong Women Stories: Native Vision and Community Survival* (Toronto: Sumach Press, 2003), 165, 166.

26 Native Women's Association of Canada, "Guide to Bill C-31," 1986, 3-4, Native Women's Association of Canada – Reports, http://www.nwac-hq.org/en/reports.html.

27 See John Borrows, *Recovering Canada: The Resurgence of Indigenous Law* (Toronto: University of Toronto Press, 2002), 21 and passim.

28 See Elaine Scarry for a brilliant analysis of the term *agency language,* in *The Body in Pain: The Making and Unmaking of the World* (New York: Oxford University Press, 1985), 17.

29 Ibid., 16.

30 Ibid., 18.

31 Ibid., 17.

32 I am indebted to Professor John Borrows for comments that helped me to develop these ideas further.

33 See Marlee Kline, "The Colour of Law: Ideological Representations of First Nations in Legal Discourse," *Social and Legal Studies* 3, 4 (1994): 455.

34 Ibid., 452.

35 See the Introduction to this volume for an overview of Indigenous feminism's goals and for debates about the social and political issues that continue to impinge upon Indigenous feminist practices.

36 Joyce Green, "Taking Account of Aboriginal Feminism," in Joyce Green, ed., *Making Space for Indigenous Feminism* (Black Point, NS: Fernwood, 2007), 20.

37 Iris Marion Young, "Gender as Seriality: Thinking about Women as a Social Collective," *Signs: Journal of Women in Culture and Society* 19, 3 (1994): 716.

38 Ibid., 722.

39 Ibid., 713, 722, 714, 723.

40 Ibid., 724.

41 Ibid., 725.

42 Ibid.

43 Ibid., 718, 728. Young explains that the collective does not depend on a *definitive* identity among individuals and thus is not constitutive of a person's entire sense of self, a view of second-wave feminism that has been strongly resisted by Indigenous women. As Young notes, "it does not define the person's identity in the sense of forming his or her individual purposes, projects, and sense of self in relation to others" (728).

44 Patricia Ewick and Susan Silbey discuss narratives and radical individuation in "Subversive Stories and Hegemonic Tales: Toward a Sociology of Narrative," *Law and Society Review* 29, 2 (1995): 217. Young also anticipates this problem of structural individuation by noting that individualist ideology works against conceptualizing women as a group, making it impossible to understand oppression "as a systematic, structured, institutional process." See Young, "Gender as Seriality," 718.

45 Ewick and Silbey, "Subversive Stories," 217, 213. "Formal legal processes," they also state, "are deliberately organized to adjudicate [among] truth claims" (215) and thus work structurally toward greater individuation.

46 Ibid., 216, 217.

47 Sharon McIvor provides an exemplary analysis of how Aboriginal women have used the Canadian courts to "advance their sex equality rights" and entitlements to citizenship, including their rights to "equal status and membership within Aboriginal communities, equal entitlement to share in matrimonial property, and equal participation in Aboriginal governance." See McIvor, "Aboriginal Women Unmasked: Using Equality Litigation to Advance Women's Rights," in Margot Young, Susan B. Boyd, Gwen Brodsky, and Shelagh Day, eds., *Poverty: Rights, Social Citizenship, and Legal Activism* (Vancouver: UBC Press, 2007), 96. McIvor has been a strong, committed, and path-breaking leader in these struggles, a prominent Aboriginal feminist, political activist, and role model whose struggle for recognition for her family has altered the political landscape for Aboriginal women in Canada. McIvor's leadership and vision cannot be overemphasized. Her work has demonstrated extensively how law can be made to remedy gendered legal provisions that have regulated without extinguishing Aboriginal women's civil and political rights and how law may be a site of intervention for Aboriginal women's equality claims. See McIvor, "Aboriginal Women's Rights as 'Existing Rights' (Canada)," *Canadian Woman Studies* 15, 2-3 (1995): 36.

48 Patricia Ewick and Susan Silbey, "Narrating Social Structure: Stories of Resistance to Legal Authority," *American Journal of Sociology* 6, 6 (2003): 1330. Ewick and Silbey's work undertakes this project in exemplary ways.

49 This expression belongs to Kathryn Abrams, who developed her crucial insight that to think concretely by remembering socially may enable feminist scholars to "establish common ground with others" by remaining receptive to the experiences of the group in assessing how that group is situated socially and "distinct from other (dominant) groups." See Abrams, "Hearing the Call of Stories," *California Law Review* 79, 4 (1991): 1051. Abrams' argument is especially important because it shows how to engage with others' stories and address the problem of experiential accounts of social disempowerment. She notes, for example, that "the valuation of experience itself provides no basis for choosing among differential experiential claims" (980), but she counters the apolitical relativism of this problem by asserting that we must "familiarize ourselves with many diverse forms of narrative" to forestall the "forced forgetting" that "imposed ... official abstraction" effects (981, 1051).

50 Ewick and Silbey, "Narrating Social Structure," 1343.

51 Ibid., 1344.

52 This knowledge is also potentially transformative: through the storyteller's "selective appropriation of events, a particular event order, the positioning of character in relation to a situation of relative powerlessness, and a sense of closure that provides a moral evaluation," the stories come to show how individuals navigate relations of relative powerlessness by "accommodat[ing] to power while simultaneously protecting their interests and identities" (ibid., 1344, 1329).

53 Ewick and Silbey, "Subversive Stories," 220-21.

54 Ewick and Silbey, "Narrating Social Structure," 1330.

55 Henderson, "Legality and Empathy," 1592; Jennifer Nedelsky, "Embodied Diversity and the Challenges to Law," *McGill Law Journal* 42 (1997): 93.

56 Ibid.

57 Emotion theory, as a field, is broad and complex and includes innovations that have challenged the transmission model of emotion by showing that emotions are both individual and social in origin. Sara Ahmed's work has been groundbreaking in this regard, for it not only analyzes emotions as a form of self-presence, it also analyzes emotions as social sites, as the expressive form that creates surfaces and boundaries that allow us "to distinguish an inside and an outside in the first place." See Ahmed, *The Cultural Politics of Emotions* (New York: Routledge, 2004), 10. Ahmed's interest is not simply in what emotions tell us or elicit as interiority but also in the work that emotions do. She asks, for example, "How do emotions work to align some subjects with some others and against other others?" She asks this question by way of urging political consciousness about how social collectives are formed and what underlying affective criteria secure their unity. For an insightful reading of the role of emotion in the formation of "whiteness" and other affiliative associations, see Ahmed, "Collective Feelings or, the Impressions Left by Others," *Theory, Culture and Society* 21, 2 (2004): 25.

58 Catherine Lane West-Newman, "Feeling for Justice? Rights, Laws, and Cultural Contexts," *Law and Social Inquiry* 30, 2 (2005): 306. The editors of the *Handbook of Emotions* also state boldly that "at the beginning of the new century, the study of emotion ... has become obvious to all." See Michael Lewis and Jeannette M. Haviland-Jones, "Introduction," in Lewis and Haviland-Jones, *Handbook of Emotions,* xi.

59 Feminist philosophy has been especially concerned to reconcile women's accounts of embodiment with entrenched notions of cognitive development that support the taken-for-grantedness of power relations. For a historical overview of these debates, see Robin May Schott, "Feminism and the History of Philosophy," in Linda May Alcoff and Eva Kittay, eds., *The Blackwell Guide to Feminist Philosophy* (Oxford: Blackwell, 2007), 53.

60 Geoffrey M. White, "Representing Emotional Meaning: Category, Metaphor, Schema, Discourse," in Lewis and Haviland-Jones, *Handbook of Emotions,* 31.

61 Sue Campbell, "Being Dismissed: The Politics of Emotional Expression," *Hypatia* 9, 3 (1994): 49. Skepticism about emotional knowledge as not to be trusted is highly gendered, as Sue Campbell explains. She notes that duplicity in emotional expression performs two functions: it calls into question the genuine nature of the emotions expressed (i.e., faking emotion), and it dismisses women for having emotions by characterizing emotional lives as unhealthy and "limit[ing] of our ways of acting in the world" (49).

62 Alison M. Jaggar, "Love and Knowledge: Emotion in Feminist Epistemology," *Inquiry: An Interdisciplinary Journal of Philosophy* 32 (1989): 164.

63 Catherine Lutz, "Emotion, Thought, and Estrangement: Emotion as a Cultural Category," *Cultural Anthropology* 1, 3 (1986): 288.

64 Campbell, "Being Dismissed," 49.

65 Jaggar, "Love and Knowledge," 167.

66 Lutz, "Emotion, Thought, and Estrangement," 304.
67 Jaggar, "Love and Knowledge," 167.
68 That emotional expression in public life is restricted, gendered, and racialized remains an important insight generated by theorists of feminist philosophy and emotion theory. As Lutz notes, emotion is often perceived as leading to danger or vulnerability for women in two ways: first, the emotional person poses a threat to the reasoning person by calling into question the individual's rationality, sense, and reliability and thus potentially does harm by undermining the "proper social coordination that has been achieved by the application of reasoned thought"; and second, by engaging in emotional behaviour, the person appears to lack control and may be perceived as "less than fully socialized, and therefore, to be dangerous." See Lutz, "Emotion, Thought, and Estrangement," 293. Sara Ahmed's work also explores how emotions mark boundaries between individuals in terms of gendering and racializing social and cultural practices, especially with regard to how emotions and emotional expression affirm differences in the "materialization of bodies" that produce "surfaces" through which the individual and the social may be delineated. Ahmed, *The Cultural Politics of Emotion* (Edinburgh: Edinburgh University Press, 2004), 17, 10. These codings are key to explaining how emotions work to secure wider social consensus for policies and social practices that target racialized groups. Ahmed shows, for example, how the language of fear is especially potent in generating the "intensification of 'threats' which works to create a distinction between those who are 'under threat' and those who threaten" (72). For an important discussion about how the affective politics of fear enable the slide from "terror" to "terrorism" in the racialization of social groups, see 71-80.
69 Campbell, "Being Dismissed," 54.
70 Lorraine Code, "I Know Just How You Feel," in Lorraine Code, *Rhetorical Spaces: Essays on Gendered Locations* (New York: Routledge, 1995), 123.
71 Ibid., 121, 123, 122.
72 Ibid., 122.
73 Ibid., 121. Michael Hardt is even more critical of the rise of affective contexts and immaterial labour in the global capitalist economy. He argues that "humanity and its soul are produced in the very processes of economic production" through binding elements such as health services and other industries that rely on caring and affective labour to "produce social networks, forms of community, [and] biopower." See Hardt, "Affective Labor," *boundary 2* 26, 2 (1999): 89-100, 91. Like Code, Hardt suggests the need to recognize that affective labour is double-edged, even as he states that the value of this labour may generate "a biopower from below" (100).
74 West-Newman, "Feeling for Justice?" 313. The calculation that West-Newman refers to concerns a person's institutional manipulability through subterranean emotions such as "commitment to the purpose at hand, loyalty to the employing organization, joy in success, trust in those with whom cooperation is necessary, envy of competitors to spur the pursuit of interests, and greed to encourage aggrandizement." Ibid., quoting J.M. Barbalet, *Emotion, Social Theory, and Social Structure* (Cambridge: Cambridge University Press, 1998), 59.

75 Jennifer Harding and E. Deirdre Pribram, "The Power of Feeling: Locating Emotions in Culture," *European Journal of Cultural Studies* 5, 4 (2002): 418.

76 Ibid., 411.

77 Ibid., 415.

78 Susan Bandes has written an important and insightful analysis of the contradictory work performed by victim impact statements in the legal context. See Bandes, "Empathy, Narrative, and Victim Impact Statements," *University of Chicago Law Review* 63, 2 (1996): 361-412.

79 Henderson, "Legality and Empathy," 1575, emphasis in original.

80 Kathryn Abrams, "Legal Feminism and the Emotions: Three Moments in an Evolving Relationship," *Harvard Journal of Law and Gender* 28 (2005): 332.

81 See the debates in *The Passions of Law,* which explore the place of emotion in law not only through arguments that analyze emotional meaning in criminal courts but also in debates about emotional content and its salience to legislation, litigation, and judging. See Susan Bandes, ed., *The Passions of Law* (New York: New York University Press, 1999). As Bandes points out, these debates show that, in law, "emotional content is inevitable" (7). The place of emotion in legal deliberations is also widely contested. Brian Rosebury, for example, seeks to impose limits on what role emotions can have in relation to larger patterns of conduct and is especially concerned about deliberations involving emotion that violate the sphere of privacy. See Rosebury, "On Punishing Emotions," *Ratio Juris* 16, 1 (2003): 37-55. Terry Maroney's research has also been crucial for advancing the research goals of the field. Maroney urges new directions in law and emotion studies, particularly in the field of critical race theory where she argues "cultural notions of the 'appropriateness' of emotional expression, social constructs as to the division of emotional labour, and other law-relevant emotion issues strongly implicate race." Maroney, "Law and Emotion," 135.

82 Susan Bandes, "What's Love Got to Do with It?" *William and Mary Journal of Women and the Law* 8 (2001-02): 99-100.

83 *McIvor v. The Registrar, Indian and Northern Affairs Canada,* 2007 BCSC 827 at para. 7 (hereafter *McIvor*).

84 Ibid., paras. 132 and 256.

85 Ibid., para. 127.

86 Ibid., para. 126.

87 Ibid., para. 128.

88 Ibid., para. 280.

89 Ibid.

90 Ibid., para. 7(d).

91 See, for example, Joyce Green's important analysis of intersecting oppressions that prevent the recognition of how "the nexus of sexism and racism shapes the lives of many indigenous women." Green, "Canaries in the Mines of Citizenship: Indian Women in Canada," *Canadian Journal of Political Science* 34, 4 (2001): 729. Green's argument uses the language of rights, difference, equality, and citizenship in sophisticated and illuminating ways. Ultimately, however, this language undermines the relationship between individuals and their stories and erodes the human dimension

that gives these concepts their practical and meaningful significance as concepts that show human relations. Feminist politics require these terms (rights, difference, equality, and citizenship) to enter into political debates to ensure the recognition and protection of women's rights. They also require language that expresses women's human capacities, commitments, feelings, and values. My argument represents an effort to widen the grounds of this debate for Indigenous feminist politics by arguing for a space that recognizes Indigenous women as feeling subjects that inflect political concepts with new objectives and meanings.

92 *McIvor,* para. 136.

93 Ibid., para. 128.

94 Ibid., para. 7(d).

95 Identity, emotion, and empowerment are intrinsically linked in new forms of political identity theorized by Indigenous legal scholars such as Val Napoleon. Napoleon asserts, for example, that experiential and individual capacities are of value to political identity through "self-determining autonomy" understood as "a capacity that exists in the context of our social relations and only in conjunction with the internal sense of being autonomous ... [T]his sense of being autonomous is felt." See Napoleon, "Aboriginal Self-Determination: Individual Self and Collective Selves," *Atlantis* 29, 2 (2005): 6. Napoleon argues here for gender empowerment not only as an ideal achieved through formal legal processes but also as a practice that begins by recognizing an individual's inherent self-worth. Martha Nussbaum also affirms this idea by arguing that judicial rationality itself, understood as the "collecting of facts about the diverse ways of life," needs to be supplemented by acts of imagination that enable judges to "enter ... into these lives with empathy [in order to] see ... the human meaning of the issues at stake in them." Nussbaum, "Compassion: The Basic Social Emotion," *Social Philosophy and Policy* 13, 1 (1996): 53.

96 Indeed, one of the complexities raised by this case is that Moses sought to eliminate an identity distinction that discriminated on the basis of gender. Thus, gender distinctions became grounds for analysis in ways that excluded recognition of gendered harms. Indigenous feminist analysis must also be attentive to these exclusions, asking if gender is not addressed, why it is absent and on what grounds. I am indebted to Jessica Rose, a member of the Law and Humanities Methods Group at the University of Toronto, for this insight.

97 *Moses II,* paras. 15 and 16.

98 Richard Posner, "Emotions versus Emotionalism in Law," in Bandes, *The Passions of Law,* 309, 313.

99 *Moses II,* para. 15.

100 Yvelaine Moses raised a further concern – that her reinstatement under section 6(1)(f) granted her a lesser category than that provided to her brother, even though the court insisted that she held the "same rights ... but by a different approach" (ibid., para. 8). The issue concerned Moses' perception that status categories differentiate among applicants both in the *kind* and *value* of the rights they are accorded. Subsequent decisions bear out her concern. In *McIvor et al. v. The Registrar, Indian and Northern Affairs Canada et al.,* 2007 BCSC 26, and *Innu Takuaikan Uashat mak Mani-Utenam v. Noël,* 2004 CanLII 1230 (Q.C.A.), the registrar refers to distinctions

between 6(1) and 6(2) as entitlements to an upgrade in status. In *McIvor,* the value-laden status provisions are conveyed through the following statement: "The only way we could *upgrade your entitlement* from subsection 6(2)" (para. 14, emphasis added). In *Innu,* the provisions are conveyed as follows: "The adoptee ... would be entitled to an *upgrade from subsection 6(2) to paragraph 6(1)(f)*" (para. 18, emphasis added). The application of these categories and their bureaucratic thinking demonstrate the additional barriers that Aboriginal women confront and the indignities they suffer when they assert their right to Aboriginal identity using the agency language instituted by this legislation.

101 The action taken by Brenda Pauline Sanderson illustrates this dilemma. Sanderson sought review of the registrar's refusal to add her name to the Indian register on the grounds that the 1985 Indian Act had allowed her great-grandmother to register under section 6(2), thereby disqualifying Sanderson from entitlement to registration. In the review application, Sanderson's claim to Indian status is all but buried beneath the respondent's challenge to the court's jurisdiction to decide Charter issues and remedies. See *Sanderson v. The Queen* at para. 3. The court dismissed the respondent's motion and concluded that it was empowered to hear and determine Sanderson's arguments (para. 31); however, in so deciding, it also delayed resolution of Sanderson's claim. These delays and uncertainties are borne by women. Like Sanderson, McIvor and her children were forced to wait several years for the resolution of their claims, which they had originally submitted on 25 September 1985. See *McIvor,* para. 98. When the British Columbia Supreme Court handed down its decision in 2007, McIvor's claim had, by then, taken twenty-two years to resolve.

102 On affective meaning and public political action, see Ann Cvetkovich, *Mixed Feelings: Feminism, Mass Culture, and Victorian Sensationalism* (New Brunswick, NJ: Rutgers University Press, 1992), 3.

103 An additional issue for Indigenous feminist practice concerns developing strategies that challenge the "atomization of social struggle" represented by this and other cases. Alan Hunt, "Rights and Social Movements: Counter-Hegemonic Strategies," *Journal of Law and Society* 17, 3 (1990): 317. The case's reasoning asserts a radical individuation of experience specific to McIvor's struggle that forces other Aboriginal women to represent their discrimination in precisely these terms. If their histories, family inheritances, and social suffering do not conform to this form of analysis, then legal remedies do not follow, as the cases cited earlier in this chapter attest. Law's focus on experience for its absolute individuality rather than its narrative exemplarity thus "impedes the visibility" of the case's "political substance" (ibid.) and prevents recognition of Aboriginal women's discrimination in historical terms. Paradoxically, these historical exclusions, legislated through Indian Act amendments, are precisely the grounds on which Aboriginal women have been forced to attempt to restore their status.

104 Code, "I Know Just How You Feel," 122.

Beyond Feminism
Indigenous Ainu Women and Narratives of Empowerment in Japan

ann-elise lewallen

In order to restore the rights of Ainu women, we need to decide what the conditions are for being an Ainu woman. We cannot say we are Ainu women unless we have our own mountains where we can gather our wood and grass. Cooking foods purchased at supermarkets is the role of modern women, not of traditional Ainu women.

– Keira Tomoko, "My Work as an Ainu Woman"

In the quotation that opens this chapter, Keira Tomoko, an Ainu activist and cloth artist, links the revival and realization of Indigenous Ainu womanhood to the earth and practices embedded in the natural environment.[1] For Ainu women, the ability to engage freely in relations with the natural world – effectively, the world in which non-human *kamuy* (deities) abide – is critical to re-creating women's subjectivities, as Indigenous and as Ainu.[2] Ecological colonialism, which began influencing Ainu lifeways from the sixteenth century, led to overexploitation of the natural environment, which fractured Ainu relations with kamuy. Today, restricted access to waterways and the land has crippled Ainu attempts to re-establish relations with the non-human pantheon. Most Ainu women today have been forced to depend on supermarkets for foodstuffs to feed their families. Yet Ainu women depend on the natural world to invoke the Indigenous knowledge and spiritual practices of their ancestors, to produce traditional foods eaten by their grandmothers, and to weave clothing worn by ancestors. After more than two hundred years of Japanese colonialism and assimilation policies in Hokkaido (the northernmost island of Japan and ancestral home of Japanese Ainu), Ainu women are now involved in recovering traditional practices to restore the ethos of these earlier generations.[3] Because reciprocal engagement with the natural world is central to reconstituting oneself as an Indigenous Ainu woman, there is a disconnect between issues of primary concern to Ainu women, such as cultural survival and human rights protection, and issues driving majority feminism, such as liberation from patriarchy.

In contemporary Japan, Ainu women self-identify as traditionalists, cultural activists, and champions of Indigenous rights, but few would describe themselves as feminists. Most would shun the notion altogether. Rather, Ainu women claim Indigenous subjectivities, align with Indigenous communities internationally, and have formed coalitions with Japanese minorities, including Okinawans, Burakumin, Resident Koreans, and immigrant groups. Most women who identify as Ainu are invested in cultural revival work – clothwork, art production, song and dance revivalism, and language revival – and do not self-identify as political leaders, even though publicly identifying oneself as Ainu and engaging in these activities constitutes a political stance in a nation that still imagines itself as homogeneous. Ainu revivalists today understand cultural practice as being bifurcated into gendered spheres of complementary economic activities, and most cultural revival efforts focus on restoring these gendered spheres as they were practised historically.[4] In contemporary Japan, persons who identify as Ainu are scattered through the archipelago and are part of a community that claims between twenty-five thousand and one million persons; however, membership and access to need-based aid administered by the largest Ainu organization, the Ainu Association of Hokkaido (4,238 members), is limited to Hokkaido residents.[5] In this chapter, I explore some of the key challenges and motivations that have propelled Ainu women in contemporary Japan to organize themselves along ethnic rather than sex or gender lines. I also consider the utility of feminism as an organizing philosophy and examine why linkages with majority feminist groups have not received support from the majority of Ainu women.

In 2003, a group of Ainu women, organized through the Sapporo branch of the Ainu Association, began coalition building with fellow Japanese minority women's groups through a non-governmental organization devoted to combatting discrimination through legal reform: the International Movement Against All Forms of Discrimination and Racism – Japan Committee (IMADR-JC).[6] Because majority feminism in Japan has failed to consider ethnic difference, minority women have chosen the practice of multiple discrimination analysis to articulate their social critiques. Multiple discrimination analysis, codified by the United Nations, enables women to identify how their dual positionality as both women and ethnic minorities produces more debilitating forms of discrimination within minority groups, among women, and within the majority society. I examine how, within a framework of multiple discrimination and human rights discourse, women are germinating an Indigenous consciousness to attend to Ainu women's specific subject positions from within the Ainu community.

In the latter part of the essay, I shift from a focus on Ainu women as a community to a focus on a group of Ainu women who are organized along the dual axes of ethnicity and sex or gender. I introduce the Ainu Women's Survey as a case study to illustrate how Ainu women have applied the tool of multiple discrimination analysis to study their social and structural positions. The Sapporo-based group of Ainu women (hereafter MD project members) initially came together as a study group to learn about the practice of multiple discrimination analysis, and they combined it with what they already knew about ethnic discrimination. MD project members developed the Ainu Women's Survey to collect data on the contemporary circumstances of Ainu women and to gauge the prevalence of multiple discrimination in women's everyday lives across Hokkaido. Project members anticipated that survey results would reveal how their compounded minority status has affected them differently than Ainu men, majority Japanese women, and other minority women in Japan. The survey results have been collated with data from the Burakumin and Resident Korean women's surveys, and in March 2007, representatives of minority women delivered individual survey reports to the Gender Equality Bureau, a cabinet-level agency responsible for promoting gender equality and ending sex-based discrimination.[7] The Japanese government, as a signatory of the Convention on the Elimination of All Forms of Discrimination against Women (CEDAW), is required to undergo periodic hearings to monitor compliance with the convention but had failed to address minority women in earlier reports. The IMADR-JC organized the nationwide minority women's survey to generate statistical data on minority women for submission to the CEDAW, to render the situation of minority women visible, and thus to demonstrate the severity of multiple discrimination in Japan. Each survey was organized locally by minority women's organizations. Ainu-identified women designed and implemented the survey among Hokkaido Ainu women, and they analyzed the results to ensure that Ainu women's circumstances would be included in the report delivered to the CEDAW.

I have chosen the Ainu Women's Survey project and project members as a focal point for this essay because this group is self-consciously addressing sex and gender issues as political concerns. And although they represent a tiny fraction of the larger Ainu community, their work suggests a paradigm shift among Ainu women and emphasizes the disconnect between strict traditionalist revivalism and more recent hybrid forms of cultural revival. Moreover, the fact that Ainu women who have attended forums in which survey results were presented have responded positively to multiple discrimination project reports suggests that women are anxious to confront and grapple with their double minority status.

This chapter emerged from my involvement with the survey project, which I describe as an exercise in engaged anthropology. I joined the MD project group during the data-recording and analysis stage of the project, and I assisted with statistical interpretation and helped to render the survey numbers meaningful to project personnel. I continued my involvement with the multiple discrimination project through 2009, helped to draft project reports, and was invited to the MD project group's bi-monthly "Empowerment Café," a meeting in which members gathered casually to discuss their current situation as Ainu women and plan future initiatives. I have made every effort to gain permission before citing personal anecdotes or comments from project members, and I will continue to respect the terms of participation and access that have been granted to me. This chapter explores the strategies Ainu women have recently adopted to empower themselves outside the frame of feminist practice.

The Complications of Speaking as Ainu versus Speaking as Women

When Cikap Mieko, an Ainu cloth artist and activist, addressed conference participants "from an Ainu woman's point of view" at the 1985 Nairobi Women's Conference NGO Forum, her presentation was criticized because, critics argued, it lacked a woman's point of view. Cikap was then criticized because of her questionable status as an Indigenous minority in Japan. Most of the criticism emanated from Wajin women activists. Wajin, or ethnic Japanese, make up the majority group in Japanese society. In response to these criticisms, Cikap argued that Ainu "are not in a position to talk about gender discrimination. There is a problem we have to face as a 'PEOPLE.' We are yet to establish the right of the Ainu nation to exist."[8]

Twenty-plus years later, Cikap's assessment of the collision between indigeneity and gender discrimination and her ranking of activist agendas remain salient for Ainu, who just received official recognition as the Indigenous people of Japan in June 2008. Nevertheless, the status of Ainu rights as Indigenous rights remains an outstanding issue because the government has not yet determined if Ainu indigeneity maps onto Indigenous rights provided under the UN Declaration on the Rights of Indigenous Peoples, which was adopted in 2007. Since the 1970s, Ainu activists have campaigned nationally and internationally for political and economic rights and an end to racial discrimination. In 1997, the Japanese government passed the Ainu Cultural Promotion Act to encourage preservation of Ainu traditional practices and material culture production. But ten years after the legislation, critics charged that the Act had improved neither the economic nor the political status of Ainu. Nor has it established a system of compensation for historical dispossession of land and livelihood. Ainu women focus their activism on the Japanese government's refusal to grant official Indigenous rights to Ainu people as their primary concern; gender discrimination remains a secondary issue.[9] In recent years, however, some Ainu women have begun to understand their dual subjectivity – as women and as Ainu – as being intertwined in complex ways and, ultimately, indivisible. Self-empowerment and consciousness raising about the compound effects of racism and ethnic and gender discrimination are enabled through a discursive practice known as multiple discrimination. By framing their subjectivity as having, simultaneously, a gendered and an ethnic dimension, Ainu women are applying the language of multiple discrimination analysis to make sense of institutions and systems that impinge on their human rights in contemporary Japanese society.

Ten years after Cikap's experiences at the Nairobi meeting, she was commissioned to write a brief article outlining Ainu women's perspectives on ethnic Wajin feminism.[10] Cikap had attended the Nairobi meeting together with a group of Wajin feminists and a fellow minority woman who was Burakumin. Burakumin are a class-segregated group of social outcasts within Japan.[11] Together, Cikap and the Burakumin representative sought to educate Wajin women in the group about their histories, ongoing oppression, and experience of erasure within majority Japanese society. As an ironic and perhaps unconscious display of this erasure, Wajin feminists responded defensively that they had never learned about minority history in school and that Ainu and Burakumin concerns should be bracketed as "North-South (i.e., regional) problems," problems that were irrelevant to majority Wajin and, by extension, feminists. The impact of these exchanges was irreversible for Cikap: "These words between us festered like a tumour, so that I had almost given up before we even left for Nairobi ... there was so little dialogue with the feminists, and my anger toward them continued to grow."[12] Nevertheless, she and other Ainu women tried to open a dialogue with Wajin women to prepare for the 1995 Beijing Women's Conference. She stated, "If we cannot create more dialogue, then we Ainu will have to respond to foreign feminists as I did in Nairobi: 'We Ainu women have no [sense of] solidarity with Japanese feminists – we simply travelled here together, that's all.'"[13]

Dialogue would be elusive, however. Solidarity building between women and across ethnic and caste divides in Japan was not rekindled until Ainu women delivered the results of the Ainu Women's Survey to the Japanese Gender Equality Bureau in March 2007. Although partnership is tenuous, majority feminists have begun to realize the gravity of minority women's issues and to take stock of inadvertent segregation within their own movement.

As echoed in Cikap's mention of the call to Ainu ethnic solidarity, MD project members have only recently begun to consider their dual subject positions as Indigenous persons and as women and to align themselves with human rights claims, largely because multilayered and entrenched systems of discrimination kept these issues hidden in the past. Although global indigeneity discourse has transformed Ainu activism since the early 1980s, feminist discourses have not resonated with Ainu women, primarily because of long-standing misunderstandings between majority Japanese feminists and Ainu and other minority women.

The disjuncture between Ainu women's activist philosophy and feminist ideology operates at several levels: in Ainu women's self-awareness and identity management and through local and international policies and legal conventions. Ainu women understand physical, emotional, and psychological abuse as inevitable and even expected because of their low social status as women inside the Ainu community and Japanese society. Over time and across many generations, these attitudes have become internalized and naturalized: to be an Ainu woman is to be subjected to violence and prejudice.[14] Because of the prevalence of anti-Ainu bullying among schoolchildren, in hiring and employment, and in marriage, and because of ongoing anti-discrimination campaigns within the association, Ainu women who are members of the Ainu Association are trained to look for instances of ethnic or racial discrimination. Sex and gender discrimination have, however, been obscured by an intense focus on countering racist attitudes in majority society. At the level of international policy making, the CEDAW and the International Convention on the Elimination of All Forms of Racial Discrimination (ICERD, adopted in 1965), both of which have been ratified by Japan, provide important mechanisms for resolving mistreatment of minority populations not protected by pre-existing state instruments. In the domestic context, although Japan introduced the non-punitive Equal Employment Opportunity Law in 1986, aiming to improve gender equality in hiring and employment practices, there is no anti-racial-discrimination law in Japan today. Minority women fall into the grey zone not protected by either convention – there are no protections mandated specifically for minority women's human rights or policies that address multiple discrimination specifically.

Ainu Women as Cultural Guardians

Ainu women's primary reasons for not embracing feminism as a movement are both linguistic and ideological. *Feminisuto* in Japanese can be interpreted as "chivalrous man," or it can refer to a well-educated middle- to upper-class Japanese woman who expects a paycheque for domestic labour.[15] Within the Ainu community, significant structural and historical circumstances have limited the utility of a Wajin-style liberal feminist agenda and have likewise made it difficult for Wajin women to understand the rationale of Ainu women's approaches to liberation. Many Ainu women seek a return to traditional value systems and to revive the sexual division of labour from the pre-colonial period (the mid-nineteenth century). Gendered labour distinctions between men and women were not interpreted as "discrimination ... It [was] through the combination of the spheres of women and men that the overall Ainu world [was] formed."[16] Women were, for example, the keepers of the home *(cisekor katkemat)*, whereas men were simply residents of the house and obliged by the women to perform ritual prayer on the women's behalf.[17]

Since the 1960s, Ainu women Elders have initiated cultural preservation and revival work to protect, transmit, and re-create traditional cultural practices passed down from ancestors and inherited from the pantheon of deities. Ainu revivalists are not in agreement about how these traditional practices should be restored. Separate camps – including traditionalists, innovators, and entrepreneurs – enact quite different revival strategies; however, all of these groups are committed to ancestral practice and intention as their basic motivation.[18] Pre-colonial Ainu communities operated according to spheres of gender complementarity and were organized by a sexual division of labour.[19] Based on oral histories and written texts, today's revival movement is bifurcated into female and male domains of cultural and economic labour. Historically, women's work included all clothwork (weaving, embroidery, mat making, and sewing), basic horticulture, gathering vegetables and shallow-water marine produce, cooking and child rearing, and care for ancestors. Men, in contrast, hunted, fished, produced all wooden implements (houses, altars, tools, etc.), and, critically, served as interlocutors between gods and humans. Men's primary economic activities – hunting and salmon fishing – were curtailed by government prohibitions in the nineteenth century. The bans remain in place today, but salmon for ritual use may be obtained through a tedious bureaucratic procedure. Thus, though men may engage in ritual practice and woodworking, traditional forms of male economic labour are no longer viable options. Kin relationships mirrored economic organization: matrilineal transmission patterns operated simultaneously with patrilineal transmission to pass down women's and men's heritage practices, lineage markers, and ancestral knowledge.

Assimilation policies produced a gendering of ethnicity,[20] whereby Ainu men were forced to adopt Japanese names and new economic roles in the public sphere, whereas Ainu women continued cultural practices in the private sphere.[21] Oral histories indicate that male Elders pressured young Ainu women to master practices from both male and female domains and in some cases, barred young girls from attending primary school to ensure that this knowledge was retained for posterity and to guarantee that deities and ancestors were properly attended.[22]

For the older generation, a sense of obligation to ancestors and spiritual practice, and the feeling that their generation forms a vital link in the chain of cultural reproduction, urges Ainu women to revive cultural heritage practice. They ask, if we Ainu women don't continue to do the work of culture and cultural transmission while the political movement for restoring Ainu rights is being waged, what degree of Ainuness will remain when political rights are finally achieved? Gendered organization in today's cultural revivalism can be understood, therefore, as a legacy of an earlier split that has reappeared in rights reclamation work: men continue to serve as political leaders for local, national, and global Indigenous rights activism, whereas women continue to work in the domain of cultural production. Because younger women tend to be less concerned with Indigenous rights recovery, few young women were involved in the MD project.

Some women revivalists view political activism as too complicated and intimidating. This sense of intimidation and hesitation may stem from the fact that Ainu political leadership is almost exclusively male. The double gender complementarity of these two spheres – female cultural production versus male economic production and women as cultural leaders versus men as political leaders – informs all efforts to reinscribe Ainu traditional values as everyday practices today. Indeed, Ainu women do not seek sexual parity or liberation from patriarchy along the same axes as do Wajin feminists; consequently, the common terrain for organizing has been limited between these two groups until now.

Gendered Identities and Cultural Expectations

Transgression of the traditional spheres of gendered labour is considered taboo, especially within ritual processes connected with the spirit world, yet some women engage in woodcarving, while very few men do embroidery. Women, who tend to be more underemployed than men, have enrolled in vocational training courses, including woodcraft classes, and therefore report higher proficiency in woodcarving (38 percent among the older generation) than men do in embroidery.[23] Traditional revivalists who seek to preserve historical practice in precise form are often in the older generation, aged fifty and older, and are more likely to insist on correct performance of gender-specific behaviours. Innovators, or revivalists who interpret Ainu cultural expression to reflect ancestral values and their generation's perspectives, tend to be in the younger generation, in their forties and younger, and are often more tolerant of gender-role transgression. On the whole, the cultural revival movement seeks to re-establish the historical sexual division of labour rather than challenge it, a stance that puts Ainu women at odds with liberal feminist mandates. Few Ainu women have registered concern with former bodily practices such as tattooing the lips, forehead, hands, and forearms as a rite of passage for adolescent women or regulating premenopausal women's participation in ritual activity to guard against women's purported impurity.[24]

Ainu women are uncomfortable labelling many gender-specific practices as sexism and insist that they need more time to investigate traditional practices to comprehend their ancestors' logic.[25] Yet, because many practices – including tattooing, speaking the Ainu language, foraging as a primary form of economic subsistence, and ritual sacrifice – were curtailed as early as

1871, Ainu women today find it difficult to locate their ancestors' rationale for cultivating certain cultural practices. For now, Ainu women endeavour to honour the practices of their ancestors and continue the process of transmission; they then work to understand these cultural logics as they gain a deeper knowledge of practice itself. Although gender segregation based on ritual impurity may today be understood as discriminatory, the disjuncture between these historical practices and contemporary political objectives has received little attention from within Ainu women's organizations. Although men today insist on maintaining the taboo against women as prayer officiates, Ainu Elderswomen were until recently well versed in prayer language. Gender role expectations may, therefore, have grown more conservative under contemporary revivalism. As Keira insists, one of Ainu women's first objectives within the cultural revival movement must be to "restore the original order of Ainu society."[26]

Whereas Wajin feminism has been critical of normative standards that require women to bear and raise children and has sought alternatives for women's reproductive capacities, within Ainu society, women's social and biological productivity (and their social worth) is still gauged to some extent by their reproductive and child-rearing capacity. The tendency to link femininity with maternity should not be interpreted to mean that Ainu women feel compelled or are encouraged to increase Ainu population numbers.[27] On the contrary, most women seek to marry non-Ainu and "dilute their Ainu blood." Until recently, some Ainu women were so anxious to marry anyone from mainland Japan (i.e., non-Ainu) that they chose criminals or abusive partners and were willing to settle for lifelong marital dysfunction as long as their children would inherit thinned Ainu blood.[28] In adulthood, Ainu women see themselves as being responsible for birthing the next generation and, in recent years, for instilling a sense of pride in their Ainu indigeneity. Gender identity for Ainu women implies expectations for childbirth and child rearing as normative responsibilities for adult women – standards that are accepted across the community.[29]

The Gap between Ainu Women's Activism and Wajin Feminism

Collective movement ideology has impeded collaboration between Wajin feminists and Ainu women activists. Despite variation between academic feminists and *shufu* (housewife) feminists, most Wajin feminists seek liberation from gender discrimination. Although Wajin women organized suffrage campaigns and literary-based organizations in the pre-war era (the 1920s), many of these groups were crushed by expanding militarism in the

1930s because they had aligned with leftist socialist organizations.[30] Under the postwar Constitution, which was adopted in 1947, women were granted universal suffrage and equal rights in marriage and divorce. The family registration system, however, still made it illegal for women to transmit Japanese nationality to their children until the Nationality Law was revised in 1985. Early postwar feminism grew out of women-led citizens' movements, critiques of ecological damage caused by rapid industrialization, and campaigns against the renewal of the Security Treaty between the United States and Japan. Feminists in the 1960s spoke first as shufu – as mothers and as consumers. They launched social critiques that developed into critiques of gender relations in Japanese society. Lobbying campaigns and the momentum gained from the 1975 World Conference on Women (Mexico City) forced Japan's hand in ratifying the CEDAW by 1985 and led to the passage of the non-punitive Equal Employment Opportunity Law in 1986.[31]

Majority women have only recently begun to acknowledge that diverse coalitions of minority women exist and that these women's concerns both overlap with and significantly diverge from their own. Majority women's groups have chosen to eschew minority women's issues because these concerns are thought to obfuscate their primary focus on gender and sex-based discrimination. Cikap's account illustrates painful divisions among women in Japan and clarifies why many Ainu women are loath to associate themselves with Wajin feminists or feminism in general. The word *feminizumu* (feminism) in Japanese is a foreign loan word; in the Ainu community, it symbolizes both yearning for Western ideas among majority Japanese and Ainu ambivalence toward Wajin pioneer-settlers and colonial administrators who modelled Hokkaido development on US settlement practices and policies toward Native American communities.

Multiple Discrimination Analysis as a Tool for Indigenous Women

Ainu women are unlikely to interpret gender-based equality issues in the same way as Wajin women not only because of attitudes toward Ainu women but also because of the ideology of sex-separate economic spheres for men and women that has shaped today's revivalism. However, while Ainu women have rejected feminist analysis in name, their work to label the systematic discrimination they experience as multiple discrimination resonates closely with nascent Japanese feminism, which sprang in part from discontent with women's subordination in pre-war socialist societies.[32] In their critiques of patriarchy, Wajin feminists have failed to address the intersection of race, class, ethnicity, and gender as sources of compound subordination. These various factors interweave to create complex experiences of discrimination that complicate identity negotiation and lead to human rights abuses, an effect now understood as multiple discrimination.[33] Multiple discrimination compounds the pre-existing conditions of subordinated groups so that a minority within a minority becomes vulnerable to more insidious forms of complex discrimination than the two minority groups in isolation. For example, fellow subjects of discrimination such as male minorities may unconsciously or purposely target weaker groups such as minority women with physical or emotional violence to ease their own experiences of subjugation.[34]

The language of multiple discrimination suits Ainu women's ambivalence toward Wajin feminism and provides a strategy to address complex layers of sex and gender and ethnic or racial discrimination.[35] Multiple discrimination analysis provides Ainu women with an avenue to issue political demands through the moral economy of human rights discourse, considered to be the hallmark of civil society. Although multiple discrimination analysis would appear to paralyze already socially marginalized groups by heightening awareness of their status as victims, MD project members reported that they instead experienced empowerment. Ainu women insist that multiple discrimination analysis facilitates a liberatory discourse that allows them to exercise agency by defining the prejudice they experience as *external* to themselves, as a systemic product of historical structures that have stripped them of autonomy. Until the tool of multiple discrimination analysis was introduced to this group of Ainu women, many understood their victimhood as natural and inherent. By providing a discursive practice for identifying and analyzing social oppression as an external phenomenon, multiple discrimination analysis frees women from a cycle of self-blame that is otherwise unrecognizable.

Tahara Ryoko, the project organizer for the Ainu Women's Survey, explained the transformative potential of multiple discrimination analysis for Ainu women:

> When I first heard about this "multiple discrimination," I had no idea what it meant. I had been aware of women's issues from before, but as an activist for Ainu people I had focused mostly on ethnic problems and work for Indigenous recognition. Resentment and anger at the Japanese government for colonizing us and then taking away our freedom to express our identity,

> this is what I felt the most. The Ainu men around me, even as they spoke about human rights abuses [against them as a minority]; within Ainu organizations and inside Ainu households, there was ongoing gender discrimination against Ainu women, and we couldn't do anything about it [because the emphasis was on ethnic issues]. No matter how much we campaigned for Ainu people, Ainu men have been deeply influenced by Japanese [majority] society [and its patriarchal institutions]. This meant that in most Ainu organizations, men occupied the leadership positions and controlled the political power. Until now, what we could do to change this was limited. When this idea of "multiple discrimination" was introduced to us, we were finally able to identify minority women's issues.[36]

As an emergent human rights discourse, multiple discrimination analysis also provides a tool for exerting pressure on state governments to protect minority rights. Minority and colonized populations that lack the right of self-determination or sovereignty rely on international bodies to intervene and safeguard their members' human rights, especially if states themselves perpetrate violence against these groups. Activist organizations collectively apply the discourse of morality to shame state governments into acknowledging and, ultimately, protecting the rights of minority populations.[37]

The Ainu Women's Survey Project

The Ainu Women's Survey was part of a nationwide survey to generate statistics on minority women's conditions for direct submission to the Japanese government and the UN-based committee to oversee the implementation of the CEDAW in signatory states. The survey designed for use among women in the Ainu, Burakumin, and Resident Korean communities included questions on education, employment, health, violence, and social welfare to gauge the overall welfare of minority women. In Hokkaido, MD project members added questions to their survey that linked discrimination to cultural transmission activities to determine whether prejudice deterred Ainu women from engaging in cultural revival activities. Other questions addressed perceptions of racism in majority society and compared perceptions of sexism in majority society with sexism in Ainu society. The survey asked respondents to evaluate the need for the transmission of traditional practices and to rank cultural elements according to priority.

The Ainu Women's Survey was administered to fifteen branches of the Hokkaido Utari Association that represented every district of Hokkaido with a significant resident Ainu population except Hidaka, which boycotted the survey. Two hundred and forty-one Ainu women participated in the survey and represented approximately 6 percent of the Utari Association's membership, or between 0.8 and 0.02 percent of the total Ainu population. (Survey results are listed in Figure 9.1.) Although Hidaka is the most densely populated Ainu region in Japan and would have afforded critical data, the Hidaka Regional Association boycotted the survey because of concerns about how its data might be circulated by external organizations.[38] MD project members suggested that male political leaders in Hidaka were probably more concerned about what the survey might reveal about the prevalence of domestic violence in Ainu households.

Although MD project team members were convinced that the survey project would eventually lead to the political and economic betterment of all Ainu women, Ainu women in the communities surveyed were less convinced of the project's merit. Some even interpreted the survey as an externally organized extractive research project that would generate wealth elsewhere but leave Ainu women in rural areas impoverished. This impression may have been influenced by the handsome compensation afforded to survey participants: each survey respondent received the equivalent of forty US dollars for participating. Payment was designed to ensure adequate participation in each community; however, some MD project members later confided to me that payment exacerbated perceptions of inequality among the haves and the have-nots in rural Ainu communities. When the number of survey respondents exceeded the amount allocated for compensation, several women – reportedly the least educated and most impoverished – were turned away and discouraged from participating in the survey. The process therefore generated inaccurate results.[39]

Several survey respondents criticized the project members' efforts to shift the focus of anti-discrimination work from racism to sexism; they argued that efforts to achieve rights as Indigenous peoples and to end the Japanese majority's racism toward all Ainu, both men and women, should be paramount. However, Ainu women's responses to survey questions about experiences of sexism and racism revealed a discrepancy between experiences of discrimination and concerns about various types of discrimination (see the "Discrimination" section in Figure 9.1). Ainu women's confusion and ambivalence about their double minority status and the unwelcome attention it garners are reflected in the survey responses.

Although the survey was designed partly to evaluate educational competence and literacy among Ainu women, its format did not suit the target community: many partially literate respondents had difficulty reading the

FIGURE 9.1

Selected results from the Ainu Women's Survey Report (2007)

Discrimination (as Ainu and as women)

- Thirteen percent reported experiencing discrimination as Ainu persons, whereas 32% reported experiencing discrimination as women. Women reported gender discrimination in the following areas: salaries (35%), sharing housework (33%), employee benefits (26%), assuming adult responsibilities (14%), marriage (10%), career options (7%), and parental expectations (6%). Women reported ethnic discrimination in the following: a general atmosphere of intolerance (26%), direct prejudice from friends or acquaintances (8%), marriage negotiations (7%), and being at a disadvantage in society (5%).
- Women reported being most concerned about the following forms of discrimination: ethnic discrimination within Japanese society (33%), gender discrimination within Japanese society (10%), and gender discrimination within Ainu society (8%).

Cultural revival and transmission

- Women reported familiarity with Ainu cultural practice in these areas: embroidery (77%), traditional clothing (57%), Ainu language (53%), traditional songs (50%), traditional musical instruments (41%), woodcarving (38%), bast-fibre weaving (36%), traditional cooking (35%), traditional ceremonies (32%), oral folklore (30%), everyday customs (20%), and hunting and fishing techniques (9%). The survey did not, however, define the degree of competence suggested by *familiarity.*
- Eighty-five percent thought cultural transmission was necessary, and 69% were currently involved in cultural activities.
- Women reported that cultural practice should be developed through the following areas: cultivating leaders and cultural guides (64%), increasing funds for cultural practice (37%), securing space for activities (26%), promoting greater understanding among community members and Japanese citizens (26%), and increasing public exhibitions and publications about Ainu issues (12%).

Education

- Sixty percent of all survey respondents graduated from elementary or junior high school but did not attend high school. Twenty-six percent graduated from high school, and 3% graduated from junior college. According to the Hokkaido Prefectural Survey of Ainu Conditions (2006), 93.5% of Ainu and 98.3% of neighbouring ethnic Japanese graduated from junior high, whereas only 17.4% of Ainu and 38.5% of ethnic Japanese graduated from high school.
- Twenty-eight percent of all survey respondents reported partial literacy; 72% claimed normal reading skills; and 67% claimed normal writing skills. The Japanese government claims a nationwide literacy rate of 97%.

▶

◄ FIGURE 9.1

Employment

- Fifty-six percent of women reported that they worked, but the survey team suspected that more Ainu women probably worked at home, in self-employed businesses or other capacities, and perhaps found the question confusing.

Household income

- Annual personal income: 20% reported an annual personal income of $4,237; 29% reported an annual income of between $4,237 and $8,475 (or 500,000 yen and 500,000 to 1 million yen, respectively).[1]
- Annual household income: 20% reported an annual household income of $8,475; 29% reported an annual income between $8,475 and $25,424 (or 1 million yen and 1 to 3 million yen, respectively).
- Only 12% of women reported that they were social welfare recipients, and 9% reported that they had received welfare assistance. According to the 2006 Hokkaido Prefectural Survey of Ainu Conditions, 38.3% of all Ainu and 24.6% of neighbouring Japanese at that time were welfare recipients.

Domestic violence

- Seventeen percent reported experiencing violence from a partner regularly; 20% reported experiencing violence once or twice.
- Twenty percent reported being forced to have sex with their partners regularly; 14% reported being forced to have sex with their partners once or twice.
- Counselling for domestic violence: 23% sought counselling help from an outsider; 33% did not seek counselling assistance.

Health

- Thirty-one percent reported having a chronic health concern. Whereas 86% are enrolled in Japanese National Health Insurance, 10% are not enrolled.
- Physical examinations in last three years: 19% had not received a physical check-up; 12% received a physical exam when they went to a clinic for treatment of an illness; 62% had regular checkups.

Note: Seventy-seven percent of all survey respondents were aged forty and older.

1 All figures are listed in US dollars.

survey and were too intimidated to seek assistance.[40] Only 26 percent of Ainu respondents had graduated from high school, and only 3 percent had graduated from junior college. Sixty percent of survey respondents had graduated from elementary or junior high school but did not continue on to high school (see "Education" in Figure 9.1). (In Japanese education, students learn Chinese ideographs from elementary through to high school. In other words, people who are unable to attend high school do not have access to a written vocabulary unless they study independently.) Even functionally literate respondents found the survey's terminology alienating – use of foreign loan words such as *minority, domestic violence,* or *reproductive health* were confusing for respondents, many of whom left these questions blank. Ironically, as one project member pointed out, "Even as we speak about 'empowerment' *(empawaamento),* just the word itself is enough to keep some women away. We have to use gentler words to express what we've been experiencing."[41]

Work on the survey enabled Ainu women to realize the gravity of multiple discrimination in their communities and the obstacles to equality that Ainu women continue to face. Inspired by the nationwide survey project but recognizing the logistical hurdles in a centrally organized project, MD project members advised that future surveys should be organized locally by and for Ainu women and should be designed to match the capabilities of Ainu women themselves. MD project members pledged to broaden the survey to include a greater diversity of age groups (77 percent of all survey respondents were aged forty and older), to increase participation of Ainu not associated with the Ainu Association (the association represents only 10 to 17 percent of Ainu) and women throughout Japan as a whole, and to involve local women from each community in the implementation of the survey. MD project organizers reported they plan to reformulate the survey to make questions relevant to Ainu women's specific situations, increase the sensitivity of questions relating to domestic violence and other difficult issues, simplify the language used in questions themselves, and add an oral component or place pronunciation keys above the Chinese ideographs to render the survey more comprehensible to partially literate respondents.[42]

Despite the optimism fostered by multiple discrimination analysis, however, survey findings revealed that the reality of limited education, limited employment opportunities, abusive or unsupportive spouses, and discrimination from Wajin society continues to challenge many Ainu women (see Figure 9.1). For persons of Ainu descent – both those who self-identify as Ainu and those who strive to pass as Wajin or "hidden Ainu" – discrimination against Ainu as an Indigenous minority, be it perceived or anticipated, bars many hereditary Ainu from exploring their Ainu identity, working to preserve and promote Ainu culture, and engaging in political action as Ainu women. Hokkaido colonization (from 1799 onward) was informed by discourses of social evolutionism and racial inferiority, which were imported from Western nations during the modernization era. Ainu phenotypic difference – including alleged hirsuteness, lighter skin tones, and more distinct facial features – came to epitomize technological and social backwardness. Early settlers and colonial authorities fetishized Ainu body hair to such a degree that *hairy Ainu,* adopted as a racial epithet, continues to be used today. Generations of intermarriage with Wajin, from self-imposed assimilation and efforts to protect offspring from prejudice against physical difference, have resulted in a contemporary Ainu population that is phenotypically indistinguishable from Wajin. Nevertheless, discriminatory practices continue.

Although not all women reported personal experiences of discrimination, many feared social ostracism and reported that they had tried to compensate by disguising their physical difference.[43] Pubescent teenaged girls are often terrified when their bodies begin to change, and Ainu women reported that they avoided romantic relationships because they feared that partners would reject them if they found their bodies to be more hirsute than those of Wajin women.[44] Fear of being "outed" has also discouraged some women from pursuing careers in nursing, acting, or professions in which their bodies may be exposed. Older tattooed women wore cold masks to disguise their heritage and protect their grandchildren from bullying. Many women bleached unwanted body hair, shaved their legs and arms, and tweezed their faces every day to hide despised markers of difference.

Empowerment or the "Power We've Always Had"

Despite formidable obstacles to its implementation, Ainu women and some survey respondents reported that they had been emboldened by the survey project. Survey organizer Tahara Ryoko said, "Because we were oppressed ['as women and as Ainu'], many of us could never realize our own abilities and strength, much less use them. Empowerment has enabled us to gain new strength, wake up to the power we've always had, and then act upon it."[45]

Although the MD project participants did not receive quantitative research training and many women remain under-educated, the Ainu Women's Survey was an exercise in action research.[46] Action research enables minority groups to design data-gathering projects specific to their needs, projects that address the social problem at hand and enable the disenfranchised population to control research design and methodology, thereby freeing the group from dependence on external scholar-experts or bureaucrats.[47] This type of research allows socially marginal communities to re-evaluate their identities, transform their awareness of group issues through new data, and rechannel this new knowledge and awareness to the majority society to increase mutual understanding. Research agendas informed by action research enable marginalized populations to exercise agency over their own disenfranchisement, leading to newfound experiences of self- and group empowerment. Although Ainu women adopted a foreign concept – multiple discrimination analysis – to appraise their circumstances, they were empowered through self-education as they simultaneously amassed data that they anticipated would illustrate the effects of multiple discrimination. In addition to multiple discrimination analysis, the collective experience of recognizing and naming the intersection of sex- and ethnic-based discrimination allowed Ainu women to link themselves to both fellow Ainu women and to minority women across Japan. MD project members reported that their self-esteem and ability to self-identify openly as Ainu were profoundly influenced by their involvement in the project.

Yet MD project members were unable to extend their personal experiences of empowerment to survey respondents, many of whom could not read survey questions or understand the foreign terminology. Respondents felt alienated rather than empowered. Core members of the survey team had difficulty indigenizing the multiple discrimination concept to resonate with concerns about racial discrimination and economic stability in the broader Ainu community. In fall 2006, MD project members hosted a Minority Women's Empowerment Forum to distribute survey results and introduce multiple discrimination analysis to Ainu women from across Hokkaido. They hoped to narrow the urban-rural gap. This was the first public airing of report findings within the Ainu community; more importantly, the forum provided an opportunity for Ainu women outside the MD project group to consider how multiple discrimination analysis can help them make sense of systemic discrimination. Multiple discrimination analysis provided a frame in which experiences of prejudice or self-blame that had been rationalized as inevitable or unavoidable were transformed into systemic problems that were not inherent to Ainu women themselves. Ainu women from around Hokkaido shared accounts of personal or secondhand discrimination, and both the speakers and audience members shed tears in solidarity as speakers described emotional wounds from prejudice and mistreatment. Finding the courage to publicly air these psychological wounds provided the speakers with some sense of respite. Several women developed goals to overcome a former sense of self-blame. Some women began saving funds to attend the meeting (scheduled for March 2007) with the Gender Equality Bureau in Tokyo, where the survey's findings would be presented to government officials. Others wanted to write up their experiences for inclusion in the Ainu Women's Survey Report booklet *Ukopar-rui* (2007),[48] which provides a record of MD project germination and development. And many women expressed a desire to initiate human rights and discrimination study groups. Although project members acknowledged that the survey had significant flaws and did not adequately attend to the diversity of Ainu women's circumstances throughout Japan today, they identified this project as a work in progress, and they plan to open it to other Ainu women throughout the archipelago as it develops further.

Conclusion

To conclude, I would like to suggest that scholars of feminist analysis who view gender equality as an equal relationship between men and women rather than as separate but equal domains for men and women have failed to incorporate the diversity of gendered experience. Ainu women possess an intersubjective identity – they define themselves as both Japanese women and as Ainu women – and their version of Ainuness is now a merging of two threads of identity. Through multiple discrimination analysis, Ainu women have come to recognize the intersection of indigeneity, gender, and Ainuness as subjectivities that, taken in combination, render their experiences different from Ainu men and majority women. Ainu value systems compel them to honour the land, the ancestors, and the deities in a way that has not yet been recognized or advocated by feminists. Ainu women's critiques may ultimately lead to a position of countermodernity and a postcolonial critique that would question capitalism, commodification, and colonialism. Ainu women's position should remind feminists in Japan and beyond that the return to gendered spheres of complementarity need not be read as subjugation of female-gendered spheres of influence in favour of male domains of productivity or rejection of women's creativity and leadership. Ainu women continue to negotiate the gap between their negative association with and experiences of Ainuness, and the possibility of a revitalized Ainuness that honours the ancestors and the pantheon of Ainu deities and, ultimately, restores honour and self-respect to each individual Ainu woman herself.

Afterword

Since I wrote this essay, I have continued my involvement with the Ainu women's MD project. In July 2009, I accompanied a group of minority women to UN hearings in New York on the implementation of the CEDAW in Japan.[49] Space limitations bar further analysis, but I feel obligated to acknowledge a changing dynamic for once-empowered Ainu women. Sadly, the Ainu multiple discrimination project was disbanded in spring 2008, when the Empowerment Café was discontinued because of a disagreement among members. The Ainu women who travelled to New York in 2009 as spokeswomen were described locally as "self-appointed representatives who couldn't possibly understand what real poverty and discrimination feels like."[50] Ainu community members anticipated a public report about the lobbying process at the UN, but feedback was prepared solely for majority Japanese donor organizations. By divulging these tensions, I do not intend to vilify these Ainu spokeswomen but aim for a more honest assessment of the real barriers to organizing. The minority women's project has been enacted largely as a top-down affair that was organized by a centralized Tokyo non-governmental organization (IMADR-JC) and extended throughout Japan. Focusing on the international sector to enact domestic change means that community-level work has been sidelined and informally organized groups such as the Ainu women's group have been weakened. These developments raise the following questions: What kind of empowerment was actually gained through the project? What are the long-term ramifications of this kind of work? I cannot begin to answer these questions here; instead, I hope to honour the voices of women whose perspectives would otherwise not be reflected in my analysis as it stands.

ACKNOWLEDGMENTS

I dedicate this chapter to the memory of Cikap Mieko – a gifted Ainu textile artist and gentle but indefatigable leader of the Ainu rights recovery movement. May her spirit be liberated as a *Cikap* (bird) in the spirit world. An abbreviated draft of this chapter was presented at "Indigenous Women and Feminism: Culture, Activism, Politics," which was held at the University of Alberta, Edmonton, in August 2005. Research for the paper, which was titled "Embracing *fuci-kewtum:* Ainu Women and 'Cultural Activism' in Contemporary Japan," was carried out from January 2004 to August 2005 during residence in three communities: Urakawa, Akan, and Sapporo in Hokkaido, Japan. I would like to express gratitude to the Ainu community for assistance with this project, especially to my fuci and host families, and to the gracious women of the Empowerment Café. I would also like to thank my advisor, Jennifer Robertson, at the University of Michigan, and my research supervisor in Hokkaido, Toshikazu Aiuchi, at Otaru University of Commerce. Many thanks also to editor Jean Barman, who provided critical commentary and to anonymous reviewers, who sent insightful criticism. This research was made possible through fellowships from the US Fulbright Commission; the US State Department; the Japanese Ministry of Education, Science, and Technology (Monbukagakusho); the Japanese Society for the Promotion of Science; the National Science Foundation; and support from the University of California,

Santa Barbara. The following institutions at the University of Michigan also made this work possible: the Institute for Research on Women and Gender, the Center for Japanese Studies, the International Institute, the Department of Anthropology, and the Rackham Graduate School. All errors in interpretation are mine alone.

NOTES

1 Following standard Japanese convention, all names will be listed with family name followed by given name.

2 In presenting Ainu women's perspectives, I do not intend to speak for Ainu women. But I do want to give voice to their concerns, especially to an English readership because most of the information written by or concerning Ainu women has been published in Japanese. Much scholarship has focused on Western colonialism and feminism as a counterpoint to Indigenous women's positions, and I would like to call attention to Japanese imperialism, carried out from 1869 to 1945 (with continued colonization in the case of Hokkaido, and with successive occupiers in the case of Okinawa). The United States has always been implicated in colonialism in Hokkaido because American advisors were hired as consultants to help with colonization and economic development. Many of these advisors had assisted with the so-called resettlement of Native Americans and drew from these experiences, along with strategies borrowed from the US Dawes Act, to help Japanese colonial administrators create Ainu policy and colonize Hokkaido.

3 In the pre-colonial era, Ainu communities were located throughout Hokkaido, and until the nineteenth century, Ainu resided in the Kurile Islands and on the southern portion of Sakhalin Island. From the seventh through to the tenth century, Ainu, or a group of people called Emishi, resided in northeastern Honshu (mainland) Japan as well. The term *Ainu* in this chapter refers to Hokkaido Ainu and Japanese Ainu in general.

4 A larger question is what span of historical practice should or can be incorporated into revival efforts. Most revivalism focuses on the pre-colonial or early colonial era (the 1850s to early 1900s), when European and American museum collectors scoured Ainu communities for so-called traditional material culture artifacts. A discussion of what constitutes the traditional and how authenticity is evaluated is beyond the scope of this essay. For further discussion of these issues, see ann-elise lewallen, "En-gendering Praxis: Ainu Women's Interventions in the Contemporary Cultural Revival Movement," in Mark Hudson, ann-elise lewallen, and Mark Watson, eds., *Beyond Ainu Studies* (Honolulu: University of Hawai'i Press, under review), and "'Hands That Never Rest': Ainu Women, Cultural Revival, and Indigenous Politics in Japan" (PhD diss., University of Michigan, 2006).

5 The Ainu diaspora extends through the Japanese archipelago and overseas. A 1988 Tokyo Prefecture survey placed the number of Ainu residents in Tokyo at 2,700, though some observers estimate the Tokyo Ainu population is closer to 5,000. Mark Watson, "Kanto Resident Ainu and the Urban Indigenous Experience," in Hudson, lewallen, and Watson, *Beyond Ainu Studies*.

6 IMADR's website states that it is an international non-profit, non-governmental human rights organization devoted to eliminating discrimination and racism, forging

international solidarity among discriminated minorities, and advancing the international human rights system.

7 IMADR-JC, *Tachiagari Tsunagaru Mainoritei Josei – Ainu Josei, Buraku Josei, Zainichi Korian Josei ni yoru Anke-to Chôsa Hôkoku to Teigen* [Minority women rise up: A collaborative survey on Ainu, Buraku, and Korean women in Japan] (Tokyo: Kaihô, September 2007).

8 Cikap Mieko, "I Am Ainu, Am I Not?" *AMPO Japan-Asia Quarterly Review* 18, 2-3 (1986): 81.

9 The UN Permanent Forum on Indigenous Issues and the UN Working Group on Indigenous Populations are two of the few international institutions that have officially recognized Ainu indigeneity. Their recognition is seen as an important source of legitimacy when claims of Indigenous rights are presented to the Japanese government. Since multiple discrimination discourse has been authored by UN forums, it appeals to Ainu women and their investment in human rights as a moral economy.

10 Cikap Mieko, "Ainu Josei kara mita Feminizumu" [Feminism as seen by an Ainu woman], in Kojima Kyoko and Hayakawa Noriyo, eds., *Joseishi no Shiza* [From the perspective of women's history] (Tokyo: Yoshikawa Bunkan, 1997), 352-54.

11 Burakumin, or *eta hinin,* are a group of social outcasts who were ostracized from mainstream Tokugawa society (1603-1868) because of their association with ritually impure labour such as the leather trade and the handling of corpses. Their minority status is defined by profession and geography – specifically, work in the leather trades, cremation, and itinerant entertainment (work defined as impure by Buddhist standards) – and does not correspond to biological, linguistic, or cultural affiliations. Alienated from society during the Tokugawa era, they were reinstated as *shin-heimin* (new commoners) along with the Ainu in 1899, but a legacy of social discrimination continues to inhibit their everyday lives, even today. Burakumin liberation groups such as the Suiheisha and later the Buraku Liberation League were influential in developing many of the protest strategies later adopted by Ainu organizations for protest in Hokkaido and Tokyo.

12 Cikap, "Ainu Josei," 353. Translation by author.

13 Ibid., 354.

14 Ainu Josei Fukugo Sabetsu Mondai Purojekuto [Ainu Women's Multiple Discrimination Problem Project], *Mainoritei Ainu Josei no Fukugo Sabetsu to Ainu Bunka Denshô ni tsuite kôsatsu suru – Ainu Josei no Empawaamento* [Regarding minority Ainu women's multiple discrimination and Ainu cultural transmission: Empowering Ainu women] (Sapporo: Hokkaido Ainu Association, Sapporo Branch, 2005).

15 ann-elise lewallen, field notes, June 2004.

16 Keira Tomoko, "My Work as an Ainu Woman," in Charlotte Bunch, ed., *Voices from the Japanese Women's Movement* (Armonk, NY: AMPO-Japan Asia Quarterly Review, M.E. Sharpe, 1996), 161.

17 Ibid.

18 lewallen, "En-gendering Praxis," 7-8.

19 See Watanabe Hitoshi, *The Ainu Ecosystem: Environment and Group Structure* (Seattle: University of Washington Press, 1973); Segawa Kiyoko, *Ainu no Kon'in* [Ainu marriage] (Tokyo: Miraisha, 1998 [1972]); Kyoko Kojima, *A Study of Ainu*

History: The Transformation of Images of Ezo and the Ainu (Tokyo: Yoshikawa Bunkan, 2003); and Emiko Ohnuki-Tierney, "Ainu Sociality," in William Fitzhugh and Chisato DuBreuil, eds., *Ainu: Spirit of a Northern People* (Washington, DC: Arctic Studies Center, National Museum of Natural History, Smithsonian Institution/ University of Washington Press, 1999).

20 The concept of *gendering of ethnicity* is based on Kojima's reading of Ainu women's history in Kojima, *A Study of Ainu History*, 395-97, and developed further in ann-elise lewallen, "'Hands That Never Rest."

21 Keira Tomoko (biographer) and Orita Suteno (recitation), *Ainu no Shiki: Fuci no Tsutaeru Kokoro* [Four seasons of the Ainu – The heart of *fuci* conveyed] (Tokyo: Akaishi Shoten, 1995); Haginaka Mie, "Kotan ni ikita Onna-tachi" [The women who lived in the Kotan villages], in Tenrikyo Doyusha Kyohen, ed., *Ainu no Kimono* [Ainu robes] (Tenri, Nara: Tenri Daigaku, 1991).

22 Hokkaido Ainu Kyoukai Sapporo Shibu [Hokkaido Ainu Association Sapporo Branch], *Ainu Josei Jittai Chousa Houkokusho* [Report on Ainu Women's Livelihood Survey] (Sapporo: Hokkaido Ainu Association, Sapporo Branch, 2006), 38.

23 See Emiko Ohnuki-Tierney, *Illness and Healing among the Sakhalin Ainu: A Symbolic Interpretation* (New York: Cambridge University Press, 1981), and Segawa, *Ainu no Kon'in*.

24 All cultural practices necessary for subsistence in the context of everyday life were virtually erased through forced assimilation policies instituted by the Tokugawa government during the period between 1799 and 1899, and the Meiji government (1868-1912). As a result, almost no Ainu persons living today retain functional knowledge or memory of the era when many practices now labelled as traditional and identified as essential elements of the cultural revival process were vital processes necessary for daily subsistence.

25 Keira, "My Work as an Ainu Woman," 162.

26 Even with the positive momentum generated by cultural revivalism, some Ainu-identified persons have called for birth campaigns to increase Ainu population numbers. Akibe I., interview with author, December 2004.

27 Kaizawa Matsutaro, "Ainu no chi sae usumereba ..." [If Ainu blood could be diluted], *Ushio* 150 (1972): 145.

28 Minority Women's Multiple Discrimination Problem Project Team, ed., *Ukopar-rui: Ainu Josei no Empawaamento* [Ukopar-rui: Ainu women's empowerment], Hokkaido Utari Association, Sapporo Branch (Sapporo: Crews, 2007).

29 See Sharon Sievers, *Flowers in Salt: The Beginnings of Feminist Consciousness in Modern Japan* (Stanford, CA: Stanford University Press, 1983).

30 Nevertheless, the majority of working women continue to work in part-time or temporary jobs or in smaller companies; thus, they are unable to benefit from the Act's provisions.

31 See Sievers, *Flowers in Salt*.

32 In international forums, the term *multiple discrimination* first appeared at the Beijing Conference on Women in 1995, was defined by the Zagreb Experts' Committee on Gender and Race in 2000, and was finally brought to bear on resolution making at the World Conference on Racism in Durban, South Africa, in 2001: "The idea of

'intersectionality' (in multiple discrimination) seeks to capture both the structural and dynamic consequences of ... two or more systems of subordination. It specifically addresses the manner in which racism, patriarchy, economic disadvantages and other discriminatory systems contribute to create layers of inequality that structure the relative positions of women, men, races and other groups, ... [and] the way that specific acts and policies create ... a dynamic of disempowerment." Moto Yuriko, "Fukugo Sabetsu to wa" [On multiple discrimination], in *Mainoritei Josei no Shiten wo: Seisaku ni! Shakai ni!* [Minority women's perspectives: Into policy! Into society!], International Movement Against All Forms of Discrimination and Racism – Japan Committee (IMADR-JC) (Tokyo: Kaihô Shuppan, 2003), 11-12. Translation by author.

33 Ibid., 13-14.

34 I use the term *racial* to underscore that most ethnic Japanese (and Ainu persons) understand the difference between themselves and ethnic minorities in Japan to be a racial difference. The late nineteenth-century discourse of race was used to support the eugenics movement to build stronger Japanese bodies for Japanese imperialism. Older Ainu also used the term *inferior race* to refer to themselves during interviews. Their language was clearly a reference to the so-called superior race science, a literal translation of the Japanese term *yûseigaku* (eugenics).

35 Tahara Ryoko, phone interview with author, 9 March 2007. Translation by author.

36 Margaret E. Keck and Kathryn Sikkink, *Activists beyond Borders: Advocacy Networks in International Politics* (Ithaca, NY: Cornell University Press, 1998).

37 Hidaka is one the most densely populated Ainu regions of Japan. Ainu constitute approximately 40 percent of the total population and 70 percent or more of the population in some communities. Discrimination is said to be so prevalent in the region that local Ainu persons refer to themselves as *Utari* (brethren/comrade) instead of Ainu. Male-dominated Ainu organizations have been reluctant to take up the problem of multiple discrimination and take seriously the complexity of gender and ethnic discrimination in the Ainu community itself. When MD project leader Tahara Ryoko presented a brief introduction to Ainu women's situation in a panel discussion on the UN Draft Declaration on the Rights of Indigenous Peoples and the Ainu community's quest for recognition as an Indigenous people, male panel participants were silent on the issue of multiple discrimination, as were audience members and the keynote speaker. Tahara Ryoko, lecture (presented at "Decade of Indigenous Peoples Memorial Event and Ainu Symposium," Sapporo, 9 February 2007).

38 lewallen, field notes, August 2009.

39 Illiteracy is likewise a considerable challenge for women in the Burakumin community, where discrimination has been linked structurally to education, and illiteracy continues to pose a challenge to all Burakumin in the older generation, particularly women. To protect the dignity of partially literate survey respondents, the Burakumin group arranged for survey questions to be read aloud to each respondent. If this strategy was insufficient, the group also appointed survey staff to work one-on-one with respondents, to read each question out loud at a pace in keeping with each woman's needs.

40 lewallen, field notes, January 2007.
41 Ibid.
42 The information in this paragraph was culled from interviews, discussions with informants, and Sakai Mina's unpublished essay "Sabetsu to Jiko Hitei no Nijûsei kara no Kaihô: Ainu Minzoku" [Ainu people: Liberation from dual-layered self-negation and discrimination], Obirin University, 2004. Copy in possession of the author.
43 Ainu women's body types are frequently ranked as less than attractive in the metrics of Japanese bodily aesthetics, which places a premium on "natural" hairlessness. See ibid.
44 lewallen, field notes, January 2007.
45 Karl Lewin first used the term *action research* to describe "comparative research on the conditions and effects of various forms of social action and research leading to social action [using] a spiral of steps, each of which is composed of a circle of planning, action, and fact-finding about the result of the action." See Lewin, "Action Research and Minority Problems," *Journal of Social Issues* 2, 4 (1946): 34-46.
46 Yunomae Tomoko, Address to the Minority Women's Survey Report Symposium, Tokyo, 2 March 2007. As a feminist scholar, Yunomae was instrumental in facilitating the development of the multiple discrimination survey as an exercise in action research for all of the three communities, Burakumin, Resident Korean, and Ainu women.
47 Ainu Women's Multiple Discrimination Problem Project Team, ed., *Ukopar-rui: Ainu Josei no Empawaamento* [Ukopar-rui: Ainu women's empowerment], Hokkaido Utari Association, Sapporo Branch (Sapporo: Crews, 2007).
48 The eight representatives included Ainu, Burakumin, Resident Korean, Okinawan, and migrant women.
49 lewallen, field notes, July 2009.

PART 3

CULTURE

10 Indigenous Feminism, Performance, and the Politics of Memory in the Plays of Monique Mojica

SHARI M. HUHNDORF

In her radio play *Birdwoman and the Suffragettes: A Story of Sacajawea,* Monique Mojica illustrates the complexities of colonial memory in the case of one of the few legendary Indigenous women in American culture. Celebrated for her role in the Lewis and Clark expedition, a foundational event in nineteenth-century US expansion, Sacajawea numbers among those Natives lauded for their complicity in the conquest of Indian lands. She was, in the words of one of Mojica's characters, the "trusty little Indian guide ... [whose] faithful servitude resulted in the successful completion of the famous expedition of Captains Meriweather [sic] Lewis and William Clark ... opening her country."[1] For this allegiance, she is memorialized in countless national sites and monuments. Yet these memorials also encourage historical forgetting: by showing Indigenous people as acquiescing to their own demise, they obfuscate the violence, and even the fact, of conquest. Although this is true of many dominant representations, the role of traitor falls most frequently to Native women, who are remembered, if at all, almost exclusively as collaborators in the invasion. They stand in stark contrast to the chiefs and warriors, gendered male in popular memory but not always in historical fact, who resisted the invaders and became the objects of an ambivalent American fascination with so-called savagery. In the gendered paradoxes of colonial memory, these commemorations accompany the silencing, trivialization, and erasure of Indigenous women and obscure their complicated historical roles. In *Birdwoman,* Mojica takes to task these understandings of Sacajawea by countering them with memories of the grandpas and grannies from her home on the Wind River Reservation. These stories depict Sacajawea instead as a revered Shoshone leader, multilingual interpreter, negotiator of treaties, and spokesperson on behalf of her nation (not incidentally, roles typically imagined as male). The play thus aims to unsettle dominant notions about Native women, expose their gendered dimensions, and replace them with oppositional histories.

Birdwoman also ties popular images of Indigenous women to the material processes of conquest. Not only has colonization involved sexual violence, the removal of Indigenous women from positions of power, and the replacement of traditional gender roles with Western patriarchal practices, it has also exerted social control through the management of Native women's bodies.[2] In particular, the representation of Indigenous women's sexuality as uncontrolled, Jean Barman has argued, served as both a primary instrument and rationale for colonialism by demonstrating the need for social reform.[3] She writes,

> The campaign to tame Aboriginal sexuality so profoundly sexualized Aboriginal women that they were rarely permitted any other form of identity. Not just Aboriginal women but Aboriginal women's agency was sexualized. In the extreme case their every act became perceived as a sexual act and, because of the unceasing portrayal of their sexuality as wild and out of control, as an act of provocation. By default, Aboriginal women were prostitutes or, at best, potential concubines. Their actions were imbued with the intent that men in power had so assiduously ascribed to them, thus vitiating any responsibility for their or other men's actions toward them.[4]

Consequent efforts to desexualize Aboriginal everyday life aimed to ensure that "the home to which women returned would emulate its colonial counterpart," illustrating the importance of domesticity to conquest.[5] The conjugation of femininity and whiteness in dominant domestic ideologies further defined Indigenous women as in need of reform, and their transformation became a means to re-create Indigenous societies according to Western norms. Because Indigenous women historically represented the so-called New World, sexuality also provided metaphors for the willing submission of Native societies and the availability of their territories, the virgin land that ostensibly offered itself for capture.

Although these processes have reshaped Native societies as a whole, they carried particular consequences for Indigenous women because they transformed sexual victimization into colonial complicity to limit women's possible roles. From the earliest days of contact, as Rayna Green wrote in a review of scholarship about Native women, "matriarchal, matrifocal, and matrilineal societies were neither acceptable nor comprehensible to members of European patriarchies."[6] Stories of so-called traitors such as Sacajawea and Pocahontas offered models of Native-European relations that became national origin stories, and because these stories came to bear on sexualized Indigenous women, they redefined these women's roles to undercut their power. "Our 'heroines' serve white males," Green continues, "and it is they, not those who fought white males, who are beloved."[7] Such stories render Indigenous women as dangerous, in need of erasure and political containment, and they have had enduring consequences in Native communities as well as in the dominant society. Even stories about militant women activists such as Bobbie Lee and slain American Indian Movement leader Anna Mae Aquash, Green continues, "rarely push the 'braids-and-shades' rhetoric of urban, militant Indian men off the newspaper page."[8] This erasure characterizes literary and scholarly writing about Native peoples as well. "While most of the studies of Pocahontas and her sisters focus on the ways in which they helped non-Indians defeat their own people," Green queries, "where is the serious study of such women as cultural brokers, working to create, manage, and minimize the negative effects of change on their people – working for Native American people and with white men and women?"[9] Conversely, because of this history, Native cultural authenticity and political resistance have been gendered male. In *Birdwoman,* Sacajawea's story exemplifies these gendered symbolic and material dimensions of US expansion. Enslaved by the Mandan and later gambled as a wife to Charbonneau, Lewis and Clark's interpreter "known for raping Indian girls," Sacajawea unwittingly joins the expedition as an unpaid member at her husband's behest in a retelling that emphasizes the hidden histories of conquest: sexual violence, the disempowerment of Indigenous women, and the exploitation of their labour.[10]

By showing gender as a key signifier and instrument of colonial power, *Birdwoman* expresses the urgency of an Indigenous feminist project that emerged in Native theatre in the 1980s and 1990s. During this period, playwrights and performers, including Mojica, began to challenge patriarchal colonialism by exploring Native women's shared experiences of sexual violence, social marginalization, and political containment across boundaries of nation, language, and culture. Their transnational perspectives showed the colonial logic and consistency of violence and narratives of Indigenous women's betrayal, and their insistence on the integral connections between patriarchy and colonialism enabled a critical analysis of Native women's place in the dominant society and in tribal communities (even though these places, both usually shaped by patriarchy, are not the same). Perhaps predictably, these efforts have not been without controversy, and Mojica's play also gestures to some of the problems of Indigenous feminism, including its relationship to mainstream movements that emerged out of predominantly white, middle-class communities.[11] In scenes that show how colonialism has shaped the relationship between Native and white women, *Birdwoman* begins and ends with suffragettes gathering to celebrate the 1905 unveiling of a Sacajawea statue in Portland, Oregon. The suffragettes themselves become catalysts of colonial memory as they recreate Sacajawea as a hero for their own cause: "I ... hunted up every fact I could find about Sacajawea," one boasts, and "out of a few dry bones I created Sacajawea and made her a living entity." Their depictions of her as the "princess of the Shoshones," "Madonna of her race," the "modest, unselfish, enduring little Shoshone squaw," along with one suffragette's fantasy of becoming an "Indian maiden dancing naked in the wilderness to the light of the bonfire!" find an uneasy parallel in the male characters' sexualized and racialized renderings. Sacajawea's transformation into a mute icon – as symbol of the suffragettes' cause and monument to the conquest – mobilizes a long history of colonial image making and exemplifies the silencing of Indigenous women scrutinized by the play: "Captured again! / Frozen! Cast in bronze, / this hollow form with my name – / Tsakakawea! / Who are these strange sisters?"[12]

Debating Indigenous Feminism

Not merely a subject of theatre, the question of Indigenous feminism has spurred contentious political, cultural, and scholarly debates that provide a crucial context for Native women's performances. Some of these performances, such as Mojica's play, highlight the disconnections between Indigenous women's politics and mainstream feminism, and others take up the relationship between Indigenous feminism and Native traditions and nationalisms. The "concept of 'patriarchy' alone is inadequate for explaining the many levels of violence that Native women face," Bonita Lawrence contends, and others point to social priorities unique to Indigenous women.[13]

In an early essay that describes Indian women's reticence to join the broader feminist movement, Kate Shanley explains,

> Issues such as equal pay for equal work, child health and welfare, and a woman's right to make her own choices regarding contraceptive use, sterilization and abortion – key issues to the majority women's movement – affect Indian women as well; however, equality *per se,* may have a different meaning for Indian women and Indian people. The difference begins with personal and tribal sovereignty – the right to be legally recognized as peoples empowered to determine our own destinies. Thus, the Indian women's movement seeks equality in two ways that do not concern mainstream women: (1) on the individual level, the Indian woman struggles to promote the survival of a social structure whose organizational principles represent notions of family different from those of the mainstream; and (2) on the societal level, the People seek sovereignty as a people in order to maintain a vital legal and spiritual connection to the land, in order to *survive* as a people.[14]

Among other points, Shanley emphasizes the connection between cultural revitalization and decolonization in Native contexts and the importance of tradition in Indigenous politics that further complicates the possibilities of Indigenous feminism. Poet Laura Tohe titled an often-cited essay "There Is No Word for Feminism in My Language" and then proceeded to recount the economically, culturally, and politically powerful roles women occupied in traditional Diné (Navajo) society. In the essay, she concludes that there is no need for feminism in a matrilineal culture, although she does concede that feminism is relevant when Native women enter the dominant society.[15] Not only does Tohe neglect the ways that patriarchy has reshaped Indigenous societies, she writes from a particular situation in which women traditionally held and, in her account, retain widespread influence (though contemporary Diné women's experiences are not as monolithic as she suggests). Others counter that women occupied a range of roles in pre-contact societies – some influential, some not – and that colonization has deformed even traditionally matriarchal cultures.[16] Advocating a more judicious stance on tradition, Emma LaRocque warns that "as women we must be circumspect in our recall of tradition. We must ask ourselves whether and to what extent tradition is liberating to us as women ... There are indications of male violence and sexism in some Aboriginal societies prior to European contact ... As Native women ... we are challenged to change, create, and embrace 'traditions' consistent with contemporary and international human rights standards."[17]

Although these arguments underscore the necessity of a feminist practice that addresses the particularities of Indigenous women's experiences within and outside of tribal communities, Indigenous feminism's uneasy fit with nationalism places it outside dominant Native politics. Although she herself insists on Indian feminist consciousness and commitments, Rayna Green observes that the "concerns which characterize debate in Indian country, tribal sovereignty and self-determination, for example, put Native American tribes on a collision path with regulations like Title 9 and Equal Opportunity."[18] In addition, Indigenous feminism's criticism of gender dynamics within Native communities and its transnational dimensions, based on connections among women across social and political boundaries, sometimes elicits accusations of divisiveness or, worse, that feminism actually undermines more pressing struggles for sovereignty. Some have even gone so far as to argue that "those who have most openly identified themselves [as feminists] have tended to be the more assimilated of Indian women activists, generally accepting of the colonialist ideology that indigenous nations are now legitimate sub-parts of the U.S. geopolitical corpus rather than separate nations."[19]

In an influential essay on the Hawaiian sovereignty movement, Haunani-Kay Trask similarly opposes feminism and Native nationalisms:

> [As] I decolonized my mind and my commitments, the political and cultural environment at home splintered my acquired feminism from my Hawaiian existence ... Given our nationalist context, feminism appeared as just another haole intrusion into a besieged Hawaiian world. Any exclusive focus on women neglected the historical oppression of all Hawaiians and the large force field of imperialism. Now that I was working among my people, I saw there were simply too many limitations in the scope of feminist theory and praxis. The feminism I had studied was just too white, too American. Only issues defined by white women as "feminist" had structured discussions ... Here, in Hawai'i, we were asserting our cultural posture, including our own style and language of argument, as defining of the political arena.[20]

Trask's critique exemplifies a broader tendency to subordinate women's concerns to those of the (ostensibly male?) nation and a reticence to identify patriarchy within Indigenous communities (illustrated, for example, in her contradictory characterization of feminism, but not nationalism, as a "haole intrusion," when both political strategies emerged from imperial contexts). Instead, she argues that feminism addresses only white women's problems, and she thus ignores the integral connections between patriarchy and colonialism identified by other Indigenous women. Trask does acknowledge the importance of Indigenous women's issues in the sovereignty movement, including those pertaining to health, reproduction, equal employment, and domestic violence; elsewhere, she describes the ways in which the colonization of Hawaii unfolded through the exploitation of Native women's bodies and the sexualization of Indigenous people.[21] Nevertheless, she argues that "the answers to the specifics of our women's oppression reside in our people's collective achievement of the larger goal of Hawaiian self-government, not in an exclusive feminist agenda" and concludes that "sovereignty for our people is a larger goal than ... equality with our men."[22]

This opposition between sovereignty and feminism positions nationalism as the sole site of Indigenous resistance to ongoing colonization, and it thus deflects questions about how patriarchy has shaped the internal dynamics of Native communities and activist movements. In a stark repetition of colonial narratives about Native women's complicity, this lack of sustained critical interrogation of nationalism from within Indigenous communities posits assimilation (an accusation frequently levelled at feminists) or submission to patriarchy as the only paths available to Indigenous women. In fact, the ways in which colonization has positioned Indigenous women require a feminist rethinking of Native politics across tribal boundaries, a task for which nationalism, as critical discourse and political practice, is inadequate.

Notwithstanding Trask's contention that sovereignty holds the solution to patriarchy, the gender politics of some Native activist groups, most famously the American Indian Movement (AIM), have elicited criticism by some prominent Indigenous women. Indeed, Lisa Mayo identifies sexism within AIM as one of the reasons that she, along with her sisters, Gloria Miguel and Muriel Miguel, formed Spiderwoman Theater, the first Native feminist drama company:

> When the women were working with the men [in the movements of the 1960s and 1970s], things came down – the women with AIM, on Alcatraz, all the different things that happened at Wounded Knee. This was early on ... [Muriel] was angry as hell because when it came down to really negotiating and talking with the powers that be, no women were allowed in the

> room. They'd say, "Go ahead. Make the coffee. Write the letters." Things like that. It was awful. So this is what we were talking about, part of what we were talking about. We said it out loud.[23]

In addition to these activists' marginalization of women – described by one critic as "male-dominated tribal politics under the guise of 'tribal sovereignty'" – scholarly accounts of these histories, some written by Native men, often erase or diminish the substantial participation of Indigenous women.[24] Although many hesitate to identify such forms of sexism and their similarities to gender dynamics in the dominant society, wary of accusations of divisiveness and alert to the possibility that these challenges draw perilously close to colonial stereotypes about Indigenous men, it is not accidental that some of these criticisms of Native politics should arise, as Mayo's comment shows, from within the theatre community. The pan-tribal origins of Native theatre companies and their multiple influences enable, as we shall see, alternative political practices and revisions of dominant literary paradigms that engage pressing transnational questions, including those surrounding gender and feminism. These issues and literary revisions came to the fore in Indigenous women's performances in the 1980s and 1990s.

Feminism and the Politics of Native Drama

Not coincidentally, drama and performance, arguably more than any other cultural or scholarly spheres, have explicitly grappled with these issues. This is true because of the political possibilities of drama as well as the particular circumstances of Native theatre groups. The first Native companies emerged in the 1960s and 1970s following the collective move of Native peoples to urban centres, also a factor in the resurgence of Indigenous activism during the same period. From the beginning, theatre and politics were closely tied, and because most Native drama groups were products of urban settings and pan-tribal educational institutions, they tended to tackle urban experiences and other issues that cut across tribal affiliations.[25] In so doing, they broaden the parameters of Native identities and experiences as they deal with political issues, such as feminism, that extend beyond tribal boundaries.

The most public of genres, theatre lends itself to such political uses. The stage, as Ngũgĩ wa Thiong'o has written of the postcolonial Kenyan context, serves as a sphere of power constituted through its "conflictual engagement with all the other shrines of power" – a position that enables social critique and potentially inspires political action.[26] In the United States, this was especially true during the activist years of the 1960s and 1970s. As theatre historian Christopher Bigsby explains, "The splintering of the audience and its reformation as a series of groups allied by race, gender or political persuasion was a reminder not of anomie but of communal strength, of a realignment with clear social and political implications ... [For these groups] theatre was in large part a means to an end, a way of clarifying process into image, of displaying the mechanisms of manipulation and suppression and thereby identifying the possibility and direction of change."[27] As a mirror of social experience, theatre provided a means for scrutinizing social relations and, ideally, compelling action aimed at social transformation. This also held true for Native companies during this period, for they often explicitly allied themselves with activists.[28] Drama also found a substantial place in mainstream feminism, and the first Native feminist company, New York–based Spiderwoman Theater, was founded in 1975 as a multiracial group with roots in feminist experimental drama and Native political activism.[29] Still active, Spiderwoman Theater is the longest-standing Native theatre company, and its groundbreaking work has heavily influenced other women playwrights and performers, including Monique Mojica, daughter of Gloria Miguel and a founding member of Native Earth Performing Arts in Toronto. From its beginnings in the 1970s, Native women's drama and performance has grown substantially, and it now comprises a rather extensive body of work, some of which explicitly engages with feminist concerns.[30]

Although the conventions of the stage – enacted through the presence of Native people and the articulation of their perspectives – counter colonial myths about the euphemistic disappearance of Indians and assert the right of Native people to define their own situations, they gain particular currency among Indigenous women, for whom problems of invisibility and cultural authority are amplified. Because Native women's occupation of public space is fraught by prior acts of containment that presumed their complicity, theatre is an important means to scrutinize gendered colonial narratives and to redefine women's political identities. In *Birdwoman and the Suffragettes* and a companion play, *Princess Pocahontas and the Blue Spots* (1990), Mojica critically examines the intertwined dimensions of patriarchal colonialism: material violence, social disempowerment, and narratives of complicity that support the political containment of Indigenous women. These plays also undertake to rewrite these narratives to show patriarchy and colonialism as inseparable and to reclaim women's activism. Countering the opposition of indigeneity and gender, the plays imagine an identity and anti-colonial politics that is *both* Native and feminist. Yet, at the same time, these performances inevitably confront the dangers of public space, which, for Indigenous women, is always sexualized, laden with histories of violence and displays of commodified Native bodies.

Issues of social presence and cultural authority central to Native theatre as a whole also come to bear on *Birdwoman and the Suffragettes.* Mojica's rewriting of Sacajawea's story reflects a broader tendency, beginning in the 1980s, in Native American literature to focus more heavily on women and draw attention to their absence in earlier literary and historical works. In the play, conflicting stories – told by Lewis and Clark, the suffragettes, Shoshone tribal members, and Sacajawea herself – vie for prominence. They contrast a silent, acquiescent, sexualized Sacajawea with a vocal resistance leader. Not incidentally, many of the characters' countermemories of Sacajawea as a resistance figure centre on voice: not only is she a translator and spokesperson on behalf of the Shoshone, her character also speaks in the first person to revise her role in the Lewis and Clark expedition. As the play draws to a close, Sacajawea exhorts listeners: "If you remember me, / remember a child fighting to stay alive / remember a slave girl gambled away / remember a mother protecting her child / remember a wife defying the whip / remember an old one who loved her people / remember I died at home on my land."[31]

Nevertheless, the play ends where it begins with the suffragettes' memorials, illustrating perhaps the intransigence of conventional narratives about Native women. Rather than a seamless narrative, the structure of the play is fragmentary and episodic; it layers conflicting stories about Sacajawea upon one another as it lets stand the gaps and erasures in the historical record. The uncertainties registered in the epigraph – "Dedicated to Sacajawea, 1786-1884 / whoever she may have been; and to / all the unnamed women who share her story" – underscore the erasures and social inscription of colonial memory even as they point to the difficulty of historical recovery. In the play, questions of memory dramatize the complexities of gender and illustrate the necessity of new stories about Native women's political places.

The Politics of Memory: *Princess Pocahontas and the Blue Spots*

Princess Pocahontas and the Blue Spots extends Mojica's concern with gendered historical memory through the stories of Pocahontas and La Malinche, Indigenous women (like Sacajawea) whose collaborations with Europeans provided the mythological foundations of colonial nation-states. The play recounts the events that have made Pocahontas an object of fascination throughout the centuries of conquest: the rescue of John Smith from execution by her father, her conversion to Christianity, her marriage to Jamestown settler John Rolfe, and the birth of their son. "My name is Lady Rebecca forever and always," Mojica's character describes her transformation, "I am a Christian Englishwoman!"[32] Although Malinche is more often disdained than celebrated, her story has the same broad outlines. Christened Doña Marina, she was interpreter for and mistress of Hernán Cortez, and she has been cursed as *la chingada* (the fucked one) and mother of the "bastard race."[33] In collaborations that seem to confirm European superiority, both women renounced their own people, abetted the invaders, adopted their cultures and, through sexual relationships with colonial figures, founded a new race.[34] Like *Birdwoman, Princess Pocahontas* criticizes and reinterprets these popular stories, but this play also explores the connections between historical memory and contemporary political practice. In *Princess Pocahontas,* Mojica's reinterpretation of Pocahontas' and Malinche's stories represents many forgotten histories of Indigenous women throughout the centuries of conquest, among them fur traders' wives who "birthed the Métis," anonymous victims of sexual violence and murder, and contemporary women who fight for tribal land and nationhood. In the play, memories of Indigenous women become a means to create a community based on shared political commitments. Countering the association of traitorous Indigenous women with colonial nationalism, the play's vision is hemispheric in scope, foregrounding the struggles for survival of Native women throughout the Americas. This alternative, oppositional history provides a precedent for contemporary Native women's resistance and demonstrates that challenges to patriarchy are integral to anti-colonial endeavours.

The opening scene, "500 years of the Miss North American Indian Beauty Pageant," parodies popular representations that disempower and marginalize Indigenous women to introduce the play's central concern – transformation. The scene features Princess Buttered-On-Both-Sides as a contestant who embodies the most egregious sexual stereotypes: she appears in a scanty buckskin dress, sings "Indian Love Call," tosses "cornnuts to the four directions," and assumes "a classic 'spiritual' Hollywood Indian pose."[35] For the talent competition, she rips off her dress and hurls herself over a precipice, "all for the loss of [her] one true love, CAPTAIN JOHN WHITEMAN."[36] The duration of the pageant, nearly five hundred years, and the name of its host, George Pepe Flaco Columbus Cartier da Gama Smith (a concatenation of the names of explorers and other colonial figures), place these images in the histories in which they are embedded and underscore connections between the material and discursive dimensions of conquest. Although she initially appears as servile and dim-witted, Princess

Buttered-On-Both-Sides, as her name suggests, is a trickster figure who embodies contradictory qualities and whose humour functions subversively.[37] Moreover, like traditional tricksters, she facilitates transformations, in this case by revising Native women's roles. The slapstick quality of this opening scene brings into question the stereotypes her character inhabits, as do her actions when she reappears later in the play. In a repetition that calls for her to again occupy the role of sacrificial maiden, this time by leaping into an active volcano, she refuses her cue with a resounding "no!" and exits the stage with the excuse, "I think I left something on the stove."[38] This repetition suggests the formulaic nature of Native women's stories, and the revision points to the ways the play undertakes to rewrite their roles. As a trickster, Princess Buttered-On-Both-Sides sets up these dual purposes: she embodies stereotypical gendered images to subject them to scrutiny, and she ultimately subverts them.

These metamorphoses are a key theme of *Princess Pocahontas*. The play is structured as a series of thirteen scenes labelled "transformations" that recast the political significance of Native women's stories. In one kind of transformation that revises conventional histories, the play shows that colonization involved the systematic disempowerment of Indigenous women in the intersecting realms of culture, politics, and representation. "Let me tell you how I became a virgin," a female deity chronicles: "I was the warrior woman / rebel woman/creator/destroyer/womb of the earth / mother of all / – married to none / but the sun himself / or maybe the Lord of the underworld / ... Of my membranes muscle blood and bone I / birthed a continent / – because I thought – / and creation came to be." But as Christianity displaced Indigenous traditions, these powerful roles gave way to notions of women as fallen, degenerate, and weak: "Separated from myself my balance destroyed, / scrubbed clean / made lighter, non threatening / chaste barren. / No longer allied with the darkness of moon tides / but twisted and misaligned / with the darkness of evil /the invaders [sic] sinful apple / in my hand! / ... without power."[39] This scene then sets the story of the women of the Puna, the founders of a women's separatist society, against the displacement of the female deity. Betrayed by their men, they flee to the highland to "honor the mother, / live without men, / demand our purity be / reclaimed."[40] The juxtaposition of one story that critically depicts the disempowerment of Indigenous women with another that shows them reclaiming autonomy and influence is a recurring strategy in the play. In addition to redefining Native women as figures of resistance, it points to the possibility of political change to anticipate its conclusion.

The disempowerment of the female deity finds a historical corollary in "Marie/Margaret/Madelaine – Métis women Transfiguration," a scene that shows the labour and sexual exploitation of Indigenous women in the fur trade (the so-called traitorous Native women in Canada's history). Marie provides sexual companionship as well as free labour for colonial expeditions, and her renaming – though she insists "my name is Atchagoos Isquee'oo" – accompanies other forms of Europeanization (she is washed, perfumed, and dressed in "proper" women's attire) that make her desirable to white men.[41] Although her story thus follows a colonial narrative about the civilization of so-called savages through the domestication and sexualization of Indigenous women, in reality these changes bring only death and destruction, for these women inhabit the roles assigned to them by European patriarchy: "We die from smallpox, syphilis, tuberculosis, childbirth. / We claw at the gate of the fort or we starve and freeze to death outside. / We birth the Métis. / When there is no more to trade, our men trade us."[42] *Princess Pocahontas* shows the hypocrisy of the colonizers' civilizing mission when women such as Marie are "turned off," a euphemism for being discarded after the arrival of a European wife. Mojica draws parallels between these historical events and the experiences of contemporary Native women, including a thirteen-year-old Chilean girl whose torturers inserted a live rat into her vagina, and Anna Mae Aquash, the AIM activist who was beaten, raped, and murdered and whose corpse was then mutilated by the FBI.

Although European colonialism is its primary target, *Princess Pocahontas* also shows the wide reach of patriarchy by scrutinizing the treatment of Indigenous women by their own tribes. In the play, Pocahontas' account of her father's neglect ("What owe I to my father? Waited I not one year in Jamestown, a prisoner? ... 'If my father had loved me, he would not value me less than old swords, guns, or axes: therefore I shall still dwell with the Englishmen who love me'") echoes in Malinche's declaration, "They say it was me betrayed my people! It was they betrayed me!"[43] Not only does this provide an explanation (though not necessarily justification) for these characters' European alliances that extends beyond willing complicity, it also castigates Native men as the real traitors because of their collusion with patriarchy. *Princess Pocahontas* undoes the colonial logic that positions Indigenous women as collaborators by casting a critical eye on gender dynamics within their communities.

These scenes illuminate the ways patriarchal colonialism has transformed Indigenous women's social places, but *Princess Pocahontas* also revises conventional gendered narratives to trace an alternative history of women's cultural and political resistance that extends into the present. Drawing a strategy from *Birdwoman and the Suffragettes*, the "Pocahontas/Lady Rebecca/Matoaka Transfiguration" depicts an adolescent Pocahontas (as Matoaka) undergoing a puberty ritual to initiate her into traditional gender roles. The scene moves backward in time, beginning with a troubadour's account of the famed rescue of John Smith and ending with Matoaka becoming a healer and entering "woman's time." By doing so, the scene replaces gendered colonial narratives with tribal ones that stress the power of women. Significantly, Matoaka uses first-person narration to tell her story, and this narrative technique underscores the importance of voice in a work that takes to task the silencing and erasure of Indigenous women. The subversive potential of words gains importance throughout the play, which reinterprets even Malinche's role as translator to the conquistadores. "I am the only one can speak to the Maya, to the Mexica," she insists, "It is my words that are of value ... I can change words. I have power ... I am a strategist. Dangerous woman."[44] This connection between words and power comes to bear on the play's final scene in which "Contemporary Woman" enlists women "word warriors," the "guerrilleras," to engage in political struggle.[45] These warriors include writers and activists, among them a courageous Kayapo woman, baby in arms, who "confronts a riot squad" and shouts, "I am here to speak for my brother and my brother-in-law ... You steal our land! I am calling upon you! I throw my words in your faces!!!!"[46] In this scene and elsewhere, *Princess Pocahontas* inverts the gendered dimensions of conventional stories by showing women as the agents of resistance and men as often unreliable supporters. In an earlier scene, when "The Man" – the "husband, the lover, the friend, the 'brother' in the struggle whose oppression is fully understood but whom the women end up carrying anyway" – is distracted by a white woman whom he follows "hungrily with [his] eyes," he occupies the role of traitor through his sexuality.[47] A reprimand by Contemporary Woman – "We're supposed to be re-building the nations, RIGHT?" – leads only to his hasty departure.[48]

More than transforming Indigenous women into oppositional figures, *Princess Pocahontas* shows the connections between patriarchy and colonialism that make feminism necessary to a politics of resistance. The play concludes at an International Women's Day celebration, and this final scene revises the gatherings of suffragettes in *Birdwoman* to represent the possibility of Indigenous feminism. Although Contemporary Woman, like Sacajawea, remarks upon the colonial tendencies of mainstream feminism, she also insists on creating a feminism that embraces the unique situations of

Indigenous women: "So many years of trying to fit into feminist shoes ... The shoes I'm trying on must be crafted to fit these wide, square, brown feet. I must feel the earth through their soles."[49] Yet, as the provisional nature of this statement suggests, feminism's specific contours, as well as its relation to tribal nationalisms (a reference point throughout the play), remain ambiguous. On the one hand, *Princess Pocahontas* revises the stories of Indigenous women so that they support tribal rather than colonial nationalisms: the assertion "we, native women, are the centre of the hoop of the nation" echoes in "women are the medicine, so we must heal the women" and "a nation is not conquered until the hearts of its women are on the ground."[50] The dominant thread of the play is, however, transnational and pan-tribal – a tendency one critic has labelled "oppositional transnationalism," a characteristic of much Native politics of the period, in which experiences of patriarchy drew together Indigenous women across space, time, and culture.[51] "Una Nacion," the title of the final scene at the International Women's Day celebration, conveys this ambiguity. Does this title suggest the necessity of eradicating patriarchy to build nations and, thus, define Indigenous feminism as a precondition of tribal nationalism? Or does it reinterpret nation to mean a separatist Indigenous women's community, like that of the women of the Puna, founded as a rejection of patriarchy? Although the play itself offers no specific answers, each of these possibilities undoes the opposition between feminism and Native politics by insisting on its crucial importance to anti-colonial endeavours.

ACKNOWLEDGMENTS

Material from this chapter is taken from Shari M. Huhndorf, *Mapping the Americas: The Transnational Politics of Contemporary Native Culture* (New York: Cornell University Press, 2009). I am grateful to Cornell University Press for permission to republish. I owe special thanks to Cheryl Suzack, Karen Ford, Jean Barman, and Jeanne Perreault for comments that greatly improved this essay.

NOTES

1 Monique Mojica, *Birdwoman and the Suffragettes: A Story of Sacajawea* (Toronto: Women's Press, 1991), 67-68.

2 On the transformation and disruption of traditional women's roles, see, for example, Paula Gunn Allen, *The Sacred Hoop: Recovering the Feminine in American Indian Traditions* (Boston: Beacon Press, 1986); Devon Abbott Mihesuah, *Indigenous American Women: Decolonization, Empowerment, Activism* (Lincoln: University of Nebraska Press, 2003); and Wendy Wall, "Gender and the 'Citizen Indian,'" in Elizabeth Jameson and Susan Armitage, eds., *Writing the Range: Race, Class, and Culture*

in the Women's West (Norman: University of Oklahoma Press, 1997), 202-29. For a discussion of the relationship between sexual violence and ongoing colonialism in the Native context, see Andrea Smith, *Conquest: Sexual Violence and American Indian Genocide* (Cambridge, MA: South End Press, 2005). Louise Michele Newman describes the relationship between Europe's civilizing mission and the instantiation of patriarchy in *White Women's Rights: The Racial Origins of Feminism in the United States* (New York: Oxford University Press, 1999), especially Chapter 5.

3 Jean Barman, "Taming Aboriginal Sexuality: Gender, Power, and Race in British Columbia, 1850-1900," *BC Studies* 115-16 (1997-98): 237-66. Barman's account focuses specifically on nineteenth-century British Columbia, but her argument illuminates colonial processes in broader historical and geographical contexts.

4 Ibid., 264.

5 Ibid., 251.

6 Rayna Green, "Review: Native American Women," *Signs* 6, 2 (1980): 250. See also Green's "The Pocahontas Perplex: The Image of Indian Women in American Culture," *Massachusetts Review* 27, 4 (1975): 698-714.

7 Green, "Review," 265.

8 Ibid., 259.

9 Ibid., 266.

10 Mojica, *Birdwoman,* 72.

11 On the controversy, see Patricia Penn Hilden, "De-colonizing the (Women's) Mind," in Patricia Penn Hilden, *When Nickels Were Indians: An Urban, Mixed-Blood Story* (Washington, DC: Smithsonian Institution Press, 1995), 157-77.

12 Mojica, *Birdwoman,* 76, 75, 83.

13 Bonita Lawrence, "Gender, Race, and the Regulation of Native Identity in Canada and the United States: An Overview," *Hypatia* 18, 2 (2003): 5.

14 Kathryn W. Shanley, "Thoughts on Indian Feminism," in Beth Brant, ed., *A Gathering of Spirit: A Collection by North American Indian Women* (Ithaca, NY: Firebrand Books, 1988), 214, emphasis in original.

15 Laura Tohe, "There Is No Word for Feminism in My Language," *Wicazo Sa Review* 15, 2 (2000): 103-10.

16 See Allen, *The Sacred Hoop,* and Mihesuah, *Indigenous American Women.*

17 Emma LaRocque, "The Colonization of a Native Woman Scholar," in Christine Miller and Patricia Chuchryk, eds., *Women of the First Nations: Power, Wisdom, and Strength* (Winnipeg: University of Manitoba Press, 1996), 14.

18 Green, "Review," 264.

19 M. Annette Jaimes and Theresa Halsey, "American Indian Women: At the Center of Indigenous Resistance in North American," in M. Annette Jaimes, ed., *The State of Native America: Genocide, Colonization, and Resistance* (Boston: South End Press, 1992), 331.

20 Haunani-Kay Trask, "Feminism and Indigenous Hawaiian Nationalism," *Signs* 21, 4 (1996): 909.

21 Haunani-Kay Trask, *From a Native Daughter: Colonialism and Sovereignty in Hawai'i* (Honolulu: University of Hawai'i Press, 1999).

22 Trask, "Feminism and Indigenous Hawaiian Nationalism," 910, 914.

23 Quoted in Ann Haugo, "'Circles upon Circles upon Circles': Native Women in Theater and Performance," in Hanay Geiogamah and Jaye T. Darby, eds., *American Indian Theater in Performance: A Reader* (Los Angeles: University of California Press, 2000), 338-39.

24 M.A. Jaimes Guerrero, "'Patriarchal Colonialism' and Indigenism: Implications for Native Feminist Spirituality and Native Womanism," *Hypatia* 18, 2 (2003): 67. Mihesuah, *Indigenous American Women,* 12. Mihesuah specifically identifies Paul Chaat Smith and Robert Warrior's neglect of women in *Like a Hurricane,* their celebrated account of AIM activism, and this underscores the patriarchal tendencies of nationalism as a critical discourse.

25 For a history of Native drama in the United States, see Shari Huhndorf, "American Indian Drama and the Politics of Performance," in Eric Cheyfitz, ed., *The Columbia Guide to American Indian Literatures of the United States since 1945* (New York: Columbia University Press, 2006), 288-318. For a history of Native women's performances, see Haugo, "'Circles upon Circles upon Circles.'"

26 Ngũgi wa Thiong'o, "Enactments of Power: The Politics of Performance Space," in Ngũgi wa Thiong'o, *Penpoints, Gunpoints, and Dreams: Towards a Critical Theory of the Arts and the State in Africa* (Oxford: Clarendon Press, 1998), 39-40.

27 C.W.E. Bigsby, *Modern American Drama 1945-2000* (Cambridge: Cambridge University Press, 2000), 268.

28 Hanay Geiogamah, "The New American Indian Theater: An Introduction," in Geiogamah and Darby, *American Indian Theater,* 159-64.

29 On theatre and mainstream feminism, see Charlotte Canning, *Feminist Theaters in the U.S.A.: Staging Women's Experience* (London: Routledge, 1996), and Sue-Ellen Case, *Feminism and Theatre* (New York: Routledge, 1988).

30 For a list of published plays, performances, and critical works, see the website of the Native American Women Playwrights Archive at Miami University, http://staff.lib.muohio.edu/nawpa.

31 Mojica, *Birdwoman,* 84.

32 Monique Mojica, *Princess Pocahontas and the Blue Spots* (Toronto: Women's Press, 1990), 31.

33 Ibid., 22-23.

34 For a discussion of the changing political meanings of Pocahontas' story, see Robert S. Tilton, *Pocahontas: The Evolution of an American Narrative* (Cambridge: Cambridge University Press, 1994).

35 Mojica, *Princes Pocahontas,* 18.

36 Ibid., 19.

37 These are general qualities of tricksters in many Native traditions. It is important to note that the nature of tricksters varies among Indigenous cultures, and Mojica's character seems not to be rooted in a single cultural tradition but is instead a kind of generic figure that has become a common feature in Native literature.

38 Ibid., 25.

39 Ibid., 35-37.

40 Ibid., 36.

41 Ibid., 43.

42 Ibid., 46.
43 Ibid., 31, 22.
44 Ibid., 23.
45 Ibid., 59.
46 Ibid., 59-60.
47 Ibid., 16.
48 Ibid., 40.
49 Ibid., 58.
50 Ibid., 39, 20, 60.
51 Ric Knowles, "Translators, Traitors, Mistresses, and Whores: Monique Mojica and the Mothers of the Métis Nations," in Marc Maufort and Franca Bellarsi, eds., *Siting the Other: Re-visions of Marginality in Australian and English-Canadian Drama* (Brussels: P.I.E. Peter Lang, 2001), 255.

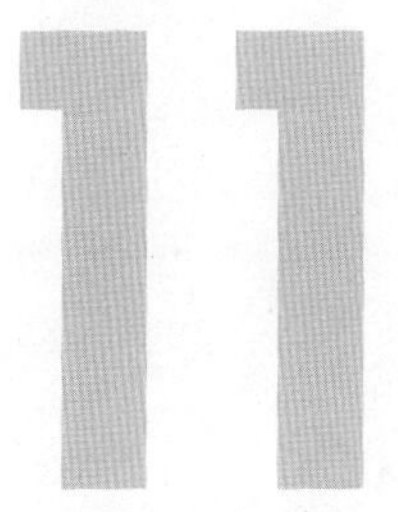

"Memory Alive"
An Inquiry into the Uses of Memory by Marilyn Dumont, Jeannette Armstrong, Louise Halfe, and Joy Harjo

JEANNE PERREAULT

> *Memory as a distinct meta-sense transports, bridges and crosses all other senses. Yet memory is internal to each sense, and the senses are as divisible and indivisible from each other as each memory is separable and intertwined with others.*
>
> – *Nadia Seremetakis,* The Senses Still

> *It's like saying "world." Memory is the nucleus of every cell; it's what runs, it's the gravity; the gravity of the Earth.*
>
> – *Joy Harjo, "A Laughter"*

In this chapter, I undertake a preliminary exploration of the role of memory – and its intimate relationship to speech, history, and the sacred – in the poetry of Marilyn Dumont, Jeannette Armstrong, Louise Halfe, and Joy Harjo. Kenneth Lincoln observes that the fulcrum of First Nations literature is a "sense of relatedness" in which "tribe means ancestral history ... an ever present religious history, not 'back there' in time, but continuously re-enacted, even as it changes form."[1] But even as I read these words, nodding in agreement, I realize that the complexity and subtlety of such an integrated intellectual, social, and spiritual context is far from my range of experience.

The way that knowledge and understanding works in this view of history, the vagueness of the word *sense* in the sense of relatedness Lincoln describes, is perplexing. Only through codes of memory could the link between history and presentness find a way into voice. N. Scott Momaday declares, perhaps metonymically, that he is aware of "the memory in [his] blood" as an aspect of his relationship to the Native parts of his heritage.[2] With pronounced authority, white scholar Arnold Krupat refutes Momaday's statement. In Krupat's words, "there is no gene for perception, no such thing as memory in the blood."[3] Krupat prefers the view that Native authors are "gifted individuals shaping a subtle and complex tradition."[4] Although one may agree with Krupat's more recent view that the important role of memory in Native literature should be examined comparatively rather than as "some sort of unique and autonomous expression of Native American culture," understanding what that role is – indeed, its variety and complexity – is also essential.[5] To stage a simple dichotomy between the two positions – memory is ever present, ancestral, and religious, *embodied* in Native literature versus there is "no such thing as memory in the blood" – might make for a good ideological argument, but it will not help us to understand the variety and complexity of memory as it appears in various Native writings.[6]

Rather than turning to the long European philosophical discussion about memory, I rely on First Nations theorists. Lee Maracle bases time itself on memory and memory on the community. Maracle explains "the structure of time of First Nations cultures" in this way: "To claim lineage memory and juxtapose it with current memory is to articulate the most sacred of one's entire thought from the beginning to the present and is intended as future memory."[7] Like Momaday, Maracle seems to refuse the vision of the artist as an independent, gifted individual. Similarly, American poet Joy Harjo has several times referred to the responsibility of remembering, and the charge of this responsibility seems to appear as a strong force for many Native writers.[8]

Memory is, necessarily it seems by conventional definition, a representation of what can no longer be directly experienced. It is often all we seem to have of the painful and elusive shimmer that divides the now from the then, the anguished slippage of life always dumbly or sharply undoing itself as it is done. Maracle's assertion of lineage memory shapes the ideas of mind and recollection along different lines from these commonplace notions of what constitutes memory. In her explanation, experience need not be individual, personal, or specific to enter memory; indeed, the word *lineage* suggests bloodlines, a heritage of the body that leaves its trace in mental effects, images, and memories. For Maracle, the personal and immediate past (which is how I read *current memory*) and the collective past available through the lineage memory of a people coalesce, but this phenomenon is not simply a given. As I read her, Maracle emphasizes the necessity of *claiming* that communal memory – actively, purposefully, and imaginatively – of juxtaposing it with current memory. Most importantly, these acts are in the realm of the articulated. What is being articulated moves beyond the everyday and into what has always been the most sacred element of our thoughts. It is this dimension of the sacred that is carried through time and is intended to be passed on as future memory.

Joy Harjo uses memory "to retrace the past not as an inducement to curl inwards on oneself, as if it were a point in time without escape route, but rather as a dynamic process to reaffirm ancient heritages and proceed forward on a path of constant renewal."[9] By bringing memory and history together in the process of retracing the past, the poet brings a personal process and a social one together. To evade the linearity of the metaphor of the path and the closure implied in circles and a curl inwards, Laura Coltelli emphasizes Harjo's image of the spiral. The "proceeding of memory" thus "spirals down the tip [of a vortex] while simultaneously expanding toward the future."[10] Harjo, Armstrong, Dumont, and Halfe each provide distinct stagings of memory and its workings, as I will show, and each participates in revealing the diverse ways memory can be conceptualized and represented to indicate its function in cultural discourses.

I lay these authors' assertions of the multiple nature and function of articulated memory alongside Roland Barthes' brief discussion "The Discourse of History."[11] Barthes refers to the "breaks in silence" that inaugurate historical discourse and claims them as the linguist's well-known performative opening to speech. Barthes makes the performative opening of historical discourse a "solemn act of foundation" based on a poetic model, the "*I sing* of the poets." But it is equally as provocative that he claims a sacred character for the breaking of silence. In reference to the anxiety of breaking silence, Barthes insists that the inception of speech is "so difficult" "or, so sacred."[12] Although it is safe to suggest that what Maracle means by *sacred* and what Barthes intends by it will diverge in significant ways, I offer Barthes' sense of the goal of historical statement. Barthes explains that "the entrance of the speech act into historical statement ... has as its goal not so much to give the historian a chance to express his 'subjectivity' as to 'complicate' history's chronological time by confronting it with another time, that of discourse itself."[13]

The introduction of the speaker, the human voice, and its audience is subsumed in Barthes' assertion that discourse itself is a kind of Platonic figure. The goal, as Barthes imagines it, is to complicate historical time. He goes on to explain that "the presence, in historical narration, of explicit speech-act signs tends to 'dechronologize' the historical 'thread.'"[14] Barthes, by using the metaphor of thread, suggests not only that narration makes a stitched pattern but also that events themselves (here, Barthes does make a claim for the real, however elusive) are linked, threaded through the needle of time. Dechronologization, the effect of explicit speech acts in historical narration, "restore[s], if only as a reminiscence or a nostalgia, a complex, parametric, non-linear time whose deep space recalls the mythic time of the ancient cosmogonies, it too linked by essence to the speech of the poet or the soothsayer."[15]

Alongside Maracle's statement, Barthes' ideas are provocative. The speaker of the past is in poetic and mythic mode (which may be Barthes' sacred mode) as the essential disturber of linearity, restoring what has been lost, bringing the past to the service of the future. So too is the speaker in Maracle's claim. In Barthes' argument, however, dechronologizing the thread of history brings into play nostalgia (with its connotation of sentimentality and self-indulgence) or reminiscence – another word that evokes misty pleasantries. Nadia Seremetakis, in her study of perception and memory, criticizes this conventional understanding of nostalgia: "This reduction of the term confines the past and removes it from any transaction and material relation to the present; the past becomes an isolatable and consumable unit of time. Nostalgia, in the American sense, freezes the past in such a manner as to preclude it from any capacity for social transformation in the present, preventing the present from establishing a dynamic perceptual relationship to its history."[16]

Seremetakis offers another way to understand nostalgia by linking it to memory through its roots in Greek thought: "'*Nostalghia*' is the desire of longing with burning pain to journey. It also evokes the sensory dimension of memory in exile and estrangement; it mixes bodily and emotional pain and ties painful experiences of spiritual and somatic exile to the notion of maturation and ripening. In this sense, *nostalghia* is linked to the personal consequences of historicizing sensory experience which is conceived as a painful bodily and emotional journey ... *Nostalghia* is thus far from trivializing romantic sentimentality."[17] Seremetakis refers to nostalgia (or *nostalghia*) as something that has a geographical element: one must have travelled in space as well as time for the longing to have developed. For First Nations peoples, exile is more fraught. Place, land, and home are often the same as they were before contact or invasion, yet they are irrevocably different. Memory is the most effective weapon against exile that is not geographical but nonetheless in effect. Although Seremetakis emphasizes the pain of loss in nostalghia, she does recognize the link of spiritual and somatic experience to the notion of maturation and ripening.

In ways similar to Seremetakis, Maracle allies linear, processual (which implies ripening or maturation), and complex (or non-linear) time with speech and thereby makes memory an active and empowering present reality in itself. The spiritual exile that Seremetakis records, however, is resisted by memory, even refuted. The assertion of a positive, even developmental or evolutionary, aspect to the embrace of memory links this classical (in the Greek sense) view of memory with that of Lee Maracle, Joy Harjo, Jeannette Armstrong, Marilyn Dumont, and Louise Halfe. I look, in part, to these poets to understand the way memory sings in the blood or, indeed, to see if this is a helpful way to think cross-culturally.[18]

Marilyn Dumont's first collection of poems, *A Really Good Brown Girl,* takes its title from her prose poem "Memoirs of a Really Good Brown Girl." This volume of personal lyric narrative, moments of insight, and social critique most often embeds memory in the body rather than in an explicit articulation of memory's force or function. In "Half Human/Half Devil (Halfbreed) Muse," for example, the visiting muse comes in violence, and for the poet "no sound, no sound" escapes as the mechanistic ("shutting off / a dripping faucet") and bestial ("dog / gnawing bone") force takes over. From "giving up to giving over" – the central one-line stanza – the muse becomes a dance (or a dancer) with a "drum rattle / gangly movement, offbeat ... blood / paint, ochre skin, ash smell." The muse figure seems to rise out of a tribal memory that is not containable in mere images but inhabits and "overtakes" the poet's body. Dumont does not say, explicitly, that the half human/half devil (halfbreed) muse is a remembered force.[19] Her title and her tone instead suggest some comic or ironic thrust: "a herd of rattles overtakes me" is an image that should make us aware that this muse might have a powerful trickster aspect.[20] Nevertheless, the only place of sound in the poem is that of the drum rattle, "pebbles encased trapped / in sound, pebbles rasp / against thin dry skin." In the drum rattles, sound becomes possible and required. This muse will neither stay contained in memory nor leave the past behind. As the poet is overtaken, she becomes able to speak.

Several pieces in the volume, including "The White Judges," appear to work directly from the rich detail of personal memory and family history, with a twist of the surreal that evokes both the child's sensibility and the adult's sharp vision.[21] "The White Judges" opens with a straightforward declarative description of the family home: "an old schoolhouse," where "all nine kids and the / occasional friend slept upstairs." The information is solid, plain, unemotional. It creates a setting and a context that includes "our walls high and / bare except for the family photos whose frames were crowded / with siblings waiting to come of age, marry or leave." Only in the last line of the first stanza-paragraph does Dumont shift into another consciousness: "At supper / eleven of us would stare down a pot of moose stew, bannock and tea, / while outside the white judges sat encircling our house." The prose breaks, and the next line stands alone: "And they waited to judge" (no punctuation). The image of the encircling judges is a powerful one, suggesting dogs or wolves resting on their haunches waiting to pounce or a group of bullies or predators, which will evoke memories of fear in many children. Who has not been in such a circle? That Dumont positions us in the physical space of the home, the family circling the stew pot, the judges circling the house, makes an almost filmic visual effect: the family scene is an easy reality, the other is a strange vision of predation, judges white (and, in my mind's eye, black-robed, male, grey-headed, intense, and staring) and waiting.

The poem recalls the moments of vulnerability with a visceral, sensual immediacy that makes the haunted, hunted feeling a kind of peripheral vision in which the white judges are intermittently perceived but never forgotten. They wait until the moments of exposure. Each section repeats how the white judges "waited till we ate tripe / watched us inhale its wild vapour ... watched us welcome it into our being ... swallow its gamey juices / until we had become it and it had become us"; and then the judges waited till the children reveal their excitement about the boxes of donated clothing: "a box transformed now / into the Sears catalogue." Joy, nourishment, desire, and intimacy all make the family vulnerable. It is these moments for which the white judges wait. Dumont describes the twilight, when her father and older brothers "would drag a bloodstained canvas ... onto our lawn" and "my mother would lift and lay it in place / like a dead relative, / praying, coaxing and thanking it." Her mother skinned and carved, "talking in Cree to my father and in English to my brothers." The image of a suburban lawn lies incongruously alongside the work of carving and skinning, which is made more difficult in the "truck-headlight-night." The mother's work is a matrix that becomes spiritual as she prays and acknowledges the animal's gift, cultural as she speaks in two languages to the different generations, and profoundly traditional as the beast is treated with reverence, "like a dead relative." The younger children drift into sleep, "bellies rested in the meat days ahead," and the mother's role is woven into the whole of the twilight scene as she takes on her tasks without emphasis. The unspoken implication is that the family, too, like the judges, has been waiting until twilight to do this work. The younger children's comfort in the murmured voices (Dumont is always "we" in reference to the children) contrasts sharply with the grim faces of the watching judges. What Seremetakis calls the sensory dimension of memory is inflected by the mixture of that which is precious overshadowed by the relentless and patient gaze of the white judges.[22]

The watchers "wait till the guitars come out." The family members dance holes into their socks and, in the last stanza, "wait till a fight broke out." The repetitions and costs of everyday life are invoked as Dumont describes the effect of the fight:

> and the night would settle in our bones
> and we'd ache with shame
> for having heard or spoken
> that which sits at the edge of our light side
> that which comes but we wished it hadn't
> like "settlement" relatives who would arrive at Christmas
> and leave at Easter.

The rhetorical repetition in which the judges wait until something "would" happen is the moment a judgment would occur – and the judgment would be made. The white judges would judge and shame would rise – not for an action or a wrong-doing but for an awareness, "for having heard or spoken / that which sits at the edge of our light side." The Métis acceptance of "our light side," the white side, is deeply conflicted. As I read them, these lines indicate that judgment (the purview of the white judges) has been picked up and brought into the family, into the centre of the circle. Shame, then, is the result of having verbalized the judges' gaze – indeed, to any acknowledgment at all. The inevitability of this revisitation is made familial; the simile brings the shame home, like other relatives who come and won't go away.

It is possible to view this memory as a "recovered utopian feeling, alterity and cultural procreation" that bears itself against official history and carries the sensory memory with it.[23] But the edges of the circle of this consoling gathering of recollections are always drawn by the attentive judges. The utopian feeling of childhood memory is removed from even a remote nostalgic sentimentality by those avid eyes. The recurring events that embed cultural identity and familial congruence are inappropriately set off from everydayness and charged with the assessment of difference and its meaning. The relationship of white judges to white readers is ambiguous. We (all readers) are invited to judge the judges and to experience the circle from the inside of that ring of eyes. If our histories provide a mirror that reflects our place in that circle of judges, then another set of memories is put into play, and with those memories may come a degree of comprehension, a revised awareness. Dumont's concern, of course, is not to examine the white judges but to provide a trope for the existence and effects of poverty, cultural specificity (Cree and English), dislocation (the lawns, the city neighbours), and the marking of racial difference and pain with the word *white.* Racism is figured in the hungry attention of the judges and the shame felt when that vision is brought home.

In "Breakfast of the Spirit," Dumont brings another aspect of memory to language.[24] In this delicate poem, the strangeness of self-knowledge and the familiarity of self-knowledge touch in the most intimate ways, being "things that are / like nothing else is." The familiar senses of one's ("your") body ("the smell of your own scent / taste of your own skin") and the familiar returns of the natural world ("the force of spring water") are indeed familiar, but they are also new, surprising, strange in the ways that "the sound of chickadees / in a stand of mute spruce" with the weight of silence lifted is always a surprise, always utterly right. The comfort of these images, with their careful placing of "you" in your own body and your own quiet spruce world, is distressed in the second stanza, where these images are brought to bear on another familiarity:

> familiar as the ripple in your throat
> waiting for your voice to return
> from the sealed-off jars of memory
> released now to feast on the preserves
> after you've slept so long
> tasted now, at the celebratory breakfast of your awakening.

The intimate tensions of sleeping and waking, silence and speech, hunger and feasting all pivot on the homely image of memory as a jar of preserves saved carefully for the moment of need. It is from this source that voice comes, and it is this store that nourishes. Individual memory may be suggested here, but the celebration and the spirit whose fast is broken in the title, "Breakfast of the Spirit," suggest another kind of remembering, one that is as personal as one's own body and as impersonal as nature. Dumont does not abstract the *idea* of memory in this poem; instead, she alerts us to the cost of amnesia and presents forgetting as a place of hunger and sleep. Memory, then, is the source of nourishment, the site of awakening, and the content of spiritual celebration.

Jeannette Armstrong's treatment of history and memory also participates in the evocation of the sacred. Although Roland Barthes might be accused of sentimentalizing the historian (by speaking of his or her essential links to poet or soothsayer), we find in Armstrong's short poem "History Lesson" a rather sharper enactment of the speaker of history.[25] In this poem, dechronologization works not only as a manifestation of the speech act in so-called paper time, as Barthes contends, but also as a collapse of sequence with a return, at the end of the poem, to consequence.[26] In this poem, Armstrong brings together the most mundane elements of everyday life in contemporary Canada – the Rice Krispies "snap, crackle, and pop" advertisement, known to every Canadian child and the pollution of rivers by "flower power laundry detergents" – and aligns them with the deadly destructive forces of Seagram's whisky. And, of course, smallpox, priests, Mounties, and miners are all jumbled together as Armstrong concludes with a devastating, and surprisingly compassionate, indictment of the colonizer.

Civilization, we are informed, in a blunt parody of the grade school history lessons we have all had, "has reached the promised land." Working from the assumption that we know the story – no question about who Christopher is – this history lesson is not about events as they follow one another in some logic of causality. The mob – whether its members are "shooting each other / left and right" (we can't ignore a political jibe here), swelling rivers with "flower powered zee," or bringing "gifts / Smallpox, Seagrams / and rice crispies" – is enacting an impulse of apparently mindless triviality, greed, and destructiveness. This impulse stands in distinct contrast to the implication of lineage and order. The "impulse" threatens "whole civilizations / ten generations," which are facing destruction. Time is compressed. A single blow can damage these "ten generations." The poem is in the present tense until the foreclosure in the last stanza: "Somewhere among the remains ... is the termination" of a "long journey / and unholy search." It is in the last stanza that Armstrong's lesson reveals that the violations caught in the jumble of linear time are not her only concern:

Somewhere among the remains
of skinless animals
is the termination
to a long journey
and unholy search
for the power
glimpsed in a garden
forever closed
forever lost.

The moment that begins this history is still happening; it is still bursting out of the belly of Christopher's ship. And the moment of termination, when the animals are all skinned and the generations mutilated, is contained in another moment, one out of historical time altogether: that is, the ongoing moment of ejection from the garden of Eden, the biblical master narrative of Western culture, the narrative that feeds not only religion but also psychoanalysis and politics (the socialist's golden age of perfect equality before private property appeared), the narrative of irrevocable loss and the tormenting promise of restoration.[27] The lesson of history that Armstrong gives us is not a single or simple one: not only is history not the past, it also cannot be explained in material or social terms. In contrast to the usual evocation of losses undergone by Aboriginal peoples, Armstrong looks at the losses suffered by the Europeans. Their loss of a spiritual power, the loss of a moment of perfect harmony, "glimpsed in a garden / forever closed / forever lost," makes their search an unconscious one. Armstrong asserts that the Europeans do not know what they have lost and cannot know what they (or we) are seeking. With this blindness, this amnesia, in place, the Europeans cannot know what the poet knows – that "somewhere among the remains," a termination to an unholy search might be found. The requirement is looking backward, facing their own spiritual loss – in other words, another kind of remembering. The inevitable desolation of the mob that burst from Christopher's ship is spiritual, but the effects of its violent and chaotic hunger have been material and unending. The needs of Europeans may be spiritual, but Armstrong asserts, as long as the search itself is unholy, the "power / glimpsed" in that garden will elude them. Memory, in other words, is an essential human requirement. Its absence creates brutal violations, stupid destruction.

Another kind of history lesson appears in Armstrong's "Threads of Old Memory."[28] "History is a dreamer," Armstrong writes, and winds these threads of old memory through the skeins made available to us by Maracle's notions of lineage memory, current memory, and future memory. Armstrong affirms her belief in those connections, linking blood and memory, but also insists upon the power of language to make other bonds possible. This recollection requires a search for the right words, the sacred words that can be "spoken serenely in the gaps between memory / the lost places of history / pieces mislaid / forgotten or stolen." This claiming of a whole history and a people in the process of "becoming" from the "imaginings of the past" is linked closely with Maracle's lineage memory, which is articulated through current memory and leads inexorably to a future memory. But blood, or lineage, itself will not carry the weight of memory for Armstrong. The narrative that links the gaps requires more than blood. Memory, it seems, does not flow easily in the blood but must be wrestled or invited into being through language.

Louise Halfe's collection *Bear Bones and Feathers* also wrestles memory into existence.[29] Halfe's poems refute an image of individual or tribal history as a location for simple sustaining recollections or the harmonious unity of humans and nature. For Halfe, the grandmothers (*Nòhkomak,* more than one grandmother; *Nòhkom,* my grandmother; *Nòhkom àtayohkàn,* grandmother of the legends) are remembered from childhood and are beings who are the stuff of memory itself.[30] Together, these grandmothers seem to encode the range of cultural and personal meanings that are attached to memory. They are not uniformly comforting presences. In "Nòhkom Àtayohkàn 1" and "Nòhkom Àtayohkàn 2," we find the contrast between menace and comfort even in the figure of the grandmother of the legends, the Nòhkom àtayohkàn. In the first of these poems, images of the Nòhkom àtayohkàn are formed of nature: hair of brome, face of soft leather cut through with ravines. The nourishing promise of this figure, and the hunger of the speaker are explicit: "I want to cup / your breast, a starving suckling child." And the address is personal, the plea fully trusting: "Old one with laughing eyes / wrap me in blanket grass ... Ground my wandering feet."[31] In "Nòhkom Àtayohkàn 2," another element appears, and this grandmother figure shows another force. From the poem's opening lushness, "Your flaming flowers / spread on my breast," the speaker observes depletion: "I've watched life / blossom and fade from / your eyes." Death images ("you've folded flies / between your lips") combine with other blossom figures ("welcomed the swirl of drinking hummingbirds"). The effect of this aspect or dimension of the Nòhkom àtayohkàn is not the endless life of the evergreen sweet pine of "Nòhkom Àtayohkàn 1." The speaker in the second poem says,

You have left me spent
lying open, dying
beneath the sun.

You, breathless,
sightless
beneath the snow.[32]

If the *me* and the *I* in this poem are understood as the lyric subject, which the poem suggests, then the passionate life force of both the ancient grandmother and the speaking woman-poet are exhausted, spent, if not yet dead, then dying, if not dying, then "breathless, / sightless." Whether under the sun or under the snow, the *I* of the poet and the *you* of the Nòhkom àtayohkàn cost each other everything in their encounter. These poems, with their links to the past, to legends snared in and by memory, carry a deliberate contradiction. Neither aspect of the Nòhkom àtayohkàn – a fundamental trope, if you will, of memory itself – can be forgotten or evaded; both have their effects in the present: one nurturing, the other totally challenging.

Similarly, the human, personal grandmother, Nòhkom, carries multiple implications and associations. A presence of power or medicine, "Nòhkom, Medicine Bear" is described in the present tense.[33] She is hardly a figure of memory, yet her existence does not seem confined to the moment. The conflation of "A shuffling brown bear / snorting and puffing" and "*Nòhkom,* the medicine woman / alone in her attic den / smoking slim cigarettes" brings human and beast together in a unity or connection whose intelligibility is wholly dependent upon cultural context. The bear and the woman are one being, yet each, in this poem, keeps its distinctiveness. She wears a red kerchief on her head, her skirt drapes over "her aged beaded moccasins," and when her work is complete, she "drapes her paws on the stair rails," leaving her "medicine power / to work in silence." The poem's references to secrets, to the darkness, to the silence all contribute to the doubleness of this poetic image. Halfe understates the mystery of how bear and woman can be one being by offering it as a given. She instead emphasizes the other mystery, the power of knowledge, of the herbs and roots and songs, the work of healing "troubled spirits" and, most profoundly, the powerful silence needed for the medicine to gather its force for its work. This Nòhkom can be claimed as grandmother, but the force of the figure and her acts seems to stand outside time or personal memory.

A very different representation of Nòhkom appears in "Off with Their Heads."[34] In this poem, Halfe sharply dispels the benevolent aura of the past, the delicate taste of memory, and any lingering illusions about inevitable and quintessential respect for nature's creatures by all Aboriginal people at all times. What is left is the image of deliberate cruelty and its effect on the child watching:

Nòhkom
used to take the
visiting tomcats
and ever so gently
wrap a snare wire
around their necks.

From the clothesline
we'd watch the cats
kicking, scratching,
clawing

until

they hung

limp.

I read this careful shaping of line and stanza, the emphatic "ever so gently" and the chilling "used to," as the wish of the poet to convey quite precisely the events of this torture. The child ("I") would later "go and examine / the stiffs." The use of the word *stiffs* – a kind of hard-boiled detective story word – must be intended here to undercut the grotesque image of the cats' struggle for life; yet the next stanzas describe the "lifeless eyes ... foam around their / mouth land-salt / on a dry lake," the eager flies and beetles and, most vividly, the child herself:

Cat stench
filled my nostrils.
I'd stumble away
clawing the invisible snare
for fresh air.

The identification of the child with the cats and the horrific surrealism of the invisible snare are underscored in the last stanza:

Nòhkom would sit at the window
with a cup of tea
puffing her pipe
staring at the tomcats.

The contemplative figure of the old grandmother with her pipe stands in almost bizarre contrast to the wilful and pointless cruelty enacted. Part of the dread conveyed by the poem is the sense of repetition: the child's curiosity and terror, repeated as the torture is repeated; the children unable to stay away from the scene of desperate suffering; the curiosity about death; and the (other) final mystery, what is the grandmother *seeing* when she stares at the dead cats? This is memory that does not seem to fulfill the wish for connection with a powerful heritage. Linking the past with the present evokes a sense of recurring panic, a scene of horror and, finally, an inexplicable silence – that of death and of the grandmother's gaze.

For Halfe, with memory comes voice, a truth indicated only in the title of "Crying for Voice."[35] Memory lives "inside marrow," and to get at it is to go through a process of detailed dissection, clearing passages, purifying and replacing some aspects of self. Each stanza of this poem identifies a necessary action in the speaker's quest for voice: "I must pull frog," and "pry its webbed feet / from snails in / my throat." Weasel will be invited to untangle braids; the "brain / eyes and tongue" of duck, rabbit, and fish must be boiled and consumed. Finding voice requires pulling out as well as taking in. Frog and tapeworm must be removed to make room for "fresh blood." Bible and tripe must be boiled and boiled and boiled to cook up this "soup," and she will "Suck marrow from tiny bones" to "fill the place / where frog left slime." The last stanza treats memory with ambivalence:

I'm fluttering wind
tobacco floating
against my face
mosquitoes up my nostrils
swatting memories
inside marrow.

The spiritual association of tobacco and wind, and the comic discomfort of mosquitoes up the nose, mix uneasily with the floating image of swatting – memories are like mosquitoes, an irritation, but "inside marrow"? The absence of a subject doing the swatting – the stanza implies the "I" – contributes to the free feeling, the fluttering and floating that "I" has achieved. The marrow sucked from tiny bones may or may not be the marrow that holds memories. What is clear in this poem is the turning of inside to outside, and outside to inside (that is, other and self shift and shift again), of the openings of throat and gut and intestine, the clearing out of innermost spaces and deepest places and, most of all, the emptying and filling in of a long process of finding voice.

In "Bone Lodge," Halfe bonds with the creature world, asserting her connection in a profound unity:

> I'm meat and bones,
> dust and straw,
> caterpillars and ants
> hummingbird and crow.
>
> Of these I know
> in the bones of the lodge.[36]

The bones are central to her image of embodied and spiritual life, and the centre of the bone is its marrow.[37] In Halfe, memory is seldom abstracted from the active voice of the poem speaking its engagement with the permeable animal, spiritual, earthly, and embodied life of the female subject. The specific memories and the evocation of legend and spirit world experience come together to produce memory as praxis, a full blurring of the categories of memory that Maracle establishes and an indication of the ways Joy Harjo's trope of the spiral might work.

I will close this preliminary consideration of memory with a reading of Harjo's "Skeleton of Winter."[38] In this poem, memory is an "other-sight" that the speaker ("I") attempts to achieve. She has remained "silent / as a whiteman's watch / keeping time." The image of the alien, disconnected circularity of the whiteman's watch, that way of keeping time, gags Harjo's speech, but the figure is a simile, and the link between her silence and herself is not integral. Rather, the implication is one of waiting. And although "It is almost too dark / for vision," the speaker finds that she has not lost the possibility of sight or speech. It is memory that allows sight, despite the darkness ("and still I see"). To figure memory as a type of seeing is to suggest, as Armstrong does, that amnesia is blindness. But Harjo does not limit memory to a single sense. As Seremetakis (in this chapter's opening epigraph) asserts, memory is a meta-sense with the power to bridge and cross all other senses.

In "Skeleton of Winter," Harjo makes all the senses part of memory: "And sound is light, is / movement. The sun revolves / and sings." Time is neither dark nor silent. With the other-sight visions of dances and births, ancient symbols are seen to be alive. The female body of the speaker takes in viscerally the vision and its effects: "A tooth-hard rocking / in my belly comes back." The labour pains of memory bring sound, echoes, to consciousness: "something echoes / all forgotten dreams, / in winter." The implication that return, echo, revolution are all in play, all part of what is to be seen and seen again, takes memory utterly out of a fixed place. The last stanza delivers the insight gained from other-sight:

I am memory alive
not just a name
but an intricate part
of this web of motion,
meaning: earth, sky, stars circling
my heart
centrifugal.

Harjo invites a connection between individual identity (a name) and cosmic sensibility. The meta-sense is not merely sensory. The lines are ambivalent: everything works in centrifugal relation to the heart – or the heart ("my heart," she says) circles the whole web of motion, the web of meaning. To say "I am memory alive" is to say memory lives in me; I live in memory; memory and I are one being; memory (that wild abstraction) is essential to identity in its narrowest (the personal name) and its widest (cosmic) implications. Again, we see that Barthes' historian, in dechronologizing, coalesces with the poet. Barthes suggests, as I mentioned earlier, that this act of speech restores non-linear time – and the gift of that time is "a deep space" that "recalls the mythic time of the ancient cosmogonies."[39] I do not want to belabour Barthes' flight of poetic speech or insight too crudely. But when, in an interview with Bill Moyers, Harjo responds to Moyers' observation that Harjo herself is "memory alive," and Harjo says, "We *all* are," Harjo seems to push the link that memory and speech make between historian and poet into a realm of the sacred that is culturally inclusive.[40] This is not to suggest that differences – cultural, historical, personal, and genetic – do not matter, nor that they do not make both meaning and matter.[41] The cultural inclusivity that I read in Harjo's "we *all* are [memory alive]" is more like a kind of possibility and a responsibility. The "Breakfast of the Spirit" that Dumont celebrates, the demanding search that Armstrong requires, and the sucking of bone marrow that brings Halfe to her truth – all these speak to memory and from memory. The *idea* of memory and the content of memory come together, and (as Ferron sings) they come apart. Those specific points and moments are what give memory its weight, and the force of memory is what holds us, individually and culturally, to our Earth ("gravity," says Harjo). Finally, then, in response to Krupat's view that there is no memory in the blood: Why not? You will find it everywhere else, if you look for it.

NOTES

1 Kenneth Lincoln, *Native American Renaissance* (Berkeley: University of California Press, 1983), 8.

2 N. Scott Momaday, quoted in Arnold Krupat, *The Voice in the Margin: Native American Literature and the Canon* (Berkeley: University of California Press, 1989), 13.

3 Krupat, *Voice in the Margin,* 13. Given that new genes are being identified all the time, I am not sure how Krupat could be quite so certain about this, even on the biological level. Readers may be interested in Thomas King's anti-essentialist stance on the issue. See, for example, the Introduction to *All My Relations: An Anthology of Contemporary Native Fiction,* ed. Thomas King (Toronto: McClelland and Stewart, 1990), ix-xvi.

4 Krupat, *Voice in the Margin,* 12-13.

5 Arnold Krupat, *The Turn to the Native: Studies in Criticism and Culture* (Lincoln: University of Nebraska Press, 1996), 48n17. Krupat is making an urgent plea for the development of a responsible critical language that "might mediate" between Native American and other fiction, an informed comparative criticism that would not "foreclose possibilities of understanding" but would allow "cross-cultural translation or ethnocriticism" that would deepen our understanding of all literatures. See his chapter "Postcolonialism, Ideology, and Native American Literature" in *The Turn to the Native* for a full discussion of these views.

6 Jodi Lundgren discusses aspects of these issues in an important article on racial and cultural syncreticity, in which she examines the emphasis various Métis writers (Beatrice Culleton, Maria Campbell, and Lee Maracle) place on culture rather than race. See Lundgren, "'Being a Half-breed': Discourses of Race and Cultural Syncreticity in the Works of Three Metis Women Writers," *Canadian Literature* 144 (Spring 1995): 62-77.

7 Lee Maracle, "Skyros Bruce: First Voice of Contemporary Native Poetry," *Gatherings: The En'owkin Journal of First North American Peoples* 2 (1991): 88.

8 Joy Harjo, "Ancestral Voices: Interview with Bill Moyers," and "The Circular Dream: Interview with Laura Coltelli," in Laura Coltelli, ed., *The Spiral of Memory: Interviews/Joy Harjo* (Ann Arbor: University of Michigan Press, 1996), 36-49, 60-74.
9 Laura Coltelli, "Introduction: The Transforming Power of Joy Harjo's Poetry," in Coltelli, *The Spiral of Memory,* 9.
10 Ibid.
11 This discussion appears under the general heading "From History to Reality" in Roland Barthes, *The Rustle of Language,* trans. Richard Howard (New York: Hill, 1986), 127-40.
12 Ibid., 130.
13 Ibid.
14 Ibid. Although I am taking Barthes out of context, I believe his assertions illuminate aspects of this discussion.
15 Ibid., 130-31.
16 C. Nadia Seremetakis, *The Senses Still: Perception and Memory as Material Culture in Modernity* (Chicago: University of Chicago Press, 1994), 4.
17 Ibid.
18 When I presented a version of this essay in Bombay, with an emphasis on the debates staged by Krupat and Momaday on the possibility of memory in the blood, I was disconcerted to observe how much of a non-issue it was to the Indian scholars I was addressing. Of course there was memory in the blood; it was too obvious to argue about. This was a corrective experience for me in that it revealed my assumption that most scholars held a scientific perspective (although the scientific perspective can also be debated, for not all genes are identified are they?) and has helped me shape this chapter in more complicated ways. I owe the women of SNDT (the Women's University) my thanks for their helpful comments.
19 Marilyn Dumont, "Memoirs of a Really Good Brown Girl," *A Really Good Brown Girl* (London, ON: Brick Books, 1996), 51.
20 Kimberly Blaeser's comic poem about being mistaken for her mother ends with the arch and pointed query, "Wonder if I'm what they call living history?" She is, of course, mocking the return to a notion of Indians as vanishing peoples that some current critical positions seem to articulate. Blaeser, "Living History," *Trailing You* (Greenfield Center, NY: Greenfield Review Press, 1994), 5.
21 Dumont, "The White Judges," *A Really Good Brown Girl,* 11-12.
22 Seremetakis, *The Senses Still,* 4.
23 Ibid., 10.
24 Dumont, "Breakfast of the Spirit," *A Really Good Brown Girl,* 41.
25 Jeannette Armstrong, "History Lesson," *Breath Tracks* (Stratford/Vancouver: Williams-Wallace/Theytus Books, 1991), 28-29.
26 Barthes, *The Rustle of Language,* 130.
27 Kimberly Blaeser examines revisionist treatments of Bible stories in Native literature in "Pagans Rewriting the Bible: Heterodoxy and the Representation of Spirituality in Native American Literature," *ARIEL: A Review of International English Literature* 25, 1 (1994): 12.

28 Armstrong, "Threads of Old Memory," *Breath Tracks,* 58-61. I have discussed this poem elsewhere at greater length and with a different focus. See Jeanne Perreault, "Speaking to Newcomers in Their Language," *Open Letter* 9, 2 (1995): 29-36.
29 Louise Halfe, *Bear Bones and Feathers* (Regina: Coteau Books, 1994.)
30 Halfe generously provides a glossary of the Cree words and phrases.
31 Halfe, "Nòhkom Àtayohkàn 1," *Bear Bones and Feathers,* 10.
32 Halfe, "Nòhkom Àtayohkàn 2," *Bear Bones and Feathers,* 11.
33 Halfe, "Nòhkom, Medicine Bear," *Bear Bones and Feathers,* 13-14.
34 Halfe, "Off with Their Heads," *Bear Bones and Feathers,* 15-16.
35 Halfe, "Crying for Voice," *Bear Bones and Feathers,* 6.
36 Halfe, "Bone Lodge," *Bear Bones and Feathers,* 3.
37 Examining anthropological practice and implication, Seremetakis looks at Greek exhumation, during which "the sensory presence of the dusted bones of the dead reawaken the memory of past commensal exchanges with the dead. Ignited by the collective memories invested in the bone as emotive artifact, the exhumers create a commensal ritual grounded on material substances." See Seremetakis, *The Senses Still,* 37. The materiality of this study limits its direct use for my reading of Halfe, but the figurative reverberations are strong.
38 Joy Harjo, "Skeleton of Winter," *She Had Some Horses* (New York: Thunder's Mouth Press, 1983), 30-31.
39 Barthes, *The Rustle of Language,* 130-31.
40 Harjo, "Ancestral Voices," 49.
41 Does *genetic* mean "racial"? I do not know, and the differences and similarities among these poets and poems have not told me.

12

To Spirit Walk the Letter and the Law

Gender, Race, and Representational Violence in Rudy Wiebe and Yvonne Johnson's *Stolen Life: The Journey of a Cree Woman*

JULIA EMBERLEY

> *Dad stands beside me, crying. A man who looks like a doctor bends over me. He opens my mouth. He says to anybody who is listening, "How do you sew up a tongue?"*
>
> – *Rudy Wiebe and Yvonne Johnson,*
> Stolen Life: The Journey of a Cree Woman

In *Stolen Life: The Journey of a Cree Woman,* Rudy Wiebe narrates the life of Yvonne Johnson, who, until 2001, was serving a life sentence for murder in the Okimaw Ohci Healing Lodge for federally sentenced Aboriginal women in south Saskatchewan.[1] Wiebe – a well-known Canadian fiction writer, historian, and cultural critic – reconstructs, at Johnson's request, her life story. The result is, in part, a serious indictment of racism and the legal systems in postcolonial Canada and the United States, including their policing operations. In addition to challenging juridical institutions and post-colonization, their book also raises important questions about the meaning of justice. In this chapter, I examine Wiebe's narrative framing of Johnson's life story and how this book addresses the representational violence of colonization to bring justice to Indigenous people in general and Yvonne Johnson in particular. While Wiebe focuses on racism in the legal system and its effect on the death of Johnson's brother Earl, Johnson's experience of sexual violence, although significant to the story, nevertheless remains supplemental to the narrative's emphasis on Earl's death. Sexual violence supplements the text of colonial violence when it is perceived through an essentialist lens and appears immutable, inevitable and, thus, ahistorical. In the case of representational violence and the question of how the law adjudicates the legitimate or illegitimate use of violence, the supplementarity of the text underscores the letter of the law but remains in the shadows as a sort of subtext. This apparitional-like story serves as the spirit of the law not only in the double sense of being a truer meaning than a literal translation of legal interpretation would allow but also in the sense of being apparitional as in immaterial and non-real. Both the ahistorical and immaterial stance toward sexual violence in colonization ensures its secondary narrative status, and yet, embedded in Johnson's testimony, I would argue, lies a different kind of power that breaks the frame of the law of narrative and transforms the official story of colonial violence.

My approach to *Stolen Life* is based, in part, on Jo-ann Archibald's theoretical work on Indigenous storytelling practices. One type of storywork, as Archibald terms it, that exemplifies Johnson's contributions to *Stolen Life* is the life-experience story. Archibald's work on Indigenous storytelling contributes to an alternative framework for reading Indigenous literary practices, as does that of Kimberly Blaeser, who writes, "We must first 'know the stories of our people' and then 'make our own story too' ... We must 'be aware of the way they [Western literary theorists] change the stories we already know' for only with that awareness can we protect the integrity of the Native American story."[2] Educated within a Western literary and theoretical tradition, I inevitably bring an inventory of knowledge to my reading of Indigenous women's writings. What I would like to do here, however, is attempt to articulate that knowledge with the new insights I have learned from Archibald's and Blaeser's work.

In Indigenous feminisms, First Nation women's experiences, their ways of knowing and being in the world, are central to theorizing racism and sexism in the colonial and postcolonial contexts of Canada. With my background in anti-racist materialist feminism, I also understand that intimate violence and colonization are embodied, material, and contingent, which is to say that the articulation of racism and sexism is constitutive of historical practices that operate in and through bodies, nations, the law, and literary (auto)biographies. Johnson's life story and Wiebe's narrative framing of that story tell a story about how intimate violence and racism function as articulated systemic modes of colonial power. In telling this story, however, Wiebe represents racial difference through the use of male and female gendered categories. He uses gendered categories to naturalize racism as masculine and sexism as feminine. This ideological blind spot maintains and furthers postcolonial power and also reproduces representational violence in its narrative construction. Blaeser's attention to the question of integrity in the Native American story furthers my understanding of how sexual violence is part of the colonial and postcolonial destruction of the integrity of the storyline, an integral part because it speaks to the destruction of the integrity of the body as well as the mind, the spirit, and the emotions.

Although I am critical of Wiebe's gendered politics in the text, I can also appreciate that Johnson's desire to restore integrity to her life and her life story established a relationship between Wiebe and herself based on principles of reciprocity and respect that cast Wiebe in the role of being a witness to her life. I read Wiebe's involvement with Johnson through the following words by Archibald that demonstrate how a work such as *Stolen Life* can help to locate "principles that address the politics of accessing publishers and producing publications, the authority to tell stories, and the need to establish collaborative relationships between First Nations Elders and storytellers and non-First Nations educators."[3] It remains to be said that not only is Wiebe a witness to Johnson's life, the reader of their book – myself included, of course – is also a witness on multiple levels, including witnessing Wiebe's own account of his position as a witness to Johnson's life and storytelling. Often, as Archibald notes, "the power of a story is shown through stories about a story."[4] There is no doubt in my mind that *Stolen Life* is a powerful text. What follows positions my anti-racist materialist feminist reading practices within the framework of Indigenous storywork to further understand the representational histories of postcolonial and sexual violence and their transformation through telling life stories.

On Being an Object of Colonial Violence

Patricia Monture-Angus notes the overwhelming attention given to violence in First Nations people's lives and how this attention rarely amounts to a sufficient analysis of the problem. In fact, more often than not, it ends up naturalizing the violence further as a seemingly inevitable condition of Aboriginal existence.[5] Nowhere, perhaps, is this more true than in the context of sexual violence toward First Nations women and children, a context in which justice is hard to come by, if the violent rape and murder of Helen Betty Osborne and the sixteen years it took to reach a conviction is any indication.[6] In their analysis of the specificity of colonial violence toward

Indigenous women and children, Anne McGillivray and Brenda Comaskey maintain that colonialism

> shaped the nature, severity and rate of intimate violence in Indigenous communities. It has influenced internal and external evaluation of the violence and created an environment in which it thrives as learned behaviour, transmitted across generations, silenced by culture. The reduction of women's roles in tribal economies and politics, the 'decentring' of motherhood in mission schooling, and the patriarchy embedded in the Indian Act, in its regulation of band membership and electoral privileges, are entwined with the targeting of childhood for 'civilization.' Residential schooling and out-group adoption separated children from mother, clan, and culture. This past continues to speak in the dynamics of intimate violence in Aboriginal communities.[7]

In her analysis of the murder of Pamela George, a woman of the Saulteaux (Ojibway) Nation and a mother of two young children who was killed in April 1995 in Regina, Saskatchewan, Sherene Razack argues that the confluence of racism, sexual violence, and spatiality created conditions for deracing the violence done to George in the legal account of what happened to her. Razack writes that "while it is certainly patriarchy that produces men whose sense of identity is achieved through brutalizing a woman, the men's and the courts' capacity to dehumanize Pamela George came from their understanding of her as the (gendered) racial Other whose degradation confirmed their own identities as white – that is, as men entitled to the land and the full benefits of citizenship."[8]

These approaches to intimate violence in the lives of First Nations women stress the interlocking contingencies of race, sexuality, and gender categories and their uneven and unequal distribution in the historical context of colonization. This understanding of how specific contingencies intersect under different hegemonic historical conditions draws attention to the fact that multiple signifiers of identity are neither universal nor static but mobile signs deployed within and against specific bodies, spaces, and institutions. In other words, it is not the identity of an Indigenous body that determines its experience of representational, political, and economic violence, it is how these bodies are turned into objects of violence within colonial institutions to maintain the equilibrium of colonial power. In the cases of Helen Betty Osborne and Pamela George, colonial power determined the inscription of their bodies as objects of racial, gendered, and sexual violence. Johnson's traumatic experience of sexual violence lies at the core of her experience of colonization. But until this specific form of colonial domination is recognized, the narrative containment of her story cannot bring about justice. In Wiebe's account of Johnson's stolen life, the trauma of her experience of sexual violence is displaced through another form of violence, the violence of writing and the law of narrative that Wiebe imposes on her fragments of memory to achieve a sequential and coherent narrative form. If justice is to come, it must be newly defined through Johnson's account of her body and through the material realities of her self-expression. At a time when the concept of legal pluralism (the multiple, and sometimes combined, use of Aboriginal law and Canadian state law) is gaining ground in the judicial system of Canada, Yvonne Johnson's life story foregrounds the problem of how the legal system can respond meaningfully to the specificity of First Nations women's and children's experience of sexualized and domestic colonial violence.[9]

Not All Vaginas Speak Equally

In a witness statement Yvonne Johnson wrote and signed 2 November 1992, which was recorded by Detective Linda Billings of the Child Abuse Unit in the Edmonton Police Service, Johnson recounts her first memory of sexual abuse at the age of two:

> My first attack happened when I was between two to three-years old. We lived in a pink house, next door to a two-storey house and down from the railroad tracks ... The attack on my body was by a grown man, by my brother Leon [eight and a half years old at that time], and later on by three other boys, one was tall with red hair. And one boy was our neighbour, and would be in later years as well.
>
> What started my rape was our babysitter [the grown man] caught Leon messing around with me behind the fridge in the kitchen. The man told him, in other words, Leon was not doing it right. I was placed on the kitchen table and the bottom half of my body stripped. He was pointing things out to Leon, saying things like this is this, and this is this. And this is where you put your prick ...
>
> I cry and try to crawl off the table. The man would yell at me and slap my ass. At first. And put me on my back. He hurt me I think by putting his finger up my cunt. I'd cry and try to get away as I was crawling off the table,

> then he started to poke my ass as well. He yelled at Leon for letting me get away ...
>
> If anyone tried to come in the kitchen, like other kids, he'd get Leon to give them a sucker and chase them away. The guy beat me to shut me up, he banged my head on the table. Then when someone came he'd put his cock in my mouth and almost kill me. But also, he'd bend my feet, to where I swear he broke them, to spread my legs and poke at me. I think he went to put lard or oil on his hands, and then Leon would bend my feet.[10]

Wiebe's account of Yvonne Johnson's traumatic experience of sexual abuse represents a scar on the surface of late colonization. It marks a time and place when and where the child's body was penetrated, both materially and metaphorically, with significance by colonial power. It would be tempting to try to suture this body back together like Mary Shelley's monster in *Frankenstein*. But although the pieces come from apparently normal and whole bodies, the reassembled body is never quite the same, never quite right; rather, it appears as an unharmonious and inelegant form riddled with unruly, infantile, and violent impulses. Neither the representation of an idealized wholeness nor an abject Other is sufficient to understand the material realities of colonial violence inscribed through and on the Indigenous child's body.

In the case of sexual violence toward children, body knowledge is often remembered in later years in a fragmented and disassembled way. This partial knowledge has become a way of identifying – and in some contexts a way of dismissing – the truth claims that emerge from women's memories of childhood abuse. Thus, representational strategies that seek to tell the truth of the body's pain, suffering, joy, and pleasure must both re-member knowledge of the body and dis-member officially sanctioned truths as to what constitutes this knowledge. This simultaneous process of re-membering and dis-membering constitutes what I would call an analytics of (dis)memberment and serves as a methodological framework for the following discussion of the significance of Yvonne Johnson's body to Rudy Wiebe's construction of the history of colonial injustice to First Nations peoples.

Early in the text, in a chapter titled "My Eyes Became My Voice," Wiebe skilfully weaves his first face-to-face encounter with Johnson in June of 1993 at P4W, the federal prison for women in Kingston, Ontario, into the fabric of her autobiographical narrative of a childhood spent in Butte, Montana.[11] Wiebe separates his textual reconstruction of this initial interview from

Johnson's autobiographical narrative by inserting *Yvonne,* in bold print, at the beginning of her excerpts. Although Wiebe constructs his own voice, as it were, as the voice of the author, the back-and-forth dialogue between Wiebe's account of this meeting and Johnson's journal entries questions the foundations of this authorial position. Initially, Wiebe's retelling of Yvonne Johnson's so-called story is a way of bringing order to the chaos that has been her life. Writing is a means to establish coherency and, thus, to make sense of the violence that has been done to Johnson and the violence she has participated in: "She's smiling at me; she has sent me tapes and videos as well, but they are so difficult to organize, her memories are so interwoven and intersnarled, that I've begged her to write only, however it comes and she remembers, but write it down; write, please" (Wiebe and Johnson, 11). Eventually, however, Wiebe situates Johnson's voice as the counternarrative to the law of narrative. Johnson says,

> I guess when I talk I express myself like I listened, story form ... I tell little stories so you can see, live, feel what I am trying to explain to you. Like I'm figuring it out, out loud. I'm always all over the place. People say I can't stay on one topic; sometimes when I just say things head-on, point blank, it drives them crazy to have to listen to me ... But the Elders say that storytelling is a gift too. If a person with a story can go deep, where people are angry, sad, where they're hiding thoughts and emotions, raise the past they've maybe forgotten and can't really recognize any more, push them to spirit-walk into themselves – to do that with a story is a gift. (ibid., 11-12)

Although the remnants of his determination to stick to the written word linger on the margins of this dialogue – "if she wants to tell her story, her words must be on paper" (ibid., 22) – Wiebe eventually submits to the limits posed by his knowledge of writing: "After forty years of work at writing, I think I know a bit about making stories, but I don't grasp the impossibilities of this one; not yet" (ibid., 24).

Of course, it is the book, *Stolen Life,* that will bring Johnson's story into the light of day, but Wiebe cannot tell the story without signalling the *impossibilities* of doing so. He tries, for example, to correct the swerves and swings of Yvonne's narrative: "I try to bring her back to her original subject: Cecilia in psychiatric care after Earl's death. And she shifts instantly, as sharp as all her memories are. In details they can be as precise as a photograph" (ibid., 85). And yet Yvonne cannot remember faces: "Why did the

Creator give me these intricate memories, this photographic mind, and yet allows me only bits and pieces of my past? So many tiny, exact snapshots branded on me. Why can't I see who the person was?" (Wiebe and Johnson, 99). To tell *her* story, to *write* her story, cannot be anything but difficult given the realities of oppression Johnson has experienced; nevertheless, she does have access to the oral and visual articulation of her experience: "If I have a visual memory, I don't doubt myself. I don't doubt the houses I lived in, in Butte, Montana" (ibid., 25).

It is through the lens of Johnson's visual memory that the reader gains entry to her early childhood memories. These memories are divided between two rental houses: the pink house, close to the open mine where her father and mother worked, and the white house, a grand house vacated by its wealthy owners and yet affordable because of the downward-bound economic conditions of the time. Johnson's notion of visual memory is linked entirely to these domestic spatial orientations. The pink and white codification of Yvonne's memories of poverty and pseudo-grandeur falls deliberately within their respective race- and class-coded boundaries, not to mention the significance of the white house to colonial governance. Whatever upward mobility the white house may represent, the spatial frontiers of Johnson's working-class family's economic situation remain firmly intact. Johnson's visual memory – along with her capacity to spirit walk through these modes of visual, spatial, corporeal, and spiritual mediations – becomes a source of healing and knowledge that enables her to break the silence about her oppression and to release her incarcerated voice. Breaking that silence, however, must be mediated through language, through the history of how Johnson's body became inscribed with value and meaning and how she resignified a historico-corporeality to re-member her life. In recounting her early childhood during the late 1950s and early 1960s, Johnson examines how the duality of predators and victims governed relationships both inside and outside the home. The explosive, frightening fights that broke out as a result of alcohol and drug abuse led Johnson to fear for her body within the house and family. Making use of her visual memory, she interprets two family photographs from the perspective of this threatening domestic violence to herself and, by contrast, to the very different sort of violence to which her older brother Earl will be subjected. In response to one photo, she describes herself sitting on her brother Leon's lap, "me with my little bare legs parted." And in response to another black-and-white photo, she writes that it was

> taken in the yard [and] shows only us kids and the Butte landscape ... and finally me, the littlest, smiling so desperately, with my arms wrapped tight around my chest, holding myself together ... and beside [Leon], tallest of all, my handsome brother Earl. He's going on fifteen, smiling, his heavy hair greased down in a curl on the right side of his face – he spent a lot of time getting the flip in his hair just so before he left for school – leaning forward a little like a Cree peering at you, his hands behind his back, and wearing a white T-shirt with a dark horizontal band. It looks like a wide rope cinched tight around his chest. (Wiebe and Johnson, 27-28)

Yvonne's images of the vulnerability of her child body and Earl's chest bound by rope anticipate the main events that will irrevocably shape Yvonne Johnson's life: her experience of sexual violence and the death, in prison, of Earl, who was the victim of police brutality and racial violence, which was covered up as suicide. It is this heteronormative logic, in which the Indigenous female body is coded as sexual object and the Indigenous male body is reduced to a representation of primitive male aggression, that overdetermines Wiebe's representation of Yvonne's and Earl Johnson's bodies as objects of colonial violence. Within this oppositional logic of sexual difference, domestic violence and sexual violence are not part of the official narrative of colonial injustice. Rather, Johnson's body and her experience of sexual violence will come to supplement the representation of the official and unofficial narratives of her brother's death.

The tension between the writerly power of the professional class that Wiebe embodies and the oral and visual power of Johnson's account of her dispossession informs the back-and-forth motion of the text, its interruptions, its narrative dissociations between past and present, its humour, surrealities, and the jarring distance between places and people: "And Yvonne is talking; truly talking. Sometimes it has to come from behind the black curtain of her hair, but she talks; her amazing, unstoppable, now utterable words trigger one memory after another and she follows that spoor like a track leading deeper and deeper into a dark forest" (Wiebe and Johnson, 31). Wiebe's romantic metaphor of the dark forest elides the integral realities of Johnson's body and its inscription of the economically depressed city of Butte, Montana, as the site of her memories and their reconstruction. Her words are like spoors that, in turn, are like a track, a map to guide Wiebe into the dark forest that is Johnson's life, the dark continent that is her landscape of memory and dispossession. The problem with Wiebe's reduction of the Indigenous female body to nature is the way in which he deploys it as a racial and sexual metonymic code for the land and territorial dispossession. In this equation, Indigenous women are neither the subject of nor the subjects in themselves of dispossession.

An Anatomy of Pain

Yvonne Johnson was born with a severe abnormality, an open palate: "Where my nose, top lip, gums, and roof of my mouth should have been, there was only folded tissue that left a gap in my upper mouth" (Wiebe and Johnson, 29). During her childhood, she received numerous reconstructive surgeries. In the book, the disfigurement of Johnson's childhood face becomes a metonymic reminder of her struggle to learn how to talk. But when Johnson says that "learning to talk took years," Wiebe's framing of her narrative produces a double layer of meaning that transcodes her physical challenge into an analytical one (ibid., 35). Johnson's birth with a cleft palate, her numerous surgeries, cosmetic as well as life-preserving, represent a problematic in Wiebe's narrative of coming face to face with the body of the Indigenous woman as the formative contradiction of colonial power.

The chapter titled "A Killing in the Family," in which Wiebe narrates Earl Johnson's death, begins with Johnson's father, Clarence, describing his response to Yvonne's birth defect: "double cleft lip and palate, the doctor called it. There was just blood in the middle of her face; he had to clean it out before he could make her breathe" (ibid., 52). Clarence shows Wiebe a photo from the clinic of Yvonne's tiny face: "A month after birth, eyes squeezed shut above the unrecognizable center of a tiny countenance, labeled on the back 'Uncorrected.' Then, six months later, 'Beginning Correction,' after the first surgery. The long, excruciating 'correction' of a 'mistake' – made by whom? – the unaware irony of medical terms" (ibid.). Correcting a mistake becomes one of the text's unspoken yet guiding tropes, as in to correct the mistaken assumption that Earl committed suicide. Rather, his death, according to Clarence, was doctored up to look like suicide. The mistake in Yvonne's body, however, is viewed as a result of natural and hereditary causes. In the oppositional contingencies of artifice-nature and savagery-civilization, Yvonne's face is coded as natural and bloody, whereas Earl's death is figured as an effect of deception, lies, and cover-ups. Although Yvonne's body can be altered and fixed by medical surgery, its meaning nevertheless remains immutable, an original mistake tied to nature's authorship and its unrelenting power over the determination of the human form. Yvonne's body becomes a conduit for telling the truth about Earl's death, as if his story must be discharged through this immutable body if the truth concerning his death is to come to light. Not surprisingly, Johnson writes, "I am like a conductor, not a human being" (Wiebe and Johnson, 11).

In another mediatory role, Wiebe describes Johnson sitting on her mom's lap as she drives into the woods and playing with forming spit in her mouth: "But I was stubborn even then when I really wanted something, and I practiced and practiced what would be so easy for any ordinary kid – to hang out of the truck window in the rushing air and try to gather a big gob of spit together into the tip of my mouth behind my lips and let it fly out just right, sail round and full and aimed so exactly to carry on the wind and bounce big off the back duals. And, finally, I did it!" (ibid., 54). This thick description, told in Yvonne's narrative voice, turns the liquid discharge from her mouth into a trail from which to follow Earl's story. What issues from Johnson's body will fill up the gaps and holes of memory, the empty spaces that, for Wiebe, represent poison: "And the Pink House where Yvonne's first memories emerge is suspended somewhere in the invisible air over that black lake, an infected space for memory only. But as indelible as poison to her ... Every house Yvonne lived in in Butte is now nothing but space" (ibid., 55, 56). But this is not a nothing space: it is the domesticated space of Johnson's life and her material experience of violence, a space that contained her body, rendered it vulnerable to sexual violence, and silenced her voice.

It is within the space of the same page that Wiebe narrates Clarence's memory of his own domestic violence and Earl's death. Domestic violence, however, is downplayed in relation to Earl's death. Clarence sees himself as the victim of the judicial system and refuses to pay the fine set by the judge as punishment for his domestic violence toward Cecilia. He would rather stay in jail. Cecilia has a full-time job, however, and needs Clarence to watch the children while she goes to work: "I said no, it was me got assaulted. I'd stay my time. So she brought the judge over, he told me he'd go easy on the fine. So I came out" (ibid., 57).

Clarence chose to remain, living alone, in Butte to unravel the truth of Earl's death. He collected newspaper articles and information to prove, over and over again, the injustice of it. The most plausible account Clarence gives of Earl's death is that Earl was being threatened by a man with whom he was once friends, the two men stole some cigarettes together, and Earl confessed to the crime. His testimony, however, indicted his "best buddy." His friend then went to Vietnam and had "a very rough time." He returned to Butte, "vowing, according to rumours floating around the bars, to get even with Earl" (ibid., 67). Wiebe, however, includes a speculative, if not mysterious, comment by Johnson on a moment of flight that takes place just before

Earl's death. It hints at something that remains unsaid and unacknowledged, precisely because Johnson cannot remember or did not know the reason for this act of flight (Wiebe and Johnson, 61). What Johnson does remember about Earl's death appears in the form of an inexplicable and mysterious event. Although she is hundreds of miles away from Earl at the time of his death, Johnson feels something like an electrical jolt to her body that throws her off her feet. The chapter concludes with Yvonne telling her mother that Earl's shadow follows her on the walls of the porch and plays hide and seek with her in the forest. In the shadow world of the outdoors and nature, Yvonne communes with Earl's discontented spirit. Johnson's brother, like her ancestor Big Bear, had been hanged in prison because of colonial injustice. Johnson's inability to remember why the family made the trip to Canada contains, if not justifies, the narrative absence of another story. Furthermore, this narrative absence is then supplemented by Johnson's mystical experience of Earl's death.

What comes through in Wiebe's reconstruction of Clarence's account of Earl's death is that it was the family that was somehow being threatened and that the family was ultimately destroyed by Earl's death. But what exactly that threat was, we do not know. At the level of the Oedipal imaginary, the greatest threat to the integrity of the patriarchal family would be incest (between mother and son). Interestingly, Wiebe's recounting of Earl's death does hint at the problem of incest in Yvonne Johnson's family. But somehow Clarence's perpetual retelling and reconstruction of Earl's death acts like a protective shield against the contamination of incest, against the writing of a story of father-daughter incest that would not only threaten the foundation of the Oedipal, patriarchal family but also utterly demystify its basis of power. Although the chapter ends with Clarence and Wiebe sharing their grief together over the inexplicable death of Earl – the consolation of fraternal bonding over the melancholic mourning for a lost son – the other narrative of incest suggestively woven into the text of Earl's death hangs like a loose thread until Wiebe informs the reader that Johnson will eventually bring legal charges against her father for sexual abuse.

The official narrative event of Earl's death and Clarence's unofficial rewriting of that narrative sets up a cycle of competing truths. The reader is drawn into the gap left between the official story and its counternarrative, only to find him- or herself still listening to a conversation between Wiebe and his Other author but unable to complete the speech act: "I have endless memories without faces. Random, separate memories with no story line, but sprinkled with possible truth" (ibid., 75). "It took years for the words with which I could explain or defend myself to be gradually, and with great pain, carved and sewn into my face" (Wiebe and Johnson, 78). Yvonne Johnson's birth defect and corrective surgeries bring a material and embodied textuality to her experience of silence. Like the fusing of her lips in a radical surgical procedure designed as a corrective measure that would eventually lead to speech, Johnson's capacity to overcome the limits of her physical reality are undone by the metonymic use of her body to act as a silent conduit for Earl's death from colonial and racial violence. The specificity of the material reality of Yvonne's embodied experience under the same regime of colonial and racial violence remains unrecognizable, however, because of her role as the conductor of Earl's death.

In the chapter that follows Wiebe and Clarence's conversation, accounts of sexual abuse, rape, and incest rupture the narrative to such a degree that the chapter remains unfocused, as it were. The residue of Earl's death still clings to memories of the family: "Earl's death remains like a mountain divide in the collective memory of the entire family; at any moment of speech or writing Yvonne will swing to that time, detailed incidents leaping into consciousness" (ibid., 92). The interventions titled "When Did This Happen? How?" that preface Yvonne's narrative accounts of sexual abuse add to the confusion – the lack of coherency, the fragments, the bits and pieces: "This was my childhood: the world even in my home is uncontrollable and can at any moment burst into violence. I can only react. If I do get caught, I was either careless or asking for it. I am always guilty." "Never sit with your legs apart, never forget to wear long pants under your dress or they'll see your panties if you forget yourself and play as a child will play, never talk back ... Be always alert and ready to outmaneuver danger before it's close enough to catch you" (ibid., 78). Wiebe intervenes: "As Yvonne and I struggle together with notebooks, letters, public records, and phone calls to find some order of chronology and fact in her past life, we need to begin again – she sees so much of her life, and consequently memory, as contained in the circle of repetition – we must begin again with her childhood place: Butte, Montana" (ibid., 80).

After Earl's death, Cecilia commits herself to a psychiatric ward. She then becomes the first and only woman truck driver at the mine (ibid., 84, 87). Another aftershock related to Earl's death is Leon's attempt to hang himself. Yvonne states,

> sometimes I think there might have been some kind of connection between Earl's death and Leon ... Perhaps that would explain why Mom became so

> obsessed with protecting Leon. Even to the point of selling me out, as it sometimes seemed to me – I don't know – or maybe I already do know and just can't remember enough to understand, but no one now, neither Mom nor Leon nor my sisters, will talk to me about this. Only Kathy says she believes I believe what I'm looking for is true – but then she cries, she won't tell me what she remembers. Dad visits and supports me as he can, but he won't, or just can't, try to explain anything about this either. (Wiebe and Johnson, 93)

Both Clarence and Leon are implicated in sexual violence toward Yvonne. Earl saves her life in one horrifying incident when she is almost murdered. The question of time is important – hence "When Did This Happen? How?" Did these events take place, for example, just before Earl's death, and is his death related to them? Yvonne remembers that Leon delivered her to an old man who sexually abused her with the help of the babysitter, and she recounts another episode in which Leon brings home lots of money and some clothes, which Cecilia then throws in the wood stove and burns, except for a plaid skirt that she gives to Kathy, who is later brought home, bleeding, after having been attacked by a gang of boys: "Kathy disappears, she is shrieking as they beat and grab at her; some of the bigger guys crowding around are opening their pants. They are clawing at her, hands everywhere as she screams, and two of them leap up above the crowd; they are trying to jump on top of her" (ibid., 88-89). Yvonne fights back with a wooden plank, and the boys disperse (ibid., 89).

These stories are woven into the history of Cecilia's involvement with the American Indian Movement (AIM) and the Trail of Broken Treaties trek to Washington in 1972, which Cecilia took up to deal with Earl's death (ibid., 105). In protest of Earl's death in Butte, AIM wants to mount a campaign, but Clarence, strangely enough, is opposed (ibid., 102-3). And finally, these unevenly remembered events end with Earl rescuing Yvonne from a violent episode in which she is brutally beaten and placed on a sawmill belt "that carries the bark from the logs up to the top of the trash cone that smokes all the time." She crashes to the ground and is taken to hospital, where she remembers the doctor saying, "How do you sew up a tongue?" (ibid., 109). These fragments of sexual abuse and the politics of AIM seem oddly disconnected from one another, divided by a semiotics of sexual difference transcoded onto public and private spaces where men do real politics (or where so-called real politics are owned by masculinity in men or women such as Cecilia), and feminine women and female children stay at home to be done in by racism, street violence, and domestic violence. Why do these worlds appear so utterly disconnected and disarticulated in Wiebe's narrative frame? Why does Johnson's body – through its own silence, through the absence of its tongue – only serve as a container of violence and for the discharge of the truth of Earl's death?

Although Wiebe may have set out to write a coherent narrative and impose the law of narrative in *Stolen Life,* he failed precisely because there is a secondary order of trauma that must be overcome – the trauma Johnson experienced in attempting to write her story to begin with. For justice to come and, along with it, for healing to take place, the originary violence of incest and sexual abuse must first be acknowledged. It is this textual component of the repetitive element of trauma that Wiebe, as a writer, should have confronted to participate in the process of telling Johnson's story.

To Spirit Walk the Letter and the Law

Although Wiebe writes that "there are so many people in your life, no story is ever only yours alone" (Wiebe and Johnson, 24), just how others become part of our stories is a complicated process, one fraught with contradictions and the overdeterminations of historical forces such as imperialism, patriarchy, and colonial occupation. Stories are themselves part of communication systems of exchange that are subject to allowable transactions that take place under political and economic structures. Under colonial patriarchy, the material realities that emerge in the stories told by women of sexual violence and abuse are not generally recognized as having authorial power and the legitimacy of transacting knowledge. Instead, materialities of sexualized violence under colonialism are rendered invisible and become mystical remainders at the mythic ends of humanity. Within Wiebe's text, Johnson emerges as a counterfigure, a phantom storyteller whose relationship to language and literature – the law of narrative – will have to be settled if her story is to be told in the biographical form. As someone victimized by a racist, colonial, and patriarchal legal system, Johnson emerges not only as a perpetrator of a violent crime but also, as her case history reveals, as someone who has experienced the racism of the legal system in Canada. Thus, Johnson is framed by Wiebe's narrative as a figure who will question both the letter of the law and the law of narrative. She will emerge in a contradictory space as someone who commits violence (in life and language) and someone who is the object of it (also in life and language).

Wiebe states for the record in his editorial Preface that "the selection, compiling, and arrangement of events and details in this book were done in a manner *the two authors* believe to be honest and accurate. Public documents are quoted selectively, but with every attempt at fairness and accuracy"; the reader assumes, of course, that Wiebe is one author and Johnson the other (Wiebe and Johnson, xii, emphasis added). But this Other author is, I think, far more ambiguous than she may initially appear, in part because Johnson does not figure as an author in a conventional sense. Rather, this Other author is mythical, if not transcendent – the *spirit* of the text and of the law – and embodied in Johnson. It is this mystical author who guides Wiebe's desire for a non-violent, rational, and textual resolution to colonial violence. When I write that Yvonne Johnson does not figure as a conventional author, I am not saying that she is not recognizable as a co-writer, but that it is Wiebe who puts her narrative threads together and carefully crafts the book as a whole. Although it is an obvious approach to try to situate Johnson as an author of *Stolen Life* in order to respond to established notions of authority claimed through identity and representation, a more interesting approach would be to try to understand how Johnson's textual contributions de-authorize and demystify the violence that is constitutive of the law of narrative and the narrative force of law.

For Wiebe, Yvonne Johnson occupies the spirit of the letter, and as such she serves to help him make a coherent narrative from an otherwise chaotic story of colonial violence. In the instance of Earl's death, Yvonne Johnson's body comes to suture the fraternal gap between Clarence and Wiebe. Johnson also comes to represent the spirit of the law, and as the apparitional Aboriginal she provides a rational and discursive solution to the failure of the law to defend the subjects most in need of justice. Generally, the protection of women by men often provides the occasion to implement justice. In Johnson's case, the man who could have, and did, protect and save her life, Earl, is dead. Thus, Wiebe steps in to become the defender of her legal rights. This does not mean that Wiebe turns himself into the hero of Yvonne Johnson's story. He does not ride in like a white knight, a white man saving brown women from brown men, to paraphrase Gayatri Spivak.[12] Wiebe's integrity as a collaborator is demonstrated on many levels. First, he is acutely aware of his physical presence: "We hug, quick and loose because for her the arms of men have mostly been dangerous, often terrible" (Wiebe and Johnson, 6). Second, he demonstrates his intellectual integrity in his rigorous research into the legal implications of Johnson's life and case history. Third, his emotional integrity manifests in his friendship with Johnson, the respect he has for her and her story, and in his numerous interviews and encounters with various members of her family. Fourth and lastly, he acknowledges the spiritual knowledge Johnson carries with her of the ceremony performed by her Grandma Flora on her child's body to heal her from her trauma of sexual abuse. Indeed, in collaboration with Johnson, Wiebe may have put on record one of the few known accounts of such a ceremony, the benefits of which, Johnson anticipates, could be far-reaching: "A child doesn't know how to protect itself, either its body or its spirit. Grandma Flora saved my spirit from being damaged beyond restoration by helping me forget, but now the Creator is again letting me remember. My question is, why?" (Wiebe and Johnson, 426). The point needs to be made, however, that Wiebe's corporeal integrity stands in direct contrast to Johnson's dis-membered recollection of her life and corporeal experience.

This leads me to wonder if affirmative justice may in fact lie in healing the violence of colonial conquest rather than in waiting for justice to arrive in a colonial judicial system. Wiebe and Johnson's text makes an important contribution to the question of justice in decolonization, but how it does so is neither self-evident nor entirely obscure. An affirmative justice exists in the folds of its narrative, somewhere between two acts of colonial violence and their narrative representation: Earl's death and the rape of Yvonne Johnson's childhood body, the imposition of narrative and Johnson's disassembled story.

Although Wiebe testifies to the impossibility of the position he places himself in, his text is most clearly a victory of sorts because it retells the story of the law and justifies the juridical aspect of decolonization that looks to its reformation and restoration within the institutions of the law itself, including the emergence of legal pluralism, a critique of the incarceration of Native women in Canada, and the racism of the judicial system. The law, however, is heterogeneous and includes the letter of the law as well as the law of narrative. What his text does not do, and where the warning flags come up, is speak *to* the law. It instead speaks *from* the law, and as a result, it fails to perceive the other law at work in Johnson's life – the law of the father under patriarchy. In other words, Wiebe's text does not question the Oedipal law of incest, its historical links to primitivism such as in Freud's Totem and Taboo, and its narrative effects.[13] In the specific case of Yvonne Johnson, the law of the father is called into existence by the crime of pedophilia, the sexualized paternal and colonial conquest of the Indigenous female child's body. Yvonne Johnson participated in the murder of a man whom, she maintained, she had reason to fear, especially for the safety of her children, because she believed him to be a pedophile. Thus, she took the law into her own hands and participated in his murder.

Humans without Justice

Wiebe's account of Johnson's participation in the murder of Chuck Skwarok, her treatment by the legal system, and its failure to treat her without prejudice represents a positive approach to the law, one that, in Walter Benjamin's words, "demands of all violence a proof of its historical origin, which under certain conditions, is declared legal, sanctioned."[14] The idea of positive law stands in opposition to natural law, which "perceives in the use of violent means to just ends no greater problem that a man sees as his 'right' to move his body in the direction of a desired goal. According to this view ... violence is a product of nature, as it were, a raw material, the use of which is in no way problematical, unless force is misused for unjust ends ... This thesis of natural law that regards violence as a natural datum is diametrically opposed to that of positive law, which sees violence as product of history."[15]

The violence of so-called primitive incest that must be subject to the prohibitions of the law of the imperial father all too normatively falls under the category of natural law and often underlies the justification of domestic violence and sexual assault because it allows "that a man sees as his 'right' to move his body in the direction of a desired goal" the right to violence as an appropriate measure to meet the naturalized and legitimized ends of domination. The ends of man incorporate the desired goals of conquest, domination, power, exploitation, and control that are sanctioned by the naturalized law of the father. Positive law, on the other hand, focuses on the means rather than the ends and demands that the meaning of what constitutes violence must be historically situated.

In the case of Johnson, the question of violence and its means are located by Wiebe in the historical violence of colonial dispossession, which is represented by the story of Johnson's ancestor Big Bear. Wiebe in fact wrote a book on the incidents surrounding Big Bear's life and recalls this work and its impact on Johnson in *Stolen Life* (10-11). Earl Johnson's death is acknowledged de jure as constitutive of this history of violence. But what of the other crime that haunts the spaces on the margins of this text, the crime that appears in the title but is never sufficiently solved – Yvonne Johnson's stolen life? How was her life stolen, and by whom? Does Wiebe's text construct a positive approach to the law in reference to Earl's death but maintain a naturalized approach to the law with reference to the question of sexual abuse and incest? If this is the case, then Earl Johnson's death is another sort of alibi, one that provides the neoliberal, postcolonial consciousness with a screen to filter the historical significance of sexualized colonial violence toward the female Aboriginal child's body and, thus, ignore its enduring effects today, as the example of Helen Betty Osborne demonstrates. Why is the violence of sexual abuse excluded from narratives of colonial violence? In the liberal consciousness of postcolonial nationalism, Yvonne Johnson's stolen life is reduced to an allegory of colonial territorial dispossession rather than a necessary condition of it. The historical narrative of colonial violence generally focuses on the European imperialist mode of territorial dispossession and its privatization of the land as capital. The experience of intimate violence by First Nations women and children complicates the narrative of colonial violence and tells a story of the dispossession of bodies and their violent transformation into objects of property in the imperial patriarchal family and the patriarchal postcolonial nation-state. Thus, it is vital that multiple forms of colonial dispossession are recognized and that they include the commodification of land *and* bodies as naturalized objects of exchange and exploitation. Sexual violence toward Indigenous women must be attended to as a fact that in and of itself is general to the history of imperialism, colonization, and globalization, not supplementary or apparitional. It is only by taking such an approach to the problem of colonialism and its neoliberal, postcolonial legacy that the corporeal memories that were stolen from Yvonne Johnson's life can be reframed in such a way that her brother's death can be seen in connection to that lost personal history. In the larger context of the present-day disappearance and murder of Indigenous women and the disclosure of widespread sexual abuse of Indigenous children in the residential school system, it is also possible to recognize the degree to which sexual violence toward Indigenous women and children was central to the formation of the postcolonial nation-state of Canada.

Postscript

When I introduced *Stolen Life* to a group of Indigenous and non-Indigenous undergraduate students in a course on theories of the body, I included as part of my teaching methods the performance techniques of Augusto Boal's *Theatre of the Oppressed.* When it came time to read and discuss this book, the students used these performance techniques to do a specific kind of body work. The students made up a performance, the crux of which was a confrontation between the official discourses of the medical profession and alternative medical practices, neither of which, as their performance explored, provided the necessary materials for healing. Alternative narratives, the students' performance suggested, do not necessarily create justice.

Rather, justice would seem to lie elsewhere, in articulating what counts *as violence* and not as something that is seemingly inevitable in people's lives.

Although the law adjudicates violence and its apparent legitimate or illegitimate use, justice comes with a qualitatively different understanding of violence. Whereas Wiebe struggles with his writing, Johnson writes through the impasse of the violence of language and writing with which Wiebe inadvertently criticizes her. She writes her story through the mediation of Wiebe, and she arrives at a place of healing. She disowns her shame and brings charges against her father for sexual abuse. The intense feeling of suffocation caused by the burning of sweet grass that Johnson describes experiencing during her grandmother's healing ceremony re-enacts the trauma of breathing difficulties that were due to her cleft palate. It also reconfigures the representational violence of a history of signification that suffocates the self. Thus, healing is about justice, and justice comes with the acknowledgment of the material limits of representational violence and not the adjudication of a violence already assumed to be either legitimate or illegitimate. Genealogies of healing through the maternal body – Johnson's grandmother, for example – are neither legitimate nor illegitimate but belong to a different order, a different materiality and materialization, of justice.

NOTES

A longer version of this chapter with a more detailed discussion of justice in relation to representational and sexual violence appears in Julia Emberley, *Defamiliarizing the Aboriginal: Cultural Practices and Decolonization in Canada* (Toronto: University of Toronto Press, 2007). This essay has been reworked to address the editorial aims of this collection.

1 In 2001, Johnson was transferred to the Edmonton Institute for Women. In September of 2005, at a hearing for early parole, the jury decided that she should be eligible to apply at a later date.

2 Kimberly Blaeser, as quoted in Jo-ann Archibald (Q'um Q'um Xiiem), *Indigenous Storywork: Educating the Heart, Mind, Body, and Spirit* (Vancouver: UBC Press, 2008), 16.

3 Archibald, *Indigenous Storywork*, 16.

4 Ibid., 85.

5 Patricia Monture-Angus, *Thunder in My Soul: A Mohawk Woman Speaks*, foreword by Mary Ellen Turpel (Halifax: Fernwood, 1995).

6 Julia Emberley, "A Critique of Post-Colonial Violence," in Melina Baum Singer, Christine Kim, and Sophie McCall, eds., *Cultural Grammars* (Waterloo: Wilfrid Laurier University Press, forthcoming).

7 See Anne McGillivray and Brenda Comaskey, *Black Eyes All of the Time: Intimate Violence, Aboriginal Women, and the Justice System* (Toronto: University of Toronto Press, 1999), and Jocelyn Proulx and Sharon Perreault, eds., *No Place for Violence: Canadian Aboriginal Alternatives* (Halifax: Fernwood, 2000).

8 Sherene H. Razack, "Gendered Racial Violence and Spatialized Justice: The Murder of Pamela George," in Sherene H. Razack, *Race, Space, and the Law: Unmapping a White Settler Society* (Toronto: Between the Lines, 2002), 126.

9 In an effort to bring about restorative justice to deal with the high proportion of Aboriginal people in Canada's correctional facilities, legislators introduced in 1996 a directive to judges to "always consider alternatives to jail in sentencing, particularly for native people." S. 718.2(e). Legal pluralism extends the idea of restorative justice but differs from it in that it uses principles based on Aboriginal cultural practices such as the sentencing circle to provide an alternative to incarceration.

10 Rudy Wiebe and Yvonne Johnson, *Stolen Life: The Journey of a Cree Woman* (Athens, OH: Swallow Press, 2000), 334-35 (hereafter cited in text).

11 The federal prison for women in Kingston, Ontario, is a topic that comes up again in the text. In 1993, Johnson was chair of the Native Sisterhood, an internal organization formed by Indigenous women. As Johnson notes, sometimes a quarter of the women in the prison are Indigenous. The organization had built a sweat lodge. One of the issues Johnson recounts deals with the relocation of several Native women to the B Range, an area of tighter security that, in Johnson's view, was an attempt on the part of prison authorities "to keep them out of the Sisterhood because they were very solid together ... Staff said the B girls helped too many kill themselves" (ibid., 34). In April 1990, *Creating Choices: The Report of the Task Force on Federally Sentenced Women* was released. The suicides of twelve Aboriginal women in P4W in 1994 prompted the Canadian government to follow up on its recommendation to close P4W. As a result of its closure and the report, the Okimaw Ohci Healing Lodge was established as, among other things, a safe place for Aboriginal women offenders. For further information, see "Institutional Profiles, Prairie Region: Okimaw Ohci Healing Lodge," Correctional Service Canada, http://www.csc-scc.gc.ca/text/facilit/institutprofiles/okima-eng.shtml.

12 Gayatri Chakravorty Spivak, "Can the Subaltern Speak?" in Cary Nelson and Lawrence Grossberg, eds., *Marxism and the Interpretation of Culture* (Chicago: University of Illinois Press, 1988), 296.

13 See Julia Emberley, *Defamiliarizing the Aboriginal: Cultural Practices and Decolonization in Canada* (Toronto: University of Toronto Press, 2007).

14 Walter Benjamin, "Critique of Violence," in Walter Benjamin, *Reflections: Essays, Aphorisms, Autobiographical Writings,* trans. Edmund Jephcott (New York: Harcourt Brace Jovanovich, 1978), 280.

15 Ibid., 278.

13

Painting the Archive
The Art of Jane Ash Poitras

PAMELA McCALLUM

In a short story titled "The Painted Drum," the Native American writer Louise Erdrich explores the reactions of a woman – part Ojibwe, part European – who unexpectedly comes upon an artifact from her past. Erdrich's protagonist is an unnamed antique dealer hired to handle the estate of a man who had been the Indian agent at the North Dakota reservation where her grandmother was born and lived until she was sent off to a residential school in Pennsylvania. The old New England house turns out to contain a superb collection of Ojibwe artifacts, wrapped and stored along attic shelves. Among the baskets, beadwork, moccasins, pouches, and bandoliers is a large, beautifully ornamented drum: "intricately decorated, with a beaded belt and skirt, hung with tassels of pulled red yarn and sewn tightly all around with small tin cones, or tinklers." What especially attracts the antique dealer's attention are the drawings on the moosehide surface. She vividly describes her first impressions of the drum in this way: "four broad tabs were spaced equally around the top. Into their indigo tongues, four crosses were set woven with brass beads ... At the very center, a small bird was painted, in lighter blue."[1] Although born in the eastern states and only an occasional visitor to the North Dakota reservation that holds her family roots, she feels the drum speak to her so intensely that she is compelled to steal it. When she relates the experience to her mother, the older woman questions her about the decoration on the drum: "I told her about the crosses." The mother's reaction is pointed and direct: "Not crosses, not Christian.

Those are stars."[2] She goes on to tell her daughter, "The drum is the universe. The people who take their place at each side represent the spirits who sit at the four directions. A painted drum, especially, is considered a living thing and must be fed as the spirits are fed – with tobacco and a glass of water set nearby ... No two are alike, but every drum is related to every other drum. They speak to one another and they give their songs to humans."[3]

In this short narrative, Erdrich dramatizes the historical erasure of cultural memory and its potential recovery. When the Indian agent acquired the drum as part of his collection of artifacts, he removed it from people who respected its sacredness and understood its communication with the spirit world; he literally imprisoned the drum in his attic, where it remained, forgotten and neglected. For Erdrich, the drum's loss of connection with cultural memory and community purpose is symbolic of the daughter's distance from her Ojibwe roots: to her assimilated eyes, the decorations on the drum are first read within Christian religious traditions as crosses; that is, they are interpreted through the teachings her grandmother encountered in the Pennsylvania residential school. And yet her mother – who represents the middle generation – is still able to instruct her in Ojibwe beliefs about the drum and its importance in their culture: the crosses are reread as stars and resituated within a different spiritual tradition. Through a conversation between the mother and daughter, what had been a disregarded artifact, a lifeless object in the archive of colonialism, is returned to people who cherish its sacred power. Erdrich's narrator fears that her audacious act of taking the drum is a huge risk to her reputation as an honest dealer (and it is!), but the story makes it clear that, within the cultural history of the Americas, the thief is surely the Indian agent.

As "The Painted Drum" incisively demonstrates, the settlement of the Americas resulted not only in massive death and destruction but also in the systematic dismantling of cultures. Artifacts from Indigenous cultures – bowls, clothing, and beadwork, the familiar objects of daily life, and sacred masks and carvings and the unearthed bones of ancestors – all ended up in private collections, research institutions, museums, and universities throughout the continent and abroad. Together with the archive of photographs and anthropological studies, these captive objects became the resources through which settler societies understood and re-presented Amerindian cultures to themselves. Yet these very objects had been torn out of the lifeworld – the day-to-day work, habits, and rituals that gave them their significance – and isolated from the cultures in which they were endowed with social value. Carved patterns on a bowl, for instance, would in traditional cultures have impressed their familiar feeling on the hands that filled the bowl with food or passed it from one person to another. In contrast, when placed in a museum – protected from use in a glass cabinet – the pattern becomes an aesthetic object subjected to the gaze of unfamiliar eyes.[4] Similarly, the early anthropological studies of Indigenous cultures often attributed Western aesthetic value to artifacts from cultures with very different conceptions of art and its relationship to society.

The Indigenous scholar and curator Gerald McMaster underlines how museum exhibitions disempower objects and cultures: "Placement of works behind glass comes to signify the distance between the cultures and between the self and the Other. The glass case protects and museumifies the culture of the Other – their objects scrutinized in medical fashion, as a sort of clinical gaze. It's a polite and aloof activity."[5] By drawing attention to the interaction between museum visitors and displayed objects, McMaster stresses how the apparently innocent activity of viewing cannot escape the relationships of politics and power that underpin museum collections. For these reasons, it comes as no surprise that he views museums and galleries as sites of struggle for Indigenous people.[6] Elsewhere, he describes interventions into the spaces of museums as strategies "to create a conscious sense of self and agency while critiquing authority."[7]

Jane Ash Poitras, a Canadian First Nations visual artist, explores these issues within a double-edged project: her artworks examine the colonial construction of Indianness and knowledge about Indigenous peoples at the same time that her own practice as an artist returns images to the cultures from which they are derived.[8] Born in the remote northern Alberta town of Fort Chipewyan, raised in Edmonton by an elderly German woman, and educated at the University of Alberta and Columbia University, New York, Poitras, who reconnected with her Indigenous relatives in early adulthood, is part of a generation of First Nations artists whose work gained public attention in the late 1980s.[9] The specific moment of the 1980s, I argue, encouraged the juxtaposition and interconnection of postmodernist aesthetic styles with a reclamation of cultural memory in the form of challenges to colonial and patriarchal representations of gender and community. Just as Erdrich's narrator discovers the symbols of the drum through her mother and grandmother, so also Poitras often evokes the connections of generations through figures of women. Her art combines an energetic aesthetics that has affinities with the postmodernist art of Robert Rauschenberg, Cy Twombly, Mark Rothko, and Helen Frankenthaler with equally powerful cultural symbols and designs from Amerindian cultures to depict urgent questions about the intersection of past and present and history and politics in contemporary Indigenous life.

In 1982, at a time when Poitras was beginning to consider art as a career and rediscovering her Fort Chipewyan family, the First Nations artist Robert Houle curated "New Work by a New Generation" at the Norman Mackenzie Art Gallery in Regina, which included works by Canadian and American artists such as Carl Beam, Bob Boyer, Domingo Cisneros, Henry Fonseca, Edward Poitras (no relation to Jane), and Jaune Quick-To-See Smith. The previous two decades had seen a growing fascination within both public and commercial galleries with Indigenous art, particularly Inuit carvings and prints, the Woodland school (Norval Morrisseau, Daphne Odjig, Alex Janvier, and others) and West Coast art. And this fascination was facilitated by such cultural institutions as the Canada Council and the Cultural Affairs Division of the Department of Indian Affairs.[10] The Regina exhibition, crucial for the construction of a nascent aesthetic, underlined the dual influences on a new generation of Indigenous artists who claimed both Indigenous traditions and contemporary Western stylistics as part of their own artistic practices. This is how Houle describes these influences in the exhibition catalogue: "The former is deeply rooted in tribal ritual and symbolism; while the latter is an irreversible influence committed to change and personal development." The result was a potent interweaving of tradition and innovation, sometimes expressed as sites of strength and longing, sometimes as sites of tension and pain. These "sensuous counterpoints" took shape as each artist negotiated personal history, Indigenous traditions, and contemporary art practices.[11]

Houle saw the commitment of artists to an ongoing dialogue with contemporary art less as a challenge to traditional cultures than as a key engagement that would open up a process of revitalization. "Such a commitment," he writes in the catalogue, "is crucial to the reconstruction of cultural and spiritual values eroded by faceless bureaucracy and atheistic technology."[12] As a creative individual "invariably and intimately involved in recording personal experiences," who is inevitably situated in a particular socio-cultural tradition, the artist can be a catalyst for transformation. Houle makes it clear that he does not view earlier generations of Indigenous artists as caught in an unproductive traditionalism: he calls Morrisseau and Scholder visionaries and innovators.[13] Simultaneously, he insists that viewers of Indigenous art ought to respond to the individual "visual recordings of human emotion and thought." Although they bear the inscriptions of the artist's personal and cultural history, they are "undoubtedly beyond ethnic definition or racial reference."[14] In other words, the moment had come when Indigenous artists wanted to be recognized as individuals who were negotiating the complexities of their heritage in the contemporary world and, like other artists of their generation, were utilizing the representational strategies of modernist and postmodernist art.

Other curators took up the challenge of "New Work by a New Generation." In 1986, the Thunder Bay Art Gallery and curator Garry Mainprize organized a travelling exhibition, "Stardusters," in which Poitras' art was included, along with that of Pierre Sioui, Edward Poitras, and Joane Cardinal-Schubert. In the catalogue, Mainprize stresses the cross-currents of Poitras' Indigenous heritage and her New York art school training: "Pan-Indian references, which also crept into her art at this time, were chosen as much for their purely artistic potential as for any other reason, and her sudden expressionistic approach to colour and form took inspiration from a broad range of sources: the colour theories of Hans Hofmann, Indian beadwork, Raphael, Kandinsky, Marcel Duchamp, Helen Frankenthaler and Kurt Schwitters, among others."[15] In the intertwining of pasts and presents, references to Indigenous traditions can be appropriated as much for aesthetic effect as for cultural resonance, and colour theory can be discovered as much in traditional beadwork as in the experimentation and theorizing of European artists. This is the sense in which these Indigenous artists can be seen as participating in what Cheryl Suzack, drawing on the work of Victor Li, calls a practical untidiness that facilitates a representation of the intersection of history and the present.[16]

It was in this politically and culturally potent moment of the late 1980s that Poitras' art began to gain recognition. Her solo show, "Sweatlodge Etchings," based on her Columbia University Masters exhibition, had been exhibited at the Museum of Anthropology in Vancouver and had travelled to other venues. In the summer of 1989, Poitras was one of a group of Native artists who took part in a landmark exhibition at the Vancouver Art Gallery, "Beyond History." Viewed from the perspective of the twenty-first century, the title of the exhibition seems puzzling. How can this art, in which the inscription of histories seems so significant, be perceived as moving beyond history? One way to begin to answer this question is to ask further questions. What history? Whose history? Far from implying that any artist is able to step beyond personal history, or that Indigenous artists have distanced themselves from the histories of their peoples, the exhibition challenged the institutional history (the dominant construction and understanding) of Indigenous art in Canada. Building on the ideas expressed in "New Work by a New Generation" and "Stardusters," the curators Tom Hill and Karen Duffek set out to bring together artwork that would both "showcase First Nations artists" and make the argument that their work was cutting-edge art – that is, the exhibition challenged viewers to respond to the art as contemporary interventions by artists who were bringing individual viewpoints to a complex, shared history.[17] As Duffek explains in the exhibition catalogue, the art in "Beyond History" "is based on more than a salvaged past. It involves a critical re-reading of history from a late twentieth-century perspective, and presents a challenge to the prevailing stereotypes of Native art through the personal aesthetic visions it reveals."[18] In other words, to move beyond history, the artists had to interrogate how their histories have been shaped by others and bring different stories from new perspectives to conventionalized narratives.

It was especially appropriate that many of the artists in "Beyond History" produced installations and assemblages. As Duffek puts it, inscribed in the art was a process of reworking materials, pulling fragments together to create something new, so that the very construction of the artwork articulated an artist's negotiation of different histories.[19] Visitors to the exhibit would have seen art that sought, in the words of Regina Hackett, "to change minds, confront, amaze and comfort."[20] Joane Cardinal-Schubert's warshirt series presented individual painted traditional garments enclosed in plastic bags. The series was a commentary on the careful preservation of objects in museums, where items are separated from those who might cherish them as legacies from their ancestors and as examples of the craft and artwork produced by earlier generations of women. Ron Noganosh created a striking installation made up of a large half-image of the Canadian flag, against which flowed an intricate cascade of tubing and liquor bottles (whose arrangements spell out "Lubicon").[21] The flag and cascade led to a skull and a beautifully embroidered garment that was both an evocation of a museum display and a body deadened by alcohol. The installation was a kind of ironic Rube Goldberg machine that reinserted itself into the contemporary politics of Canada's Native peoples. Robert Houle's *Lost Tribes* presented a line of brightly painted horizontal panels that had "the solemnity of headstones."[22] "Like open pages of a long, narrow book," each panel was inscribed with the name of a tribe destroyed by disease, war, or assimilation.[23] Intersecting the panels were the yellow and black slashes of caution signs (allusions to Rauschenberg? Warhol?), a warning of the violence of history and of the persistence of that violence. In her critique, Duffek underscores the defamiliarization that these artists worked on viewers' expectations: "Instead of using their art to reinforce the notion that continuous tradition alone defines Native identity, they throw into doubt our expectations of (and nostalgia for) 'authentic' culture."[24] With references to modernist and postmodernist art layered into narratives about the politics of contemporary Native communities, the varied works in "Beyond History" articulated a commitment to move beyond traditional conceptions of Native art and beyond the apolitical formalism of some modernist or postmodernist art.

As Ingrid Jenkner notes, the use of postmodern stylistics, a "bricolage of signifiers" in Poitras' artworks, functions to "assert and reclaim the strength of Native cultures in a postcolonial context."[25] Poitras' exploration of photography often centres on the extraordinary archive of photographs accumulated by American photographer Edward Curtis. In the late nineteenth and early twentieth centuries, he travelled throughout the continent accumulating some forty thousand images of Amerindian peoples for his twenty-volume work, *The North American Indian.* Although Curtis conceived of his project as a strategy to preserve what he saw as a disappearing way of life, a common assumption of his time, it is amply evident to a viewer in the next century that his photographs pose their subjects in idealized stances that foreground a nostalgic construction of Native cultures.[26] In *The Truth about Stories: A Native Narrative,* Thomas King points out that Curtis carried "boxes of 'Indian' paraphernalia – wigs, blankets, painted backdrops, clothing" to persuade his subjects to dress in the way he imagined they should look.[27] Stoicism is the predominant emotional tone of the images, and they put into circulation a kind of freezing of affect that downplayed the expression of pain and suffering. The genuine problems Amerindian peoples faced as their traditional ways of living were being dismantled by modernity and European settlement – starvation following the destruction of the buffalo herds, children taken from their families to attend residential schools, loss of languages, poverty, and addiction – are conspicuously absent from Curtis portraits. In the words of Anne Makepeace, "we do not see missionaries preaching in the plazas or on the Plains in his pictures, or medicine men being arrested for performing outlawed ceremonies, or Indian children being hauled off to boarding schools, or the abuse they suffered there."[28] Nor does Curtis present any Native resistance to these devastating losses.

And yet, it would not be correct to suggest that for Curtis the Amerindian peoples he was so preoccupied with photographing were without a power that aroused his desire. In *Mimesis and Alterity,* the anthropologist

Michael Taussig draws attention to "the soulful power that derives from replication" or "the magical power of replication, the image effecting what it is an image of, wherein the representation shares in or takes power from the represented."[29] Taussig's use of *soulful* echoes the belief – common in the early days of the technology – that photography could steal one's soul, but it also underscores the economy of affect that circulates from the represented. In the uncanny clash that circulates around mimesis and alterity, Curtis' subjects are not only the passive objects of his camera lens but also remarkable presences whose spirit haunts the photographs, waiting, perhaps, for the stroke of the artist's brush to transform them.

Poitras' aesthetic provides a particularly impassioned example of the affective potential that can be mobilized from the archive of anthropological photography. Curtis' photograph "Hopi Mother and Child" shows a carefully composed portrait of a woman carrying her child in a shawl on her back. The child gazes with security at his mother's shoulder, and the woman stares fixedly outside of the photograph's frame. It is an image typical of Curtis' work. It focuses on the social dyad of mother and child, a conventional signification of intimacy, which in this case is represented in the small hand against the skin of the adult's shoulder. The photograph is of a "primitive" Madonna presented as an object for the gaze of colonial documentation.

In Poitras' revision of Curtis, also titled *Hopi Mother and Child,* she repositions the image on a background of varied reds, blues, and purples and produces an impression of the ancient stones on which the Hopi people wrote their stories in rock art. The top of the painting reaches upward into a row of sacred stars, and the photograph itself is contained within a frame of traditional fabric designs and paintings. Put somewhat differently, an image stolen by Curtis' photography is restored to the enclosure and protection of familiar Amerindian artwork. Resituated within their culture, the woman and child regain strength and historical presence; they are no longer positioned as objects of the camera's gaze. In Carolyne Chatel's view, the reworking of the photograph is a process of reclaimed memory or "a gesture [of] respect for her ancestors."[30]

But this is not all. Having reappropriated the photography from the files of the anthropological archive, Poitras opens up the focus with a second photograph that tells a different story about the historical moment of Curtis' project. In this photograph, the viewer is confronted with a group of children of various ages who stand before the unmistakably Westernized wall of a brick building. Like a page torn from a schoolbook, the image contains handwritten notations: "confinement on reservations during the nineteenth century resulted in a changed way of life." These children, awkward in settler clothing – jackets for the older boys, checked dresses for the girls – perhaps stand in front of a school in which they are being taught to reject their Elders' way of life. By interjecting a historical reference to residential schools, Poitras not only critiques idealization of the Curtis photograph but also mobilizes recognition of the basic family unit that was broken by snatching children from their communities to attend school. She also challenges the viewer to think about how gender functions within communities and about how the basic social relationship between mother and child can be manipulated through idealization and violent severing.

At the same time, Poitras depicts the persistence of traditional beliefs by painting over the photograph images of mounted warriors and horses. The transparency of the images suggests their connection with the spirit world, and they seem to be protectors of the children who represent the children's connection to traditional sacred values. In Poitras' hands, *Hopi Mother and Child* tells a story about generations, about the passage of knowledge and cultural memories over decades and centuries. Her artwork reverses Curtis' isolation of the mother and child by reinscribing them within Hopi and other Indigenous cultures. By appropriating photographs from the anthropological archive and resituating them within her own aesthetic practices, Poitras re-empowers Indigenous women.

One of Poitras' most poignant reinterpretations of this astonishing archive of anthropological photography is her mixed-media-on-paper work, *One Dollar Please*. The central photograph portrays a woman and child standing alone on the vast grassland of the central Plains. Carefully posed, photographed from behind and below, the woman stares out into an apparently empty distance; only her baby, too young to comprehend the exchange between adults, catches the viewer's gaze with a skeptical look that belies immaturity. It is an image that strengthens the stereotypical figure of the lone Indian, a solitary individual within a boundless expanse of nature. This effect is especially ironic because a mother and child can also be read as symbols of a basic unit of community.

The political aesthetic of Poitras' art resituates the photograph in the lifeworld of Native societies and communities and appropriates conventional responses (mother and baby, the exotic other, the lone Indian) to the authority of the artist. Blue and red borders, sacred colours, are positioned at the top of the painting, and they echo around the photograph. The intense blue in the colouring of the sky dissolves the boundaries between photograph and painting, returning the image to the symbolic world of the artwork. Similarly, the painted grasses (vibrant strokes of green, white, yellow, red, and blue) restore a vitality to what, in the photograph, seems to be a barren, empty space. Poitras' brush gently outlines the embroidery and beadwork on the papoose. The effect emphasizes the art created by the woman in the photograph and challenges the viewer to think of her not as a mute object from the past but as an active agent within her culture. Drawings of sacred shamanic figures and spirit animals – which inspire her people, land, and culture, and which connect the contemporary artwork to the photograph – float around the photograph, enacting its reincorporation into a living spiritual world. As if to underline the reclamation of the photograph by life, Poitras incorporates porcupine quills into the grasses. The ivory shading and straight lines of the quills provide an aesthetic counterpoint to the curves of the blades of grass; at the same time, they are a touching reminder that part of a living creature has entered into the creation of the artwork.

The exchange values of the European world, however, still haunt *One Dollar Please*. Poitras has explained that the title comes from a story about a man who asked for one dollar to have his photograph taken.[31] This fee, relatively modest even in its time, is represented by the stencilled *One Dollar* – the *r* is obscured – across the top of the painting and by the Monopoly money collage underneath the large letters. Poitras' evocation of the famous board game that permits players to act out control of large fortunes (perhaps the reason for its continuing popularity?) not only suggests the European drive for power and domination over the Americas, it also underscores the monopoly of images, the colonial archive of photographs by Curtis and others, that has helped to construct non-Indigenous understandings of Indigenous peoples. It is this monopoly of representations that Poitras' art contests when her own artistic practices reappropriate images as part of a process of returning them to the cultures of her own people while simultaneously foregrounding the initial acts of objectification for discussion and critique.

Marilyn Daniels has commented that the geometrical composition of Poitras' paintings endows the artworks with "a sense of self-contained balance, clarity and stillness."[32] At the same time, however, "the works are multilayered: those who stay with the works may uncover a quiet tension despite the initial impression of calmness and balance."[33] The layering of Poitras' art often works to open up unexpected historical connections. Her artwork titled *woman creates so man can survive* (1998) displays a compositional style similar to *One Dollar Please*. A background washed with deep greys and blues gives the impression of ancient slate walls. In the centre is a square band of buff, terracotta, and black patterns that surrounds a photograph of two women. The photograph, difficult to place in time (is it the late 1800s? the early 1900s? mid-century?), portrays two women – one seated, one standing – who gaze impassively at the camera. Seeming to look out across a vast void into an unfamiliar world, and dressed in Western clothing, the women stand in front of a partially dismantled shelter. They appear to inhabit a culture in transition; they are caught between traditional and settler ways of life. At the bottom of the painting are four small circles made of antlers; at the top is a band of brightly coloured fabric. Life moves from the natural world of the animal to the human world of the fabric: women's work draws material from nature to remake it into the intricate lines of woven cloth, a creativity that often passes unnoticed. Both the circles and the strip of fabric repeat the colour red, which shadows into rose on the background and spills across the photograph. There is a double irony in this dripping red: it is both the blood flowing from people who have suffered centuries of domination and the pulsing blood of a way of life that has survived that domination.

The title of the painting, *woman creates so man can survive,* creates a playful reflection on the generic use of *man* to mean "humankind," a linguistic strategy that erases women from their familial, social, and cultural roles within communities. The images in Poitras' painting resituate women in the centre (literally) and celebrate their work, which sustains human societies.

A particular site of cultural collision is the intersection of traditional figural drawings and patterns with contemporary marketing practices. The appropriation of Indigenous imagery to produce objects for mass-market sales around the world has continued largely unquestioned, even in the contemporary period, which claims to be sensitive to intellectual property. Images are assumed to be readily available for reproduction and are simply taken, without any recompense to the peoples from whose tradition the design derives. Joane Cardinal-Schubert describes the frenzied production of Indianness after the success of the Woodland School and Inuit art in the late 1960s: "White artists began to paint Native children with teardrops in their eyes; there was an attempt to romanticize the Indian, they were curiosities. Tourist shops abounded with fake artifacts and jewellery."[34]

One of the most widely appropriated images is the silhouetted flute player Kokopelli, a figure derived from Hopi culture and rock paintings, who has been widely marketed in popular Santa Fe fabrics, jewellery, scarves, T-shirts, notepaper, postcards, and restaurant, bar, and motel names. The list could go on almost indefinitely, for Kokopelli has become a shorthand signifier of southwest Indianness. There is little agreement about what makes Kokopelli so appealing for commercial exploitation. In *Kokopelli: The Making of an Icon,* the archaeologist Ekkehart Malotki suggests that the figure conjures up the "near universal appeal of the flute and the magic its music can evoke" and New Age nostalgia for "something a bit exotic and mysterious."[35] In a way that parallels the fascination of modernist artists with *art negre,* Kokopelli might connect with "a number of psychological needs, such as that for mystery and wildness in what many see as an increasingly sterile and impersonal world."[36] A more pessimistic, more ideological process at work in the commercialization of Kokopelli is suggested by J.D. Lewis-Williams, who argues in regard to South African rock art that colonizing cultures need to dismantle and disempower what had been held sacred by Indigenous cultures. Late stages of this process, when assimilation is nearly complete and conflicts are not as sharp, are characterized by "a gloss of fun" and depictions that are "in numerous trivializing ways solely for commercial gain."[37] Read in this way, the relentless marketing of Kokopelli participates in a process of cultural erasure in which the flute player is emptied of traditional sacred power and recirculated as a floating signification of southwestern style. Every Kokopelli T-shirt bought by a tourist as a souvenir of Arizona, every Kokopelli brooch cherished as Indian jewellery, every Kokopelli emblazoned on a coffee mug to associate a mass-market product with the look of ancient pottery shares in a process by which the figure is disengaged from a specific culture and history to become little more than another decorative pattern. From such a perspective, the borrowed power of cultural appropriation is often a process of neutralizing traditional sacred power within the anonymous exchange values of the marketplace.[38]

To contemporary viewers, Poitras' incorporation of Kokopelli can hardly fail to function as a visual reminder of how art produced by Native societies has been wrenched from them for someone else's profit. At the same time, her art returns the figures and designs to Indigenous culture.[39] In a compellingly symbolic gesture of composition, Kokopelli, a spirit bird, and traditional patterns from pottery that the ancestors of these women produced become part of a frame that encloses the photograph, thereby protecting and surrounding the women with their own culture. If the photograph is a reminder of how settler societies have appropriated the representation of Amerindian peoples, then Poitras' artistic practices work to resituate the two figures within the cultural figurations of the world that photographs by Curtis and others failed to represent.

By returning Kokopelli to a configuration of southwestern cultures, Poitras reanimates traditional associations with the Hopi figure. The name Kokopelli, Malotki argues, is a corruption of Kookopölö, the name of a Hopi kachina god of fertility whose humpbacked bag of seed symbolizes fertility for both the human and natural worlds. The figure is also associated with Maahu, the cicada insect whose buzzing sound is said to be fluting and whose appearance in the summer warms the land and foretells good crops.[40] For the peoples who created the southwestern rock drawings, the fertility of nature and humanity was integral to survival and the continuance of life; therefore, Kookopölö was one of the most powerful gods. By framing *woman creates so man can survive* with a Kokopelli figure, and therefore with echoes of the Hopi kachina, Poitras stresses the fundamental creativity, both biological and cultural, through which women sustain their societies. As in *One Dollar Please,* Poitras retrieves the photograph of anonymous women from cultural constructions of Indianness and uses her own artistic intervention to reposition the two women in a world of life and continuity with their peoples. Women are a crucial part of culture: their all-too-often unnoticed work and activities are essential to the meanings and conventions of cultural expression.

In a very different style, Poitras deals with similar questions in the 1991 painting *The Flute Player.* In this painting, she defamiliarizes Kokopelli so that the conventional silhouette of the flute player disappears in a tangle of brilliant colours: his feathered head is barely visible at the right side. Rather than bending forward, as the popular Kokopelli silhouetted figures do, this flute player bends backward like a jazz saxophonist, a reminder that Kokopelli's power is not locked into the archaeological past but can take its place within the musical traditions of the Americas. Instead of the single Kokopelli popularized by innumerable commercial appropriations, Poitras repositions the Hopi kachina within a community of sacred figures from various Indigenous cultures. Near the top right is a warrior and horse from the tradition of Plains buffalo robe painting; at the left is a Cree shamanic figure; in the centre, partially visible, is the head of a red Northwest Coast bear. Kokopelli's flute is wrapped around an eagle, as if this sacred bird has been conjured by magical music. Dominating the foreground is an intriguing green figure marked with traces of blue lettering. In his book *Kokopelli,* Malotki shows petroglyphs from Arizona and New Mexico that portray a flute player who is "uncharacteristically ... pot-bellied rather than humpbacked."[41] Poitras may echo this figure in order to defamiliarize the conventionalized Kokopelli and to participate in a process of returning this all-too-often appropriated image to Hopi traditions. The words written over the figure – *pride* is legible, others are traces of letters might suggest the reading *rising pride* as a reclamation of tradition. In the composition itself, the riot of colours and the intertwining shapes create a vibrant, dynamic surface in and through which powerful spirit figures move. Poitras' art revives the flute player as part of the potent domain of an Indigenous spirit world.

The Flute Player nonetheless raises a persistent puzzle in its imagery. If I earlier described the eagle as a sacred bird, it is impossible to forget that this formidable predator also has strong symbolic affiliations with the United States. The stars emerging from the flute, together with the red and white stripes formed by the head of the bear shaman, render an unmistakable stars-and-stripes pattern – the flag of colonial and contemporary America. Why does Poitras include a figuration of the nation that over decades and centuries has led such a brutal campaign of colonization against Indigenous peoples? One answer lies in her stress on the living presence of the past in Amerindian cultures: the flute player, Kokopelli, is not a dead remnant of cultures long past; instead, this Kokopelli is part of contemporary society, an energetic and vigorous musician who might be found playing riffs in Chicago, New York, or Montreal. By refusing to portray her flute player simply as the familiar silhouette from primitive rock paintings, Poitras challenges her viewers to reimagine an overly conventionalized archival image as a spirited, robust contemporary musician. Another answer might reside in Poitras' dialogue with the past. By situating the eagle midway between the stars and stripes and an image of a Plains community, Poitras retrieves the figure of the eagle, a sacred bird in many Indigenous cultures, from its symbolic encoding as the national sign of the United States. The painting therefore attempts an act of reappropriation in which the borrowed power of the eagle is relocated alongside Kokopelli and the other sacred creatures of Amerindian societies. The ambiguity of the images may also suggest a reading that is all too often resisted by viewers who assume stars and stripes and red, white, and blue must signal the flag of the United States: these stars and stripes are depicted in a process of dispersal, being made available for configurations other than the American flag. Just as the narrator of Erdrich's "The Painted Drum" learned to see crosses as stars, so also are the viewers of Poitras' painting challenged to think differently about familiar images. Finally, it is important to stress that *The Flute Player* does not invoke a nostalgic return to the past. The contemporary style of the painting, together with the Fauvist colours, makes it clear that Poitras' dialogue with the past reclaims symbolic figures from Indigenous cultures to reanimate their energy for a present moment.

How might Poitras' artworks be considered part of a wider process of Indigenous feminism? Questions of gender are often a pivotal issue in Poitras' artworks. As the images of the mother and child in *One Dollar Please* or in *Hopi Mother and Child* suggest, Poitras celebrates the transmission of cultural values across generations and within communities. Like the narrator of "The Painted Drum," she is aware of the crucial connections among daughters, mothers, and grandmothers. Perhaps, as an adoptee, she is intensely aware both of the painful distress of breaking these connections and of the possibilities of remaking them. She has also been a strong presence in social activist projects that can be situated within a broadly described feminism. As an artist and citizen, she has participated in acts of gender politics. In 1992, she took a stand against the sex trade that had developed in her inner-city Edmonton neighbourhood: using the weapon of an artist – paint – she wrote on the pavement the licence plate numbers of men cruising the streets to pick up women. The men soon disappeared. "The secret," she commented, "was making the johns lose their anonymity." But this feisty act of resistance has another darker side: her crusade began, in her account, "the day a man jumped out of his truck and grabbed her arm, telling her he could make her rich."[42] Hearing about this incident makes it impossible to ignore how easily an Indigenous woman is assumed to be raw material for prostitution and how many Indigenous women are caught within the crippling life of the sex trade, often with attendant substance abuse and addictions. By painting licence plate numbers on pavement, Poitras also protested against the assumptions society makes about these women.

In a similar gesture of political activism, Poitras participated in an exhibition of art dedicated to raising awareness about breast cancer. A cancer survivor herself, she contributed an installation artwork titled *Courage Blanket*. In this work, by employing the familiar shape of a tombstone, Poitras memorializes individual women whose names are noted and whose photographs (including a striking profile of a woman who has lost her hair in chemotherapy treatment) form a central strip across the artwork. The most remarkable aspect of *Courage Blanket,* however, is the opposite side – a blackboard on which Poitras writes to invite viewers to inscribe the names of those who have succumbed to breast cancer: "I encourage all those who have lost someone to this disease to write that person's name on the blackboard side of this installation." By involving exhibition visitors in the ongoing evolution of the artwork, if only in a small way, Poitras recognizes the feminist value of community and offers an opportunity to memorialize a beloved friend or family member. It is an act of creation that draws those who see *Courage Blanket* into participating in its construction and in the healing work of making art. Poitras also includes an album of hundreds of letters and photographs that were sent to her from cancer victims or their families and friends. It is a poignant way to make many seemingly insignificant acts part of a collective act of feminist practice.

Indigenous feminism, nevertheless, has sometimes been characterized as a contradictory positioning that asks women to choose between their ancestry and their gender. As Helen Hoy comments in *How Should I Read These? Native Women Writers in Canada,* "for minoritized groups, internal struggles around gender must often coincide with group solidarity in the face of shared external threats."[43] In *Journeying Forward: Dreaming First Nations' Independence,* Patricia Monture-Angus, a Canadian activist and legal theorist, rejects feminism with the following assessment: "My problem with feminism is quite simple. The reference point for feminism is the power and privilege held by white men of which I aspire to neither."[44] Monture-Angus is certainly justified in turning away from a politics that seeks control over others, but her definition of feminism is dangerously narrow. Elsewhere in *Journeying Forward* she outlines her understanding of ethical commitment: "Maintaining good relationships with your family, clan and nation, but the rest of the living world as well (by which I mean the environment and all things around us), means that you are fulfilling one of your basic responsibilities as a human being. It is this web of relationships which provides the support, encouragement and instruction necessary to living a good life. It is this web (or the natural laws) that is the relationship that has been devastated by colonialism."[45] By describing these situated interconnections, Monture-Angus comes much closer to depicting the feminist practices that inform Poitras' artworks. Her art engages with colonial constructions of Indianness, often by laying hold of archival images of women isolated from any sense of community and reframing them within symbolic representations of Indigenous communities. In the case of *One Dollar Please, woman creates so man can survive,* and other paintings, her artwork incorporates found objects – antler fragments, cloth, and porcupine quills – that gesture toward the concrete materiality of an Indigenous world. The juxtaposition of imagery and symbols drawn from Indigenous cultures within and alongside the aesthetic style of postmodernist painting underlines the hybridity of contemporary Indigenous communities and stands as a refusal to reproduce familiar romanticized notions of the so-called Indian. In a similar and related way, Poitras' art snatches Kokopelli from circulation in mainstream contemporary cultures and restores this widely appropriated figure to an Indigenous context. All of these artistic practices challenge viewers to reflect on questions about history, gender, and indigeneity in new ways.

NOTES

1 Louise Erdrich, "The Painted Drum," *New Yorker,* 3 March 2003, 79.

2 Ibid., 80.

3 Ibid., 81.

4 Joane Cardinal-Schubert, an artist whose warshirt series explicitly addresses the question of museum collections, comments, "Although the works [Indigenous artifacts in museums] were aesthetically pleasing, they were frozen in time – objects lifeless without their function." See Cardinal-Schubert, "In the Red," *Fuse* 13, 1-2 (1989): 27. For further analyses of museum practices and Indigenous artifacts, see Deborah Root, *Cannibal Culture: Art, Appropriation and the Commodification of Difference* (Boulder, CO: Westview Press, 1996); Bruce Ziff and Pratima V. Rao, eds., *Borrowed Power: Essays on Cultural Appropriation* (New Brunswick, NJ: Rutgers University Press, 1997); and Phyllis Mauch Messenger, *The Ethics of Collecting Cultural Property: Whose Culture? Whose Property?* (Albuquerque: University of New Mexico Press, 1991).

5 Gerald McMaster, "Museums and Galleries as Sites for Artistic Intervention," in Mark A. Cheetham, Michael Ann Holly, and Keith P.F. Moxey, eds., *The Subject of Art History: Historical Objects in Contemporary Perspectives* (Cambridge: Cambridge University Press, 1998), 258.

6 Gerald McMaster, "Object (to) Sanctity: The Politics of the Object," *Muse* 10, 3 (1993), www.museums.ca/publications/muse/1993.

7 Gerald McMaster, "Museums and the Native Voice," in Griselda Pollock and Joyce Zemans, eds., *Museums after Modernism: Strategies of Engagement* (London: Blackwell, 2007), 75.

8 Pamela McCallum, "Linked Histories: Recent Art by Three First Nations Women," *Alberta Views* 2, 4 (Fall 1999): 18-23. *First Nations* is a Canadian term put forward by Indigenous peoples. It functions as a counterdiscourse to federalist language that refers to the two (French and English) founding nations of Canada.

9 Jane Ash Poitras, "Autobiographical Statement," *Matriart* 2, 1 (1991): 28-29; Carol Podedworny, "First Nations Art and the Canadian Mainstream" *C Magazine* 31 (Fall 1991): 23-32; Tom Hill, "Beyond History," in Tom Hill and Karen Duffek, eds., *Beyond History* (Vancouver: Vancouver Art Gallery, 1989), 5-15; Karen Duffek, "Beyond History," in Hill and Duffek, *Beyond History,* 27-38.

10 Hill, "Beyond History," 7-9.

11 Robert Houle, "The Emergence of a New Aesthetic Tradition," in Robert Houle, *New Work by a New Generation* (Regina: Norman Mackenzie Art Gallery, 1982), 2.

12 Ibid., 3.

13 Ibid., 4.

14 Ibid., 2.

15 Garry Mainprize, *Stardusters* (Thunder Bay, ON: Thunder Bay Art Gallery, 1986), 10.
16 Cheryl Suzack, "Forum: On the Practical Untidiness of Always Indigenizing," *English Studies in Canada* 30, 2 (2004): 2.
17 Karen Duffek, interview with author, Vancouver, February 2003.
18 Duffek, "Beyond History," 27.
19 Duffek interview.
20 Regina Hackett, "Powerful Show by Indian Artists," *Seattle Post-Intelligencer*, 31 May 1989, 1.
21 The Lubicon Cree are a small band in east central Alberta whose land claims came to national and international prominence when they led a boycott of "The Spirit Sings" exhibition of Indigenous artifacts that took place during the 1988 Calgary Olympics. Sadly, two decades later the federal government has not settled the land claim.
22 Duffek, "Beyond History," 28.
23 Hackett, "Powerful Show by Indian Artists," 13.
24 Duffek, "Beyond History," 27.
25 Ingrid Jenkner, *Image Rites* (Halifax: Mount Saint Vincent Art Gallery, 1997).
26 Thomas King points out that settler societies have been fascinated with the figure of the disappearing Indian – Cooper's Chingachgook, Stone's Metamore, Longfellow's Hiawatha, and so on – from the early nineteenth century. See King, *The Truth about Stories: A Native Narrative* (Toronto: Anansi, 2003).
27 Ibid., 34.
28 Anne Makepeace, "Edward Curtis," American Masters, http://www.thirteen.org/americanmasters/curtis/.
29 Michael Taussig, *Mimesis and Alterity: A Particular History of the Senses* (New York: Routledge, 1993), 2.
30 Carolyne M. Chatel, *Jane Ash Poitras: Cycle of Life* (Ottawa: Galerie D'Art Vincent, 2002), 8.
31 Ibid., 10.
32 Marilyn Daniels, "Erasure and Retrieval in Mixed Media," *Fuse* 18, 3 (1995): 43.
33 Ibid., 44.
34 Cardinal-Schubert, "In the Red," 26.
35 Ekkehart Malotki, *Kokopelli: The Making of an Icon* (Lincoln: University of Nebraska Press, 2000), 2, 4.
36 Ibid., 139.
37 Quoted in ibid., 4.
38 Ziff and Rao, *Borrowed Power*.
39 Poitras has spent considerable time visiting Indigenous southwestern communities and therefore may be especially interested in the appropriation of Kokopelli. See Poitras, *Who Discovered the Americas: Recent Work by Jane Ash Poitras* (Thunder Bay, ON: Thunder Bay Art Gallery, 1992), 7-10. Martin P.R. Magne and Michael A. Klassen argue that a possible Kokopelli figure in rock paintings east of Banff National Park in Alberta suggests contact among Cree and southwestern peoples. See Magne and Klassen, "A Possible Fluteplayer Pictograph Site Near Exshaw, Alberta," *Canadian Journal of Archeology* 26, 1 (2002): 3-23.

40 Malotki, *Kokopelli,* 61-63.
41 Ibid., Plates 6 and 10.
42 "Native Artist Uses Brush to Shame Johns," *Regina Leader Post,* 14 August 1992.
43 Helen Hoy, *How Should I Read These? Native Women Writers in Canada* (Toronto: University of Toronto Press, 2001), 21.
44 Patricia Monture-Angus, *Journeying Forward: Dreaming First Nations' Independence* (Toronto: Fernwood, 1999), 156.
45 Ibid., 160.

14

"Our Lives Will Be Different Now"
The Indigenous Feminist Performances of Spiderwoman Theater

KATHERINE YOUNG EVANS

The core members of Spiderwoman Theater – sisters Lisa Mayo, Gloria Miguel, and Muriel Miguel (Kuna-Rappahannock) – have crafted over twenty all-woman shows since the group's inception in 1975, each multilayered production disarming the often mutually reinforcing forms of racism and sexism directed at Native women.[1] In several of their performance pieces, the sisters reappropriate and undermine colonial stereotypes; they overlay two-dimensional images of Indian Princesses and Noble Savages with their three-dimensional bodies and raucous humour. Using an original performance technique called storyweaving – a technique that combines mythic stories, personal and familial memories, popular culture references, songs, movement, and video clips – Spiderwoman Theater brings to diverse audiences the active presence, in Gerald Vizenor's words, of Native American women within both Euro-American society and contemporary Native artistic production.[2] This presence challenges Native studies critics to see gender identity as a critical lens through which to analyze Native writing, and it demands scholars focus more attention on live performance as a site of revitalization for contemporary Native communities fractured by centuries of colonialism. Along these lines of inquiry, this chapter examines three pieces of Spiderwoman Theater's prolific oeuvre: *Sun, Moon, and Feather* (1981), *Winnetou's Snake Oil Show from Wigwam City* (1989), and *Power Pipes* (1992). In similar and distinct ways, each piece wields and transforms the tools of theatre and of feminism to critique the complex cultural, racial, and gender oppression facing Native women in the United States.

Because of its embodied and aural nature, live performance can both respond to colonization and affirm individual and communal identities on intellectual, emotional, and physical levels. As they are enacted, Spiderwoman Theater's works become, as critic Jaye T. Darby describes the work of playwright Hanay Geiogamah (Kiowa-Delaware), "ceremonial literature" that tries "to restore balance and harmony within the community at all levels, from the personal to the cosmic."[3] Building on the scholarship of artists and intellectuals such as Geiogamah, Darby, Drew Hayden Taylor (Ojibway), Diane Glancy (Cherokee), and Elizabeth Theobald (Cherokee), who see theatre as an extension of Native storytelling techniques and as an important location to enact healing ceremonies for Native peoples, I argue that Spiderwoman Theater's performances indigenize European and Euro-American theatre techniques and feminist tools of analysis gleaned from the New York City artistic community in which the group began. By integrating these tools into both Native storytelling structures and their own understandings of the spiritual and cultural power of Native women that have been passed on by their family and the pan-tribal Indigenous community in which they live in New York, Spiderwoman Theater is able to launch a complex critique of twentieth-century modes of racial and gender oppression both within and without Native communities while remaining firmly committed to the survival and revitalization of these communities.

Early critics and reviewers of Spiderwoman Theater concentrated mainly on how the group drew upon feminist performance traditions and noted, quite rightly, that Miguel's work with Joseph Chaikin's Open Theater in the 1970s and the group's involvement with the East Village experimental feminist theatre scene in the late 1970s and 1980s had contributed significantly to its performance aesthetic.[4] Although the alternative gynocentric performance spaces of the Lower East Side offered the group an open and provocative environment within which to work, and although non-Native performers such as Lois Weaver and Peggy Shaw, now of the lesbian group Split Britches, contributed extensively to early pieces, critics have only recently devoted attention to the group's place in the history of Native American performance. Beginning with the publication of Ann Haugo's essay "Negotiating Hybridity: Native Women's Performance as Cultural Persistence" in 1995, Native studies critics have offered insightful, if still too few, perspectives on the group's work as Native theatre. In her 1999 article in the *Journal of Dramatic Theory and Criticism,* Haugo argues that Spiderwoman's work destabilizes the stereotypes imposed by Euro-American society on Native peoples. She identifies how colonial privilege continues to limit the critical conversation about Native performance by focusing on the appropriateness of terms such as *Indian* and the cultural authenticity of urban Native performers. This investment in critiques that avoid "political questions of identity and commodification" in favour of "apolitical questions of semantics and labels," she argues, neglects the transformative and healing power of Spiderwoman Theater's work for Native women and men living in North America today.[5]

The collections *American Indian Theater in Performance: A Reader* and *American Indian Performing Arts: Critical Directions,* both co-edited by Hanay Geiogamah and Jaye Darby, emphasize a more productive focus for Native American theatre criticism: locating dramatic works in the cultural contexts that inform their creation, recognizing the diversity and complexity of Native theatrical production, and celebrating the ritual traditions and "restorative quality of the mythic found in much of contemporary Native theater."[6] This chapter strives to do all three. It identifies how Lisa Mayo's, Gloria Miguel's, and Muriel Miguel's intergenerational and intertribal relationships with women have informed their interlocking critiques of misogyny and colonial oppression and how their use of mythic stories and ceremonies has contributed to the regeneration of Native communities, particularly of Native women. Although some critics argue, as does Laura Tohe (Diné), that gender-based critique is unnecessary when considering traditional Native cultures because they have complementary and equally respected gender roles, the material realities of Native women who live in North American cities, such as the members of Spiderwoman Theater, require indigenized feminist frameworks from within which to analyze and intercede in their disempowerment, both inside and outside of Native communities.[7] A commitment to the decolonization of Native America, as Yup'ik scholar Shari Huhndorf asserts, does not relegate a focus on gender relations to the margins of contemporary scholarly work. In fact, such a commitment necessitates the development of a culturally specific feminism with which to fight the overlapping modes of sexual and racial oppression in the colonial world today.[8] Robert Warrior (Osage) makes this point in an essay in *American Indian Literary Nationalism* (2006), in which he agrees with scholars such as Huhndorf and Cheryl Suzack (Batchewana Anishinaabe) that feminist tools of analysis and the acknowledgment of women's collective agency need to be connected with tribal history and Native community identity to, as Suzack writes, "restore gender identity as an analytical category to discussions of tribal politics and community values."[9] This chapter adds to conversations on both Native theatre and Indigenous feminism by considering how Spiderwoman Theater's arguments for women's safety, sexuality, and self-fulfillment in its performances rely on its cultural, spiritual, and political ties to an intertribal Native community.

Sun, Moon, and Feather, an exploration of the three sisters' relationship as they grew up in a predominantly Italian neighbourhood in Brooklyn, layers stories of sibling rivalry over those of urban Indian identity, economic disadvantage, racial prejudice, and lesbian sexuality.[10] The pain of displacement runs as an undercurrent and, as Lisa Mayo points out in a 1992 interview, is a point of entry for many Native people: "The first time we performed [the play] for an all-Native audience was very thrilling. They got things that non-Indians didn't get. They saw it on another level ... They understood what we were saying about being uprooted."[11] Throughout the piece, the trio negotiates the intersection of joy and despair by pairing witty humour, physical comedy, and flashy costumes with painful stories about growing up poor and Native in white America. Instead of solemnity, the sisters choose to articulate their memories through irreverent and imaginative stories, impersonations, and songs.

The piece opens with a tape recording of the three sisters describing the hopelessness they felt as impoverished cultural outsiders in Brooklyn, but the show quickly undercuts the despair of the "poverty tape," as they call it, with their quirky, campy brand of humour. The sisters' recorded voices reveal their alienation from the Italian families around them and their own family's pain and suffering. Gloria recalls, "There wasn't much hope. When you came home after school to a cold house, no food, a drunken father, a depressed mother, a neighborhood that's very hostile to you." But while the tape plays and Mozart's "K.546 Adagio and Fugue in C minor" blasts from the speakers, images of the San Blas Islands, the homeland of the Kuna Nation, and home movies of the sisters' Kuna father and uncles appear on a white sheet at the back of the stage.[12] The audio of despair clashes with the visuals of family, community, and nation. In the grainy images, their father laughs and smiles alongside family and friends, while the women's voices detail their "worthlessness, selflessness, coming out of being poor, being dirty, not having enough to eat." The disjuncture of words and images replicates the fracture that occurred for the father when he left the San Blas Islands to take a sailing job and stayed in Brooklyn.

Already in this opening sequence, we see the sisters trying to alleviate the symptoms of their parents' distress, though with little success. Mayo's voice describes how "we used to clean the house ourselves. When we tried to clean the house they would get so upset. Mama gave up. Mama gave up a long time ago."[13] Attempts to cover up the Miguel sisters' circumstances met with resistance from their parents. What was needed was not an external cleaning but an internal healing, a process to which *Sun, Moon, and Feather* contributes by animating the bonds that hold the sisters together and connect them to previous generations of Kuna and Rappahannock family members.

The set for *Sun, Moon, and Feather* offers another visual representation of the sisters' connection to their Kuna heritage, as well as of the intertribal influences on their work. The backdrop for the play is a large patchwork quilt made mostly of large embroidered cloth pieces called *molas,* an important cultural and economic production of Kuna women.[14] The centre of the quilt consists of a large mola donated by Gloria, and smaller molas and other pieces of quilt and calico that Muriel received during the giveaways at her first Sun Dance surround it.[15] Over the group's thirty-year history, non-Native collaborators also added material, but representations of their Kuna womanhood remain at the literal heart of the quilt. The quilt exemplifies Spiderwoman Theater's artistic method (to layer stories through storyweaving) as well as the larger impetus behind its work (to heal some of the ruptures the sisters and others in the American Indian community have experienced because of colonization). Muriel Miguel discusses how the group stitches together both stories and community in a 2002 interview with Ann Haugo: "We do this layering; we put things together; we piece things together. We piece a lot of things together to make a whole."[16] The mola – a layered work that emphasizes aesthetic pleasure, cultural connectedness, and women's power in Kuna society – serves as a physical manifestation of the wholeness enacted by Spiderwoman Theater's performances.

Throughout *Sun, Moon, and Feather,* the expression of gender identity joins Native women together but also highlights diversity and difference within Native communities, among Native women, and between Indigenous women's lived experiences and the white ideals of middle-class femininity. Early in the play, Lisa ropes Gloria into a make-believe tea party, complete with a cadre of stuffed animals and dolls to serve as honoured guests. Lisa attempts to create an elaborate fantasy world of privilege by imagining that two empty plastic plates are laden with delicate desserts, that plastic cups are "the most delicate china that was made in the world," and that a plastic measuring cup is a magic teapot from the Ming Dynasty that "is never empty because if it's empty, you just turn it over and it's full again."[17] At each step, Gloria tries to thwart the game by throwing the cups and plates and using the "pure damask linen napkins" (really just paper napkins) to wipe a doll's bottom. Lisa tries to subdue Gloria and instruct her in the behaviour of the white leisure class: "You must keep your pinky up like this and talk fancy."[18] Positioned immediately after the poverty tape, Lisa's tea party underscores the distance between the sisters' lived experience and the ideal of white womanhood. By using obviously fake replicas of a fancy tea service and forcibly commanding Gloria to imitate upper-class Anglo women, Lisa's game calls attention to the performativity of the ideal, an ideal able to be performed only by a select few based on economic advantage, skin colour, and cultural background. Moreover, the audience is meant to laugh both at Lisa's imaginative refiguring of the props and at Gloria's attempt to sabotage the tea party. As a result, the audience takes sides against the ideal of white, upper-class femininity and diffuses its power through laughter as the actors parody its markers.

But the parody does not fully counteract the self-hatred experienced by a child who is too dark and too poor to fulfill the dominant cultural ideal of young womanhood in mid-twentieth-century New York. Gloria Miguel, the darkest-skinned of the three sisters, immediately follows Mayo's tea party with her own memory of race-based prejudice both within and without a Native community:

> *Gloria (playing with doll):* Elizabeth, do you remember when Aunt Ida and Uncle George and Uncle Frank used to take you out and leave me home? I used to sit at the window for hours wondering, why couldn't I go? There you were all dressed up with a big bow in your hair, going out and I had to stay home. I used to think there was something terribly wrong with me.[19]

By playing with the doll (a light-skinned doll in the performance) as she speaks, Gloria brings her childhood self and the pain she experienced into the present. Because of colour hierarchies imposed by colonization, family members preferred the light-skinned Lisa (called Elizabeth by her family) to the darker-skinned Gloria, for she could better fulfill the ideal of white female beauty with her fancy dress and bow in her hair. Such a distinction within the family resulted in a sibling rivalry played out through the youngest sister, Muriel. Lisa wanted Muriel "to be an Indian and carry on the traditions of the family, so I could leave," whereas Gloria, perhaps more painfully aware of the burden of Indianness in white America, "wanted her to be clean ... to be educated ... to be cultured."[20] Both Lisa and Gloria want in some way to leave their identity as Native women behind because of the limitations it puts on their social status in the United States. At the same time, *Sun, Moon, and Feather* is a loving tribute to their family and a boisterous parody of the oppressive structures and pop culture images that instantiated these limitations.

One of the most memorable of these parodies appears near the end of the play, when the trio re-enacts "Indian Love Call," the saccharine love song from the 1936 MGM movie musical *Rose-Marie*. In the movie, red-haired, fair-skinned Jeanette MacDonald plays the beautiful and stubborn American opera singer Rose-Marie de Flor, and Nelson Eddy is the swashbuckling Canadian Mountie, Sergeant Bruce. *Rose-Marie* follows the pair's search for de Flor's brother, John Flower (played by a young Jimmy Stewart), who has escaped from prison and is somewhere in the Canadian Rockies. MacDonald and Eddy display their vocal virtuosity through numerous songs, including "Indian Love Call." While camping out in the wilderness, they hear an eerie howl, and an answering high-pitched wail echoes off the mountain cliffs. Sergeant Bruce reassuringly explains that the sounds are a young Indian man and woman calling to each other across a great distance, and he takes the opportunity to serenade the shaken de Flor with a syrupy melody about romantic true love. Eventually picking up on the words, de Flor joins him in the chorus.

In *Sun, Moon, and Feather,* Gloria and Lisa argue about who will get to play Jeanette MacDonald, the paragon of white femininity, success, and beauty. After some debate, Gloria wins out, climbs up on a chair, and begins the duet. Lisa plays Nelson Eddy, while footage from the actual movie plays on a screen in the background.

Gloria (sings): That is the time of the moon and the year.
When love dreams to Indian maidens appear.
And this is the song that they hear.
Lisa and Gloria (sing): When I'm calling you oooo ooo
Will you answer too oooo oooo
Gloria (sings): That means I offer my love to you
To be your own
Lisa (sings): If you refuse me
I will be blue and waiting all alone.
Gloria and Lisa (sing): But if when you hear my love call ringing clear

> *Gloria (sings):* And I hear your answering echo so clear
> *Lisa and Gloria (sing):* Then I will know
> Our love will come true
> *(Gloria gets off chair):* You belong to me
> I belong to you
> *(They run to each other and dramatically kiss three times).*[21]

This scene renders humorous the sentimentality of monogamous, heterosexual romantic love, an emotion portrayed as primitive, mysterious, and slightly melancholy, much like the Indians calling to each other in the wilderness. In the movie, whiteness and heterosexuality are defined against disembodied Indian voices and a misappropriated tribal ritual. In chivalric fashion, Sergeant Bruce allays de Flor's fears of danger in the mountains, but he does so by simultaneously assimilating Native people into white cultural norms (Indians in a heterosexual love relationship) and marking them as ultimately different (Indians as inarticulate, wailing primitives). The parody of "Indian Love Call" in *Sun, Moon, and Feather* relies on the visual disjuncture between the Hollywood image of white, conventionally attractive, young lovers projected behind middle-aged, plus-size Native women.

It also relies on the virtuosity and skill demonstrated by Gloria and Lisa as they perform the elaborate vocal arrangement a cappella. By performing with vibrancy, skill, and humour, Gloria and Lisa call attention to the misidentification of Indian peoples as primitive savages or relics of the past. Instead, their performance offers a fortifying image of creative Native persistence by positioning Native voices and bodies at the centre of a cultural production meant to relegate them to the periphery. Through their inclusion of "Indian Love Call," they acknowledge the destructive capacity that pop culture material holds for Native individuals who are unable to identify with either limited option – primitive savage or heroic white protagonist. They also acknowledge the pain of their own childhoods, when they were "bombarded by movies, TV, Barbie dolls" that made them want to be "blue-eyed ... thin ... tall," like the Jeanette MacDonalds of the world.[22] Their humorous parody of the song also transforms the material's potential danger into an opportunity to explode preconceived notions about appropriate Indians who, as Haugo explains, have been "deemed authentic by Hollywood."[23] "Indian Love Call" reiterates the centrality of humour to coping and survival and provides another opportunity for the sisters to respond to the interconnected forms of gender, socio-economic, racial, and cultural oppression.

In *Winnetou's Snake Oil Show from Wigwam City*, the members of Spiderwoman Theater, joined by Hortensia Colorado (Chichimec Otomi), satirize the 1892 Karl May novel *Winnetou* and skewer the New Age movement for its support of plastic shamanism and Wild West shows that deploy Indian stereotypes to shore up what Richard Slotkin calls the myth of the frontier.[24] The play opens with the theme to the *Magnificent Seven* playing and scenes from the movie projected onto the screen at the back of the stage. Wild-Eyed Sam, "a cantankerous know-it-all" racist, and Gunther, the German protagonist of May's novel, enter as if they were hunting in the woods of the American West.[25] Wild-Eyed Sam, played by Hortensia Colorado, regales Gunther, played by Lisa Mayo, with stories of the creatures of the wilds, especially bears and Indians. When a bear, played by Gloria Miguel, attacks them, Gunther springs to action, killing it with "a hit on the head, a shot in the eye, and a stab in the chest."[26] Because of its references to hypermasculinized Hollywood westerns and the tradition of rugged frontiersmen, this opening scene introduces gender identity as a necessary lens through which to read the play as a whole.

Euro-American westward expansion generated a specific code of white masculinity on the frontier that relied on the subjugation and physical domination of Indigenous peoples, land, and animals. In Spiderwoman Theater's rendering of the Winnetou story, the appropriation of Native knowledge at the expense of Native peoples is also a feature of Euro-American culture. Gunther learns much from Winnetou, the Apache who befriends him out of respect for his daring conquest of the bear, but this knowledge only makes Gunther believe he is now an expert on the local Indians:

> *Winnetou:* Hear that? That is Indians talking to each other. We must be very careful.
>
> *Gunther:* Yes, but they are not ready to attack yet.
>
> Among Indians, the leader gives the signal with a scream, then the rest join in.
>
> *(Winnetou is making faces because Gunther really is a know-it-all.)*
>
> The screaming is intended to scare the shit out of people.[27]

Although intended as humorous, this exchange of knowledge has real consequences for both Winnetou and the attacking Indians in this scene. "Hordes of Indians" (the two other actors) capture Winnetou and challenge Gunther to a duel, which leads to the death of Hordes #2, played by Gloria. At the close of the show, Winnetou, abandoned by Gunther, "creeps about in corners like a mangy cur," a symbol to May and his European readers of all Indians. Gunther pronounces, "Here lies the Indian, a sick and dying race," though the absurdity of such a statement is underscored by the very presence of Native bodies and stories on stage and in the audience.[28] By inserting four twentieth-century Native women into the hypermasculinized and stereotypical characters of frontiersmen and savages, Spiderwoman Theater highlights the absurdity of May's demeaning and reductive story.

Interspersed with the Winnetou scenes is an acerbic and parodic rendering of the Indian princess stereotype of the Wild West shows.[29] Each of the four actors takes the role of an Indian princess – Princess Pissy Willow, Minnie Hall Runner, Ethel Christian Christiansen, and Mother Moon Face. In their performance of the Winnetou Snake Oil Show from Wigwam City, the three sisters draw on their own experiences performing in their father's snake oil shows as children.[30] Although they underscore the artificiality of these shows by transparently faking their skills with the bull whip, horseback riding, precision shooting, and rope handling, the sisters' own background in Indian show business points to the complicated forms of colonial oppression that forced their family to sell snake oil and charge money for false representations of Native rituals. As in *Sun, Moon, and Feather*, Spiderwoman Theater's use of home movies – this time of pow-wows from the mid-twentieth century – creates a visual disjuncture between the meaningful expression of Native spirituality on screen and the commodified version parodied on stage.[31]

The most memorable scene in *Winnetou's Snake Oil Show* comes in the latter half of the performance, when the Indian princesses choose a white male spectator to turn into an Indian, complete with personal and tribal names such as Old Rocking Chair of the Wishee Washee tribe.[32] This so-called ceremony is elaborately low-budget: sacred spaces are denoted by bath mats, and the essence of sweat lodge comes from a plastic spritz bottle.[33] Although absurd, the selling of honorary Indian status to non-Native people by plastic shamans, both Native and non-Native, poses a real threat to Native communities. This process ignores the very real power dynamics and social inequities that shape Native experience and representation in North America. Moreover, it dematerializes the very culture these spiritual seekers desire to access as it simultaneously commodifies it. As Philip Deloria observes, these followers gain access to an Indianness that relies "not upon spiritual experience, cultural crossing, or accidents of birth, but upon economic exchange."[34] In this configuration of culture, Euro-Americans have access to Native cultural traditions but continue to deny Native people access to white privilege. Muriel Miguel asserts, "We couldn't go into their community and easily adapt because they don't want us there. We'll always be the oddity. It's the paradox that they want what we have but they don't want us."[35] *Winnetou's Snake Oil Show* demands responsibility from New Agers who, like the Hollywood studios of the 1930s, erase the real presence of Native peoples in favour of a romanticized and two-dimensional view of their culture that generates high revenues.

A key element of Spiderwoman Theater's storyweaving process is the inclusion of the members' own stories and histories alongside mainstream images. In one scene about halfway through *Winnetou's Snake Oil Show,* a character identified as Demon #1, played by Gloria, addresses the audience:

> My father believed in demons. Listened to Chief Nele and captured tortoise. At the age of thirteen, his body was covered with blue dye from the Poli Wala tree. And he slept three nights and three days alone in the rain forest ... He left Nargana on the San Blas islands and became an able-bodied seaman ... To chase away the demons, he gulped down a bottle of whiskey ... He never returned to Nargana. He still believed in demons. He believed in demons until the day he died.[36]

Gloria's description of her father's coming-of-age ceremony, in contrast with the parodic skewering of plastic shamanism, works to re-forge spiritual and cultural bonds, rather than render them absurd. Standing centre stage while a home movie of her family at a pow-wow plays behind her, Miguel brings into the present moment the complex history of her father's – and her own – relationship to a Kuna cosmology. A belief in demons, a belief that for Gloria's father never dissipates, brings an affirmation of Kuna spirituality. Yet this same belief when transferred to the alien culture of Brooklyn produces the conditions for alcoholism in the same man. By inhabiting the mythic creature of the demon, Gloria Miguel partakes of the spiritual power it possesses, transforming her body into a crucible for positive transformative potential to bring her father – and herself – back into a nourishing connection with Kuna spiritual beliefs. As a microcosm of the play as a whole, this scene demonstrates how tribal spiritualities offer individual and collective wholeness when used with respect by those within a Native community. But they can also undercut Native people's agency when they are divorced from the proper cultural context.

The performers work through this ambivalence toward their own Native identities throughout the play. In addition to Gloria's enactment of the demon, the women recall the spiritual lessons passed down to them by mothers and grandmothers. Lisa recounts how her Rappahannock mother was born with a caul, "an extra piece of skin covering her head," that her grandmother said gave her special psychic powers. Although as a child Muriel "would have liked her [mother] to be like every other mother in the neighborhood," she and her sisters came to take pride in her mother's status as a revered wise woman.[37] As in Gloria's recollection of her father's ceremonial entrance into Kuna manhood, the sisters' story of their mother's gift, a gift they now acknowledge as their own, revitalizes their connection to Native spiritual beliefs and contrasts sharply with the New Age movement's decontextualized appropriations of these beliefs. Following their personal story of a spirituality that "has alternately shamed and mystified them,"[38] Muriel, as the character of Ethel Christian Christiansen, details the spontaneous transformation of a white woman into an Indian:

> *Ethel Christian Christiansen:* I used to be a white woman. It's true. I was Irish ..., German ..., Norwegian ...? Then one day, my skin turned bronze and I became a shamaness. I must share with you this vision I had. I was in the subway, waiting for the F train and there was this noise and I looked up and a white light was coming towards me. No, it wasn't the F train. It was a white buffalo. And seated on that white buffalo was a noble savage, naked ... except for his loin cloth. His skin was the color of bronze, with just a touch of gold. His hair was the color of Lady Clairol No. 154, midnight blue. He wore it in long braids, intertwined with rattlesnake skins. And growing out of his skull was an eagle feather, signifying he was a chief. He is a chief, I am a shamaness.[39]

In performance, this scene ridicules the essentialized vision of Indians that defines plastic shamanism. As Ann Haugo points out, "once her skin turns beige, Ethel Christian Christiansen discovers her Indian soul" and is then visited by the stereotypical Indian male, complete with loin cloth, braids, and feather, riding a white buffalo.[40] The performance destabilizes the connection of skin colour to spiritual knowledge as it implicitly derides Ethel for assuming that bronze skin makes one a shamaness. Moreover, it calls attention to the labour exercised by colonial stereotypes to make the "beads and buckskin" image of Indians seem authentic and to effect the erasure of actual Native peoples through stereotype. The midnight blue hue of the Indian chief's braids is more like Lady Clairol hair dye than any naturally occurring colour.

What also stands out about Ethel's tale of transformation is its sexual overtones. As in *Rose-Marie*, a heterosexual love relationship finds footing in reductive images of Native primitivism. In Ethel's story, her desire for Indian identity is both spiritual and sexual, and both characteristics objectify and simplify what is desired. Instead of a complex tribally specific web of beliefs, rituals, and mythic history, Ethel sees only easy access to becoming a shamaness, a flattened, simplistic rendering of the female spiritual power the three sisters had detailed in the previous scene. Instead of the complex material realities of Native men living in North America in the twentieth century, Ethel sees a dehistoricized nearly naked caricature of Indian masculinity, whose "eyes pierced [her] skin and seared [her] heart."[41] We find this condensing of spirituality and sexuality in Native women throughout Euro-American history in images of Pocahontas, Sacajgawea, and La Malinche. By depicting an Indian man in the same terms – seemingly participating in the spiritual and sexual exploitation of Native cultures – Spiderwoman Theater flips the corrosive stereotype of Native women as promiscuous, passive, and disloyal. The sisters also expose the harmful power white women yield to entrench stereotypes of Native men as consumable eye candy. Not only does this undermine Native men's effectiveness in the public sphere, it also disregards the violence they perpetrate on both themselves and the women in their lives. Scenes like this in *Winnetou's Snake Oil Show* limit Native women's potential to form alliances with white women who neglect to deal honestly with contemporary Native issues and their own complicity in the continued subjugation of Native peoples, whether effected through spiritual appropriation or a self-serving sense of sisterhood.

Winnetou's Snake Oil Show from Wigwam City is an affirmation of the centrality of Native ways of knowing, which are exemplified by the final sequence in which the actors, as a chorus, repeat "now I telling you. Watch me. I'm alive. I'm not defeated. I begin. Now I telling you" directly to the audience.[42] The continuous present tense of the chorus, "Now I telling you," evokes a realization that, despite attempts to erase, co-opt, or destroy them, Native women continue to survive and will forever be "telling" themselves into being through stories. Moreover, the grammar echoes that of the sisters' uncle Joe, their father's brother from the San Blas Islands. According to Lisa, "when he wanted to tell you something, he'd say, 'NOW I TELLING YOU!'"[43] This inclusion of Uncle Joe's words, like the inclusion of the home movies in both *Sun, Moon, and Feather* and *Winnetou's Snake Oil Show,* not only testifies to a strong Kuna presence in the current generation, it also acknowledges the presence of previous and future generations that will continue on in the telling.

Gloria Miguel revisits her father's coming-of-age ceremony and contemplates the healing this ritual could provide for her in *Reverb-ber-ber-rations* (1990) and *Power Pipes* (1993). In the former, in a scene titled "Unfinished Business," she tells the audience, "After my father's death, I knew I had to return to Naragana. My father's blood, my blood, our blood. He wanted to close open wounds. Rectify his guilt. He died, I returned for him. To find his son, my brother ... Through me my brother is connected with his father. My father's blood, my blood, our blood."[44] Through her rhythmic repetition of "my father's blood, my blood, our blood," Gloria collapses the boundaries between herself, her father, and her brother. Her telling of the story is the ritual that maintains her closeness with Naragana and members of her family. Together, the family closes the open wounds, and they seal their blood as one, regardless of the boundaries of death, distance, time, or gender. In the ritual, these boundaries disappear. Yet for an audience attending a performance by the longest continually running feminist theatre group, Gloria's emphasis on her blood as healer brings to mind the life-giving power of menstrual blood.

In *Power Pipes,* Miguel, as the character Mesi Tuli Omai, makes this connection more explicit. She returns again to Naragana, this time without ever leaving New York. She relates the following story:

> All alone. (She crosses to center stage with her stool and sits. Music recording of panpipes) I found a way to escape. Just stay in one place. Just sit down in one place, close your eyes and go off. It was hot in the city the summer I got my first moon. On my eleventh birthday. That same week my only friend was struck and killed by a car. I was so sad ... I sat by my window, closed my eyes, and went off on a faraway trip. (Droning sound) I traveled many miles, all the way to Naragana, on the San Blas Islands, where my father came from, where the Cuna people would have a special celebration for me. A traditional healing ceremony for me. There I found myself naked, sitting in a clay tub of water. Men and women were dancing around me. A special woman cut my hair, another woman poured water over me ... Home again, sitting by the window, I thought, "My life will be different now."[45]

During the ceremony, Mesi Tuli Omai's body, much like Miguel's father's body during his own coming-of-age ceremony, is "covered in blue dye" from the fruit of the polly-walla tree. Afterward, her father leads her around the island, blowing a large conch shell and pronouncing that "today my daughter is a woman ... Today she is ready to be a wife."[46] Although this experience is reminiscent of the ceremony for men, Mesi Tuli Omai's coming-of-age ceremony is bound up tightly with her identity both as a woman and as a Kuna displaced from the San Blas Islands. The pain she feels at losing her best friend, the discomfort of the hot New York summer, and the combined thrill and anxiety over her first period are all subsumed within the structure of the Kuna ceremony. Within the womb-like clay tub, the rituals enacted by the women gathered around her cradle and comfort her, alleviating the feelings of aloneness that begin the passage. Her father, in this vision of the ceremony, ceases the destructive alcoholism Miguel witnessed as a child in exchange for embedding his daughter – and re-embedding himself – in Kuna spiritual life. He and the "special" women act as mediators for Mesi Tuli Omai's transition to womanhood. By announcing "today my daughter is a woman," her father makes it reality in a Kuna cosmology.

But how does this translate to contemporary life in New York City? Even though Mesi Tuli Omai is a great distance from the San Blas Islands, she is able to transcend the geographic boundaries that hold her in New York. Likewise, she is able to transcend the boundaries that keep her separated from a community of Native women. As she says, her "life will be different now" that she has joined the female lineage made available through menstruation and her connection to Kuna spirituality.[47] Her need for this community of women stems partially from her distance from it, from her experiences growing up poor, female, and Native in a city dominated by non-Native definitions of womanhood, beauty, and wealth. The "material realities of Native life," as Warrior describes it, which seek to disempower Native women through the overlapping and interlocking forces of racism, sexism, and classism in state and legal institutions as well as popular media mandate the massive strength mustered through women-focused rituals, stories, and conversations.[48]

A moving example of this mobilization occurs immediately following Mesi Tuli Omai's story in *Power Pipes*. In Part 1 of Scene 12, "Rape Story," She Who Opens Hearts, played by Hortensia Colorado, is gang raped by seven men on a subway; the rape is portrayed in a pantomime sequence in which rattles and drums mark the increasing terror and violence. Mesi Tuli Omai witnesses the attack but exits without helping She Who Opens Hearts. Leading up to the attack, warning sounds punctuate She Who Opens Hearts' inner monologue and emphasize her instinctual distrust of the man staring at her and the other men walking toward her. Although She

Who Opens Hearts perceives the imminent threat, she dismisses it as "just [her] imagination" until it is too late.[49] In Part 2 of "Rape Story," the same sequence is repeated, but instead of exiting, Mesi Tuli Omai comes to the aid of She Who Opens Hearts, and together they fight off the gang, screaming "RAAAAPE!!!!!!"[50] In the third depiction of "Rape Story," the scene's beginning is the same but four deities join the two women to offer their support. The deities join the warning sounds heard in the earlier versions and urge She Who Opens Hearts to "listen to your warning" and "answer the voices." They ask, "who are your protectors?"[51] With the deities alongside her, offering their protection and power, She Who Opens Hearts springs at her attackers verbally and physically, ably defending herself against the rape.

The threat of sexual violence is thus contained through collective action by Native women in Part 2 and through an openness to the lessons and support of the spiritual world in Part 3. Through a coalition of mortal and mythic women, She Who Opens Hearts defends herself against the violence intended by the gang. Although the menace of sexual violence encroaches on Native women's lives in real ways, the rape also serves as a metonym for the larger threat to Native women's survival posed by colonization and the subsequent dissolution of gender equity within tribal communities. Both women's collective action and a spiritual connection serve the same end purpose – the deflection of violence and the empowerment of Native women. Combined, they constitute a profound response to the specific challenges facing Native women today. In the "Rape Story" scene, Spiderwoman Theater demonstrates the transformative potential of Native women acting and speaking out against injustice in concert with one another and the spiritual and cultural legacies that inform their identities.

Power Pipes itself can be seen as an empowering ceremony for Native communities in general, but specifically for Native women. It was created collaboratively by six Native women, and its cast has included five members and two generations of the same family in varying configurations. Monique Mojica, Gloria Miguel's daughter and a successful performer and writer in Toronto, originally helped Spiderwoman Theater develop the piece, and Murielle Borst, also a performer and writer and Muriel Miguel's daughter, later took her role as Wind Horse Spirit Warrior. Sisters Hortensia and Elvira Colorado, who perform regularly as Coatlicue Theater Company's Colorado Sisters, also participated in the creative process and played the roles of She Who Opens Hearts and Obsidian Woman, respectively. Haugo declares that *Power Pipes* "best exemplifies Spiderwoman Theater's legacy" because of its reliance on the contribution of personal stories and histories from so many women.[52] Spiderwoman's storyweaving process, which takes the individual contributions of the performers (often developed during improvisation sessions) and interlaces them in a non-linear tapestry of story, film, sound, and movement, requires the honesty, trust, and willingness to take risks that the company has demonstrated over thirty years of existence. It also requires respect for and a connection with each performer's own cultural identity, however complicated, and a commitment to the survival and revitalization of Native communities in contemporary North America. It is these communities, specifically communities of Native women, to whom Spiderwoman Theater speaks.

Muriel Miguel has remarked that "when Indians gather, there's always a lot of laughter" and that performing for an all-Native audience is "a totally sizzling and uplifting experience."[53] These comments point to the potential of Native theatre – specifically Spiderwoman Theater's combination of irreverent comedy, personal stories, and mythology – to heal communities through live performance. By grounding their work in their personal experience, the members of Spiderwoman Theater disarm attempts by Euro-Americans to circumscribe Native identity. Through stories that rejuvenate tribal traditions and through parodies of demeaning pop culture, Spiderwoman Theater offers a multifaceted model for navigating the process of decolonization and articulating Indian self-definition. The sisters' own lived experience – complete with tears, laughter, and anger – offers a rebuttal to the myth of the vanishing Indian by asserting a vibrant presence in mainstream culture and a crucial vision of the uses of Indigenous feminist theatre.

NOTES

1 Throughout this essay, I identify the specific tribal nation of the Native writers, performers, and intellectuals I mention, relying on each individual's self-designation in my terminology. Not only does this practice underscore the diversity within Native America today, but it also delineates Native communities as distinct political entities, rather than ethnic or racial minorities within the US and Canada.

2 Gerald Vizenor, *Fugitive Poses: Native American Indian Scenes of Absence and Presence* (Lincoln: University of Nebraska Press, 1998), 15.

3 Jaye T. Darby, "'Come to the Ceremonial Circle': Ceremony and Renewal in Hanay Geiogamah's *49*," in Hanay Geiogamah and Jaye T. Darby, eds., *American Indian Theater in Performance: A Reader* (Los Angeles: UCLA American Indian Studies Center, 2000), 197.

4 See Charlotte Canning, *Feminist Theaters in the U.S.A.: Staging Women's Experience* (New York: Routledge, 1996); Jill Dolan, *The Feminist Spectator as Critic* (Ann

Arbor: University of Michigan Press, 1988); and Rebecca Schneider, *The Explicit Body in Performance* (London: Routledge, 1997).

5 Ann Haugo, "Negotiating Hybridity: Native Women's Performance as Cultural Persistence," *Women and Performance* 7, 2 (1995): 125-42. Ann Haugo, "Colonial Audiences and Native Women's Theater: Viewing Spiderwoman Theater's *Winnetou's Snake Oil Show from Wigwam City*," *Journal of Dramatic Theory and Criticism* 14, 1 (Fall 1999): 135.

6 Jaye T. Darby, "Introduction: A Talking Circle on Native Theater," in Geiogamah and Darby, *American Indian Theater in Performance,* xiii.

7 Laura Tohe, "There Is No Word for Feminism in My Language," *Wicazo Sa Review* 15, 2 (Fall 2000): 110.

8 Shari Huhndorf, "Literature and the Politics of Native American Studies," *PMLA* 120, 5 (2005): 1626.

9 Cheryl Suzack, quoted in Robert Warrior, "Native Critics in the World: Edward Said and Nationalism," in Jace Weaver, Craig S. Womack, and Robert Warrior, eds., *American Indian Literary Nationalism* (Albuquerque: University of New Mexico Press, 2006), 212.

10 Spiderwoman Theater, *Sun, Moon, and Feather,* in Hanay Geiogamah and Jaye T. Darby, eds., *Stories of Our Way: An Anthology of American Indian Plays* (Los Angeles: UCLA American Indian Studies Center, 1999), 287-314. Muriel Miguel identifies as lesbian. Although sexual identity plays an important role in individual and collective forms of feminism, as I demonstrate later in this essay, I forego discussion of Miguel's sexuality in favour of readings that highlight the possibilities Spiderwoman Theater's performances hold for the empowerment of communities of Native women of all sexual orientations. For astute critical readings of the intersection of sexuality and feminist theatre in the work of the Spiderwoman Theatre, see Canning, *Feminist Theaters in the U.S.A.,* 90-95 and 189; Dolan, *The Feminist Spectator as Critic,* 71-72; and Schneider, *The Explicit Body in Performance,* 153-74.

11 Lisa Mayo, Judy Burns, and Jerri Hurlbutt, "Secrets: A Conversation with Lisa Mayo of Spiderwoman Theater," *Women and Performance* 5, 2 (1992): 176.

12 Spiderwoman Theater, *Sun, Moon, and Feather,* 290. Kuna Yala, the name of the autonomous Kuna territory, includes the San Blas Islands and a several-hundred-mile-long strip of land along the Caribbean coast of Panama, bordering Colombia.

13 Ibid., 291.

14 For discussions of molas in Kuna culture, see James Howe, *A People Who Would Not Kneel: Panama, the United States, and the San Blas Kuna* (Washington, DC: Smithsonian Institution Press, 1998), and Mari Lyn Salvador, *The Art of Being Kuna: Layers of Meaning among the Kuna of Panama* (Los Angeles: UCLA Fowler Museum of Cultural History, 1997).

15 Ann Haugo, "Weaving a Legacy: An Interview with Muriel Miguel of the Spiderwoman Theater," in Roberta Uno with Lucy Mae San Pablo Burns, eds., *The Color of Theater: Race, Culture, and Contemporary Performance* (London: Continuum, 2002), 225.

16 Ibid.

17 Ibid., 294.

18 Ibid., 293-94.
19 Ibid., 294.
20 Ibid., 296.
21 Ibid., 311-12.
22 Muriel Miguel, quoted in Anna Kay France and P.J. Corso, eds., *International Women Playwrights: Voices of Identity and Transformation – Proceedings of the First International Women Playwrights Conference, October 18-23, 1988* (Metuchen, NJ: Scarecrow Press, 1993), 117.
23 Haugo, "Colonial Audiences," 138.
24 Slotkin's study of the myth of the frontier traces how white American writers crafted a coherent and celebratory view of westward expansion through a combination of two genres: the captivity narrative and tales of the hunter-warrior. What resulted was an image of a frontiersman who was both primitively violent and a harbinger of Euro-American progress, cultural and physical, across the continent. The most applicable book in Slotkin's trilogy on the frontier myth is *Gunfighter Nation: The Myth of the Frontier in Twentieth-Century America* (New York: Atheneum, 1992).
25 Spiderwoman Theater, *Winnetou's Snake Oil Show from Wigwam City,* in Jaye T. Darby and Stephanie Fitzgerald, eds., *Keepers of the Morning Star: An Anthology of Native Women's Theater* (Los Angeles: UCLA American Indian Studies Center, 2003), 231.
26 Ibid., 237.
27 Ibid., 249.
28 Ibid., 260.
29 Rayna Green's article "The Pocahontas Perplex: The Image of Indian Women in American Culture" *Massachusetts Review* 16, 4 (1975) details competing images of Native women in the Euro-American imagination. Native women were seen as both highly refined princesses sympathetic to Euro-American cultural norms and as savage squaws, exploitable for hard labour and sexual pleasure.
30 Ann Haugo, "Native Playwrights' Newsletter Interview: Lisa Mayo," in Geiogamah and Darby, *American Indian Theater in Performance,* 326; Haugo, "Weaving a Legacy," 227.
31 Spiderwoman Theater, *Winnetou's Snake Oil Show,* 234.
32 Ibid., 256-57.
33 Ibid., 255-56.
34 Philip J. Deloria, *Playing Indian* (New Haven, CT: Yale University Press, 1999), 169.
35 Haugo, "Weaving a Legacy," 230.
36 Spiderwoman Theater, *Winnetou's Snake Oil Show,* 247-48.
37 Ibid., 252.
38 Haugo, "Circles upon Circles upon Circles," 240.
39 Spiderwoman Theater, *Winnetou's Snake Oil Show,* 254.
40 Haugo, "Colonial Audiences," 137.
41 Spiderwoman Theater, *Winnetou's Snake Oil Show,* 254.
42 Ibid., 262.
43 Mayo, Burns, and Hurlbutt, "Secrets," 177.

44 Spiderwoman Theater, *"Reverb-ber-ber-rations," Women and Performance* 5, 2 (1992): 202-3.
45 Spiderwoman Theater, *Power Pipes,* in Mimi Gisolfi D'Aponte, ed., *Seventh Generation: An Anthology of Native American Plays* (New York: Theatre Communications Group, 1999), 173.
46 Ibid., 174.
47 Ibid.
48 Warrior, "Native Critics in the World," 211.
49 Spiderwoman Theater, *Power Pipes,* 175.
50 Ibid., 176.
51 Ibid., 176-77.
52 Haugo, "Circles upon Circles upon Circles," 241.
53 Kallen Martin, "Spiderwoman Theatre," *Akwesasne Notes* 1, 3 (31 December 1995): 133.

15 Bordering on Feminism
Space, Solidarity, and Transnationalism in Rebecca Belmore's *Vigil*

ELIZABETH KALBFLEISCH

Feminism without borders is not the same thing as borderless feminism. It acknowledges the fault lines, conflicts, differences, fears, and containment that borders represent. It acknowledges that there is no one sense of a border, that lines between and through nations, races, classes, sexualities, religions, and disabilities are real, and that a feminism without borders must envisage change and social justice work across these lines of demarcation and division.

– *Chandra Talpade Mohanty,* Feminism without Borders: Decolonizing Theory, Practicing Solidarity

Space, place, land, and, indeed, the border – both real and imagined – hold particular significance to Aboriginal people and figure strongly in the production of many artists working today. The manner in which these important themes relate to feminist concerns is not always as apparent, given the complex relationship between feminism and Aboriginal art. *Vigil,* the 2002 performance of Anishinaabe artist Rebecca Belmore, suggests a point of mediation. Thematically, space, place, and the border are germane to the work, but their impact intensifies as they imbricate with the performance's feminist tenor. Aboriginal art remains undertheorized from a feminist perspective; transnational feminism, however, imagined as a "feminism without borders" by feminist scholar Chandra Talpade Mohanty in the passage cited above, suggests a means for a renewed feminist interlocution into Aboriginal contemporary art.

Because contemporary feminist theory – particularly that of the third wave, which has sought to be more inclusive – has not integrated cohesively into Aboriginal cultural practice, the suggestive trope of the border is an impressive means by which to negotiate this integration. Borders are barriers that exclude, but they also provide safe demarcated space. Penetrable borders also suggest a meeting point where communication and exchange can occur. Harnessing the border's potential to facilitate exchange – among feminists cross-culturally, between artists and spectators, and among citizens – even as it maintains distinct spaces, offers a new, positive turn on the divisive feminist and cultural politics that short-fuse the relationship between Aboriginal art and feminism.

In this chapter, I draw on two of Mohanty's contributions to transnational feminism – "Under Western Eyes: Feminist Scholarship and Colonial Discourses" and *Feminism without Borders: Decolonizing Theory, Practicing Solidarity* – to situate Belmore's performance (and Aboriginal women's art practice more generally) in a feminist cross-cultural context. By approaching Belmore's *Vigil* by way of transnational feminism, I apply an ethical model of engagement that establishes a hospitable working space for feminist subject positions occupied by Aboriginal women. Territory and cultural difference still carry great importance for many Aboriginal people. Thus, rather than insisting on dismantling borders, feminism without borders allows feminist connections to be made within and across existing ones. Feminism without borders has the potential to exert much influence as a strategy for cross-cultural communication. Its capacity to articulate the relationship between a subject and space sets transnational feminism apart as a site with the potential for truly dynamic engagement. As individuals and populations move through space, crossing national and cultural borders, feminism takes their cue, reflecting this reality and acknowledging multiple and varied allegiances. In this chapter, Mohanty's politics of shared feminist values across borders frame my discussion of Belmore's *Vigil*, the space of her performance, and the terrible crimes against women that her work addresses.

Vigil and Its Context

On 23 June 2002, Rebecca Belmore staged *Vigil* in an empty and otherwise unremarkable lot at the corner of Gore and Cordova Streets in Vancouver's

Downtown Eastside. The work was presented as part of the Talking Stick Festival of First Nations performance. *Vigil* was a response to the alarming number of Aboriginal women who have disappeared from the Downtown Eastside over the past twenty years and pointedly, to the increasing number of Aboriginal women who have vanished since 1995. Too frequently, the Downtown Eastside is described with pejorative adjectives such as *grim, gritty,* or *seedy;* the *Washington Post* calls it "a version of hell populated by prostitutes, drug addicts and pimps."[1] Located just beyond the city's affluent commercial shopping district, the neighbourhood has come to signify hardship: signs of poverty, drug addiction, prostitution, and mental illness are visible on its streets and in its residents. The public, at local and national levels, so closely identifies the Downtown Eastside with the city's social problems that accounts of Vancouver's drug trade, prostitution, and poverty invariably invoke this neighbourhood as their nexus. This notoriety resonates with area residents, many of whom are Aboriginal and have migrated to western Canada's largest city from other parts of the province.

Newspaper accounts report that most of the disappeared worked in the sex trade and coped with addictions; many, too, were afflicted by mental health problems.[2] Of the sixty-nine women on the missing list released by the Royal Canadian Mounted Police (RCMP) in October 2004, more than half were identified as Aboriginal.[3] For years the police did not pursue these unsettling disappearances, leaving the loss of each woman and its attendant ambiguous circumstances to be marked only by the woman's friends and family. Not until 2001 – after prodigious lobbying by families and friends, the Native Women's Association of Canada (NWAC), and other outreach and women's groups – did the authorities react. They established the Missing Women Task Force, a joint venture of the RCMP and the Vancouver Police Department. In the winter of 2002, police charged Robert Pickton, the owner of a pig farm near Port Coquitlam, a small community on the outskirts of Vancouver, with the murder of two women. As the investigation of the pig farm continued, the number of dead rose. Due to DNA or remains uncovered at the site, Pickton was charged with the murder of twenty-six women. In December 2007, he was convicted on six counts of second-degree murder. He has yet to be tried for the deaths of the other twenty women. If the Crown were to pursue and achieve convictions on all charges, the case would be the largest serial murder in Canadian history. During the investigation, the farm was designated as a crime scene and as a mass grave. Yet the Downtown Eastside, the site of the disappearances, has a far more complex status.

Although the Pickton murders were particularly heinous, the crimes against the women of Vancouver's Downtown Eastside are seen by many Aboriginal people as part of an extensive and ongoing history of oppression in Canada. Amnesty International attests to this in a scathing report.[4] In this sense, it follows that the attacks on women that inspired *Vigil* parallel the colonial assault on Aboriginal people, thus making a case for allegiance between feminist and Aboriginal activism. The artist's reclamation of the missing women's home space reiterates the prior claim of Aboriginal people to (land) space in Canada. This prior claim imbues Belmore's use of the performance space with double meaning. The chilling racist and sexist language used by the police, and sometimes by the media, with reference to the women who disappeared rendered Belmore's claim all the more pointed: repeated references to hookers, drug addicts, and so-called Indians overdetermined the missing according to the stereotypes about Aboriginal people and the Downtown Eastside.[5] Belmore located her performance in a part of the Downtown Eastside where many of the missing and murdered women had worked on the streets. The Downtown Eastside is at once a place, location, or destination and a non-place, where women vanish and where residents do not easily fit in and often cannot be accounted for.

In the performance, which runs nearly forty minutes, the artist marks the loss of women from the place; she mourns their absence and acknowledges the violence and misogyny that their deaths have revealed. The performance's title, *Vigil*, sets the tone for what follows: a memorial, a vigil, but at a most basic level, an occupation. Belmore establishes her presence in the street space she has selected and prepares it for her occupation. The performance begins as she enters, carrying two buckets of water and a canvas shopping bag full of supplies. She sets these things down and pulls out smaller bags of candles, rags, hammer and nails, clothing, and a bouquet of roses. These items are tossed on the pavement deliberately and with haste; seconds later, the artist pulls on red rubber kitchen gloves, picks up a small whisk-style broom, and begins to brush the pavement.

Belmore smoothly integrates the preparation of the site, a small parking lot, into the performance itself. Her efforts to establish her space are indistinguishable from the subsequent action that takes place within it. As she moves through the space, sweeping with the small broom, the site's limits, effectively quasi-barriers, are defined: a tall black wrought-iron fence closes off the back, and a chain-link fence defines a side. Action takes place on both sides of this fence, but the fence itself figures as a central feature of the performance. Belmore's small audience, a crowd of about twenty, loops around the other open sides, thus closing the artist in from the street. Belmore fixes these boundaries as she begins to clean the space inside them. In doing so, she territorializes and exerts control over a public space, something that, ostensibly, is difficult to enact, perhaps more so in a space such as the Downtown Eastside that seems to elude order and cohesion. By marking off her territory, Belmore takes control of the site as a safe space and constructs a personal space within a public one. Her action suggests that these spaces are not as mutually exclusive as we might think.

As much as Belmore seeks to define her site, the porousness of the border complicates the space. She attempts to light candles in the foreground. Although these candles would provide another boundary of sorts, they are immediately extinguished by the wind. Belmore diligently defines her territory, but people can still pass through its borders. They can cut through the crowd or walk around or climb over the fences, much like any outsider can cross into the Downtown Eastside, pass freely through it, and still not be a part of the taxonomic space identified for its residents. The territorialization of the performance space, of the street itself, renders non-place into place. This is not a gratuitous transformation. The notoriety of the area coupled with the supposed transience of its inhabitants makes for a precarious sense of place. Questions about its nature, about who lives there and who goes there (questions that are fed by sensational media accounts), evade the human, the specific, and the concrete. By doing so, they give rise to a non-place; they posit a place that is a synecdoche, built upon the fictions and fears of outsiders.

The mantle of non-place has fostered ambivalence about the Downtown Eastside. The Vancouver police respond sluggishly to missing persons cases; in turn, they attribute their indifference to the alleged rootlessness of the women themselves. Critics charge that because the victims have largely been identified as Aboriginal street-level prostitutes and substance abusers, their social status has pre-empted adequate attention and expedited investigations. The police offer up these same identifiers to rationalize their reluctance to pursue the women's cases. According to the police, many of the women are difficult to trace because they lived transient lives, estranged from their families.[6] This logic reveals an unsettling disconnect between the totalizing manner in which the Downtown Eastside is represented and the individual experiences of its inhabitants. The area had a notorious reputation before the Missing Women Task Force was founded and certainly before the police charged Robert Pickton with the murders. The Downtown Eastside location is firm and fixed with mappable coordinates.

Yet its cartographic certitude does not extend to its inhabitants: the fixity of the Downtown Eastside does not cohere with the supposed transience of its population. The area's troubles prohibit it from being granted the status of home for its residents. As a localized concept, place shares many attributes with the idea of home; however, the features of the Downtown Eastside that are employed repeatedly to construct it eschew those associated with home. In 2002, the *Ottawa Citizen,* for example, marvelled that though many of the missing women "lived a street life, others still retained family connections, cared for their children, even had bank accounts," as if these quotidian concerns are obsolete in the Downtown Eastside.[7]

Belmore's *Vigil* sanctifies this place by accounting for it. As her performance continues, she prepares the site further as its primary occupant. Kneeling, she scrubs the asphalt vigorously with a brush from one of the buckets, to which she has added cleaning fluid. She pulls a rag from a bag and mops up some of the water – somewhat futilely, for the wet pavement immediately drenches the rag, leaving it filthy. As she cleans, the artist becomes breathless, her jeans damp, and her brow furrowed with concentration and activity. Belmore's intense engagement with this task suggests a profound commitment to it; the flurry of activity resonates on several levels and sets the performance's tone. Belmore's actions allude to funerary preparations, during which the body of the deceased is ritually cleansed – often by women – and prepared for burial rites. In the absence of bodies, the artist prepares the site from which the missing disappeared, the ground from which they vanished, the ground that swallowed them up. Cleaning the street also fixes the site for its occupants, whose transitory movements disallow the status of home. Home and place are unseated signifiers that fail to correspond. Belmore's actions acknowledge the site as a home worthy of respect, protection, and care, but they also warn that the streets where some of the victims made their homes are unsafe. This staging also signifies in patent terms domestic work and women's labour. Belmore's actions remind us that all the victims were women, that she mourns a group of women. At a basic level, the act of cleaning connotes the menial work of women, work generally unaccounted for and often conducted by Indigenous people, illegal aliens, or new immigrants far from their homeland.

Homeland and Aboriginal Diaspora

The theme of homeland reappears again and again in the work of many contemporary Aboriginal artists. Belmore's own body of work provides a case study for the prevalence of politically charged land-based issues in

Aboriginal art. In an early performance, *Exhibit #671B,* which was staged in the winter of 1988, Belmore sat cross-legged and wrapped in blankets outside of the Thunder Bay Art Gallery, a location close to her own hometown of Upsala, Ontario. The performance coincided with the passing of the Olympic torch as it travelled to Calgary, where the Olympic Games were subsequently held. For this work, Belmore positioned herself as a living exhibit to protest a now notorious major exhibition of First Nations art, "The Spirit Sings: Artistic Traditions of Canada's First Peoples," which was mounted during the Olympics. The exhibition was sponsored by Shell Oil, a company whose drilling on Lubicon Cree land had angered Aboriginal people and upset difficult protracted negotiations for rights. Another of Belmore's works, *Ayum-ee-aawach Oomama-mowan: Speaking to Their Mother* (1991), featured a huge megaphone constructed from natural materials. The artist travelled with the work to Aboriginal communities across Canada and, in so doing, collaborated with scores of individuals. The work afforded Aboriginal people the opportunity to speak directly, by means of the megaphone, to the land itself. This act empowered many participants by effectively redirecting their voices of protest away from deaf ears in government to a different order of power and authority – the land. By serving as a facilitator, Belmore reaffirmed the cultural centrality of land for many Aboriginal people while maintaining an engagement with ongoing political and legal struggles over homeland.

Homeland is a far more complicated construct in *Vigil,* for Belmore does not explicitly address land issues. Indeed, it is difficult to refer to homeland as a construct, given the political realities associated with continuing struggles toward its realization and maintenance. It is useful, however, to consider the ways in which homeland is an idea and the power that can be derived from having an ideology as a foundation of identity. How one feels at home often depends on less tangible notions about homeland. Homeland as a construct does not diminish its importance collectively or individually. Codifying the idea of homeland in this way allows Aboriginal diasporic communities to exist in the same political territory – Canada – as their Indigenous homelands.

Homeland also has an ideological value for urban Aboriginal populations, something to which the many exhibitions designed around the theme of land over the past quarter-century attest.[8] Despite the cogency of the politics of traditional land, the land-centred identity construct presents a particular set of relational conditions to urban Aboriginal populations. The

2001 Canadian census found that 49 percent of Aboriginal people live in urban areas – off reserve and out of rural settings – a number up slightly from the 1996 census.[9] These figures suggest that large numbers of Aboriginal people are experiencing culture and community in ways different from those who live in reserve communities and on ancestral lands. Living space therefore takes on a new level of significance as Aboriginal people make their homes in urban areas. Some have migrated to these areas; others have never lived in exclusively Aboriginal communities, on reserves, or off the land. This development calls for the recognition of an ideological home, one that is central to cultural memory and political agency and to maintaining the relevance and currency of the adopted inhabited home. The experiences of diasporic populations help to theorize the migration of Aboriginal people to cities, especially when one considers, as Avtar Brah does, the range of movement and living spaces that constitute diasporas. Over and above geographic borders, *diaspora* also describes positions that result from the crossing of cultural and psychic borders.[10]

It is crucial to emphasize the theme of boundaries and space in *Vigil* because these themes recur in contemporary Aboriginal art. The manner in which they function in *Vigil* suggests the complexity of issues associated with these themes and implicates them in a feminist project. Because the affirmation of borders continues to be of a dire order, addressing the possibility of borders in flux and, moreover, conceiving of such spaces as positive or enriching is an unstable proposition. Reconciling a cultural identity bound in so many important ways to land and borders with notions of identity informed by contemporary cultural politics is an assiduous challenge.

Feminism's stake in the Aboriginal diaspora relates not only to the changing cultural terrain but also to the economic conditions experienced by women. Migrant workers contribute to the transnational flows that form diasporas, and women, axiomatically, constitute a large percentage of that labour force. The global labour market depends on women as domestic workers, for home-based piecework, in garment or other sweatshop industries, and as sex workers. Moreover, the economic duress experienced by many Aboriginal women because of their gender can compel their relocation. Critics hold that provisions in the Indian Act, the long-standing and contested Canadian legislation that governs Aboriginal people, discriminate against women and fail to provide them with adequate legal standing on reserves.[11] For example, some women find themselves homeless after a divorce because their former husband's claim to the matrimonial home on the reserve is usually upheld.[12] Economic factors therefore often drive women from reserves to urban areas to seek employment. This movement demonstrates resounding parallels with the situation of women throughout the developing world and beyond.

How does one talk about the primacy of location and of inhabitation while still allowing for the flow of traffic in the global world? How can we talk about the conditions this migration creates for women without invoking a monolithic woman? What is the relevance of transnational feminism to Aboriginal women, and how does it apply to art and visual culture? Transnational feminism has potential as a mode of feminist ethics for studying (art) cross-culturally. Although a tension exists in the exchanges between Aboriginal and non-Aboriginal women, transnational feminism attempts to navigate this difficult terrain. Its goal in part is mediatory; consequently, transnational feminism offers a means to situate feminist positions held by Aboriginal women in a manner that does not diminish the politics of land and sovereignty, which are often used to separate Aboriginal and feminist priorities. By acknowledging the continuing relevance of borders for some, despite travel and dispersal, transnational feminism allows Aboriginal women to keep important culturally specific issues of community and land-based identities in play as they actively engage with issues of gender, power, and cross-culturalism.

Feminist Occupations

If an overriding objective of feminism is to reform the social relations of power entrenched in gender, and if it is acknowledged that gender inequities are found in some form in all cultures, then feminism can play a role in challenging these subordinations in all contexts, including Aboriginal ones, despite claims to sovereign cultural status. Belmore's occupation of the street site in *Vigil* marks the reclamation of a specific unstable and dangerous space that Aboriginal women themselves occupied. It also marks an urgent claim to a feminist space that is both Aboriginal and cross-cultural. Highlighting the feminist politics in Belmore's performance does not undermine the discomfort that many Aboriginal women have with certain feminisms. Highlighting the metaphor of spatial occupation does, however, bring different orders of feminist commitments to light. The ways in which Belmore's occupation can be interpreted are manifold in that this occupation can be understood as a hostile intrusion, as a placeholding or, more generally and ingenuously, as the actualizing of a lived space. Belmore's presence maintains some of this ambiguity, and her own complicated identity, replete with shared investments, adds nuance to her use of place. As feminist, as woman, as Aboriginal, as Anishinaabe, as Lac Seul Band member, as artist, as urbanite, as public figure, as stranger, as insider, and as outsider, Rebecca Belmore maintains multiple identities; she occupies multiple spaces, and these slippery assignments simultaneously or sequentially ease and hinder her claim.

Aboriginal and non-Aboriginal women share interests, particularly in situations that arise from occupying spaces mutually or simultaneously. Despite variations in their roots (and routes), points of access, and experience, women who live in close proximity actively share relationships and investments in their space. They mutually occupy it. By simultaneous occupation, I mean independent occupations of a given physical space, the experience of which is so mediated by individuating factors that it becomes mutually exclusive. Although occupants define the space differently, they nonetheless cohabitate it. An occupation, furthermore, may at times be mutual and at other times simultaneous. With Aboriginal people increasingly calling metropolitan areas home, these assertions speak overwhelmingly to the occupation of city spaces and the particular conditions these spaces imply. Shared spaces mean that women who experience different realities often identify with divergent histories; although they adhere to distinct cultural traditions, they may also grapple with mutual experiences.

Contemporary Aboriginal artists are urbanites in increasing numbers and regularly draw on complicated patterns of identity and experience in their artistic practice. Belmore's own migratory history is a case in point. Born in 1960 in Upsala, Ontario, she lived apart from her family as she attended high school in Thunder Bay. She studied at the Ontario College of Art (now the Ontario College of Art and Design) in Toronto in the late 1980s and then returned to northern Ontario. She now lives in Vancouver. Belmore travels and exhibits throughout the country and internationally, and notably, she represented Canada at the 2005 Venice Biennale with a video-based performance installation titled *Fountain*. Reading contemporary Aboriginal art through feminist theory may in part help to parse these multiple contexts and locations. In return, the work of a number of these artists, Belmore among them, challenges feminism's claims by strengthening the critical discipline of feminist theory with the voice of women whose experiences have been neglected.

In 1997, Marcia Crosby, a scholar of Tsimshian and Haida ancestry, curated an exhibition, "Nations in Urban Landscapes," at Vancouver's Contemporary Art Gallery. The exhibition considered the practice of three prominent Aboriginal artists and their relationships to their urban surroundings. It signalled a bold move for Crosby, who had risen to prominence in the early 1990s with the publication of "Construction of the Imaginary Indian," a powerful confrontational essay about the relationship between Aboriginal and non-Aboriginal Canadians. The more recent project was not conciliatory; the accompanying exhibition catalogue includes some harsh criticism of non-Aboriginal attitudes toward Aboriginal people. Crosby does, however, recognize hybridity as an active identity phenomenon, and she also acknowledges that although Aboriginal people's experiences of urban spaces may prove to be radically different, Aboriginal and non-Aboriginal people do occupy the same spaces. Crosby acknowledges that identity informed by contemporary urban experience is an important theme in Aboriginal art. In the exhibition catalogue, she argues that the relegation of Native authority exclusively to reserves and traditional land bases impoverishes the complexity of First Nations subjectivity. She writes, "these conventions are not used as a platform for authenticating the land and resource dispute between First Nations and Canadian governments, but ... they have also emerged as a measuring stick for 'Indianess.' As a political strategy, this excludes the historical gaps and the hybrid individual and communal histories of contemporary aboriginal societies."[13]

Thinking about space may help to bridge this divide. Mediations on spatial occupation are part of continuing processes of decolonization as they relate to the particularities of location and inhabitation. Belmore's own biography attests to the issue of location in *Vigil.* As an urban Indian, a term that has become prevalent in the contemporary Aboriginal cultural lexicon, Belmore occupies a living space that intersects and overlaps with multiple cultural and gender profiles. Space, a thematic constant in Aboriginal art, has further nuance when engaged by an urban artist who shares living space with people of different cultural backgrounds. Urban life, moreover, as the Downtown Eastside disappearances attest, presents a number of challenges to Aboriginal women that are shared with women of other backgrounds.

Transnational Feminism

Transnationalism is by no means a firmly designated signifier. Varying terms – including *world feminism, global feminism,* and *transnational feminism* – all appear frequently and sometimes interchangeably. I deliberately use the latter term because, in my view, it implies the particular designation I would like to give it, and it offers the most ideological potential. I am most comfortable reiterating the term *transnational,* primarily because of its semantic insistence on the nation and the implication of borders that are crossed or exist to be crossed. As an alias, *transnational* is far more suggestive of actual global realities – as well as of the nature of an individual's own sense of (national) identity, despite global traffic – than is implied by the holistic-sounding qualifiers *world* or *global*. Although the result may be inadvertent, this vocabulary may encourage the elision of specific national allegiances and the particularities of citizenship. The magnitude of borders does persist, both as geo-physical or political boundaries and as psychic determiners. The very universalizations that the practice of this kind of feminism seeks to undo are ultimately reinforced by words that connote a singular community, as in one world, one globe.

Mohanty, because of her innovative scholarship two decades ago and her continued commitment to anti-racist, provocative feminism, remains the key thinker in transnational feminism. She has helped to shape it into a dynamic collective practice that attempts to grapple with feminist issues cross-culturally as it actively seeks to broach – and then avoid – the pitfalls of universalizing feminist concerns. Not all Aboriginal women endorse alliances with feminist groups, least of all those that extend across cultures. Writer and scholar Lee Maracle's account of her relationship to feminism testifies to an established disconnect: "Before 1961, we were 'wards of the government,' children in the eyes of the law. We objected and became, henceforth, people. Born of this objection was the Native question – the forerunner of Native self-government, the Native land question, etc. The woman question still did not exist for us. Not then. I responded, like so many women as a person without sexuality. Native women do not even like the words 'women's liberation' and even now it burns my back."[14]

As a result of its high-stake risks, however, transnational feminism offers an ethical model for feminist scholars doing cross-cultural work, and it establishes hospitable working spaces for feminist subject positions occupied by Aboriginal women, women of colour, non-Western women and, potentially, those outside of academia. In addition to its ethical mandate as a methodology, transnational feminism informs an epistemological model of subjectivity – that is, the collective models of identity it embraces allow for a subjective sense of self in the world. Although Mohanty's work reflects her formidable experience and ability to address the most difficult ethical and theoretical quandaries of recent feminist discourse with regard to race and identity, solidarity and multivocality, and global politics and economies, her position betrays a certain misapprehension of the global world and of the experiences of its citizens. Mohanty's desire to downplay political borders and reiterate other formal lines of identity formation reflects a deeper desire to keep the specificities of identity politics in play – something she believes that recent critical theory has denied.[15] A retrieval of identity-based bordered states undermines the political, cultural, and economic power that political borders continue to exert. The importance of this cannot be understated, particularly given that critical theory – and feminism itself – continues to promote global culture as it corresponds to diasporic populations for whom political borders supposedly have diminished importance.

In what became the defining essay on transnational feminism, "Under Western Eyes: Feminist Scholarship and Colonial Discourses," Mohanty proposes a working philosophy for what she terms third world feminisms. She also commits her model to a critique of the hegemony of Western feminism and to forging a new autonomous feminism, one that will emerge from – and be accountable to – geographic, historical, and cultural specificities. Her model constitutes a feminism that is, in Mohanty's words, simultaneously about dismantling and deconstructing and building and constructing.[16] Mohanty's contribution to scholarship can thus be recognized as a rethinking of the objectives and practice of feminist theory but also as an uncompromising critique of Western feminism.

Two decades after its initial publication, "Under Western Eyes" maintains its intellectual and cultural relevance. This status suggests, however, that much work remains to be done in the field of transnational and antiracist feminism. Even so, by amending Mohanty's founding principle for transnational feminism – to achieve a balance between dismantling and building anew – the scholarship will better reflect and guide a truly contemporary endeavour. Specifically, given my focus on Aboriginal art practice, larger feminist concerns can best be served by placing the emphasis on this second aspect, that is, by producing new and viable feminist thought or, indeed, feminist art practice. This ordering allies itself with Mohanty's critique of the dominance of hegemonic ideologies in feminism, hegemonies that have been pervasive for too long. Critiques of earlier or existing feminist theories are by no means dismissible: the ways in which feminism speaks or fails to speak to non-Western (or Indigenous) women testifies to the challenges that lie ahead and the possibilities that remain.

To a great extent, even well-intentioned proponents of transnational feminism perpetuate the construct of the monolithic third world woman. The unfixed and sometimes paradoxical positioning of Aboriginal women in the global world challenges this figure. Geographic location – homeland – situates Aboriginal people in the heart of the developed world, although they continue to struggle with processes of decolonization that, in many ways, situate them as so-called third world peoples. Some Indigenous scholars locate the complex and unique positioning of Indigenous peoples as the fourth world.[17] Belmore's early performance, *Exhibit #671B,* worked to unseat this tendency. In it, Belmore inserts herself, as a living spectacle, into the dominant culture's exhibitionary paradigm for Aboriginal culture. Resistance to, and exclusion from, discourses of Western feminism confers outsider status on Aboriginal women, who, like many women from the developing world, are not served by dominant models.

The strategies of transnational feminism can be used to theorize working models for Aboriginal women, and specifically, for Aboriginal women's art. In this sense, transnational feminism offers a political mode of thinking that corresponds to the political, social, economic, and cultural specificities of Aboriginal people. The continuing processes of decolonization in which Aboriginal people are engaged do not occur in cultural isolation – they parallel the experiences of other Indigenous and decolonizing peoples globally. Importantly though, isolating the impetus of transnational feminism and its philosophical underpinnings figures as a distinct methodological strategy, an ethics of transnational feminism. In the Introduction to her recent and important book *Feminism without Borders,* Mohanty strives to justify her title and the book's chief conceit. By rethinking feminism and its contemporary global objectives, Mohanty calls for the transcendence of some borders and the acknowledgment and acceptance of others. In this way, her title misleads, for by no means does she endorse the obliteration of borders that an internationalist feminist project, understood in its most literal sense, might imply. Mohanty rejects the universalizing tendencies with which so many Anglo-American feminists have been charged. Borders that protect cultural difference (and territory) for Aboriginal women may remain in place, just as feminist connections may be initiated within and across those borders. Furthermore, Belmore's movements and use of performance space in *Vigil* are consistent with transnational feminism's potential to communicate a subject's relationship to space and movements through it. This is particularly relevant with regard to the experiences of some of the Aboriginal women that the performance evokes.

Feminist geographers such as Gillian Rose work from the premise that geography itself implies a masculine subject position. The discipline, she argues, is founded on the notion of a detached, rational being mapping space. This role cannot be comfortably inhabited by a feminine subject, for this subject, in contrast to the male subject, inherits characteristics that would disrupt the geographer's work.[18] By contrast, Belmore occupies the performance space in an anti-masculinist manner, for her movements defy that of the geographer, the model of masculine rationality that the discipline continues to harbour. In *Vigil*, Belmore maps the space with her body. Through the use of her body, Belmore's practice demonstrates the body's ties to a feminist tradition of performance art. Her body registers the signs of her labour and grief through her actions. Her body literally frames her communion with the missing women: their names are written in black marker across her skin. Midway through the performance, Belmore looks down at her marked skin, reads the names, and shouts them out, each name, as it were, re-entering and exiting her body. Grief is irrational, despite Belmore's attempts to manage it. Geographically speaking, so too is Vancouver's Downtown Eastside, for the neighbourhood evades place, placement, and order.

Scholars and artists position land and its importance to Aboriginal women as a provocative but volatile thread of inquiry. The multiple ways women relate to land in Aboriginal cultures make it a defining but often unfixable feature in the formation of an individual's relationship to her cultural community, her sense of self and, thus, her subjectivity: land is key for many, but not always in the same ways. Land also has overwhelming resonance with regard to the changing socio-political experience of Aboriginal women in Canada today. Thus, I position the engagement with land and the meaning it affords to contemporary Aboriginal identity as a critical intersection within feminist theory to highlight its potential as a means to work through the diversity of identities raised by transnational feminism today. With this in mind, *Vigil* is no less about land than is Belmore's earlier iconic work *Ayum-ee-aawach Oomama-mowan: Speaking to Their Mother*. Both works probe the artist's relationship to place. Belmore's unspoken call for a safe space for women in *Vigil* makes a claim to place that resembles her direct appeal to the land in her earlier piece.

Decolonization suggests the dismantling of some borders and boundaries as it calls for the maintenance and determination of others. Borders, as I have discussed, figure substantively in Belmore's performance in the sense that the artist delimits a space and then occupies it. Space, Belmore's use of it, and the importance of the location of her act all draw on the idea of bordered, bounded space. Aboriginal people have long attributed a supreme status to borders that transcends the political, the social, and the cultural. Borders protect and uphold the political integrity of Aboriginal nationhood and, indeed, many less tangible forms of cultural sovereignty and identification. With this primacy comes the need to recognize the volume and frequency of cross-border traffic, of living on the frontiers, and of individual and collective negotiations of boundaries. Not the least of these spaces are those occupied by Aboriginal women today. Many Aboriginal artists have sought to express their particular spatial occupations and lived experiences with specific reference to gender. In *Vigil,* as Belmore concludes her performance, a pickup truck pulls up to the site; James Brown's classic "It's a Man's Man's Man's World" is playing within. She pauses before getting into the truck, and this pause compels reflection. For Aboriginal people, a man's world may very well represent the colonization of territory; the lyric also, with chilling precision, cuts to the indignity of violence against women. If scholars are at a loss to identify a vocabulary with which to address in feminist terms the practices of Aboriginal women artists, in this moment Belmore cinches these complex orders of consciousness, identification, and activism coherently and emphatically.

Reflective Solidarity

Belmore's *Vigil* is a personal response; however, because it occurs in a public space, it is also a call to others. In this respect, it can be seen as coalition building. A theory of reflective solidarity, as articulated by Jodi Dean, acknowledges relationships between women – between feminists – the respective identities of whom have denied a collective cohesion. This form of solidarity is, as Mohanty notes, germane to Belmore's performance of *Vigil* and the feminist response to it.[19] As a performance, *Vigil* depends on its audience, for the medium engages with an audience more actively and directly than other art forms. Alliance figures prominently in Belmore's performance as the artist extends herself – bodily through her work – to an audience of spectators. This overture, and the alliance it fosters, lays the groundwork for a more meaningful relationship among strangers. Belmore's performance stands as an invitation. When the artist gathers a crowd around her at the corner of Gore and Cordova Streets, she issues an invitation. She implicitly echoes Jodi Dean's call: "*I ask you to stand by me over and against a third*."[20] The act of performance is itself an invitation: the spectators who gather curbside to watch, whether by premeditated intent or because they happened upon the performance, respond. Their presence, enacted through spectatorship, signals solidarity with the artist and solidarity with the feminist tenor of her performance.

As *Vigil* continues, Belmore takes a rose from the bouquet she left on the ground at the outset. She looks at her arms: "Sarah!" she yells, "Helen!" The invocation is also an invitation, a call to the spectators, and perhaps to those beyond on the street, to carry the mantle of those names. By writing the names on her arms, Belmore uses her own body to link these women to the site of their disappearance; by calling out their names, in what has thus far been a silent performance, she implicates the spectators in their absence: I ask you to stand by me over and against a third. The nuance attributed to the category "we" means that an alliance is dynamic, active, and rendered through interaction, that alliance can be understood dialogically. The "we" in Belmore's work operates on multiple levels. It emerges from the performance – it is the product of the artist's invitation to the spectators to share in her work. Less immediate though still forceful, this "we" has another life in the gallery space, as mediated through the video screen in the exhibited version of *Vigil*, the video installation *The Named and the Unnamed* (2002). Contained by the intimate quarters of the gallery space, the video initiates a "we" as each new spectator breaks into the continuous video loop. This break, triggered by entry, creates another level of noise and a counter-presence that works toward the formation of an active "we."

Watching a performance, or a video, is not a passive act. Belmore's performance commands an incredibly distressing subject matter that the spectator must command with her. We flounder in our grief and in our helplessness in the face of this enormous loss. Tacitly, to be moved, we must acknowledge the disturbing circumstances that motivated Belmore's performance, chiefly, that dozens of women have disappeared with little public outcry. We are disturbed by the circumstances of many of these women's lives, their vulnerability, and what we imagine to be their private despair. This knowledge is highly upsetting and overwhelming; the performance offers comfort by uniting us, silently, with Belmore's outcry.

Naming maps the women to the place from which they vanished. By the naming of individual women, Belmore's solidarity takes its form by the recognition of others. Naming centres her performance by means of the most basic reference to another person – her name. Naming gestures, in this sense, to both the specific and the overwhelmingly general: specific in the sense that these women disappeared or died nameless, in obscurity and without a public outcry; general in the sense that the name is just that, the casing of an individual we do not or cannot know. A name, furthermore, can always belong to another; it can be claimed entirely and legitimately by another. Thus, Belmore's act of naming is both felicitous and frustrated as she draws herself – and the spectators – closer to the disappeared only to find that very propinquity thwarted. The video's title, *The Named and the Unnamed*, comes to stand not only for those who have been named and those who remain unaccounted for but also for the futility of knowing another, in this case, others who have truly lost their voice.

As she calls out the women's names, Belmore bites at roses, taken one by one from the bouquet. She tears at the soft petals and thorny stalks with her teeth. She takes it all into her mouth, and then, sometimes gagging, she spits the matter onto the street. Later, she puts on a long red dress. With a hammer, she nails the fabric to a telephone pole and then tears herself free, each time ripping the dress more. She repeatedly nails and tears the fabric, to the pole and to the wooden plank at the base of the fence. She tatters the dress until all that remains is shredded and hanging from nails. As the trial for the murder of some of the missing progresses and disturbing details are made public, these acts are a chilling and ultimately accurate portrayal of the violence and suffering to which the women were subjected.

Yet Belmore's acts – although referential, evocative, and moving – gesture ultimately to the integrity of the artist's subjectivity, which is distinct from the localized, individuated women for whom she created the performance. Belmore's body language is in part her own, for as a performance artist, she has distinguished herself by her refined corporeal communication. This language belongs to a performance art tradition: Belmore's act is not random. She has gallery support and performs using a vocabulary shared by those with a fluency in contemporary art, performance, and discourses of the body. In this way, she uses her tools as an artist to communicate the tragedy of the missing and murdered women. She approaches her subject with a shared sensibility that stems undoubtedly from her residency in Vancouver and her experiences as a woman and Aboriginal person. However, recalling her differences – her identity as an artist being the most important – is a useful reminder to be wary of the generalizations identity politics maintain.

"Bordering on Feminism," the title of this chapter, conveys a useful rhetorical image for the issues that *Vigil* evokes, but also, more generally, for Aboriginal feminist practices. Belmore's performance signals an act of reflective solidarity with the missing women; it is both an act of solidarity with the missing and an appeal to others to stand with her in her action. An implicit "we" girds the work of many Aboriginal artists. This collective "we" implies the bonds that unite, in solidarity, a diverse Aboriginal population. It enables Aboriginal peoples of varied backgrounds to stand together on certain fronts of common concern. But the feminist "we," with its potential for cross-cultural positioning, lends new optimism to the contemporary transnational feminist project. As spectators alone, as witnesses, we can offer reflective solidarity, an offering that difference previously denied. This offering represents a kind of active stillness in which individuals may remain in their own respective spaces. But it also suggests the crossing of borders that heretofore kept us divided.

NOTES

1 DeNeen Brown, "On Willy's Pig Farm, Sifting for Clues; Canadian Police Think They've Found the Pieces of a Grisly Puzzle, and 15 Missing Women," *Washington Post,* 5 September 2004, D01.

2 Ken MacQueen, "Streets of Fear," *Maclean's,* 25 March 2002, 36; Greg Joyce, "Six Women Allegedly Murdered in BC Led Lives of Desperation, Disappointment," *Canadian Press,* 14 April 2002.

3 Robert Matas, "Missing-Women List Grows to 69. Police in Vancouver Add 8 New Names; DNA of One Found on Pickton Pig Farm," *Globe and Mail,* 7 October 2004, A11. This list represents women who vanished between 1991 and 2000; it was determined by a review of more than 220 missing persons cases from British Columbia.

4 Amnesty International, "Stolen Sisters: Discrimination and Violence against Indigenous Women in Canada – A Summary of Amnesty International's Concerns," 4 October 2004, AMR 20/003/2004, http://www.amnesty.ca/.

5 A high-profile police spokesperson, who was also the police liaison with the victims' families, was quoted as saying that because women who were addicted to drugs had ruined their looks by the time they arrived in the Downtown Eastside, it was hard for them to get dates. The Vancouver police chief initially supported the liaison, but he was later forced to resign after the families cried foul. See Robert Matas, "Pickton Case Spokesman Resigns Over Comments: Police Chief Stands By Him, but Brother of Missing Woman Calls Remarks Offensive," *Globe and Mail,* 9 November 2002.

6 MacQueen, "Streets of Fear," and Daniel Girard, "Missing Women, Missing Answers," *Toronto Star,* 20 April 2002, H01.

7 "Public Pressure Spurred Police Probe: Police Ignored Missing Women Because They Were Sex Workers and Drug Users," *Ottawa Citizen,* 8 February 2002, A3.

8 These exhibitions include the following: "Staking Land Claims" at the Walter Phillips Gallery at the Banff Centre for the Arts, 1997; "Land, Spirit, Power: First Nations at the National Gallery of Canada," 1992; and "Our Land/Ourselves: American Indian Contemporary Artists" at the University Art Gallery, University at Albany, SUNY, 1990.

9 Statistics Canada, *Aboriginal People of Canada: A Demographic Profile, 2001,* Statistics Canada, http://www12.statcan.ca/.

10 Avtar Brah, *Cartographies of Diaspora: Contesting Identities* (London: Routledge, 1996), 193-94.

11 See Judith F. Sayers, Kelly A. MacDonald, Jo-Anne Fiske, Melonie Newell, Evelyn George, and Wendy Cornet, eds., *First Nations Women, Governance, and the Indian Act: A Collection of Policy Research Reports* (Ottawa: Status of Women Canada Policy Research Fund, 2001), and Wendy Cornet, "First Nations Governance, the Indian Act and Women's Equality Rights," in ibid., 117-66.

12 Sue Bailey, "Native Women's Group Sues Indian Affairs Minister (Jane Stewart): Land Legislation Seen as an Infringement of Constitutional Rights," *First Perspective* 8, 7 (1999): 6; Beverley Jacobs, *Native Women's Association of Canada Submission to the Special Rapporteur Investigating the Violations of Indigenous Human Rights,* 2 December 2002, http://www.sistersinspirit.ca/engdocuments.htm.

13 Marcia Crosby, "Nations in Urban Landscapes," in Marcia Crosby, *Nations in Urban Landscapes: Faye Heavyshield, Shelley Niro, Eric Robertson* (Vancouver: Contemporary Art Gallery, 1997), 11.

14 Lee Maracle, *I Am Woman: A Native Perspective on Sociology and Feminism* (Vancouver: Press Gang, 1996), 16.

15 Mohanty, *Feminism without Borders,* 6.

16 Ibid., 17. The page reference cited refers to a reprint in *Feminism without Borders,* 17-42. The essay was originally published as "Under Western Eyes: Feminist Scholarship and Colonial Discourses," *boundary 2* 12, 3 and 13, 1 (1984): 338-58.

17 See, for example, Grace J.M.V. Ouellette, *The Fourth World: An Indigenous Perspective on Feminism and Aboriginal Activism* (Halifax: Fernwood, 2002).

18 Gillian Rose, *Feminism and Geography: The Limits of Geographical Knowledge* (Cambridge: Polity Press, 1993), 4.

19 Mohanty, *Feminism without Borders,* 7.

20 Jodi Dean, *Solidarity of Strangers: Feminism after Identity Politics* (Berkeley: University of California Press, 1996), 3.

16

Location, Dislocation, Relocation
Shooting Back with Cameras

PATRICIA DEMERS

The art of film is located on the same semiological "plane" as literary art: the properly aesthetic orderings and constraints – versification, composition, and tropes in the first case; framing, camera movements, and light "effects" in the second – serve as the connoted instance, which is superimposed over the denoted meaning.

– *Christian Metz,* Film Language: A Semiotics of the Cinema

The chronotope mediates between two orders of experience and discourse: the historical and the artistic, providing fictional environments where historically specific constellations of power are made visible.

– *Robert Stam,* Subversive Pleasures: Bakhtin, Cultural Criticism, and Film

We associate *documentary* primarily with the medium of film. And, with the encouragement of etymology (*documentum* "pattern, warning, or proof," from *doceo, ere* "to teach"), we also anticipate an instructive experience. Conveying visual history and enlivening actual events with archival footage, dramatic re-enactments, symbolic images, interviews, and voice-overs, the documentary – like all artistic forms – can be engrossing and moving. Its effects – resulting from narrative order, reflections of other points of view, the interplay of connoted and denoted meanings, and the foregrounding of specific people, happenings, and objects – are not unlike those of literature, both fiction and non-fiction. Image track and verbal narration can reinforce or defamiliarize a central idea; they can "obliquely reflect another take on it, or contest it."[1] One of the central questions I want to explore concerns our responses as twenty-first-century viewers and readers of documentary. Are viewing and reading comparable, mutually illuminating activities or discrete audience-targeted undertakings? Does documentary's "indexical relation to the real" align it more logically with non-fiction than with fiction?[2] Does the fact that documentary in general is neither fractured nor disjunctive render problematic any possible association with the pastiche quality of postmodern writing and its deliberately jagged edges? Most pressing for this project, how is the connection between aboriginality and historical narrative, between the crucial specificity of affiliation with a First Nation and the relation of a specific moment or series of moments in time, announced, facilitated, and complicated by filmmaking?

In addition to the relationship between viewing and reading, another key pervasive element of this exploration involves identity. Since the documentary filmmakers I want to discuss are Indigenous women and feminists, it is necessary to explain the significance – and position my understanding – of both *Indigenous* and *feminist*. Three Indigenous documentary filmmakers – Loretta Todd (Métis), Alanis Obomsawin (Abenaki), and Catherine Martin (Mi'kmaq) – a selection of whose work I discuss, exemplify the tenets and questioning stance of third-wave feminism. Revisiting and undoing essentialist definitions of femininity and the white middle-class ethos of second-wave feminism, these filmmakers are deeply committed to criticism that does not perpetuate stereotypes or protect the powerful. Their critical stance, as I see it, is entirely in keeping with what Joan Wallach Scott has recently described as "one that seeks to interrogate and disrupt prevailing systems of gender, one that assumes that what worked in the late 1980s might not work in the early years of the new millennium, one that is committed to self-scrutiny as well as to denunciations of domination and oppression, one that is never satisfied with simply transmitting bodies of knowledge but that seeks instead to produce new knowledge."[3] As documentarists, these filmmakers reassemble facts about the treatment of Native veterans, the Mohawk view of the Oka crisis, and the execution-style murder of Anna

Mae Pictou Aquash. Their appeal to these experiences is more than "an originary point of explanation" but rather builds a series of questions about "discourse, difference, and subjectivity, as well as what counts as experience and who gets to make that determination."[4] In other words, the documentary serves as a medium to explore "the discursive nature of 'experience'" and "the politics of its construction."[5]

Moreover, the condition of unresolved tension that shuttles back and forth between the terms *Indigenous* and *feminism*, a tension many Indigenous women have remarked upon, needs to be acknowledged. Eschewing the distance of an ethnographic approach to an object of study, I am not suggesting a fixed Indigenous identity or a merely curious aberration. Rather, my understanding of indigeneity and, specifically, Indigenous feminism has been heightened by Robert Dale Parker and Devon Abbott Mihesuah, in whose scholarship I have discovered succinct articulations of many of my own views.

Parker, the first editor of the poetry and prose of Jane Johnston Schoolcraft (1800-42), adroitly strips away the veneer of authenticity attached to the white student of Indian culture who is viewed as "a better, more authentic source of knowledge about Indian culture than a knowledgeable Indian" to reveal the misogyny and belittlement the veneer masks.[6] Refusing to overestimate Henry Rowe Schoolcraft's oft-vaunted contributions to the history of anthropology, Parker concentrates instead on Jane Schoolcraft's middle-ground Indianness as evidence that "Indian cultures, like any cultures, have always been changing" and that "Indian cultures' adaptation to the white invasion does not necessarily make their new forms any less Indian, even though they are differently Indian."[7] Schoolcraft, who wrote and lived in English and Ojibway, "offers a history and a specially valuable model of bilingual and multicultural life and writing for American Indians and for American culture and literature at large."[8] Parker's study of the complex layers of Schoolcraft's often muffled existence and of her culture as appropriated by others points to the importance of the Schoolcraft moment within a changing colonialist culture, the need to uncover traditional Ojibway elements within an English discourse, and the detection of anxiety as a familiar world unravels. His editorial work also succeeds in bringing together two worlds: "scholarly questions" and "the larger audience that makes such questions meaningful in the first place."[9] His lively descriptors of bringing "that larger audience's practicality and directness into the fusty corners of scholarly arcana" suggest a parallel to this project's blending of reportedly widespread viewing and less common reading and the ways these activities might enlighten each other.[10]

Adaptations, mixtures, and a frank assessment of misogyny from within and beyond one's circle also affect an understanding of Indigenous women as feminists. Indigeneity can encompass a variety of affiliations, and feminism's influence on art, expression, and culture and its commitment to principles of equality and social justice mean that it, too, is not "a style, or a formal approach" but "a philosophy, an attitude, a political instrument."[11] Although art critic Roberta Smith notes that "feminism is not of itself an aesthetic value," she insists it "will be around as long as it is necessary for women to put a name on the sense of assertiveness, confidence and equality that, unnamed, has always been granted men."[12] Devon Abbott Mihesuah probes the multiple modes and political instrumentality of such assertiveness. Instead of adducing one feminist theory to encapsulate Native women's thought, she sketches "a spectrum of multi-heritage women in between 'traditional' and 'progressive'" who possess "a multitude of opinions about what it means to be a Native female."[13] She argues, moreover, that the concept of Indigenous feminism is not monolithic but influenced by a range of circumstances: "How we as Native women define ourselves as female and how we relate to the concept of feminism, to feminists, and to each other, how we define colonialism, and how men and women should behave depend on our relation to our tribes, our class, appearance, life partners, education, and religion."[14] Mihesuah characterizes many Indigenous feminists, whether white or Native in attitude, as "Native activists ... concerned with more than just female marginalization ... fight[ing] for fishing, land, water, and treaty rights, and at the same time ... [not wanting] to be called inferior by anyone because they are women."[15] For some, the divide between feminism and activism or tribalism is very clear-cut. Other Native women have declared that they do not have time for feminism, either because they are "secure in their identities as tribal women" or because they "worry about survival."[16]

An understanding of or appeal to indigeneity and Indigenous feminism or activism, then, needs to acknowledge the contingent, constantly negotiated and renegotiated values and roles that are bound up in these terms. As in any attempt to grapple with ideology, the assurance of fixity is facile and misleading. On the contrary, what is required is an agile ability to perceive a range of activities, possibilities, and circumstances.

As a member of a Department of English and Film Studies, one who has, however, concentrated mainly on literary texts, I am interested in exploring how reading cinematic devices as discursive literary strategies can help to enlarge our understanding of the art of the documentary. Without setting up a hierarchy of values or installing either what Laura Marks calls ocular-centrism or textuality as a benchmark, I want to comment on the work of three Indigenous documentary filmmakers as artistic creations in their own right by investigating how linguistic patterns, narrative design, and visualized images widen the field of vision.[17] The aim is not to elevate or impose literary standards, to effectively enshrine another form of colonialist mentality, or to suggest a hierarchy that underestimates Native art by disembedding it. On the contrary, investigating complementarities between cinematic and literary forms of expression should reinforce and amplify the realities of exclusion and neglect that haunt the films.

In addition to their cinematic techniques and feminist commitment, these three Indigenous documentary filmmakers share a remarkable number of intertextual allusions. Loretta Todd's *Forgotten Warriors* (1996), Alanis Obomsawin's *Rocks at Whiskey Trench* (2000), and Catherine Martin's *The Spirit of Annie Mae* (2002) all deal with histories of treachery, loss, and attempted extermination; the withholding and distorting of information; the non-Native invasion and appropriation of sacred spaces and strategies to reclaim them; and a series of poignant ironies. Their shared feminist understanding foregrounds issues of equality and justice by focusing on dispiriting lapses, moments when these values have been noticeably absent. In *Forgotten Warriors,* Aboriginal volunteers who enlisted as commandos, medics, and engineers to fight fascism in Europe come home to face fascism in Canada. In *Rocks at Whiskey Trench,* the Mercier Bridge that the Mohawks of Kahnawake blocked to resist the destruction of sacred land is built and enlarged by a sizable contingent of Mohawk ironworkers. In *The Spirit of Annie Mae,* an inquiry into the brutal murder of Anna Mae Pictou Aquash on the Pine Ridge Reservation near Wanblee, South Dakota, is led by her daughter, a Native peace officer in Pictou County, Nova Scotia. Despite the erosion of promises and seizure of lands, these Canadian Indigenous documentary filmmakers are directing attention through the purposiveness and critical lens of their medium to the restoration of long-delayed justice, to renewed pride, and to fully realized selfhood.

Although the National Film Board of Canada's (NFB) initiatives in the mid-1980s to develop Aboriginal filmmaking were reduced by 1996, that year inaugurated a decade-long explosion of work by Aboriginal filmmakers. Many independent film companies that sought to reclaim and celebrate Indigenous histories emerged in this period, such as Gil Cardinal's Kanata or

Great Plains Productions, the Cree-owned Blue Hills Productions, and Mohawk Shelley Niro's Turtle Night Productions. Christine Welsh's film *Women in the Shadows,* about her great-great-great-grandmother, Margaret Taylor, the country wife of Hudson's Bay Company governor George Simpson, is in Welsh's own words, an "affirmation of the importance of Native women's experience" and "a celebration of survival."[18] The films discussed in this chapter, however, were all made and distributed through the NFB.

Filmmaker Loretta Todd – of Cree, Iroquois, and Scottish ancestry – works mainly in Alberta and British Columbia. She had already investigated the work of the Sacred Circle Program in the Edmonton public school system in *The Learning Path* (1991), celebrated four Aboriginal artists in *Hands of History* (1994), and explored the topics of HIV-AIDS in *Healing Our Spirit* (1995) and solvent abuse in *No More Secrets* (1996) before she released *Forgotten Warriors.* According to Carol Kalafatic, Todd is a keeper of stories who can "wield semiotically loaded, cinematic 'madeleines' that have the power to bring layers of cultural memory to life." Todd herself acknowledges that "the filmmaker has the image, the sound ... to help *others* bring [the whole history] alive." Space and light, she adds, become "smell, touch, tears, laughter ... They don't just go into the ears; they also go into the *spiritual plane,* into the *basket.*"[19]

The basket of *Forgotten Warriors,* which contains evidence of withheld information and delayed acknowledgment, is woven of motifs that signal paradox, contrasts, and perspectival shifts. With voice-overs of Native veterans who themselves emphasize the paradox, we hear that Native Canadians, despite the opposition of their parents, felt they had "more right than anybody else to fight" and that they had "a duty to maintain relationships with the land." But entitlement is tinged with a threat to treaty rights as the owner of one voice admits that he was told that "the Queen needs your help and, if she's defeated, your agreement goes down with it." The names of decorated veterans listed by narrator Gordon Tootoosis – among them Tom Longboat, Private Norwest, Mary Grayeyes (the first Indian woman to enlist), George Munroe (winner of the military medal for bravery), and Sargeant Tommy Prince (of the Elite Special Service, winner of eleven medals, including the Silver Star from the US Army) – reverberate with ironic or tragic contrast. Mary Grayeyes relates that during her enlistment an officer found her Grade 8 education superior to the preparation of others with Grade 12 or 13. No one glorifies or minimizes the carnage. George Munroe from the John Smith Reserve north of Prince Albert faces the camera and offers a tense-lipped account of hunting the enemy like

Mary Grayeyes *Forgotten Warriors* © 1997 National Film Board of Canada, all rights reserved

moose. Clifford George, who led the return to Native land at Ipperwash (where his relative Dudley George was killed in a confrontation with the Ontario Provincial Police) notes in a matter-of-fact voice that it took almost fifty years "to invite Native veterans to lay a wreath in Ottawa on Remembrance Day." The most moving contrast concerns Sargeant Prince, of the Broken Head Ojibway, who is discovered in a derelict hotel room on Winnipeg's skid row. A female friend who relates the encounter is overcome when this old man, dressed in cast-offs, snaps to attention and salutes at the mention of his serial number.

Forgotten Warriors relates the main issue of systemic neglect through direct-to-camera declarations that have the effect of witness statements. Senator Len Marchand speaks bluntly about lands that went to white veterans by the terms of the Veterans' Land Act; a narrative voice-over relates the dismal record of withheld information about land grants, training programs, and family benefits, and with the Soldier Settlement Act, the appropriation of reserve land for white veterans. Native veterans, whose claims were mishandled by the Department of Indian Affairs, were often told that, as treaty Indians, they could not own property.

The Soldier Settlement Act (1917) provided for the purchase of land for returning veterans. Although about 35 percent of Native Canadians "who were of eligible age for service" enlisted for combat, Native veterans of both world wars experienced a real disparity upon their return.[20] As one official explained, "these returned Indian soldiers are subject to the provisions of the Indian Act and are in the same position as they were before enlisting."[21] Since the Department of Indian Affairs had been given sweeping control to seize lands that were deemed insufficiently used, many bands lost a sizable portion of their land base, and the transfer of fertile lands primarily benefitted non-Native veterans. The Act allowed settlement for some, fuelled alienation for others, and excused the appropriation of valuable treaty land for non-Indian use.

The visual medium heightens the affective power of this narrative of neglect. Shifts in perspective happen through uniquely cinematic means. Native actors – not Hollywood stereotypes – re-create scenes of leaving the family home, watching anxiously in the trenches, and relaxing in a pub and at a homecoming dance. The frames for this documentary, an eagle in flight at the opening and a distribution of eagle feathers to Native veterans at a ceremony at Douglas College in Vancouver at the close, reinforce the final words spoken by a veteran – that his experience in the Second World War "wasn't a wasted time." The note of dejection, albeit one denied, continues to resonate. It can prompt us to replay the film, and it can also germinate

Ceremony at Douglas College

Chateauguay residents lobbing rocks *Rocks at Whiskey Trench*

reflection. Oblivion – with its probable source in neglect, disregard, oversight, or aimlessness – and the sense of the unfulfilled that the word *wasted* denotes are all conveyed through the vocal testimony and ironic echoes of *Forgotten Warriors.* Todd's film remains a powerful indictment of the obliteration of traditions and an interrogation of ways of seeing.

In these documentaries, introductions and conclusions are more than bookends: they are assertive narrative devices that punctuate a thesis and locate a human identity in a place or event. The opening of *Rocks at Whiskey Trench* – written, narrated, directed, and produced by Alanis Obomsawin – is unforgettable. It is a bloody and "living testament," in the words of the Mohawk woman whose welling eyes rivet the viewer, of what really happened on 28 August 1990, when a convoy of seventy-five cars carrying women, children, and Elders left Kahnawake and crossed the Mercier Bridge. The bridge had been blocked by Mohawk to protest the appropriation of sacred land to enlarge a golf course. While the Sûreté du Québec passively prevented a full-scale attack and occasionally stepped aside to allow rocks to be thrown, the enraged residents of Chateauguay, who used the Mercier Bridge to commute to Montreal, pelted the convoy with an avalanche of rocks as it passed through a narrow access route that was called Whiskey Trench because of the Seagram's distilleries on either side. The residents shattered windshields, terrorized drivers and passengers, and injured babies and eighty-year-old grandparents who were huddled under blankets and mattresses in back seats. As one survivor summarizes, "these were rocks to kill us."

Rocks at Whiskey Trench is the fourth instalment of Obomsawin's quartet of documentaries about the Oka crisis. It was preceded by *Kahnesatake: 270 Years of Resistance* (1993), *My Name Is Kahentiiosa* (1995), and *Spudwrench: Kahnawake Man* (1997). The latter two are accounts of a Mohawk woman and man involved in the standoff. The first documentary charts the period when Mohawk land was appropriated by the Sulpicians. As Obomsawin reiterates in a radio interview, "the Mohawks knew it was their land."[22] Hailed by American Indian filmmaker Beverly Singer as "Canada's most celebrated Aboriginal filmmaker," an officer of the Order of Canada, and the subject of a retrospective at the Museum of Modern Art in New York, New Hampshire–born and Quebec-raised Obomsawin, winner of a Governor General's Award and holder of several honorary degrees, has had a distinguished career with the NFB.[23] Her productions confront audiences "with further evidence of the disturbing injustices that still face many modern young Aboriginal people."[24] Yet she has sidestepped didactic documentary by instead reworking "documentary conventions and plac[ing] representation at the service of a Native political and aesthetic agenda."[25] As Zuzana Pick observes, "Obomsawin's approach to human emotion is premised on creating a place for empathy that promotes the circulation of affect between protagonist and viewer."[26]

Obomsawin's remarkable footage from inside the Mohawk community – before, during, and after the event – combines with historical accounts of the Sulpician seigneury and Mohawk longhouse traditions. Obomsawin herself spent seventy-eight days with the Mohawk behind the barricades. *Rocks at Whiskey Trench* creates and circulates empathy by continuously contrasting attitudes inside and outside Kahnawake. While tabloids flash announcements of "Le Pont Mercier – un champ de bataille" and "des heures sombres," the narrator's voice informs us of the ways of the Wolf (pathfinder), the Bear (keeper of medicine), and the Turtle (wisdom). The narrator tells us of the determination to stop the desecration of the area called the Pines and of the decision to block the Mercier Bridge to support the community at Kahnesatake (the Canadian army planned to use Kahnawake as an approach to Kahnesatake). Among the Mohawk commentators, Kahnawake resident and Olympic gold medallist Alwyn Morris outlines the issue bluntly: "The fact that it happened here, in this country, suggests some very deep problems." On the other side, we see the angry lobs of rocks from Chateauguay residents (this is on-the-spot footage, not a re-enactment), learn that only thirty were arrested (many with conditional discharges, some with weekend detentions or fines), and hear a proud Chateauguay merchant

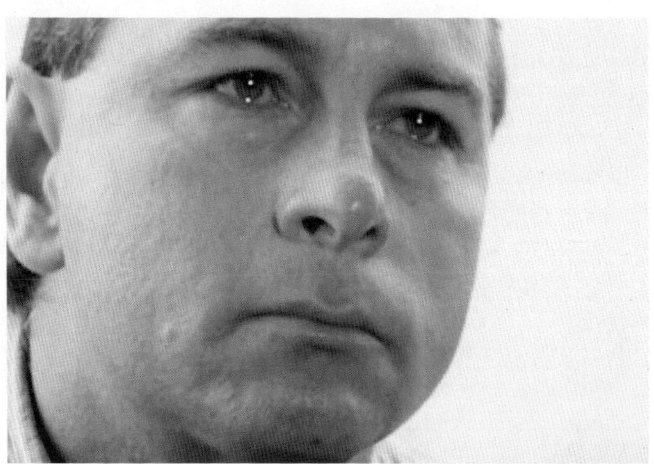

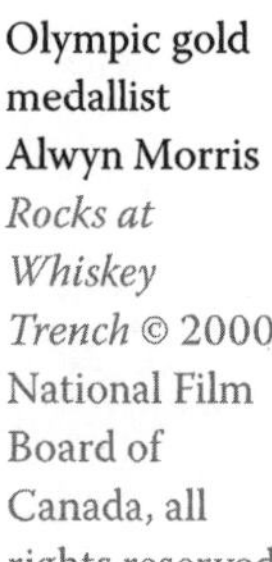

Olympic gold medallist Alwyn Morris *Rocks at Whiskey Trench* © 2000 National Film Board of Canada, all rights reserved

declare belligerently to the camera, "ça n'a changé rien de ma vie" (it didn't change anything in my life).

The retributive justice depicted in *Rocks at Whiskey Trench* is predictable. Kahnawake residents pelt the army with stones as its members attempt to cross the bridge and occupy the longhouse. Predictable yet unsatisfying – and necessarily so. After the seventy-eight-day siege, Mohawk warriors face criminal charges; a healing circle is established. But only a thin layer of tolerance for Chateauguay remains. A tearful Mohawk teenager, reliving her family's narrow escape a decade earlier, wonders if "it can happen again," and an older woman, admitting that she should "never have left," boldly declares Mohawk pride: "They could never beat that out of us, not even with rocks!" As events from a decade earlier filter through the footage of *Rocks at Whiskey Trench*, suspicion hangs in the air. Oka was a moment of radicalization for Obamsawin, a moment stronger than being afraid, a moment that entwined an intense love of the land with "a love for human beings and human rights."[27]

Sides taken and loyalties declared are essential components of the work of these Indigenous filmmakers, whose worldviews are anything but ethically neutral. Although Catherine Martin's account of the life and murder of Anna Mae Pictou Aquash at the age of thirty opens with Aquash's daughter staring down a rifle barrel and features many grisly details, the mood of *The Spirit of Annie Mae* is celebratory and, despite the brutal crime, positive. Aquash's family refer to their lost sister, mother, and cousin as Anna Mae, but most references use the name Annie Mae. By contrast, Obomsawin's

Tearful teenager *Rocks at Whiskey Trench*

film, with its community-wide focus and simmering tensions, could not possibly convey this attitude. Martin, from the Millbrook Reserve in Truro, emerged in the 1990s as Nova Scotia's first Indigenous filmmaker and has continued the healing power of Mi'kmaq storytelling traditions.[28] The positive energy of *The Spirit of Annie Mae* is maintained largely through the direct on camera testimonials of women (Aquash's two daughters, two older sisters, and two activist friends, artist Buffy Sainte-Marie and journalist Minnie Two Shoes) and through Aquash's letters home, which are neatly written and error-free and read by her daughter. In other forums, Martin has declared, "I knew that Annie Mae Aquash (Pictou/Maloney) had a story to tell and wasn't given the chance when she was murdered in 1975. She was silenced by someone who had no right to make judgment on another's right to life. I knew she wanted to tell a story and one day, I would help her tell that story. That has become my role as a storyteller who uses film as a medium to reach the audiences, to help others tell the story of the people."[29] She has also underscored the importance of largely female narration: "For the most part the story was told from a female perspective shedding light on a period in history that has mainly been told from a male point of view."[30]

According to Devon Abbott Mihesuah, "The life of Anna Mae Pictou-Aquash demonstrates what it means to be a modern Native woman aggressively fighting racial, cultural, and gender oppression."[31] Although members of Aquash's family, who were sharecroppers, did not consider themselves poor, they had no electricity or running water on the Shubenacadie Reserve, where such amenities were enjoyed only by the nuns, priests, and Indian

Anna Mae Pictou Aquash's daughter
The Spirit of Annie Mae © 2002 National Film Board of Canada, all rights reserved

agent. Aquash's curiosity about Mi'kmaq traditions was piqued by a Native mentor at Indian Island. Her life in Boston as a packer and later a seamstress also contributed to her growing interest in the sacredness of Native culture. She was associated with the Boston Indian Council and then with the American Indian Movement (AIM). Her studies at Wheelock College New Careers Program led to "a satisfying job as a teacher's aide in an all-black child care centre."[32] She did not take up a scholarship offered by Brandeis University.

In Martin's words, as a "story from within, from our minds, our hearts, and our memory," the film uses vivid language to propel its narrative.[33] In the documentary, we hear from Aquash herself that the FBI is "a racist organization" and from her letters that, as "a raggedy ass Indian," she does not intend to venerate any "raggedy ass pilgrims." "No sweat, I'm an Indian all the way," she affirms, when jailed on a charge of possession of explosive devices. Her former husband and father of her children, Jake Maloney, describes her as "a grizzly bear mom." Female friends make it clear that the mixture of spirituality and activism with promiscuity, drugs, and alcohol in AIM upsets her. During her short-lived stint as a waitress at the nightclub the Cave in Boston, she refused to serve alcohol to Native patrons. She complained about the sacrilege of drinking and drugs at a Sun Dance. She so antagonized the bootlegger chief of the Pine Ridge Reservation that he called in the GOON (Guardians of the Oglala Nation) squad; despite the acronym, they were essentially thugs dispatched to eradicate AIM.

The close of Aquash's story on film is a murky pool of unanswered questions. Her participation in the occupation of the Office of Indian Affairs in Washington, DC, as part of the Trail of Broken Treaties and her participation in the seventy-one-day occupation of the camp at Wounded Knee, the site of the massacre of Chief Big Foot and three hundred of his followers, made Aquash a target for FBI investigations. She was apprehended but eventually released. The circumstances of her murder have become clearer. Following an investigation of Aquash's cousin Robert A. Pictou-Branscombe, "a highly decorated Mi'kmaq combat Marine veteran," it has been revealed that her death was ordered by American Indian Movement (AIM) officials.[34] The Bellecourt brothers, Vernon and Clyde, and the Means brothers, Russell and Ted, are alleged to have conspired in the murder. Also, "Theda Nelson Clark, Arlo Looking Cloud, and teenager John Boy Patton, at least, were involved in the execution."[35] She was buried as Jane Doe but exhumed and reinterred. Only a second independent autopsy in 1976 confirmed the presence of a bullet in the back of her head, a finding that overturned the earlier official report of death by exposure. Women cut the cold March ground to dig her second grave in South Dakota. Despite three grand jury investigations and evidence of a cover-up within AIM, official charges have yet to be laid. Although the crime is revealed if not resolved, her daughter closes the film with the resounding declaration: "She's never just another dead Indian to us; she's our mother." Although the identity of Anna Mae's murderer or murderers was at one point undisclosed and the resolution in *The Spirit of Annie Mae* is delayed because of legal incertitude or obfuscation, the film's conclusion reverberates as an explosive indictment of delays and cover-ups.

In these documentaries, eagle feathers, rocks, and rifle barrels are both physical objects and aggregative symbols. Their prominence as cinematic frames allows us to understand how visual media can function as chronotopes, "mediating between the historical and the artistic" and "making historically specific constellations of power ... visible."[36] They resonate connotatively with tropes of loss, neglect, and betrayal and affectively with voices of reclamation, reassertion, and realization. It is significant, moreover, that women – as blood relations, ideological allies, and artist-creators – spearhead and advance these insights as they militate for change. Moreover, we can consider eagle feathers, rocks, and rifle barrels fetishes and fossils inasmuch as they "refer to the power of memory images to embody different pasts" and "encode material conditions of displacement."[37] In Laura Marks' argument, "they are those historical objects that contain the histories produced in intercultural traffic."[38] The sorts of intercultural exchanges highlighted in *Forgotten Warriors, Rocks at Whiskey Trench,* and *The Spirit of Annie Mae* expose degradation and obliviousness as they discomfit smugness and challenge the upbeat rhetoric of royal commissions and reports. In bearing witness to forgotten, neglected, or muffled histories, these fetish-like or fossil-like objects convey and capture – emblematize, really – the layers of historical interpretation that have distanced viewers from an original communal meaning or significance.

These documentaries also affirm the political instrumentality of feminism. Recognizing the potential hallucinatory and subversive qualities of fossil and fetish, these three film treatments – decidedly instructive and enabling – succeed by carrying within them "histories that, once unraveled, make the fixity of the present untenable."[39] These filmmakers concentrate on the interconnected worlds of "self, family, community, tribe ... and country."[40] As Todd's work shows, their focus is not exclusively on women. Through respect for tradition and ceremony, the integrity of storytelling, and the honesty of a personal, direct voice, these films activate their revisionist impulse to document the fight for justice and redress. Their immediacy and ineluctable presence make this struggle urgent. By foregrounding both seeing *and* reading – as a seeing inside – these documentaries combine outward didactic motivation and inward reflection to drive home and embody, on behalf of First Nations people, the supremely human tenets of recognition, dignity, and survival.

NOTES

1 Julia Lesage, "Women's Fragmented Consciousness in Feminist Experimental Autobiographical Video," in Diane Waldman and Janet Walker, eds., *Feminism and Documentary* (Minneapolis: University of Minnesota Press, 1999), 312.
2 Laura U. Marks, "Fetishes and Fossils: Notes on Documentary and Materiality," in Waldman and Walker, *Feminism and Documentary,* 228.
3 Joan Wallach Scott, *Women's Studies on the Edge* (Durham, NC: Duke University Press, 2008), 6.
4 Joan Wallach Scott, "The Evidence of Experience," *Critical Inquiry* 17, 4 (Summer 1991): 777, 790.
5 Ibid., 797.
6 Robert Dale Parker, ed., *The Sound the Stars Make Rushing through the Sky: The Writings of Jane Johnston Schoolcraft* (Philadelphia: University of Pennsylvania Press, 2007), 63.
7 Ibid., 64.
8 Ibid., 73.
9 Ibid., xv.

10 Ibid.
11 Roberta Smith, "They Are Artists Who Are Women: Hear Them Roar," *New York Times,* 23 March 2007, B35.
12 Ibid.
13 Devon Abbott Mihesuah, *Indigenous American Women: Decolonization, Empowerment, Activism* (Lincoln: University of Nebraska Press, 2003), 6-7.
14 Ibid., 159.
15 Ibid., 162.
16 Ibid., 160, 168.
17 On ocularcentrism, see Marks, "Fetishes and Fossils," 224.
18 Christine Welsh, "Women in the Shadows: Reclaiming a Métis Heritage," in Ajay Heble, Donna Palmateer Pennee, and J.R. (Tim) Struthers, eds., *New Contexts of Canadian Criticism* (Peterborough, ON: Broadview Press, 1997), 65.
19 Carol Kalafatic, "Keepers of the Power: Story as Covenant in the Films of Loretta Todd, Shelley Niro, and Christine Welsh," in Kay Armatage, Kass Banning, Brenda Longfellow, and Janine Marchessault, eds., *Gendering the Nation: Canadian Women's Cinema* (Toronto: University of Toronto Press, 1999), 116, emphasis in original.
20 Olive Patricia Dickason, *Canada's First Nations: A History of Founding Peoples from Earliest Times* (Toronto: McClelland and Stewart, 1992), 326.
21 James Dempsey, "Problems of Western Canadian War Veterans after World War One," *Native Studies Review* 5, 2 (1989): 5-6.
22 Eleanor Wachtel, "Interview with Alanis Obomsawin," *Wachtel on the Arts,* CBC Radio 2, 13 January 2009.
23 Beverly R. Singer, *Wiping the War Paint off the Lens: Native American Film and Video* (Minneapolis: University of Minnesota Press, 2001), 58.
24 Heather Norris Nicholson, ed., *Screening Culture: Constructing Image and Identity* (Lanham: Lexington Books, 2003), 131.
25 Zuzana Pick, "Storytelling and Resistance: The Documentary Practice of Alanis Obomsawin," in Armatage et al., *Gendering the Nation,* 77.
26 Ibid.
27 Wachtel, "Interview with Alanis Obomsawin."
28 Nicholson, *Screening Culture,* 133.
29 Catherine Anne Martin, "The Little Boy Who Lived with Muini'skw (Bear Woman)," in Renée Hulan and Renate Eigenbrod, eds., *Aboriginal Oral Traditions: Theory, Practice, Ethics* (Halifax/Winnipeg: Fernwood/Gorsebrook Research Institute, 2008), 56.
30 Ibid., 57.
31 Mihesuah, *Indigenous American Women,* 115.
32 Ibid., 117.
33 Martin, "The Little Boy," 58.
34 Ibid., 125.
35 Ibid., 126.
36 Robert Stam, *Subversive Pleasures: Bakhtin, Cultural Criticism, and Film* (Baltimore: Johns Hopkins University Press, 1989), 11.

37 Marks, "Fetishes and Fossils," 227-28.

38 Ibid., 228.

39 Ibid., 229.

40 Mihesuah, *Indigenous American Women,* 162.

Contributors

Kim Anderson (Cree-Métis) is an adjunct faculty member in the Department of Women's Studies, University of Guelph. She is the author of *A Recognition of Being: Reconstructing Native Womanhood* and co-editor, with Bonita Lawrence, of *Strong Women Stories: Native Vision and Community Survival.*

Jean Barman is a professor emerita at the University of British Columbia and a Fellow of the Royal Society of Canada. Among her books are *Stanley Park's Secret: The Forgotten Families of Whoi Whoi, Kanaka Ranch and Brockton Point* and, with Jan Hare, *Good Intentions Gone Awry: Emma Crosby and the Methodist Mission on the Northwest Coast.*

Patricia Demers is Distinguished University Professor of English and Film Studies at the University of Alberta and the past president of the Royal Society of Canada. Her recent publications include *Women's Writing in English: Early Modern England,* an edition of Hannah More's *Coelebs in Search of a Wife* (1808), and a third edition of *From Instruction to Delight: Children's Literature to 1850.*

Laura E. Donaldson (Cherokee) is an associate professor of English at Cornell University. She is the author of *Decolonizing Feminisms: Race, Gender,* *and Empire-Building* and co-editor, with Kwok Pui Lan, of *Postcolonialism, Feminism and Religious Discourse*.

Julia Emberley is a professor of English at the University of Western Ontario. She is the author of several books, including *Thresholds of Difference: Feminist Critique, Native Women's Writings, and Postcolonial Theory; The Cultural Politics of Fur;* and, most recently, *Defamiliarizing the Aboriginal: Cultural Practices and Decolonization in Canada*.

Katherine Young Evans is a doctoral candidate in English at the University of Texas at Austin, where she completed a master's thesis on Spiderwoman Theater. Her current research, supported by a fellowship from the American Association of University Women, focuses on how performance texts by Indigenous women impacted late nineteenth- and early twentieth-century Native rights debates.

Minnie Grey (Inuit) has worked actively throughout her career to improve the quality of life in northern Canada. She is the lead negotiator for the creation of the Nunavik Regional Government and continues to hold key positions representing the Inuit of Nunavik.

Patricia Penn Hilden (Nez Perce) is a professor emerita of Ethnic Studies at the University of California at Berkeley. She is the author of *When Nickels Were Indians: An Urban Mixed-Blood Story* and, most recently, of *From a Red Zone: Critical Perspectives on Race, Politics and Culture*.

Shari M. Huhndorf (Yup'ik) is a professor of Ethnic Studies and Women's and Gender Studies at the University of Oregon. She is the author of *Going Native: Indians in the American Cultural Imagination* and *Mapping the Americas: The Transnational Politics of Contemporary Native Culture*.

Elizabeth Kalbfleisch received a doctorate in visual and cultural studies from the University of Rochester, New York. She teaches in the Department of Art History at Concordia University in Montreal.

Leece M. Lee (Blackfeet) is a doctoral student in comparative ethnic studies at the University of California at Berkeley. Her research examines US continental expansion and its contemporary legacies, focusing on how patriarchy and racial domination in early colonialism affected Native American women's political roles and practices.

ann-elise lewallen is an assistant professor of modern Japanese cultural studies at the University of California at Santa Barbara. Her work focuses on cultural revitalization, Indigenous governance, eco-tourism, and the intersection of gender and ethnicity in Japan. She is concerned with research ethics and designing collaborative research that benefits host communities. She has worked with the Japanese Ainu community as an advocate-anthropologist since 1998.

Pamela McCallum is a professor of English at the University of Calgary and a Life Fellow of Clare Hall, Cambridge University. She co-edited, with Wendy Faith, *Linked Histories: Postcolonial Studies in a Globalized World* and recently edited and introduced a new edition of Raymond Williams' *Modern Tragedy*.

Jeanne Perreault is a professor of English at the University of Calgary. She co-edited, with Sylvia Vance, an anthology of Indigenous women's writing, *Writing the Circle,* and is the author of *Writing Selves: Contemporary Feminist Autobiography.* She co-edited *Tracing the Autobiographical* with Marlene Kadar, Linda Warley, and Susanna Egan, and most recently, with Marlene Kadar and Linda Warley, co-edited *Photographs, Histories, and Meaning.*

Cheryl Suzack (Anishinaabe) is an assistant professor cross-appointed with English and Aboriginal studies at the University of Toronto. Her research interests include law and literature studies, Indigenous women's writing, Indigenous law and literature, feminist theory, and postcolonial theory. She has published articles on Indigenous women writers from Canada and the United States.

Rebecca Tsosie (Yaqui) is Willard H. Pedrick Distinguished Research Scholar, a professor of law, and executive director of the Indian Legal Program at Arizona State University. She has written and published widely on doctrinal and theoretical issues related to tribal sovereignty, environmental policy, and cultural rights, and serves as a Supreme Court justice for the Fort McDowell Yavapai Nation.

Teresa Zackodnik is a professor of English and Film Studies at the University of Alberta. She is the author of *The Mulatta and the Politics of Race* and editor of the multivolume *African American Feminisms, 1828-1924* and *"We Must Be Up and Doing": Early African American Feminisms.*

Index

Note: (f) after a page number indicates a figure or illustration; the italic letter *n* in a page number indicates a note.